GIRLS' OPS 002

SWORD ART ONLINE
GIRLS' OPERATIONS

ART: NEKO NEKOBYOU
ORIGINAL STORY: REKI KAWAHARA
CHARACTER DESIGN: abec

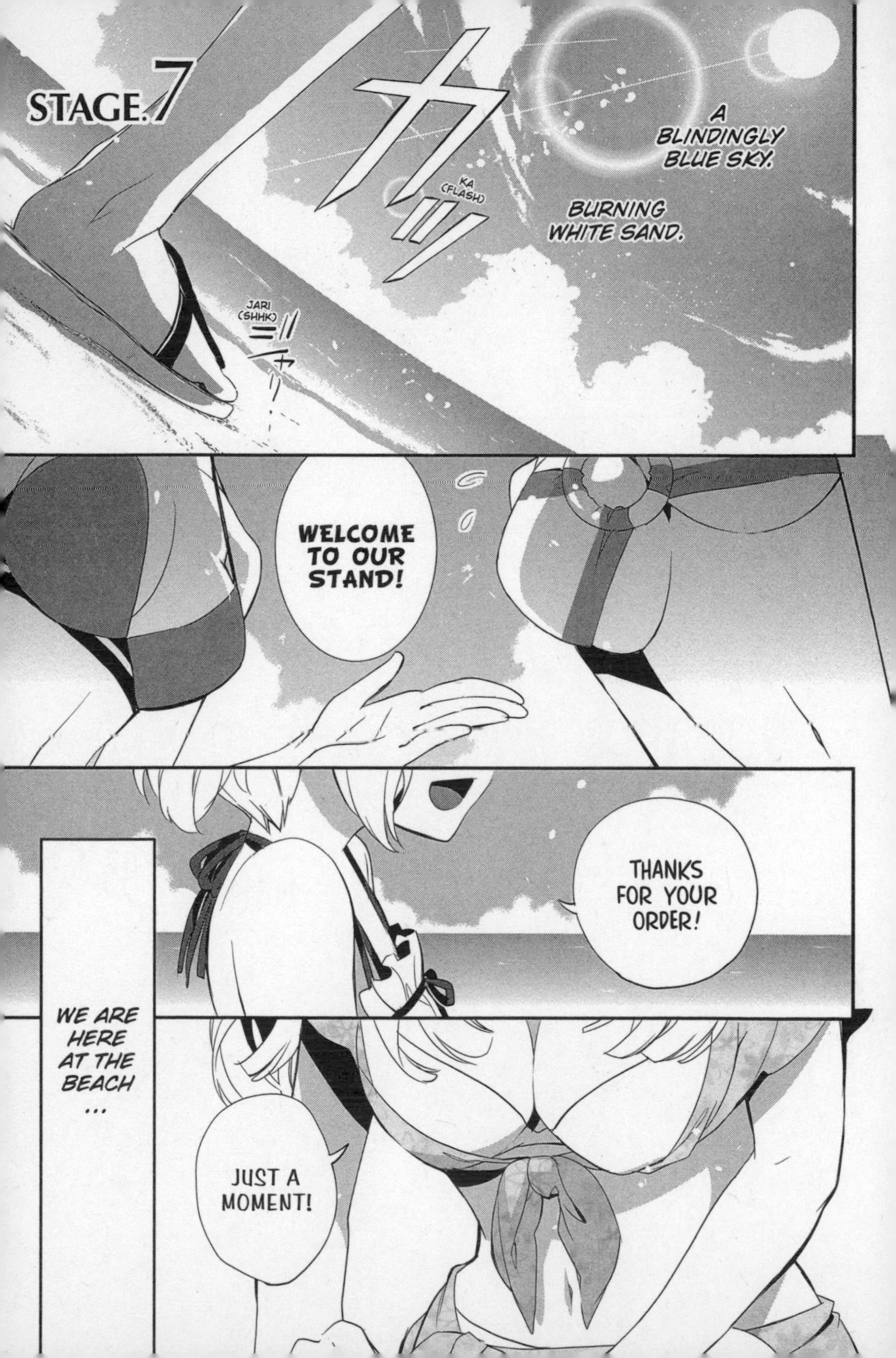
STAGE.7
A BLINDINGLY BLUE SKY.
KA (FLASH)
BURNING WHITE SAND.
JARI (SHHK)
WELCOME TO OUR STAND!
THANKS FOR YOUR ORDER!
JUST A MOMENT!
WE ARE HERE AT THE BEACH ...

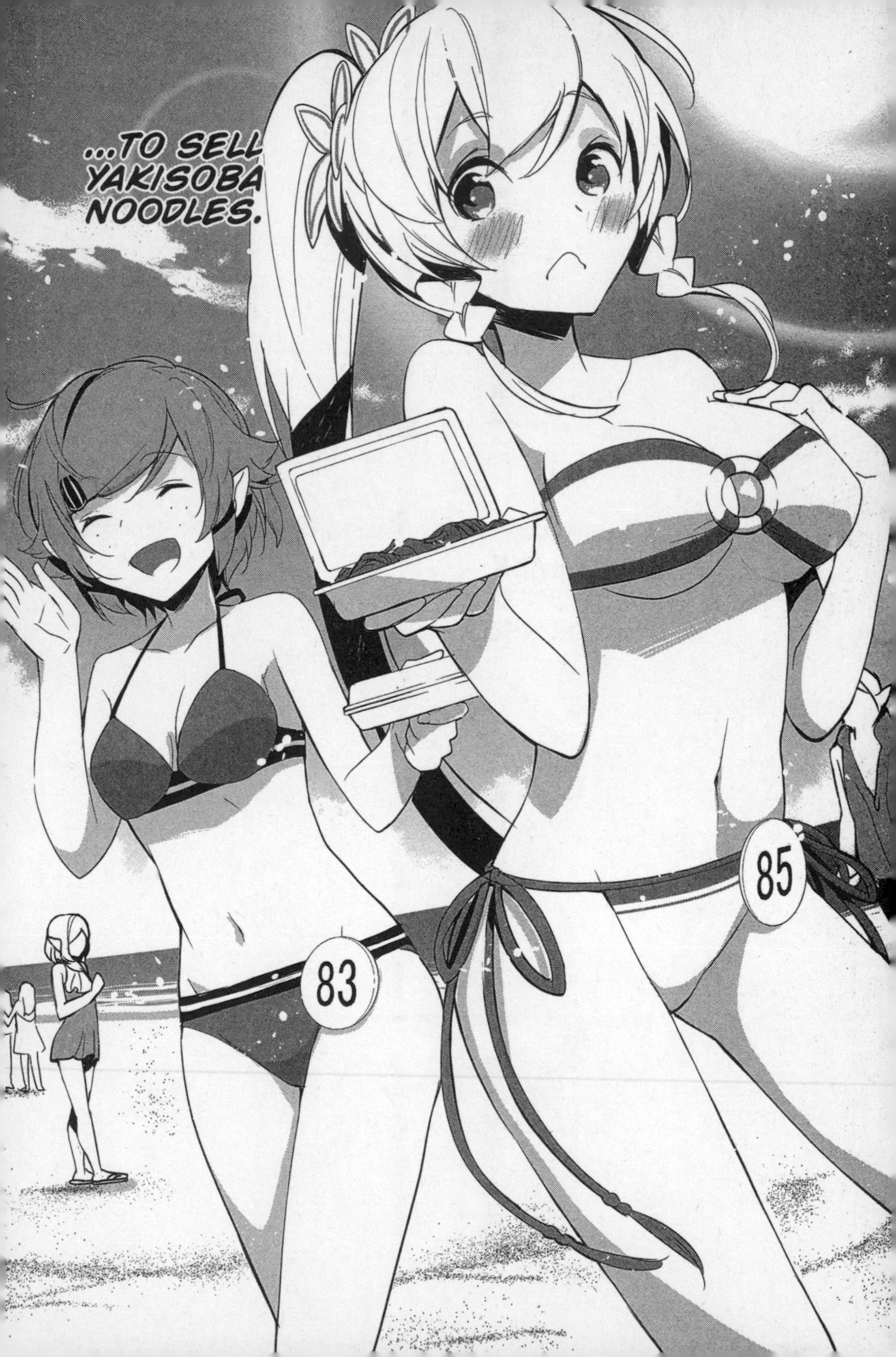
...TO SELL YAKISOBA NOODLES.
85
83

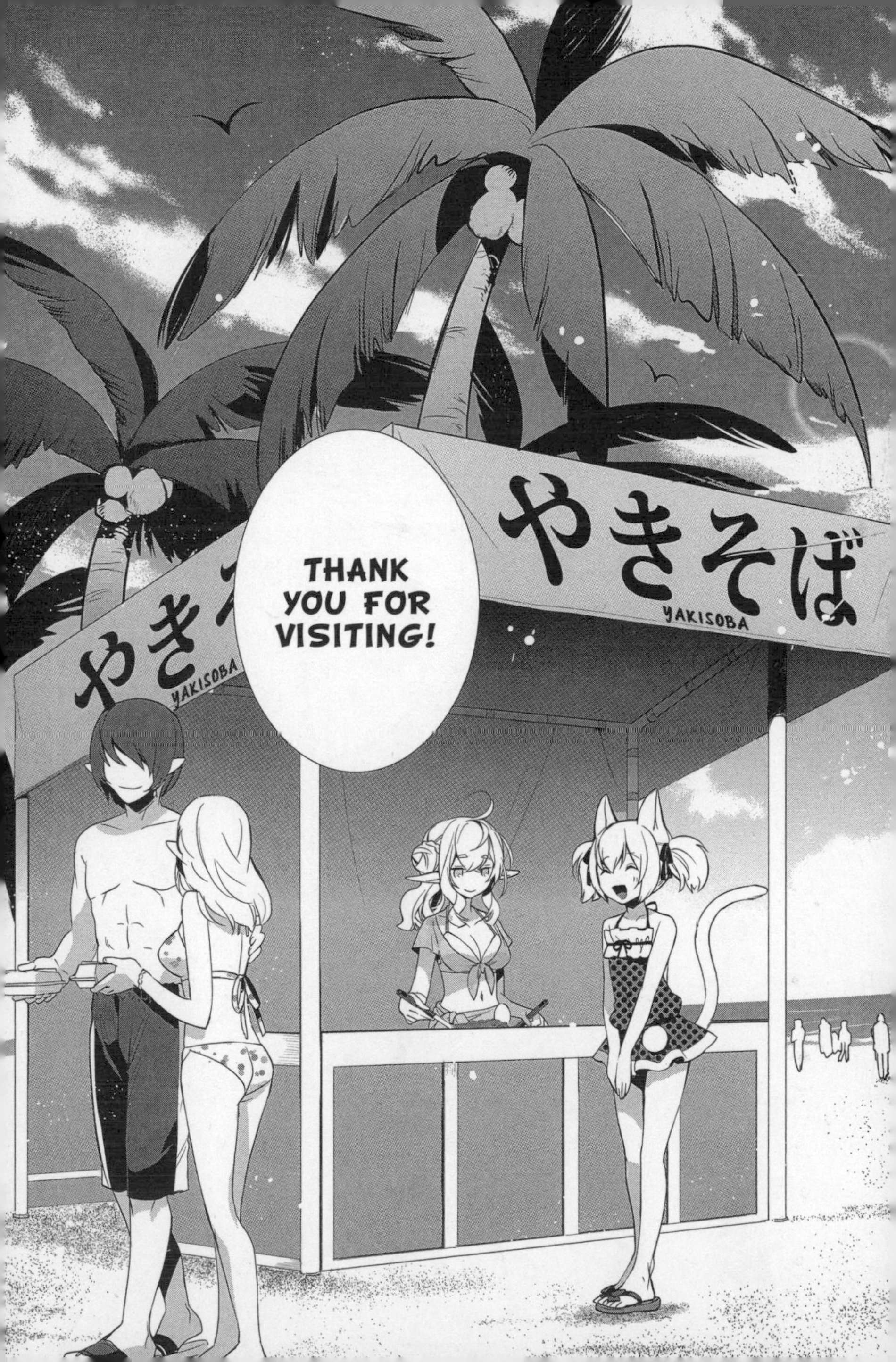

やきそば
YAKISOBA
THANK YOU FOR VISITING!
やき
YAKISOBA

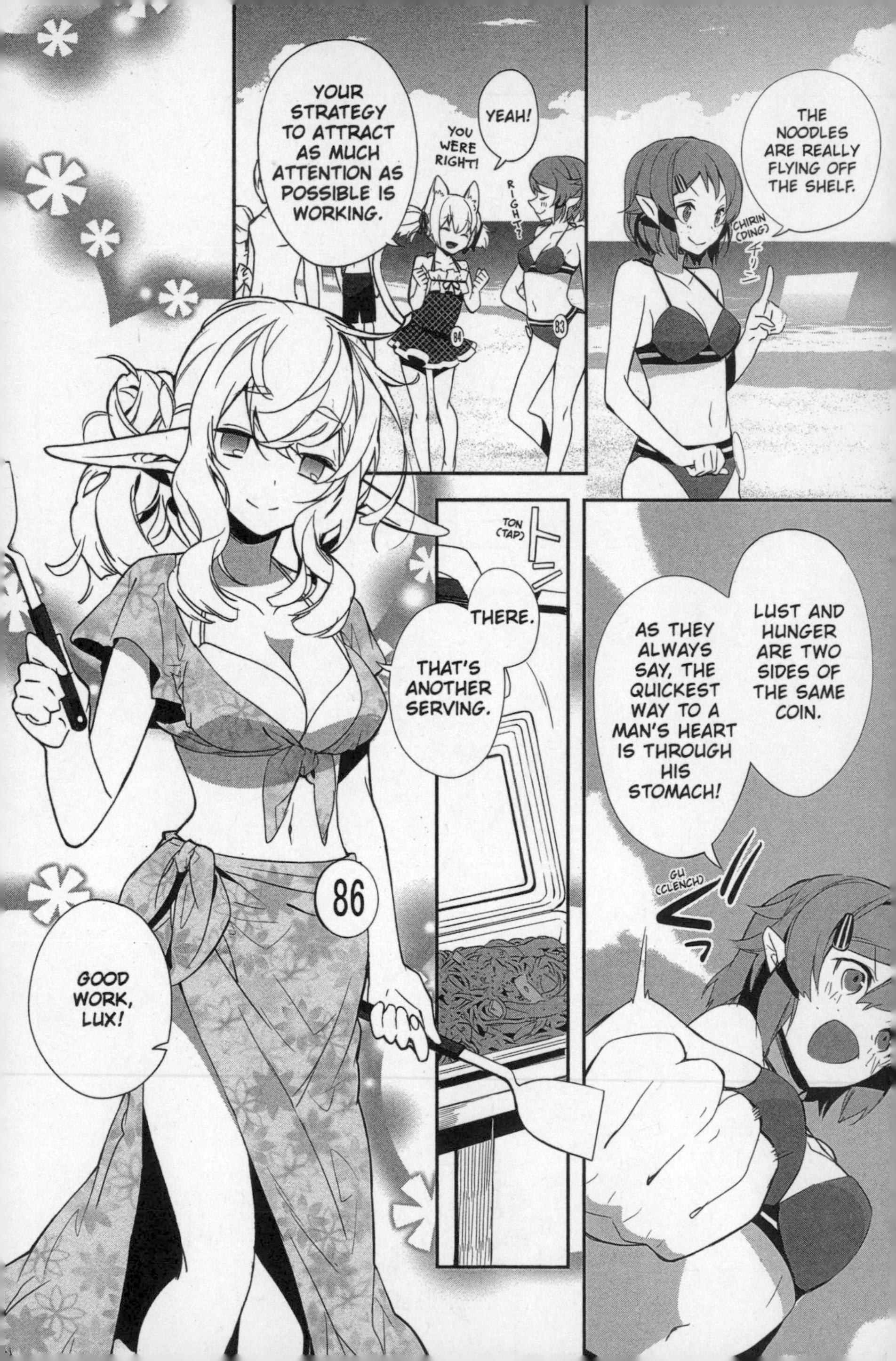
THE NOODLES ARE REALLY FLYING OFF THE SHELF.
CHIRIN (DING)
YEAH!
YOU WERE RIGHT!
RIGHT
YOUR STRATEGY TO ATTRACT AS MUCH ATTENTION AS POSSIBLE IS WORKING.
84
83
LUST AND HUNGER ARE TWO SIDES OF THE SAME COIN.
AS THEY ALWAYS SAY, THE QUICKEST WAY TO A MAN'S HEART IS THROUGH HIS STOMACH!
GU (CLENCH)
TON (TAP)
THERE.
THAT'S ANOTHER SERVING.
86
GOOD WORK, LUX!

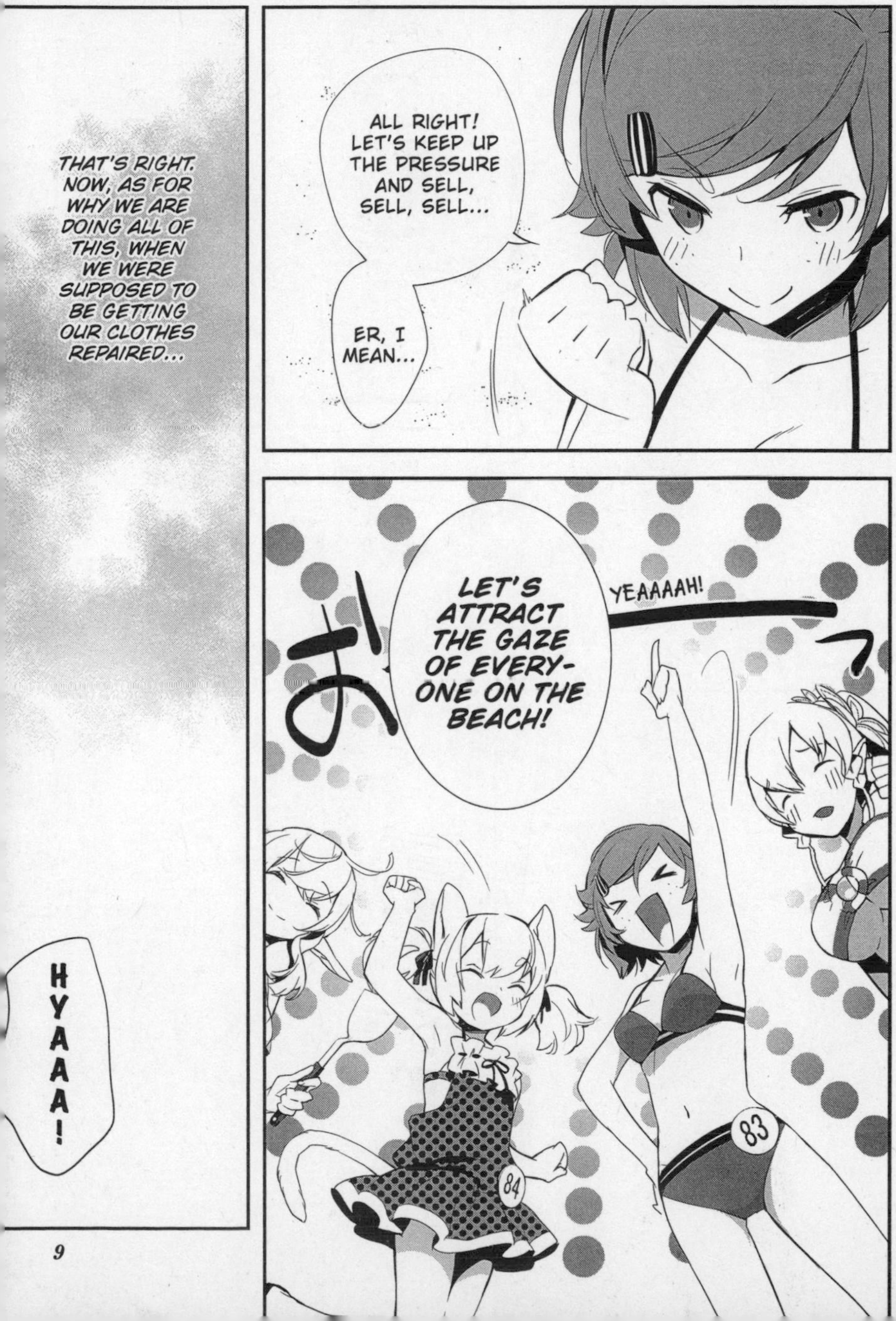
ALL RIGHT! LET'S KEEP UP THE PRESSURE AND SELL, SELL, SELL...
ER, I MEAN...
THAT'S RIGHT. NOW, AS FOR WHY WE ARE DOING ALL OF THIS, WHEN WE WERE SUPPOSED TO BE GETTING OUR CLOTHES REPAIRED...
LET'S ATTRACT THE GAZE OF EVERY-ONE ON THE BEACH!
YEAAAAH!
お!
HYAAAA!

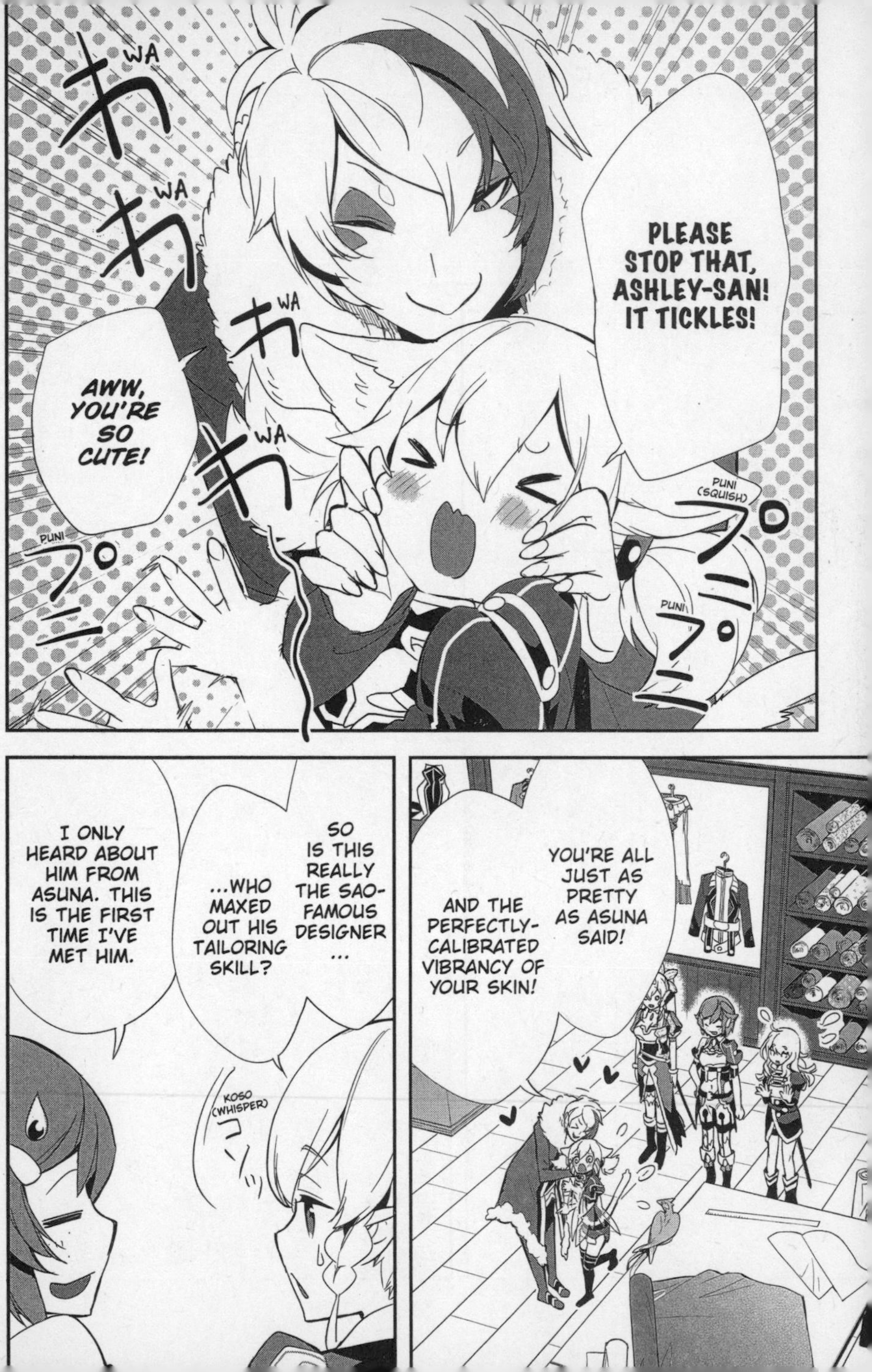

WA
WA
WA
WA
PLEASE STOP THAT, ASHLEY-SAN! IT TICKLES!
AWW, YOU'RE SO CUTE!
PUNI (SQUISH)
PUNI
PUNI
YOU'RE ALL JUST AS PRETTY AS ASUNA SAID!
AND THE PERFECTLY-CALIBRATED VIBRANCY OF YOUR SKIN!
SO IS THIS REALLY THE SAO-FAMOUS DESIGNER ...
...WHO MAXED OUT HIS TAILORING SKILL?
I ONLY HEARD ABOUT HIM FROM ASUNA. THIS IS THE FIRST TIME I'VE MET HIM.
KOSO (WHISPER)

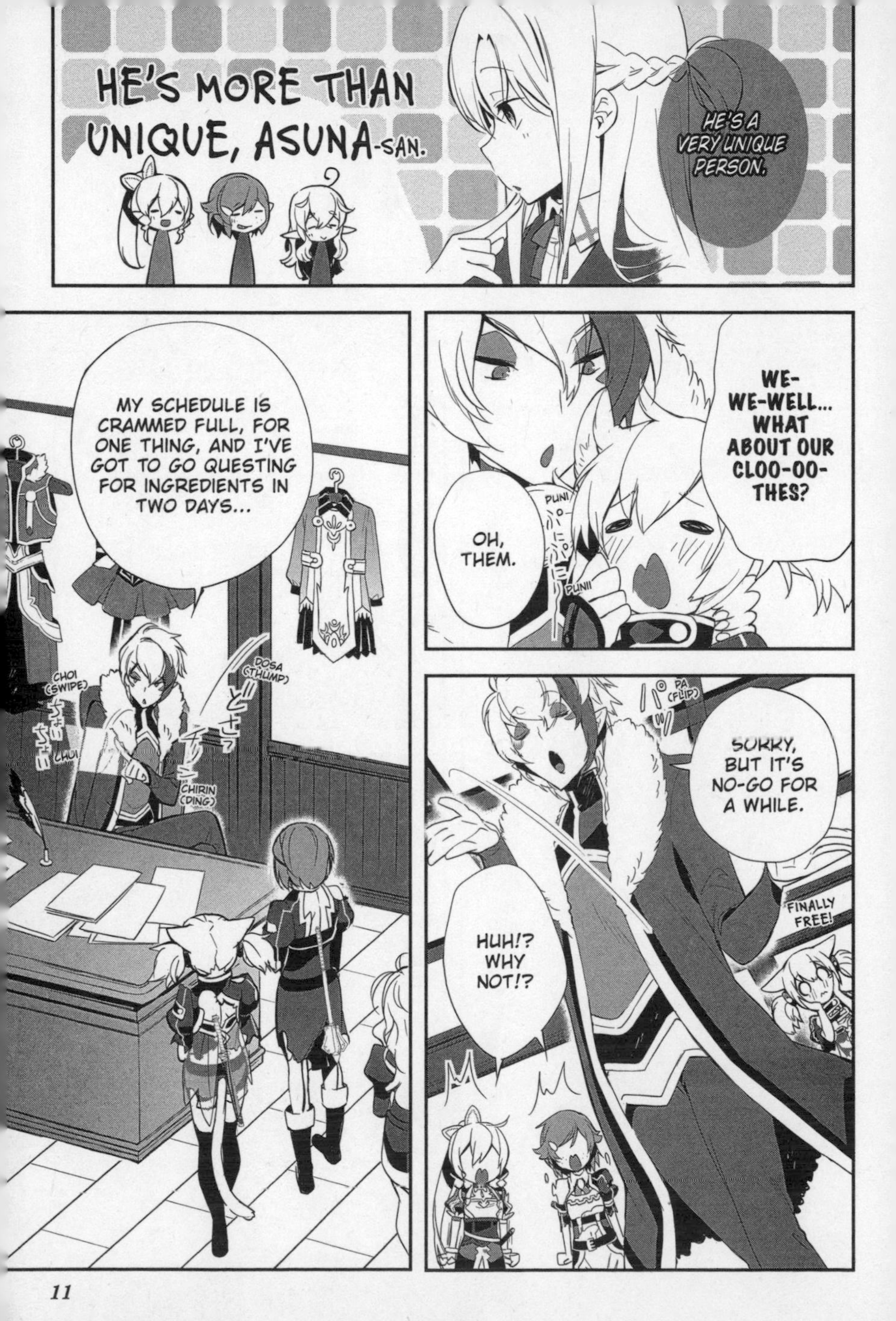
HE'S A VERY UNIQUE PERSON.
HE'S MORE THAN UNIQUE, ASUNA-SAN.
WE-WE-WELL... WHAT ABOUT OUR CLOO-OO-THES?
OH, THEM.
PUNI
PUNII
MY SCHEDULE IS CRAMMED FULL, FOR ONE THING, AND I'VE GOT TO GO QUESTING FOR INGREDIENTS IN TWO DAYS...
DOSA (THUMP)
CHOI (SWIPE)
CHUI
CHIRIN (DING)
PA (FLIP)
SORRY, BUT IT'S NO-GO FOR A WHILE.
HUH!? WHY NOT!?
FINALLY FREE!

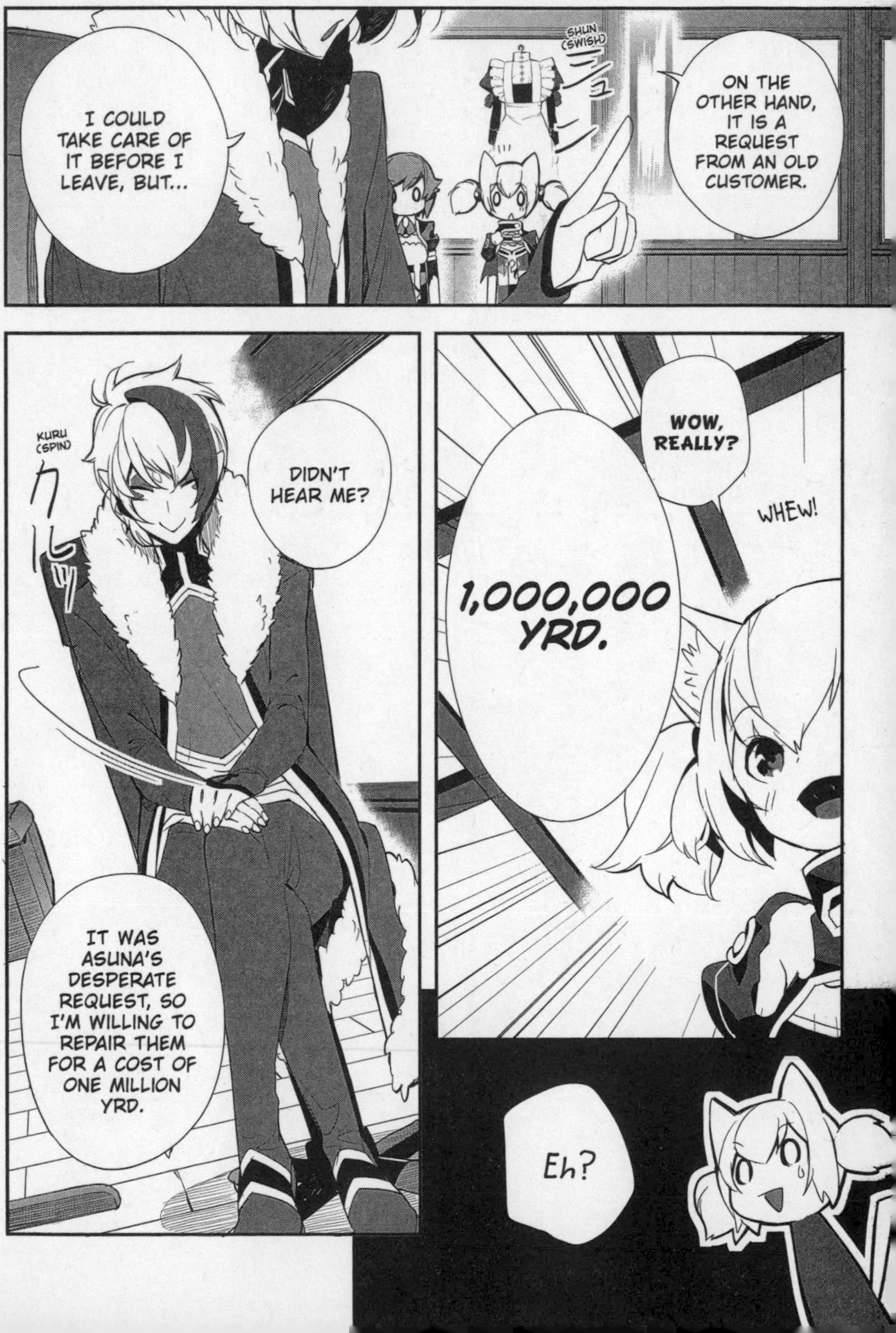
ON THE OTHER HAND, IT IS A REQUEST FROM AN OLD CUSTOMER.
SHUN (SWISH)
I COULD TAKE CARE OF IT BEFORE I LEAVE, BUT...
WOW, REALLY?
WHEW!
1,000,000 YRD.
DIDN'T HEAR ME?
KURU (SPIN)
IT WAS ASUNA'S DESPERATE REQUEST, SO I'M WILLING TO REPAIR THEM FOR A COST OF ONE MILLION YRD.
Eh?

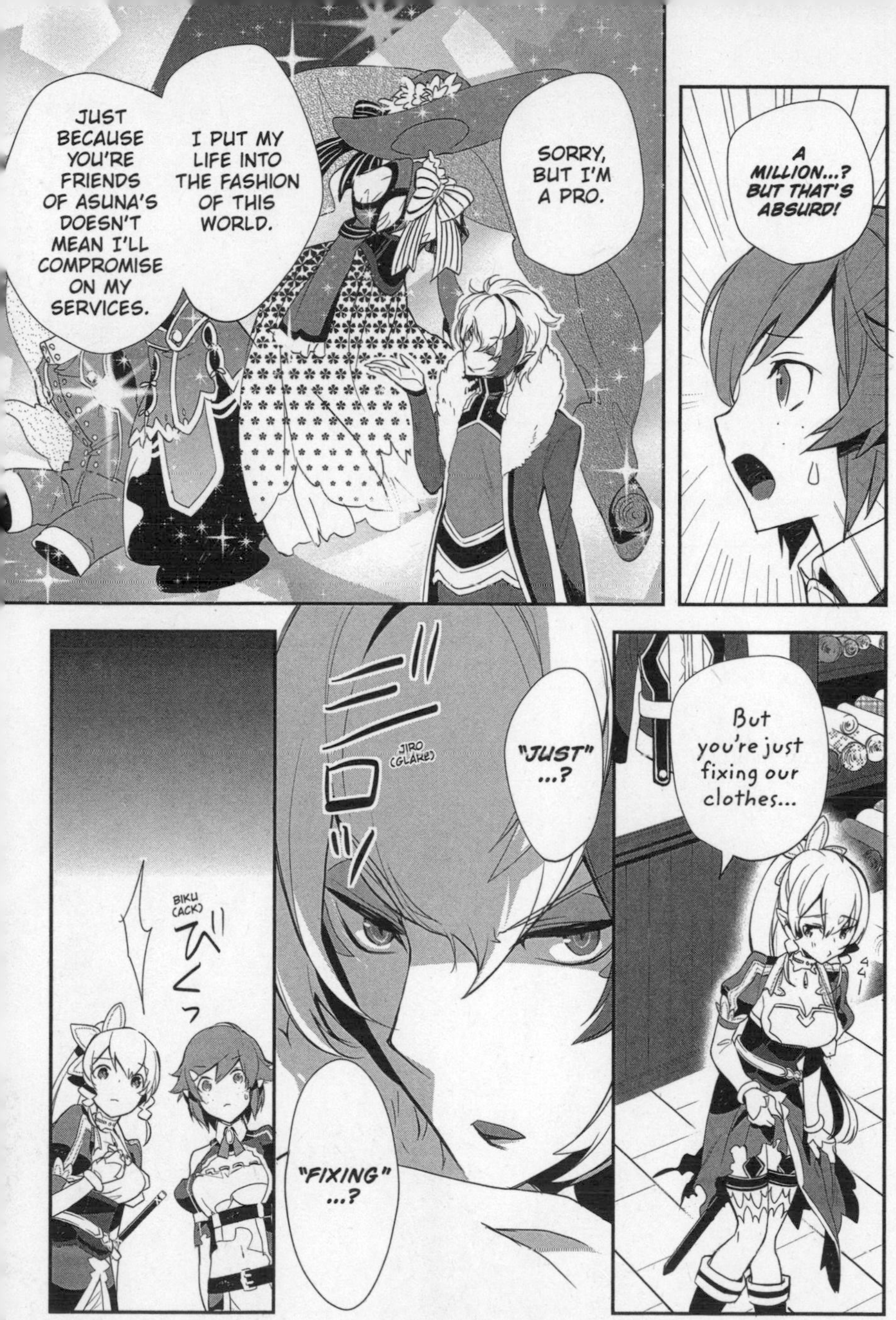
A MILLION...? BUT THAT'S ABSURD!
SORRY, BUT I'M A PRO.
I PUT MY LIFE INTO THE FASHION OF THIS WORLD.
JUST BECAUSE YOU'RE FRIENDS OF ASUNA'S DOESN'T MEAN I'LL COMPROMISE ON MY SERVICES.
But you're just fixing our clothes...
"JUST" ...?
JIRO (GLARE)
"FIXING" ...?
BIKU (ACK)

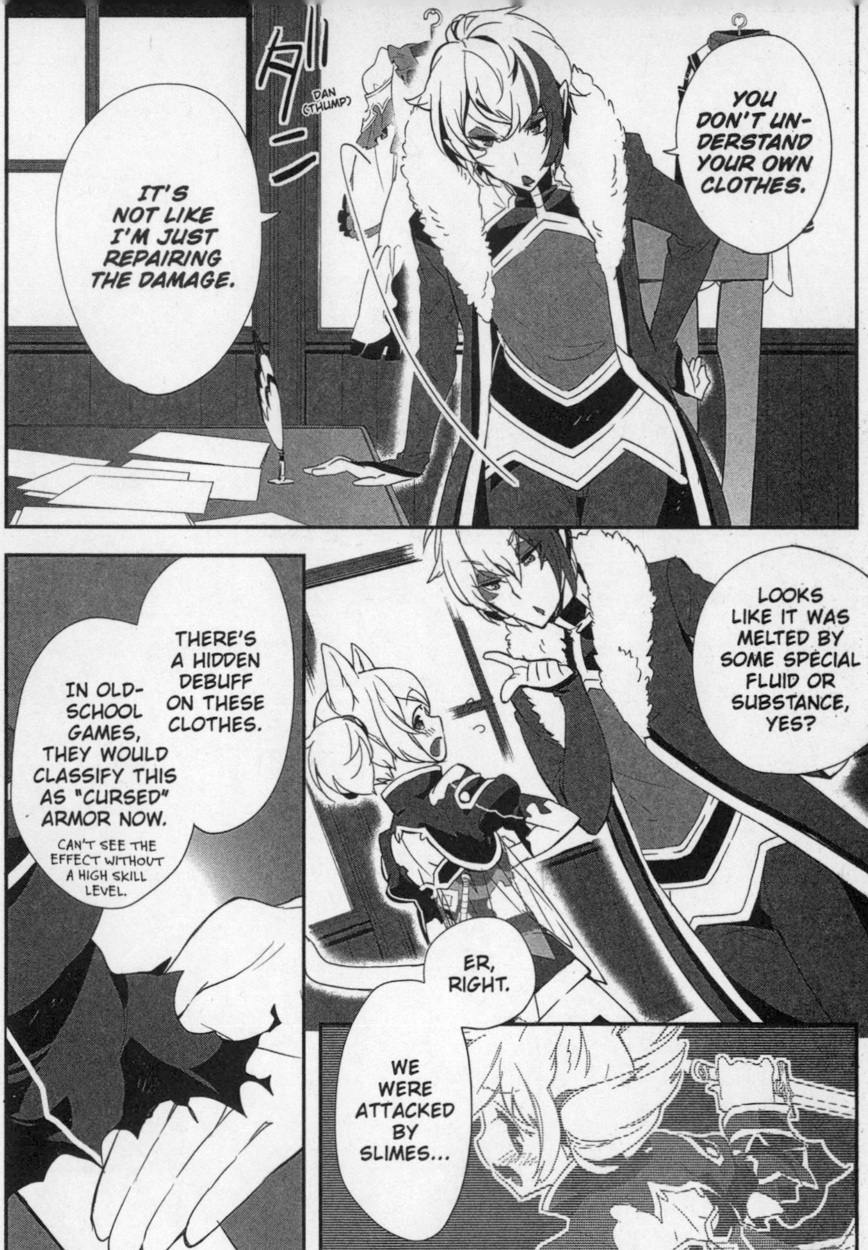
YOU DON'T UN-DERSTAND YOUR OWN CLOTHES.
DAN (THUMP)
IT'S NOT LIKE I'M JUST REPAIRING THE DAMAGE.
LOOKS LIKE IT WAS MELTED BY SOME SPECIAL FLUID OR SUBSTANCE, YES?
ER, RIGHT.
WE WERE ATTACKED BY SLIMES...
THERE'S A HIDDEN DEBUFF ON THESE CLOTHES.
IN OLD-SCHOOL GAMES, THEY WOULD CLASSIFY THIS AS "CURSED" ARMOR NOW.
CAN'T SEE THE EFFECT WITHOUT A HIGH SKILL LEVEL.

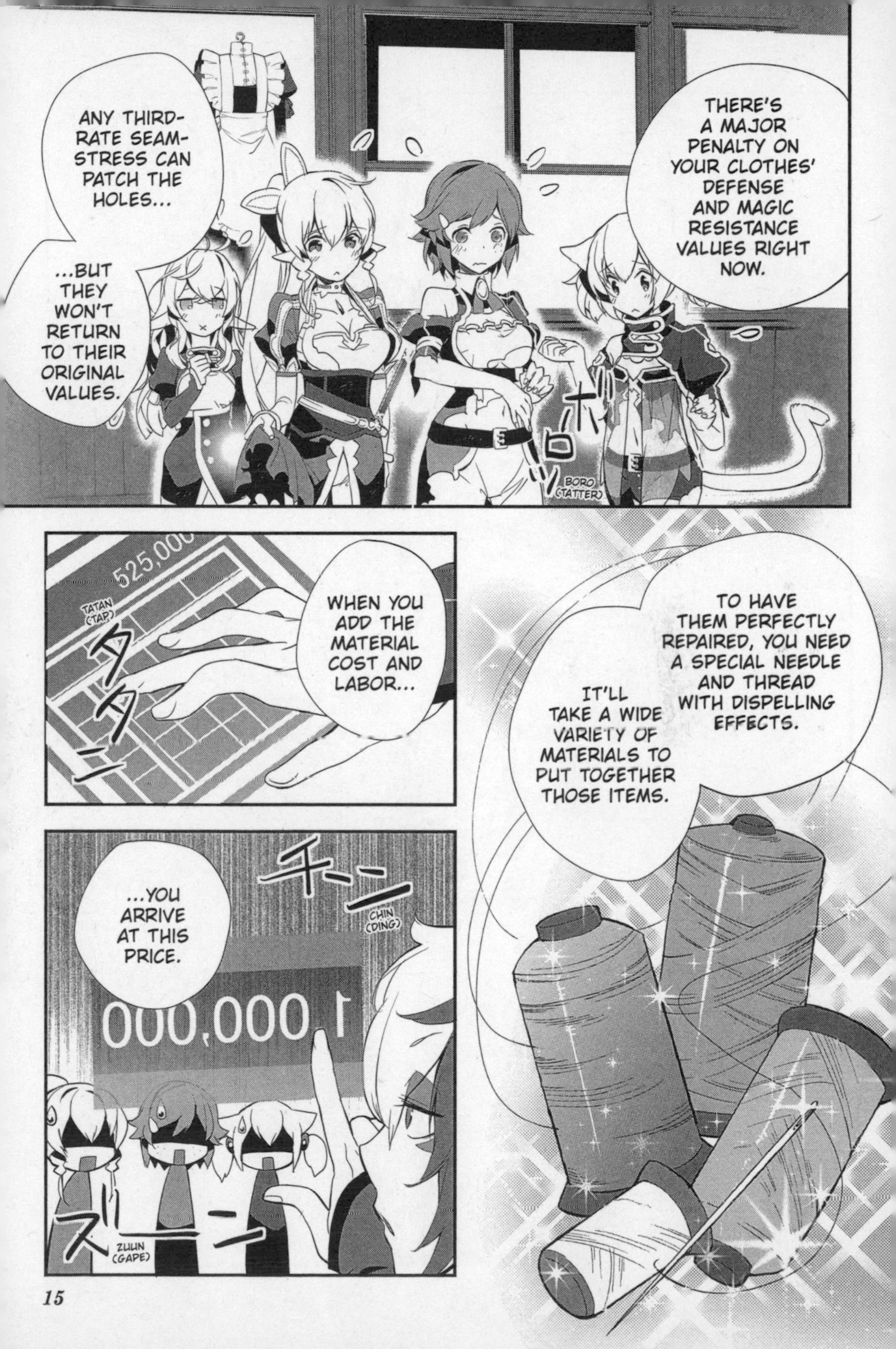
THERE'S A MAJOR PENALTY ON YOUR CLOTHES' DEFENSE AND MAGIC RESISTANCE VALUES RIGHT NOW.
ANY THIRD-RATE SEAM-STRESS CAN PATCH THE HOLES...
...BUT THEY WON'T RETURN TO THEIR ORIGINAL VALUES.
BORO (TATTER)
TO HAVE THEM PERFECTLY REPAIRED, YOU NEED A SPECIAL NEEDLE AND THREAD WITH DISPELLING EFFECTS.
IT'LL TAKE A WIDE VARIETY OF MATERIALS TO PUT TOGETHER THOSE ITEMS.
525,00
WHEN YOU ADD THE MATERIAL COST AND LABOR...
TATAN (TAP)
...YOU ARRIVE AT THIS PRICE.
CHIN (DING)
ZUUN (GAPE)

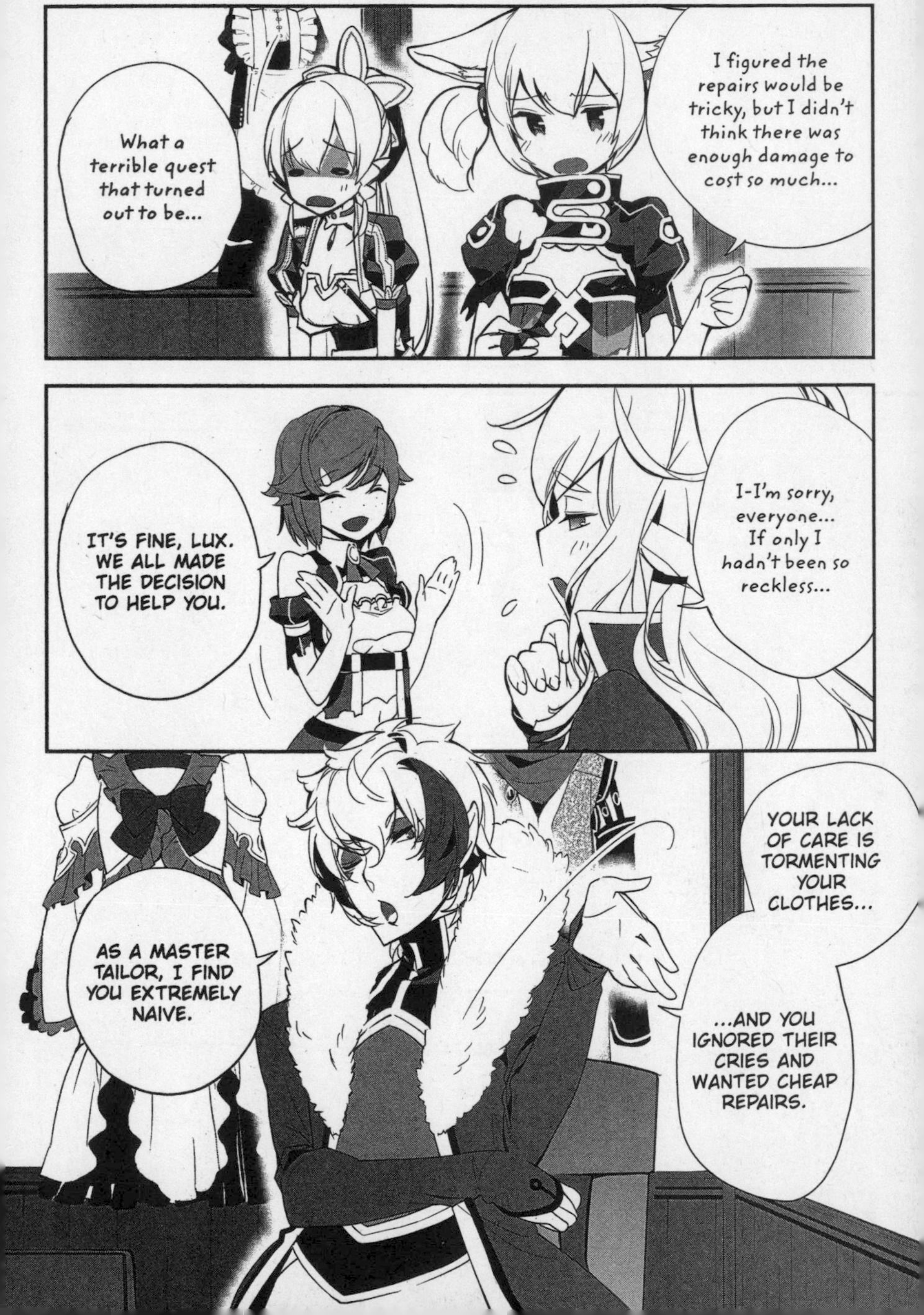
I figured the repairs would be tricky, but I didn't think there was enough damage to cost so much...
What a terrible quest that turned out to be...
I-I'm sorry, everyone... If only I hadn't been so reckless...
IT'S FINE, LUX. WE ALL MADE THE DECISION TO HELP YOU.
YOUR LACK OF CARE IS TORMENTING YOUR CLOTHES...
...AND YOU IGNORED THEIR CRIES AND WANTED CHEAP REPAIRS.
AS A MASTER TAILOR, I FIND YOU EXTREMELY NAIVE.

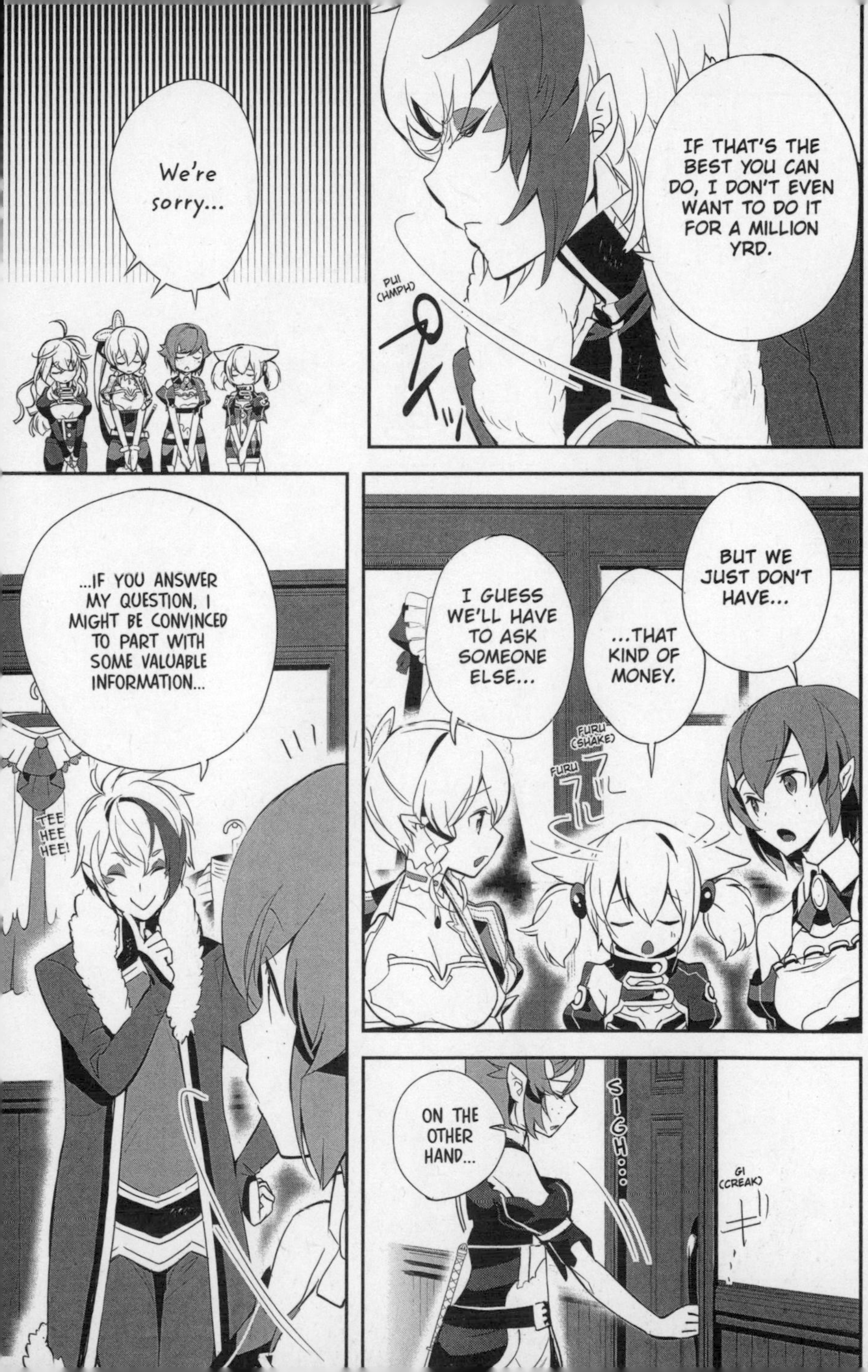
IF THAT'S THE BEST YOU CAN DO, I DON'T EVEN WANT TO DO IT FOR A MILLION YRD.
PUI (HMPH)
We're sorry...
BUT WE JUST DON'T HAVE...
...THAT KIND OF MONEY.
FURU (SHAKE)
FURU
I GUESS WE'LL HAVE TO ASK SOMEONE ELSE...
ON THE OTHER HAND...
SIGH...
GI (CREAK)
...IF YOU ANSWER MY QUESTION, I MIGHT BE CONVINCED TO PART WITH SOME VALUABLE INFORMATION...
TEE HEE HEE!

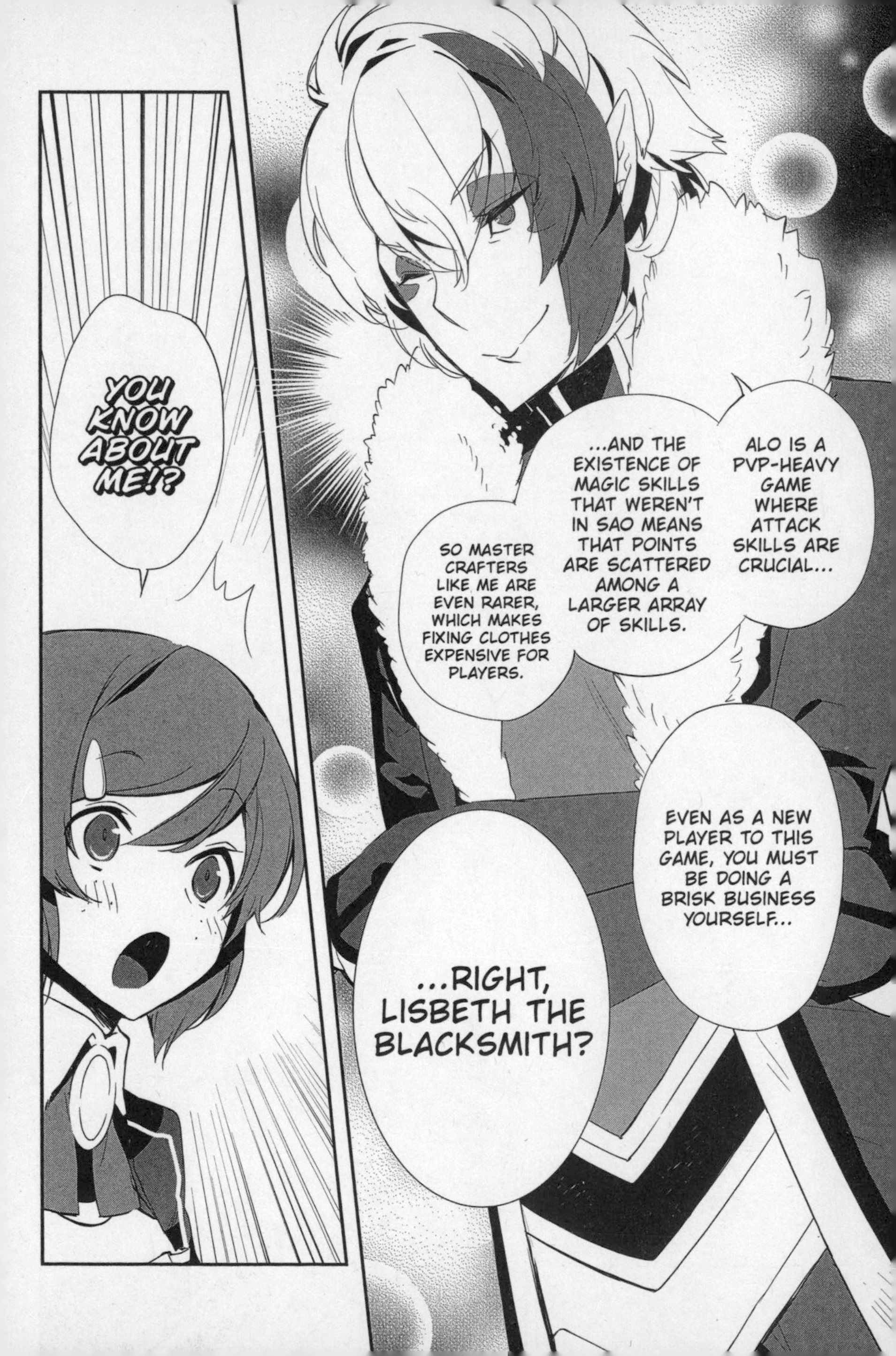
ALO IS A PVP-HEAVY GAME WHERE ATTACK SKILLS ARE CRUCIAL...
...AND THE EXISTENCE OF MAGIC SKILLS THAT WEREN'T IN SAO MEANS THAT POINTS ARE SCATTERED AMONG A LARGER ARRAY OF SKILLS.
SO MASTER CRAFTERS LIKE ME ARE EVEN RARER, WHICH MAKES FIXING CLOTHES EXPENSIVE FOR PLAYERS.
EVEN AS A NEW PLAYER TO THIS GAME, YOU MUST BE DOING A BRISK BUSINESS YOURSELF...
...RIGHT, LISBETH THE BLACKSMITH?
YOU KNOW ABOUT ME!?

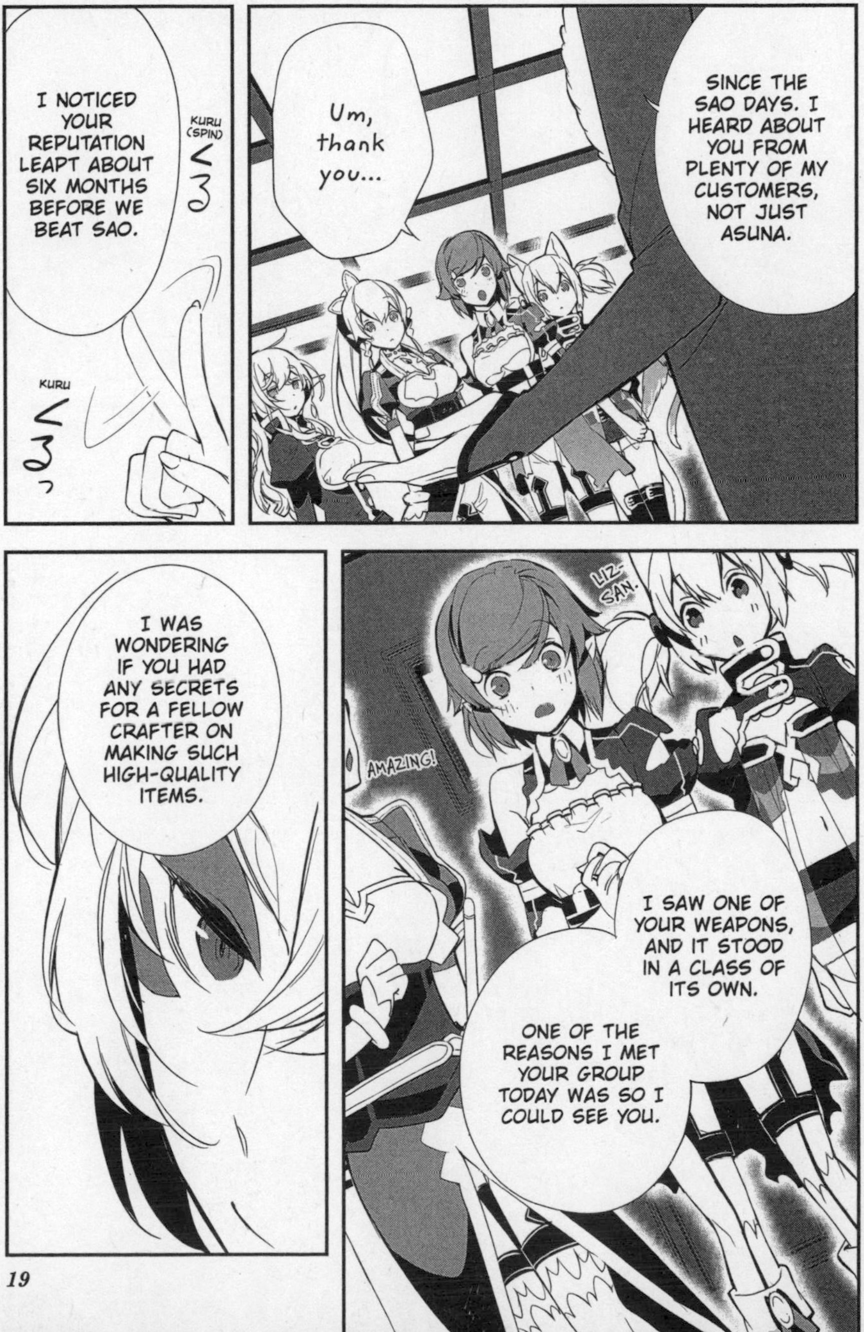
SINCE THE SAO DAYS. I HEARD ABOUT YOU FROM PLENTY OF MY CUSTOMERS, NOT JUST ASUNA.
Um, thank you...
KURU (SPIN)
I NOTICED YOUR REPUTATION LEAPT ABOUT SIX MONTHS BEFORE WE BEAT SAO.
KURU
LIZ-SAN.
AMAZING!
I SAW ONE OF YOUR WEAPONS, AND IT STOOD IN A CLASS OF ITS OWN.
ONE OF THE REASONS I MET YOUR GROUP TODAY WAS SO I COULD SEE YOU.
I WAS WONDERING IF YOU HAD ANY SECRETS FOR A FELLOW CRAFTER ON MAKING SUCH HIGH-QUALITY ITEMS.

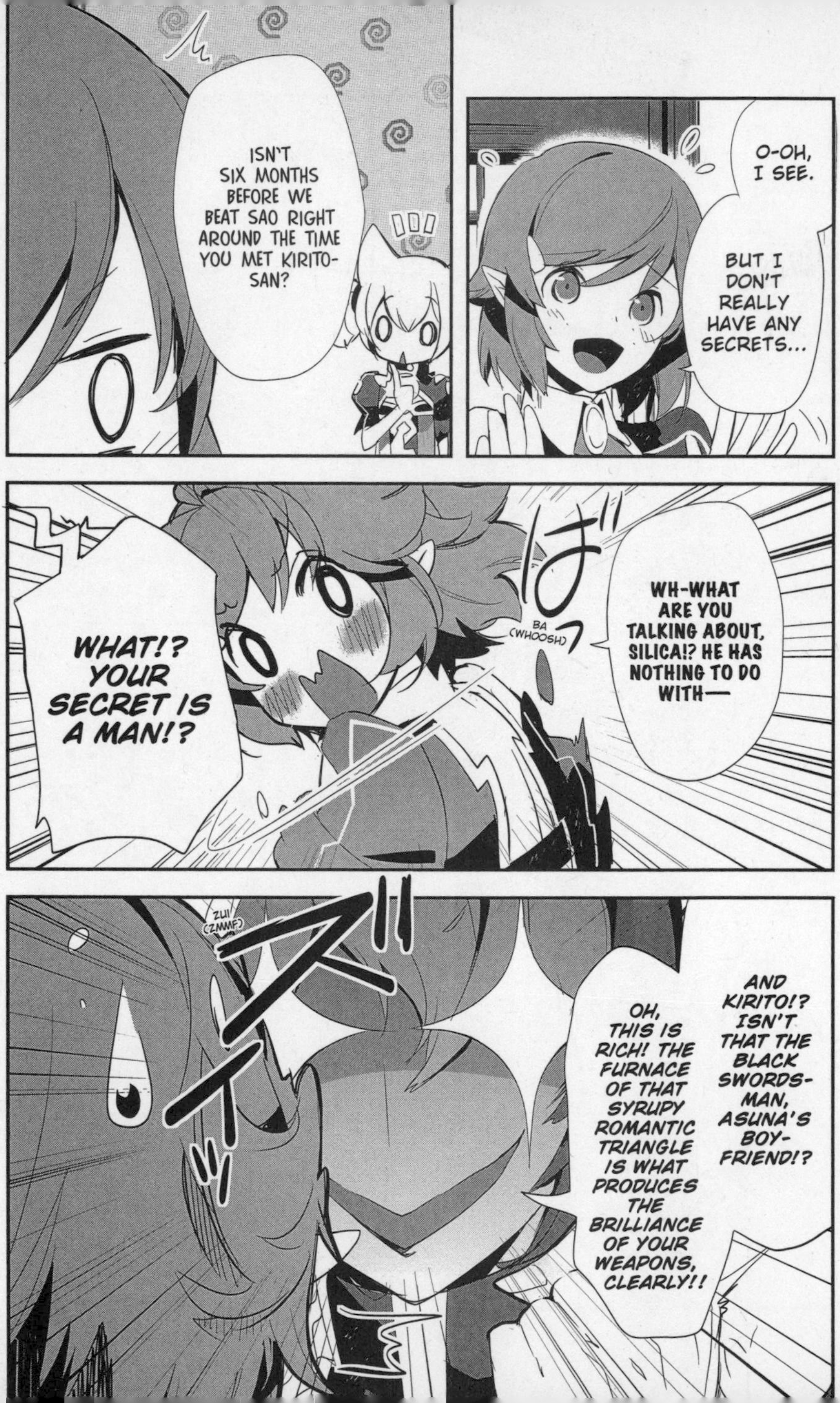
O-OH, I SEE.
BUT I DON'T REALLY HAVE ANY SECRETS...
ISN'T SIX MONTHS BEFORE WE BEAT SAO RIGHT AROUND THE TIME YOU MET KIRITO-SAN?
BA (WHOOSH)
WH-WHAT ARE YOU TALKING ABOUT, SILICA!? HE HAS NOTHING TO DO WITH—
WHAT!? YOUR SECRET IS A MAN!?
ZUI (ZMMF)
AND KIRITO!? ISN'T THAT THE BLACK SWORDS-MAN, ASUNA'S BOY-FRIEND!?
OH, THIS IS RICH! THE FURNACE OF THAT SYRUPY ROMANTIC TRIANGLE IS WHAT PRODUCES THE BRILLIANCE OF YOUR WEAPONS, CLEARLY!!

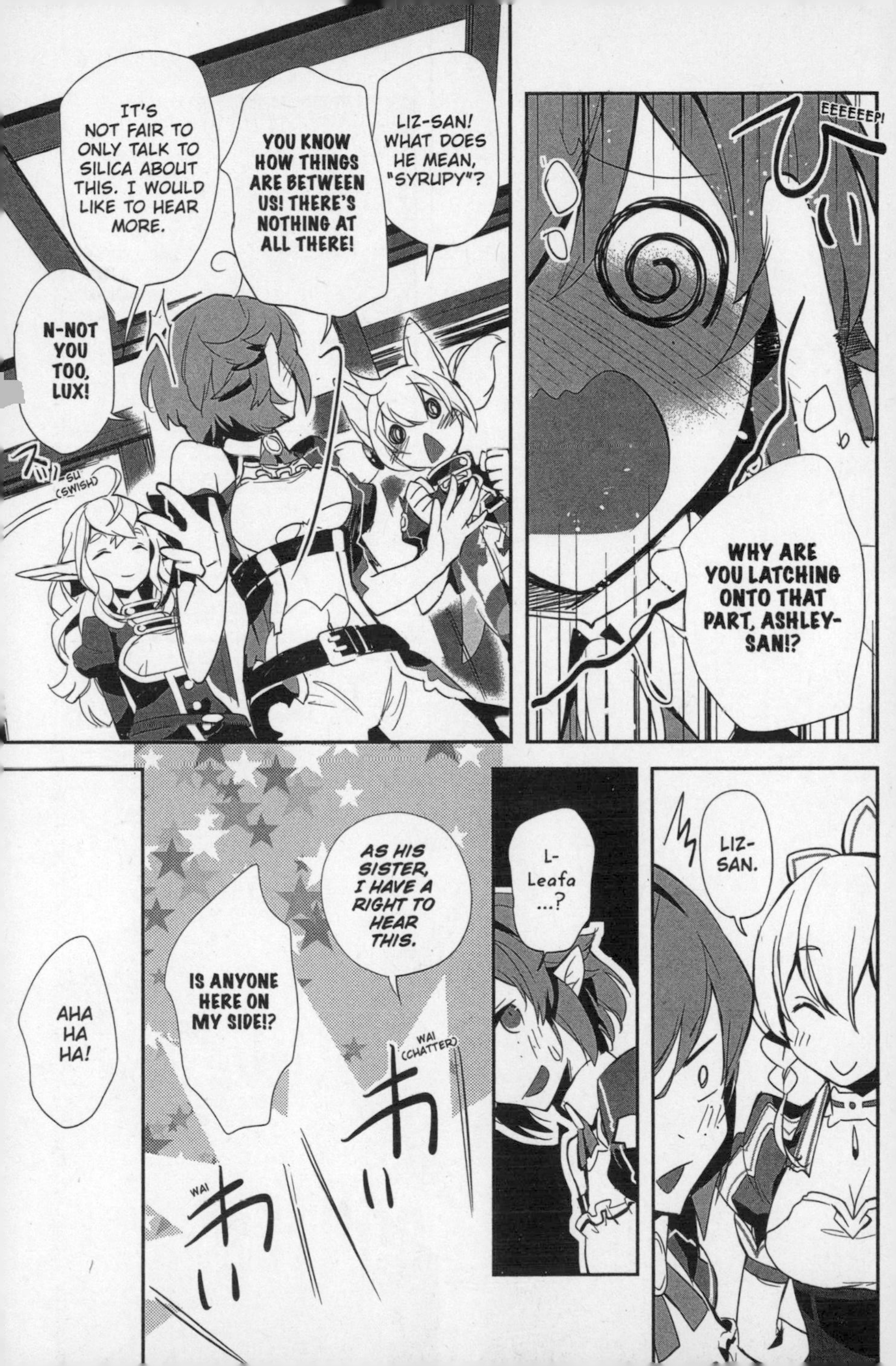
EEEEEEP!
WHY ARE YOU LATCHING ONTO THAT PART, ASHLEY-SAN!?
LIZ-SAN! WHAT DOES HE MEAN, "SYRUPY"?
YOU KNOW HOW THINGS ARE BETWEEN US! THERE'S NOTHING AT ALL THERE!
IT'S NOT FAIR TO ONLY TALK TO SILICA ABOUT THIS. I WOULD LIKE TO HEAR MORE.
N-NOT YOU TOO, LUX!
SU (SWISH)
LIZ-SAN.
L-Leafa ...?
AS HIS SISTER, I HAVE A RIGHT TO HEAR THIS.
IS ANYONE HERE ON MY SIDE!?
WAI (CHATTER)
WAI
AHA HA HA!

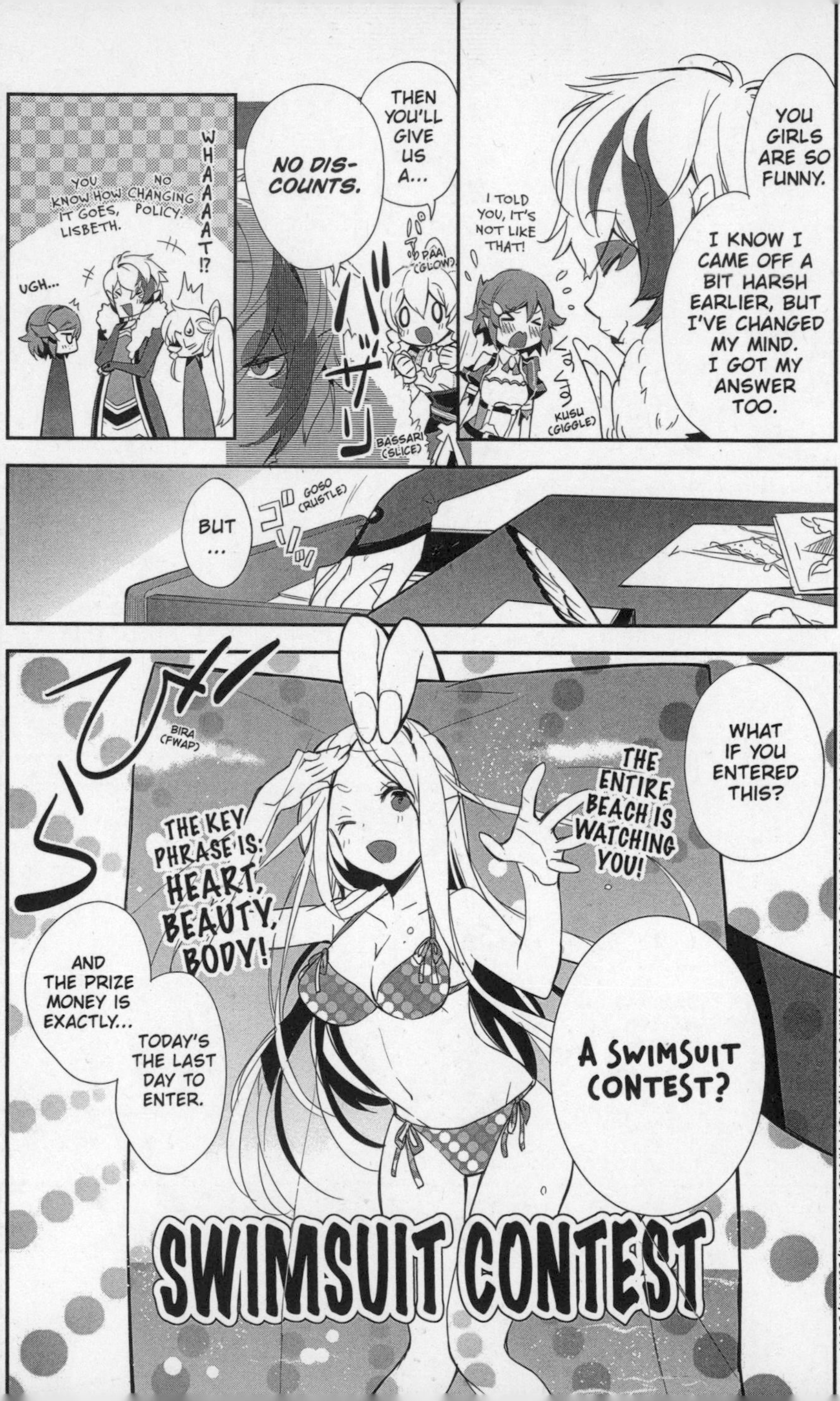
YOU GIRLS ARE SO FUNNY.
I TOLD YOU, IT'S NOT LIKE THAT!
KUSU (GIGGLE)
I KNOW I CAME OFF A BIT HARSH EARLIER, BUT I'VE CHANGED MY MIND. I GOT MY ANSWER TOO.
THEN YOU'LL GIVE US A...
PAA (GLOW)
NO DIS-COUNTS.
BASSARI (SLICE)
WHAAAAAT!?
NO CHANGING POLICY.
YOU KNOW HOW IT GOES, LISBETH.
UGH...
BUT...
GOSO (RUSTLE)
WHAT IF YOU ENTERED THIS?
BIRA (FWAP)
THE ENTIRE BEACH IS WATCHING YOU!
THE KEY PHRASE IS: HEART, BEAUTY, BODY!
A SWIMSUIT CONTEST?
AND THE PRIZE MONEY IS EXACTLY...
TODAY'S THE LAST DAY TO ENTER.
SWIMSUIT CONTEST

POSTER: SWIMSUIT CONTEST, THE ENTIRE BEACH IS WATCHING YOU! THE KEY PHRASE IS: HEART, BEAUTY, BODY!

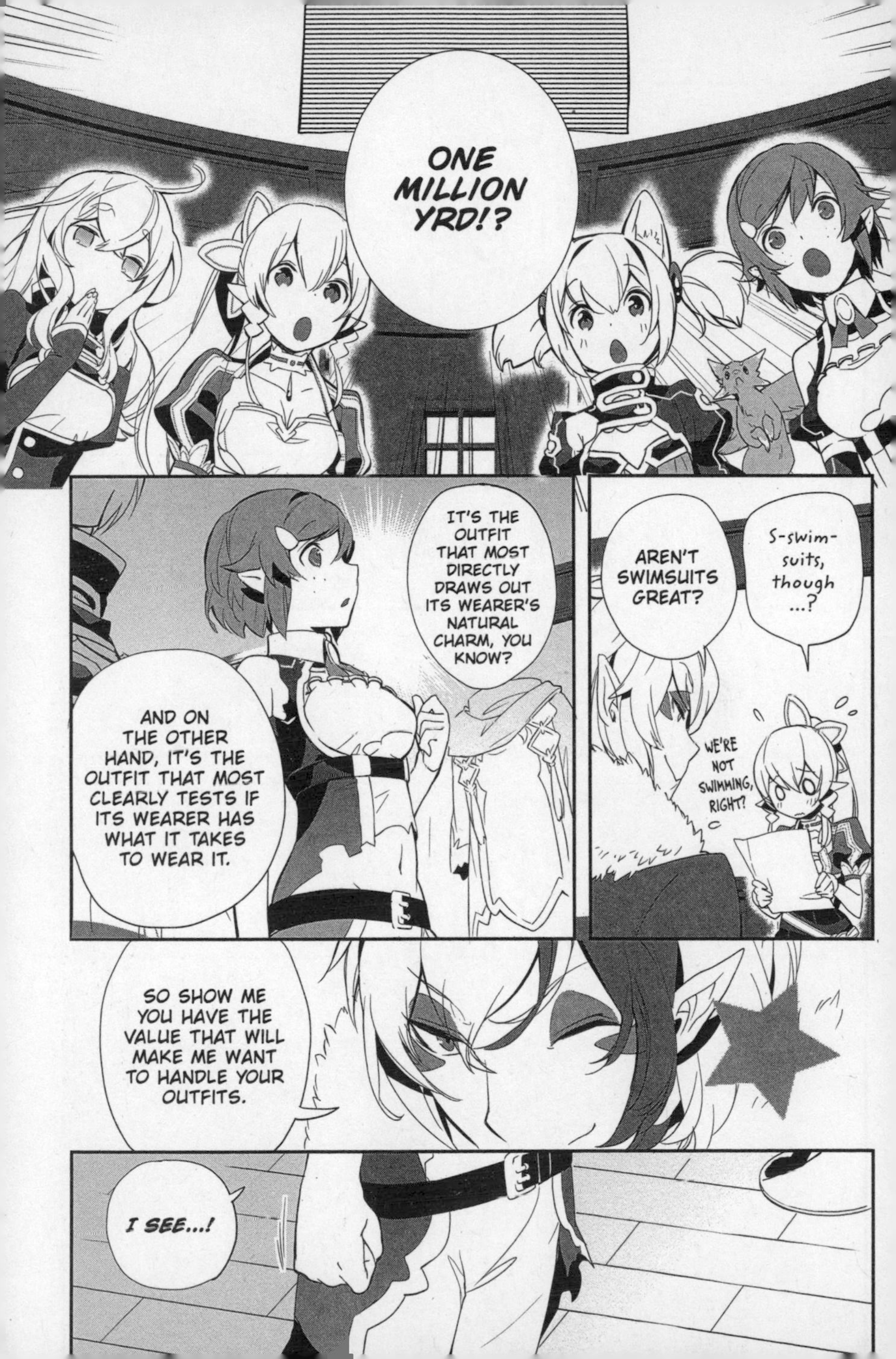
ONE MILLION YRD!?
S-swim-suits, though ...?
AREN'T SWIMSUITS GREAT?
WE'RE NOT SWIMMING, RIGHT?
IT'S THE OUTFIT THAT MOST DIRECTLY DRAWS OUT ITS WEARER'S NATURAL CHARM, YOU KNOW?
AND ON THE OTHER HAND, IT'S THE OUTFIT THAT MOST CLEARLY TESTS IF ITS WEARER HAS WHAT IT TAKES TO WEAR IT.
SO SHOW ME YOU HAVE THE VALUE THAT WILL MAKE ME WANT TO HANDLE YOUR OUTFITS.
I SEE...!

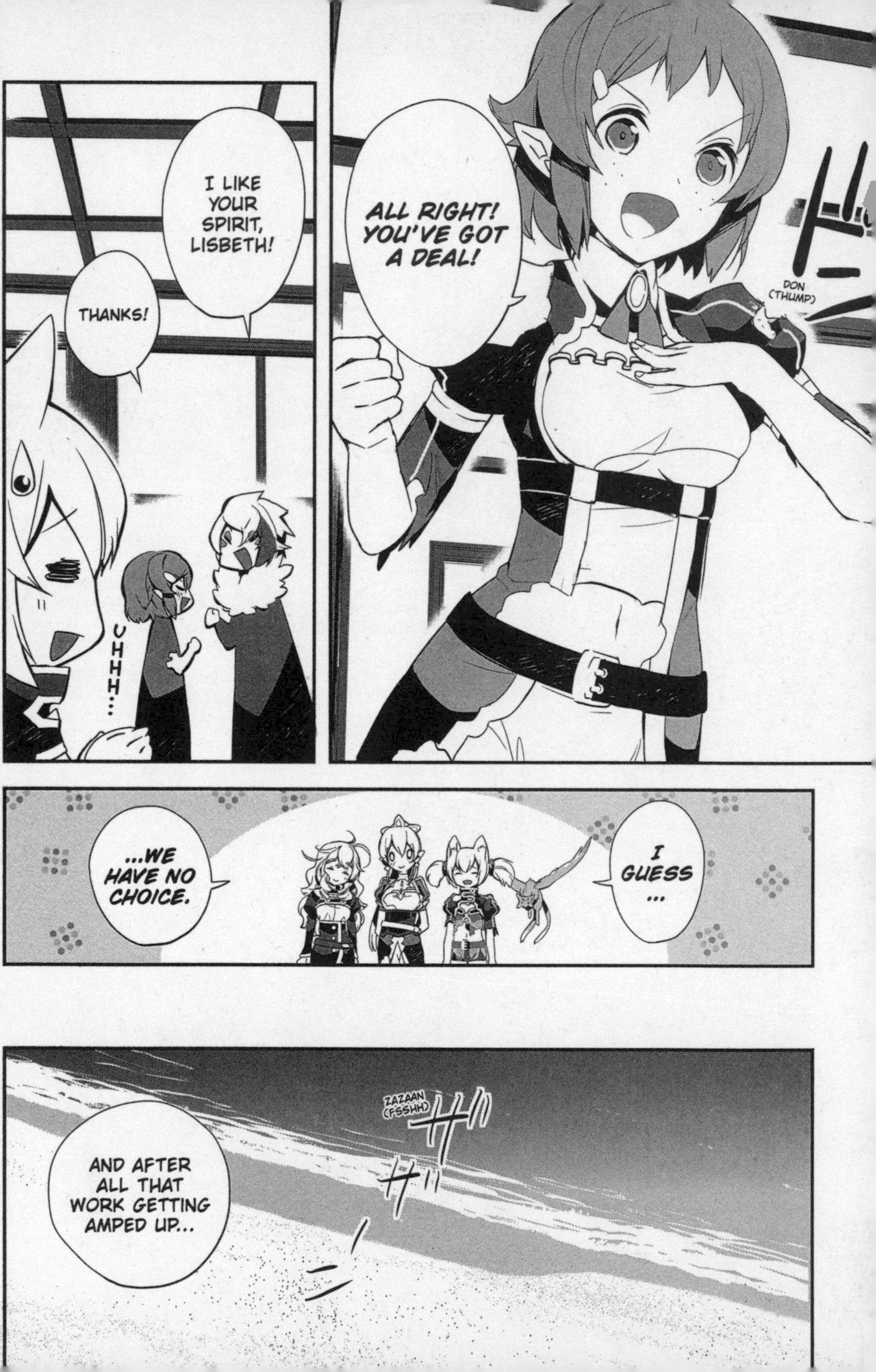
ALL RIGHT! YOU'VE GOT A DEAL!
DON (THUMP)
I LIKE YOUR SPIRIT, LISBETH!
THANKS!
UHHH...
I GUESS...
...WE HAVE NO CHOICE.
ZAZAAN (FSSHH)
AND AFTER ALL THAT WORK GETTING AMPED UP...

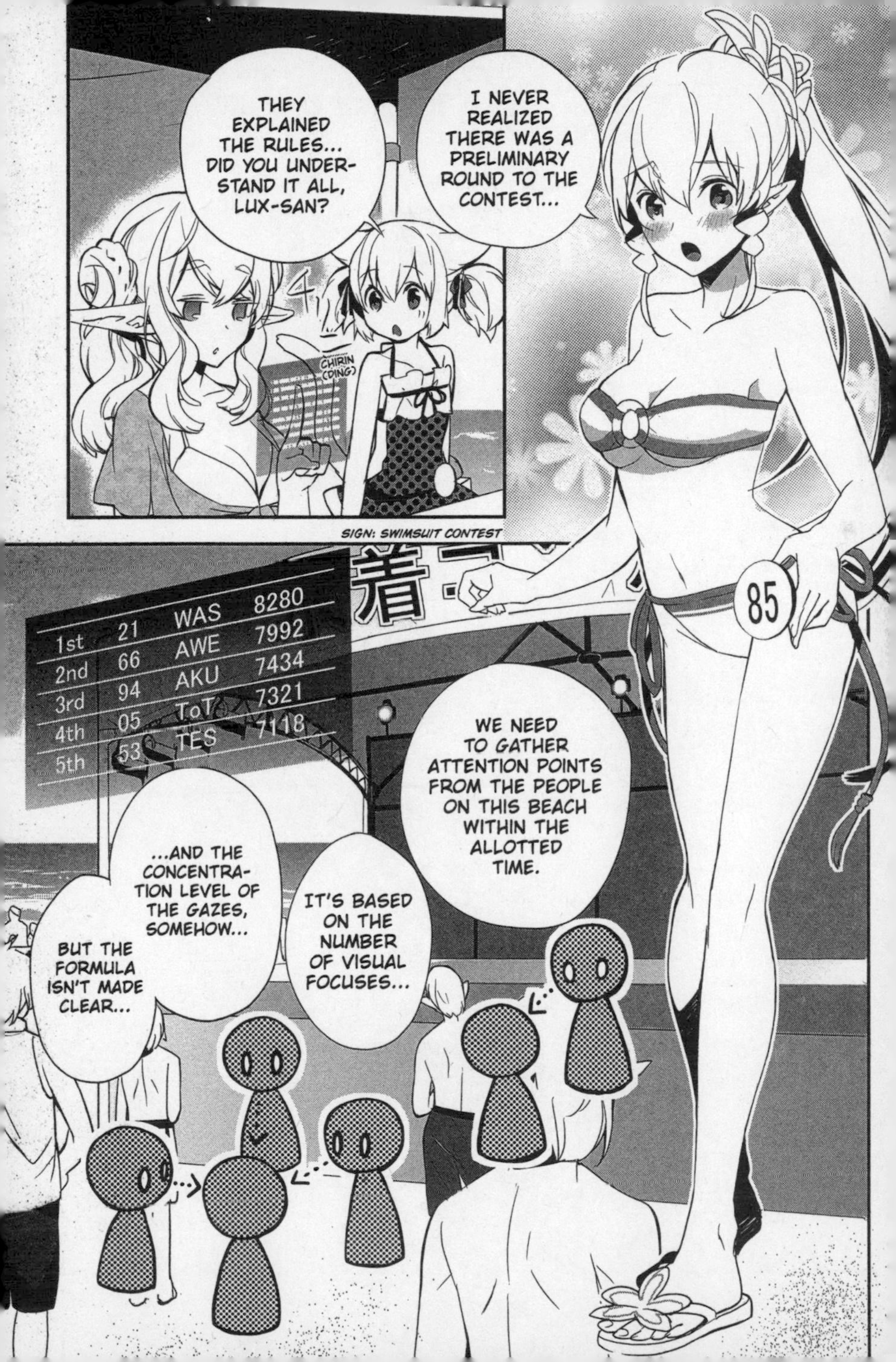
I NEVER REALIZED THERE WAS A PRELIMINARY ROUND TO THE CONTEST...
THEY EXPLAINED THE RULES... DID YOU UNDER-STAND IT ALL, LUX-SAN?
CHIRIN (DING)
SIGN: SWIMSUIT CONTEST
1st 21 WAS 8280
2nd 66 AWE 7992
3rd 94 AKU 7434
4th 05 ToT 7321
5th 53 TES 7118
85
WE NEED TO GATHER ATTENTION POINTS FROM THE PEOPLE ON THIS BEACH WITHIN THE ALLOTTED TIME.
IT'S BASED ON THE NUMBER OF VISUAL FOCUSES...
...AND THE CONCENTRA-TION LEVEL OF THE GAZES, SOMEHOW...
BUT THE FORMULA ISN'T MADE CLEAR...

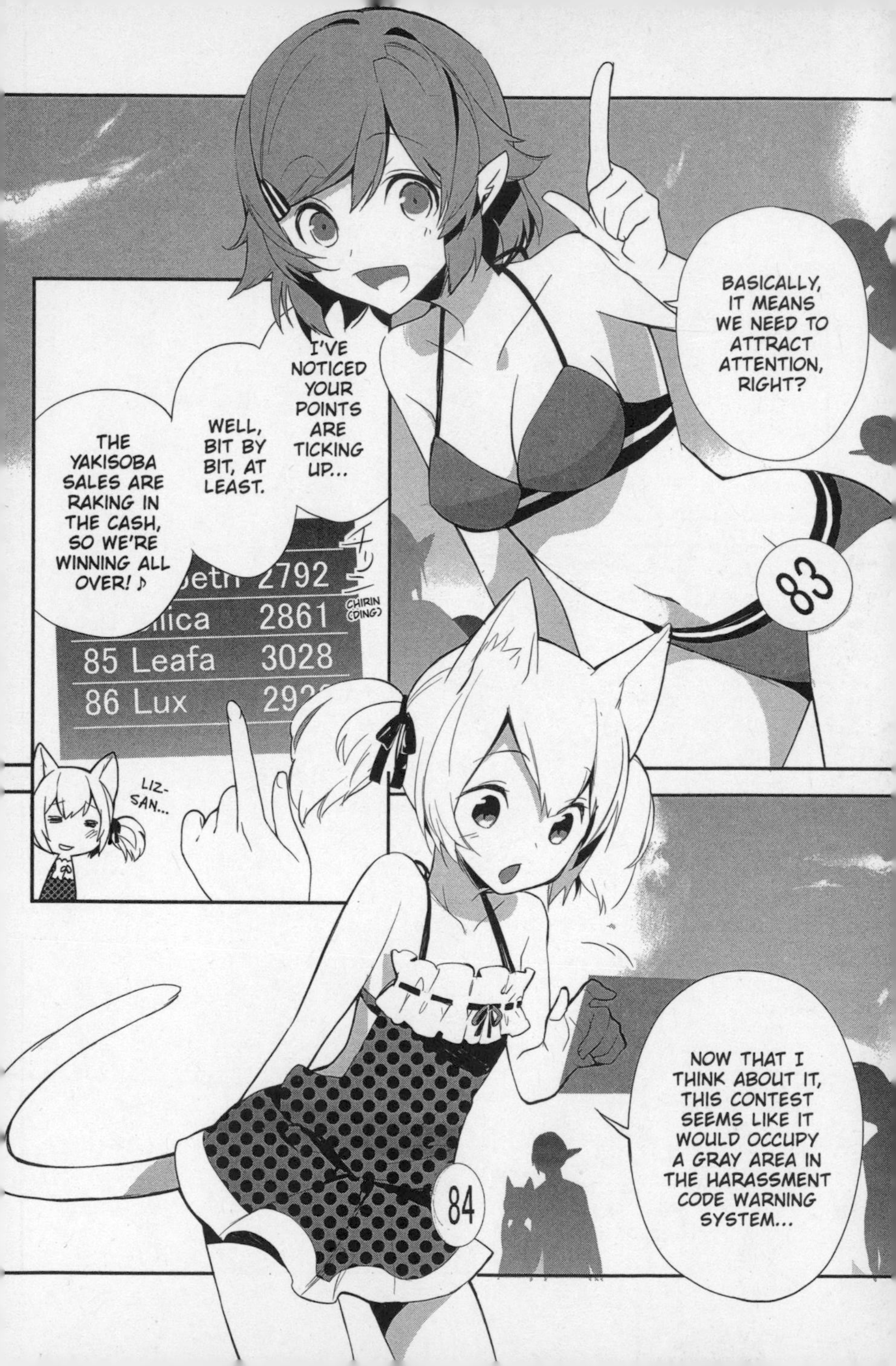
BASICALLY, IT MEANS WE NEED TO ATTRACT ATTENTION, RIGHT?
I'VE NOTICED YOUR POINTS ARE TICKING UP...
WELL, BIT BY BIT, AT LEAST.
THE YAKISOBA SALES ARE RAKING IN THE CASH, SO WE'RE WINNING ALL OVER! ♪
CHIRIN (DING)
83
85 Leafa 3028
86 Lux
LIZ-SAN...
NOW THAT I THINK ABOUT IT, THIS CONTEST SEEMS LIKE IT WOULD OCCUPY A GRAY AREA IN THE HARASSMENT CODE WARNING SYSTEM...
84

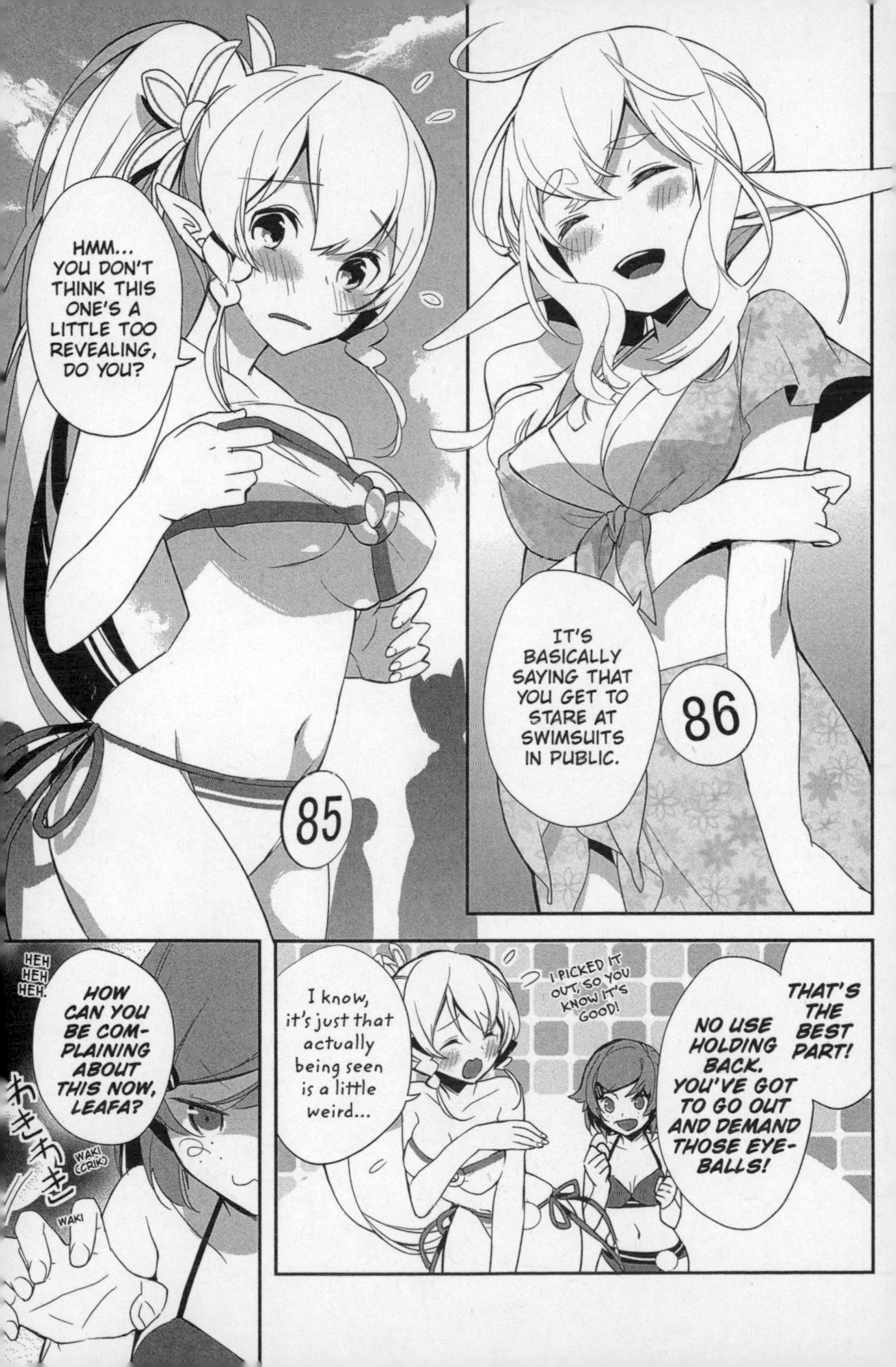
IT'S BASICALLY SAYING THAT YOU GET TO STARE AT SWIMSUITS IN PUBLIC.
86
HMM... YOU DON'T THINK THIS ONE'S A LITTLE TOO REVEALING, DO YOU?
85
THAT'S THE BEST PART!
NO USE HOLDING BACK. YOU'VE GOT TO GO OUT AND DEMAND THOSE EYE-BALLS!
I PICKED IT OUT, SO YOU KNOW IT'S GOOD!
I know, it's just that actually being seen is a little weird...
HOW CAN YOU BE COM-PLAINING ABOUT THIS NOW, LEAFA?
HEH HEH HEH.
わきわき
WAKI (CRIK)
WAKI

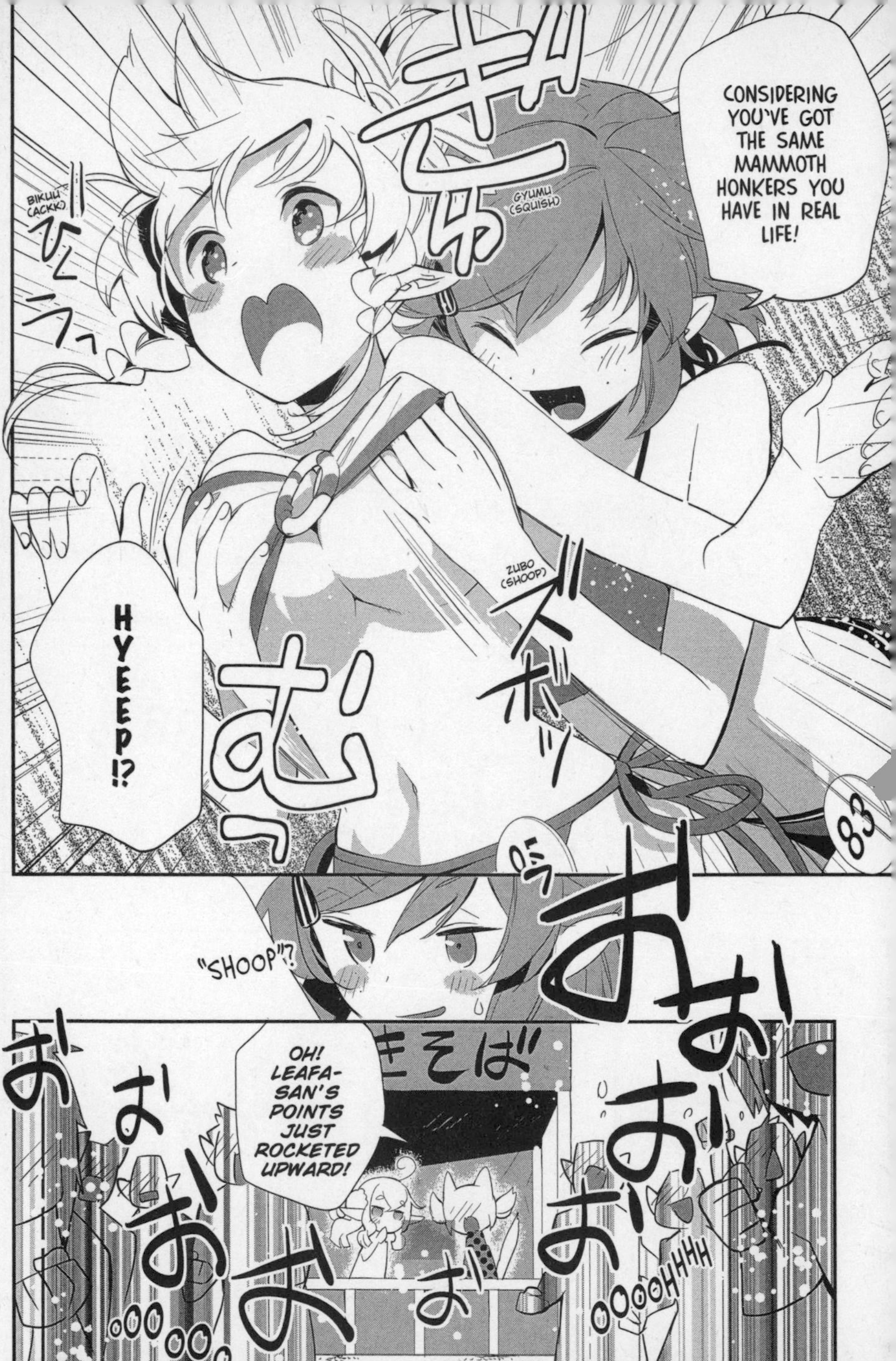
CONSIDERING YOU'VE GOT THE SAME MAMMOTH HONKERS YOU HAVE IN REAL LIFE!
GYUMU (SQUISH)
BIKULI (ACKK)
ZUBO (SHOOP)
HYEEEP!?
83
"SHOOP"!?
OH! LEAFA-SAN'S POINTS JUST ROCKETED UPWARD!
きそば
OOOOHHHH
...OOO...OOO...
SIGN: YAKISOBA

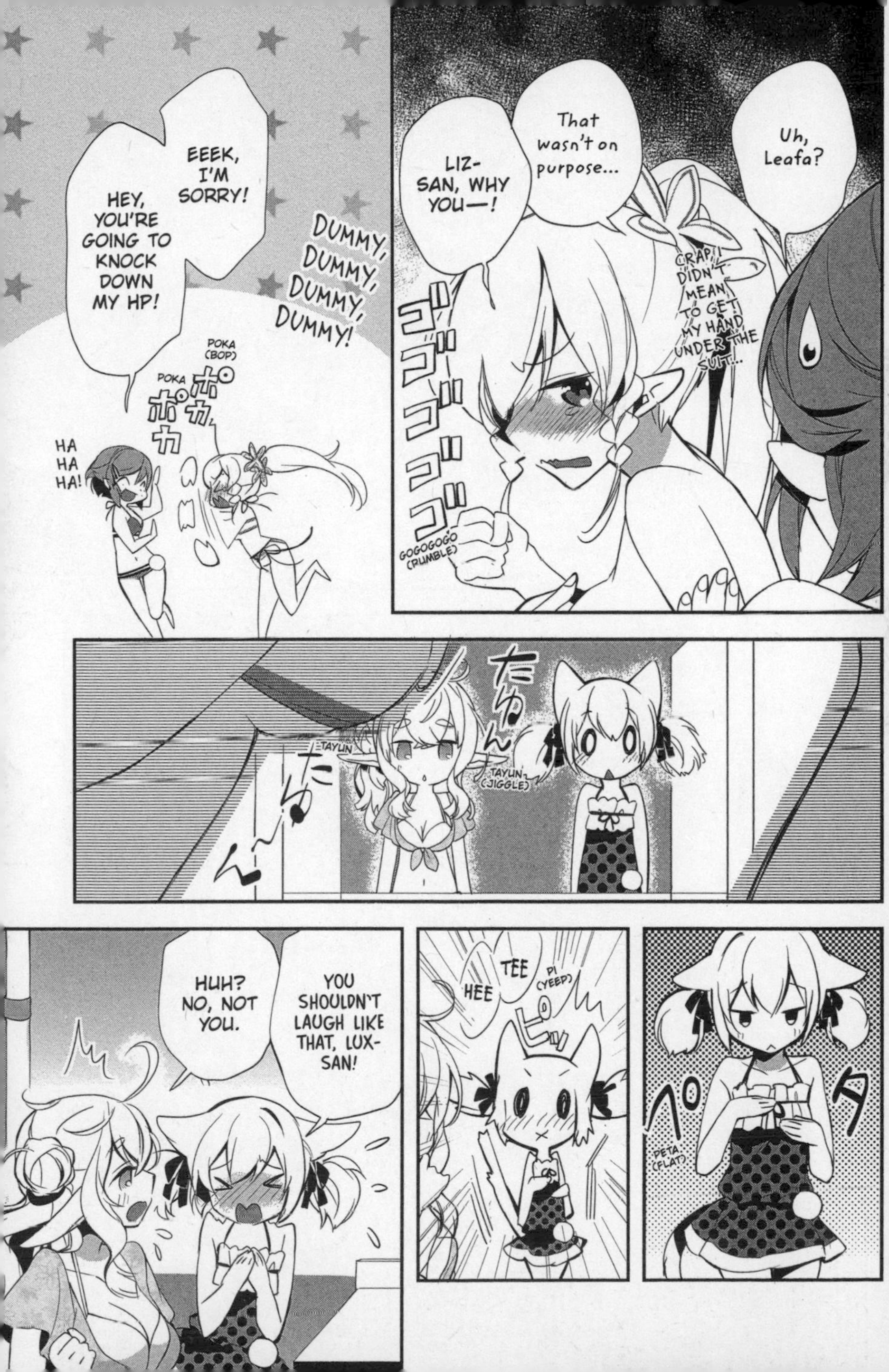
Uh, Leafa?
That wasn't on purpose...
LIZ-SAN, WHY YOU—!
CRAP, I DIDN'T MEAN TO GET MY HAND UNDER THE SUIT...
ゴゴゴゴ
GOGOGOGO (RUMBLE)
EEEK, I'M SORRY!
HEY, YOU'RE GOING TO KNOCK DOWN MY HP!
DUMMY, DUMMY, DUMMY, DUMMY!
ポカ
POKA (BOP)
ポカ
POKA
HA HA HA!
たゆん
TAYUN (JIGGLE)
たゆん
TAYUN
ペタ
PETA (FLAT)
TEE
HEE
ピッ
PI (YEEP)
YOU SHOULDN'T LAUGH LIKE THAT, LUX-SAN!
HUH? NO, NOT YOU.

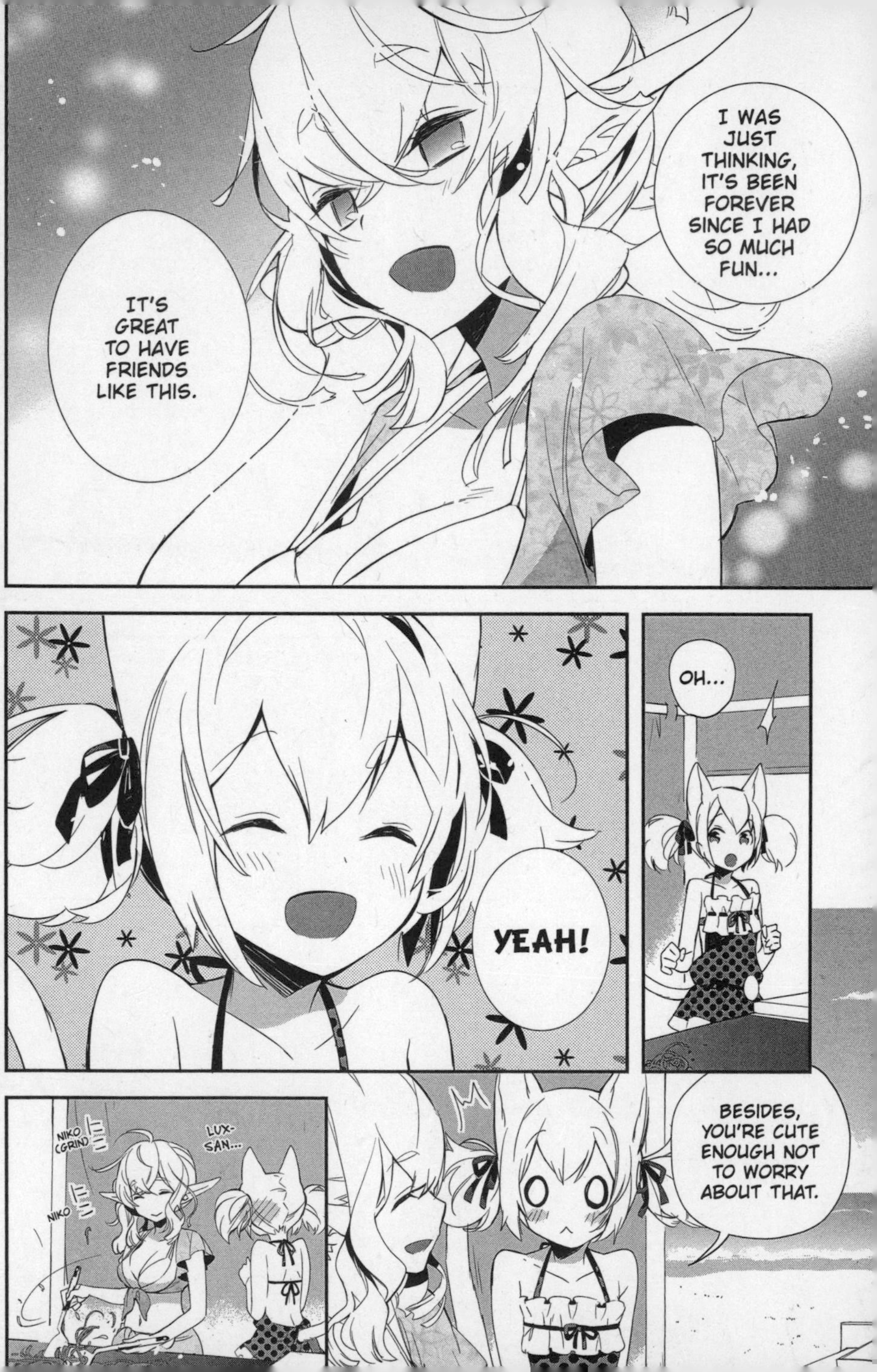
I WAS JUST THINKING, IT'S BEEN FOREVER SINCE I HAD SO MUCH FUN...
IT'S GREAT TO HAVE FRIENDS LIKE THIS.
OH...
YEAH!
BESIDES, YOU'RE CUTE ENOUGH NOT TO WORRY ABOUT THAT.
LUX-SAN...
NIKO (GRIN)
NIKO

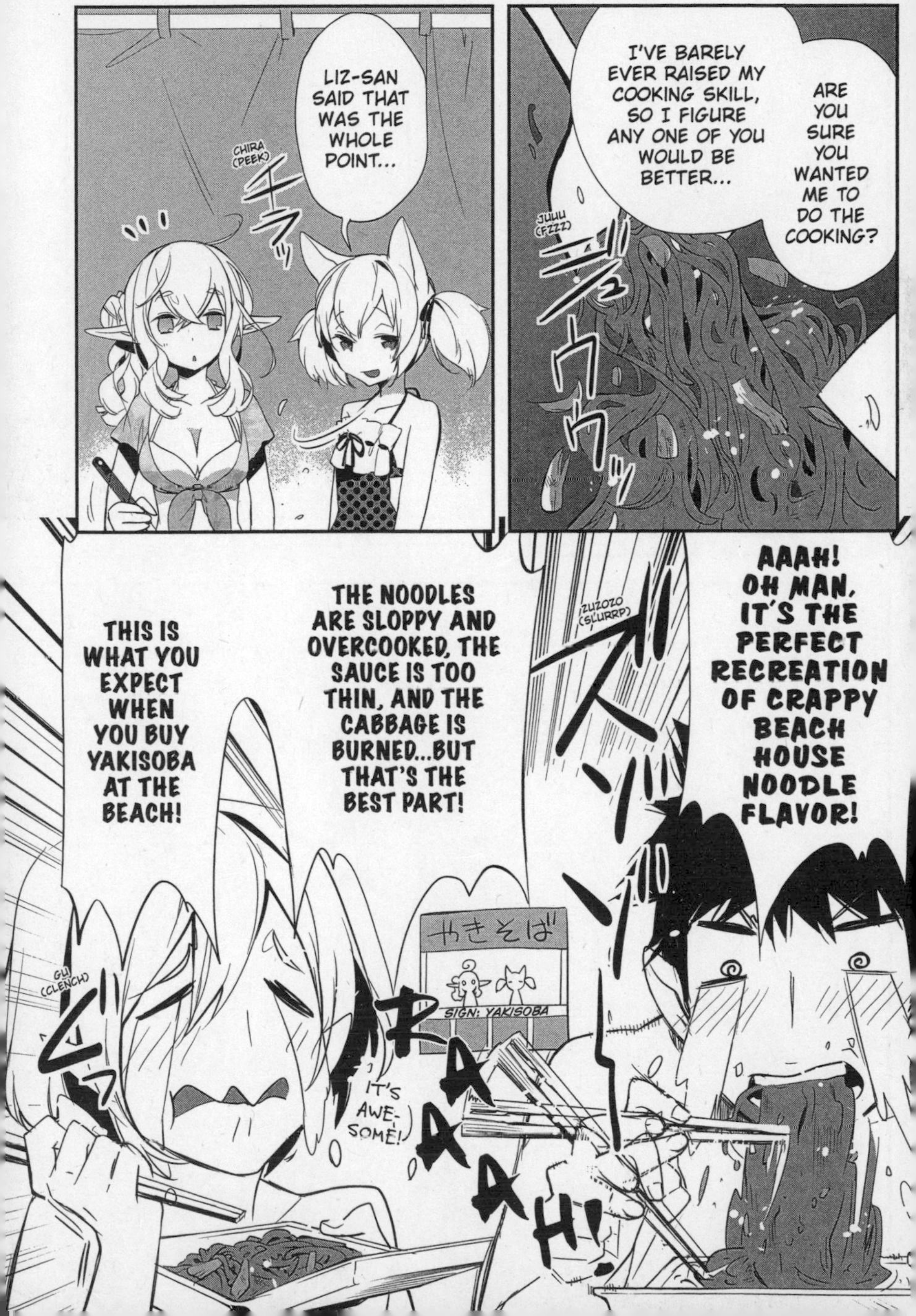
ARE YOU SURE YOU WANTED ME TO DO THE COOKING?
I'VE BARELY EVER RAISED MY COOKING SKILL, SO I FIGURE ANY ONE OF YOU WOULD BE BETTER...
JUUU (FZZZ)
LIZ-SAN SAID THAT WAS THE WHOLE POINT...
CHIRA (PEEK)
AAAH! OH MAN, IT'S THE PERFECT RECREATION OF CRAPPY BEACH HOUSE NOODLE FLAVOR!
ZUZOZO (SLURRP)
THE NOODLES ARE SLOPPY AND OVERCOOKED, THE SAUCE IS TOO THIN, AND THE CABBAGE IS BURNED...BUT THAT'S THE BEST PART!
THIS IS WHAT YOU EXPECT WHEN YOU BUY YAKISOBA AT THE BEACH!
やきそば
SIGN: YAKISOBA
RAAAAH!
IT'S AWE-SOME!
GU (CLENCH)

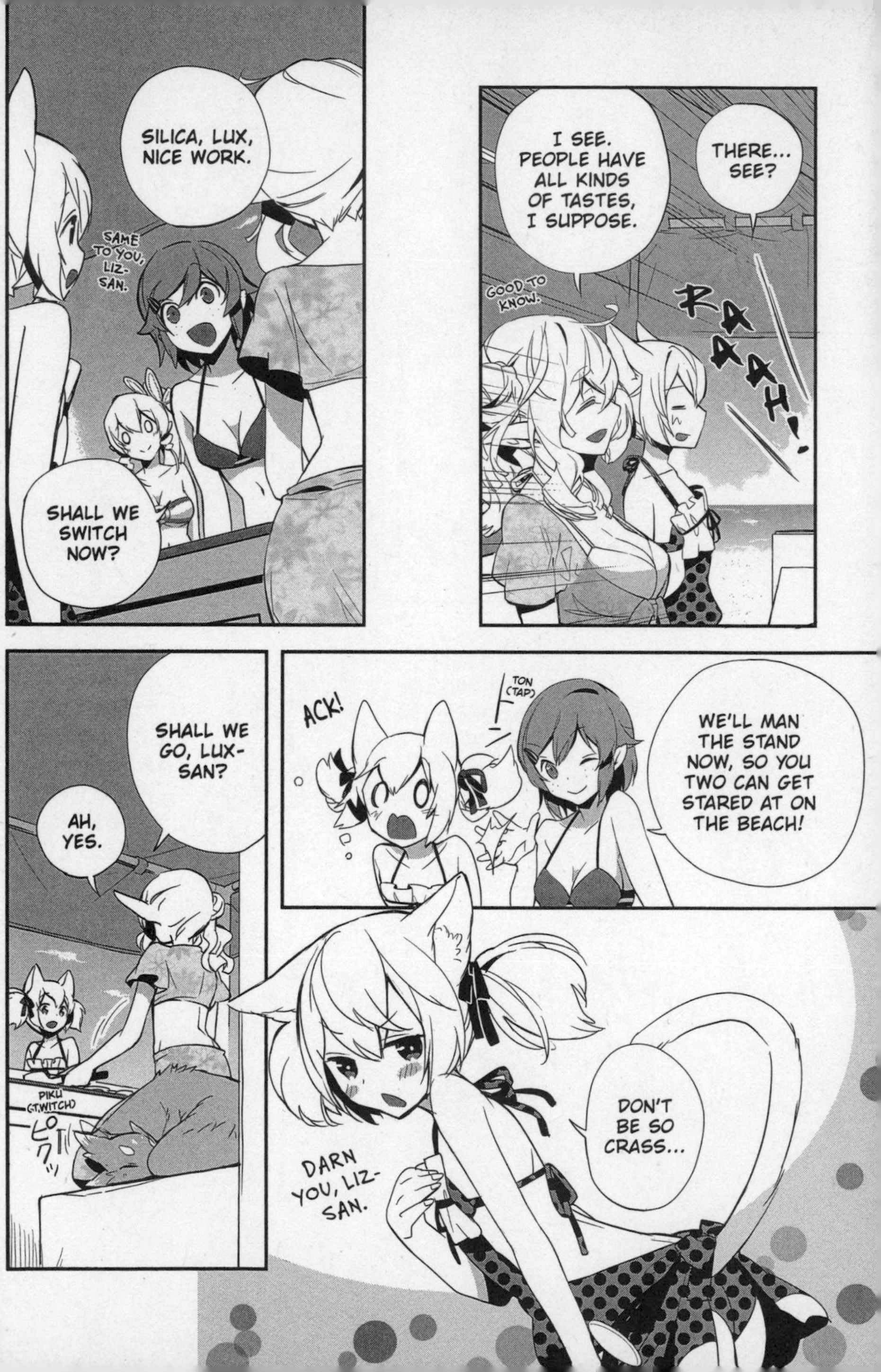
THERE... SEE?
I SEE. PEOPLE HAVE ALL KINDS OF TASTES, I SUPPOSE.
GOOD TO KNOW.
RAAAH!
SILICA, LUX, NICE WORK.
SAME TO YOU, LIZ-SAN.
SHALL WE SWITCH NOW?
TON (TAP)
WE'LL MAN THE STAND NOW, SO YOU TWO CAN GET STARED AT ON THE BEACH!
ACK!
DON'T BE SO CRASS...
DARN YOU, LIZ-SAN.
SHALL WE GO, LUX-SAN?
AH, YES.
PIKU (TWITCH)

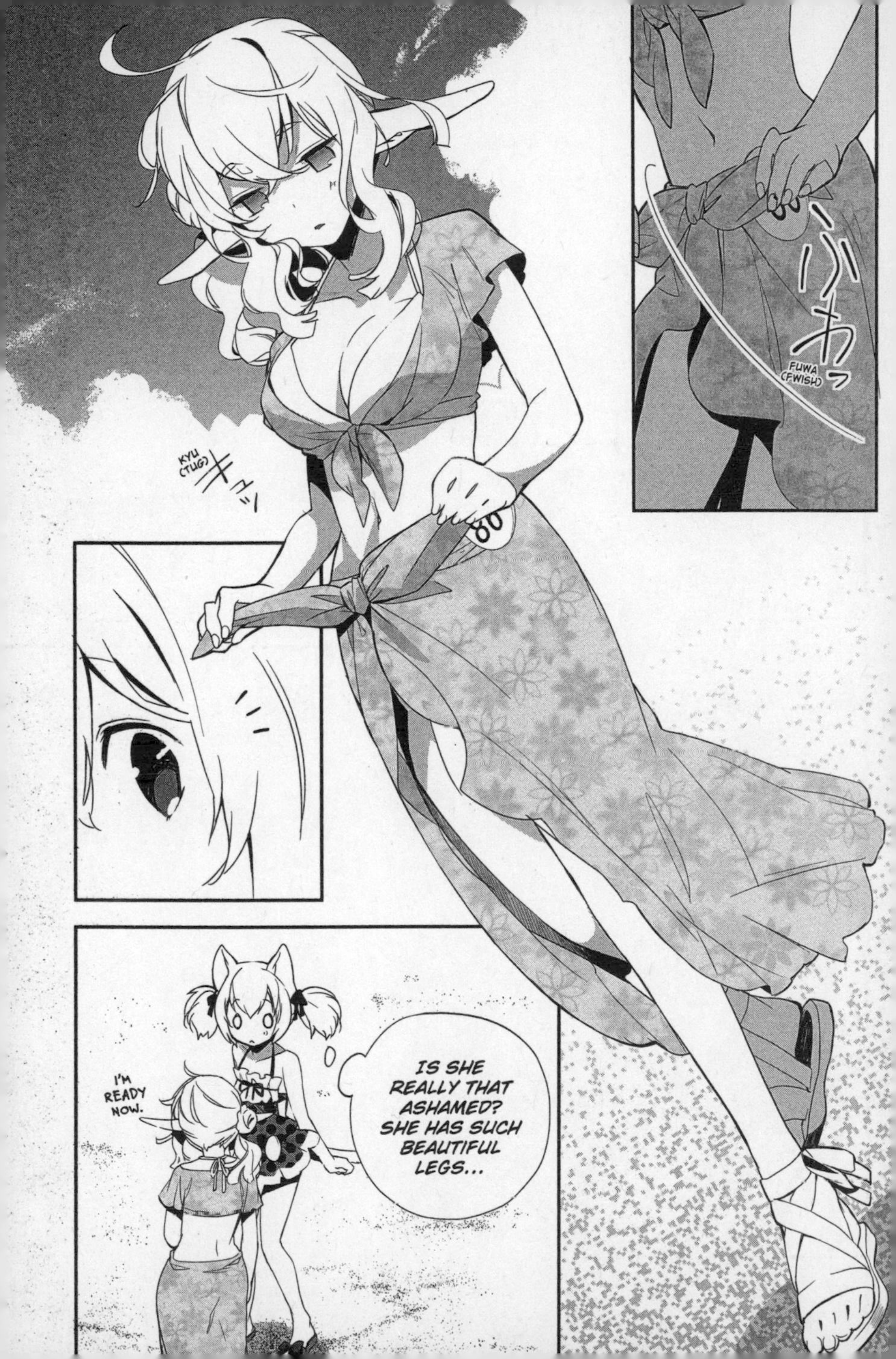
ふわっ
FUWA (FWISH)
KYU (TUG)
IS SHE REALLY THAT ASHAMED? SHE HAS SUCH BEAUTIFUL LEGS...
I'M READY NOW.

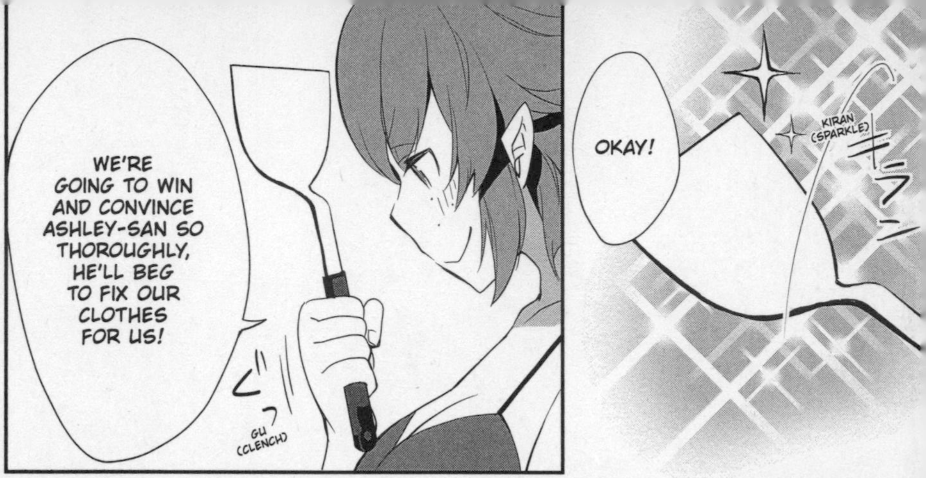
OKAY!
KIRAN (SPARKLE)
キラン
WE'RE GOING TO WIN AND CONVINCE ASHLEY-SAN SO THOROUGHLY, HE'LL BEG TO FIX OUR CLOTHES FOR US!
ぐっ
GU (CLENCH)

SIGN: YAKISOBA

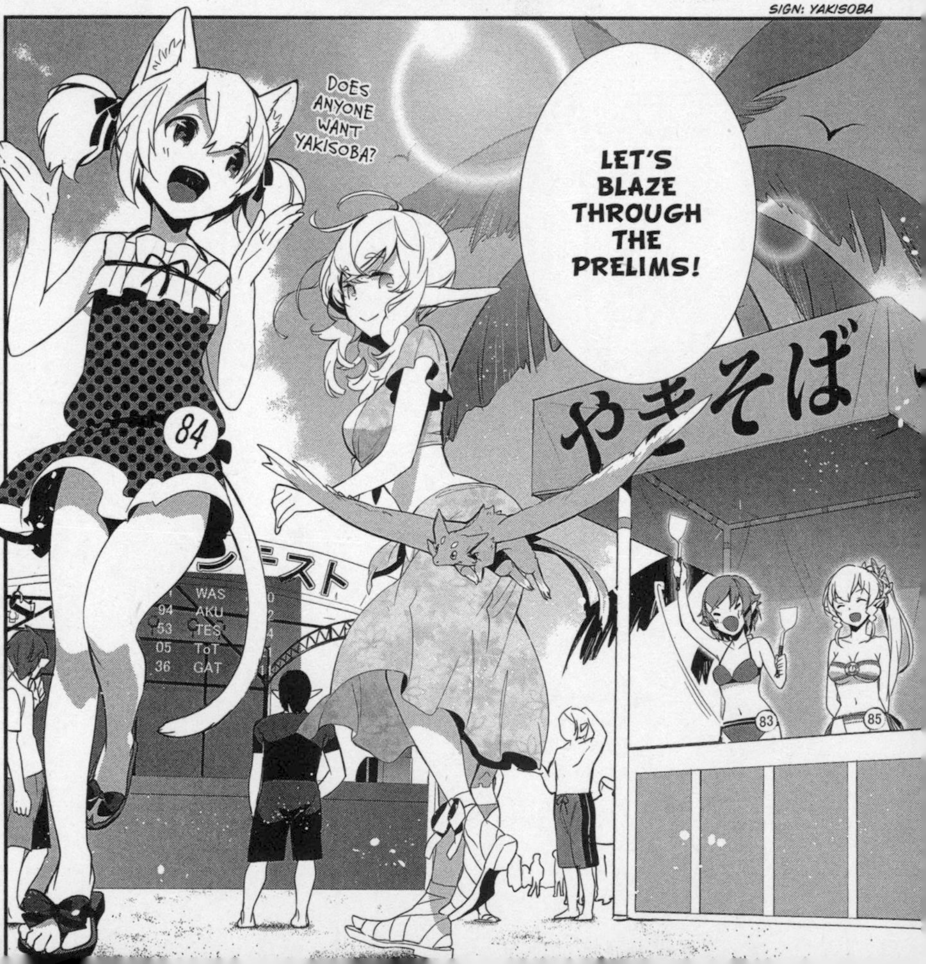
LET'S BLAZE THROUGH THE PRELIMS!
DOES ANYONE WANT YAKISOBA?
やきそば
84
WAS
94 AKU
53 TES
05 ToT
36 GAT
83
85

SWORD ART ONLINE
GIRLS' OPS

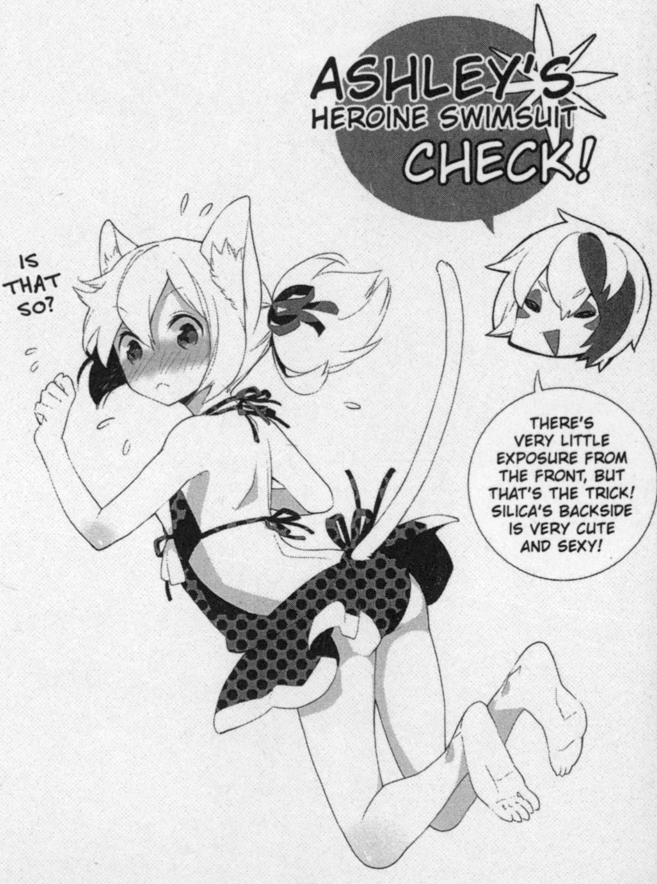
ASHLEY'S HEROINE SWIMSUIT CHECK!
THERE'S VERY LITTLE EXPOSURE FROM THE FRONT, BUT THAT'S THE TRICK! SILICA'S BACKSIDE IS VERY CUTE AND SEXY!
IS THAT SO?

STAGE. 8

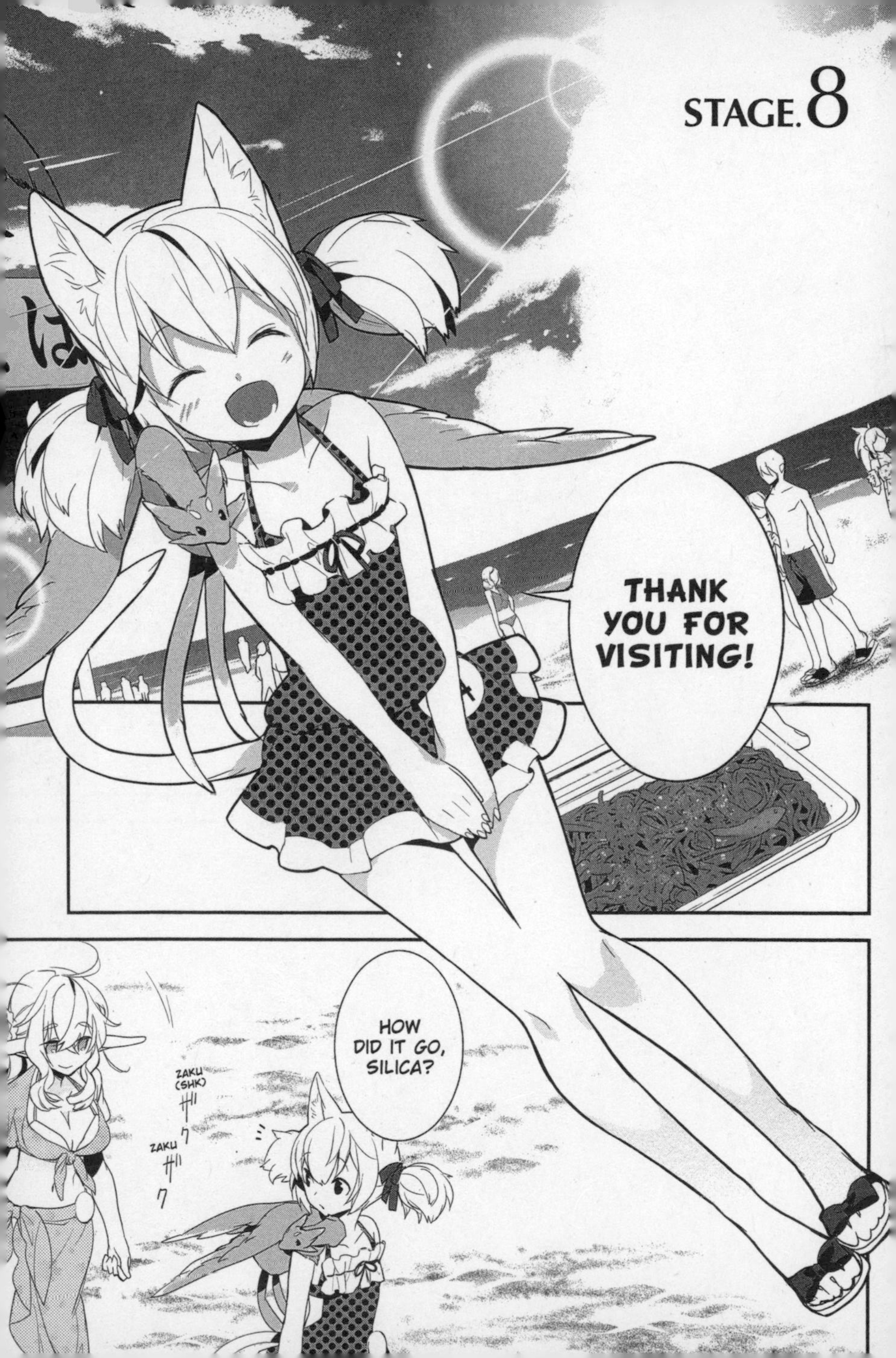
THANK YOU FOR VISITING!
HOW DID IT GO, SILICA?
ZAKU (SHK)
ザク
ZAKU
ザク

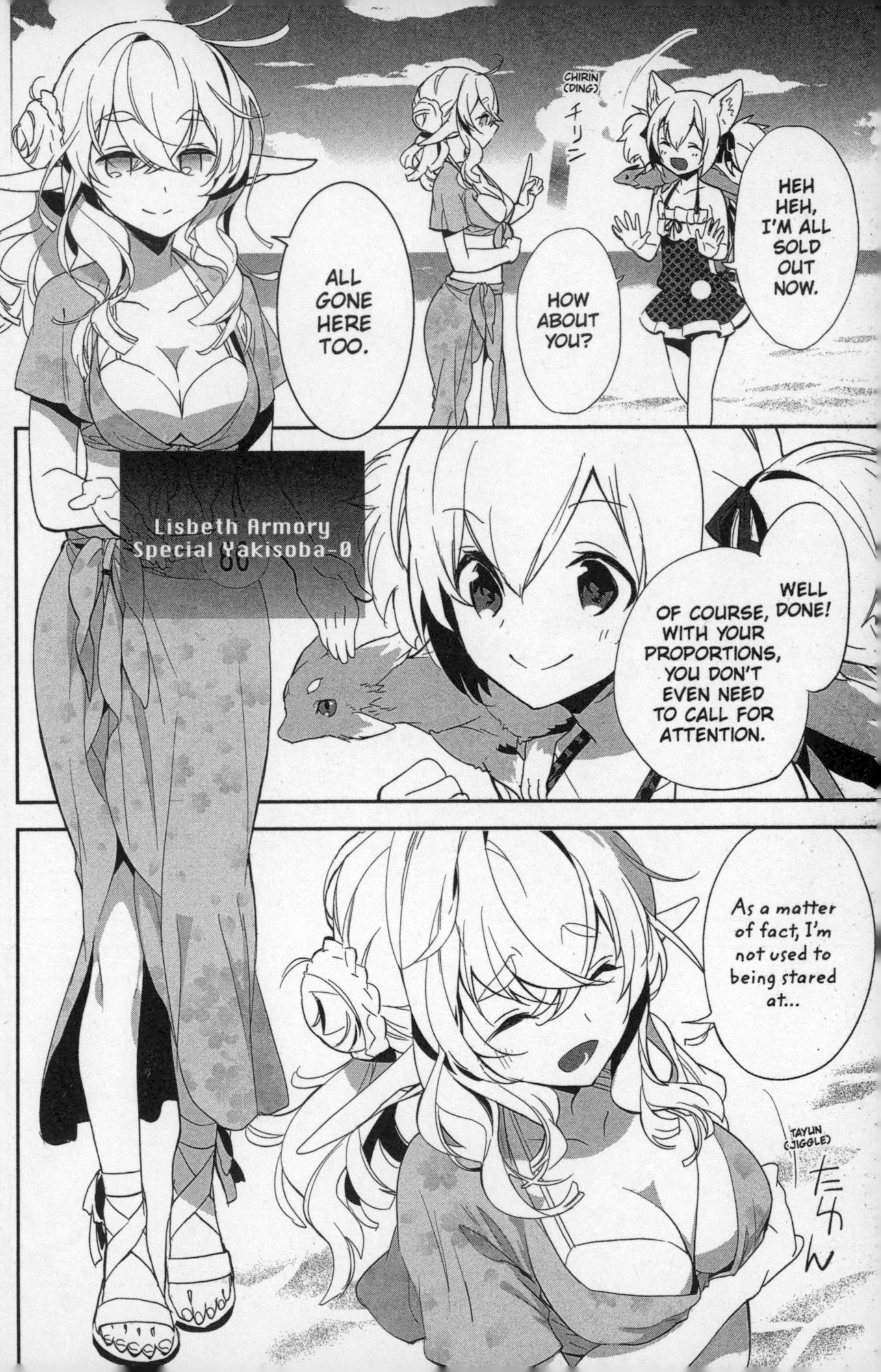
CHIRIN (DING)
チリン
HEH HEH, I'M ALL SOLD OUT NOW.
HOW ABOUT YOU?
ALL GONE HERE TOO.
Lisbeth Armory
Special Yakisoba-0
WELL DONE!
OF COURSE, WITH YOUR PROPORTIONS, YOU DON'T EVEN NEED TO CALL FOR ATTENTION.
As a matter of fact, I'm not used to being stared at...
TAYUN (JIGGLE)
たゆん

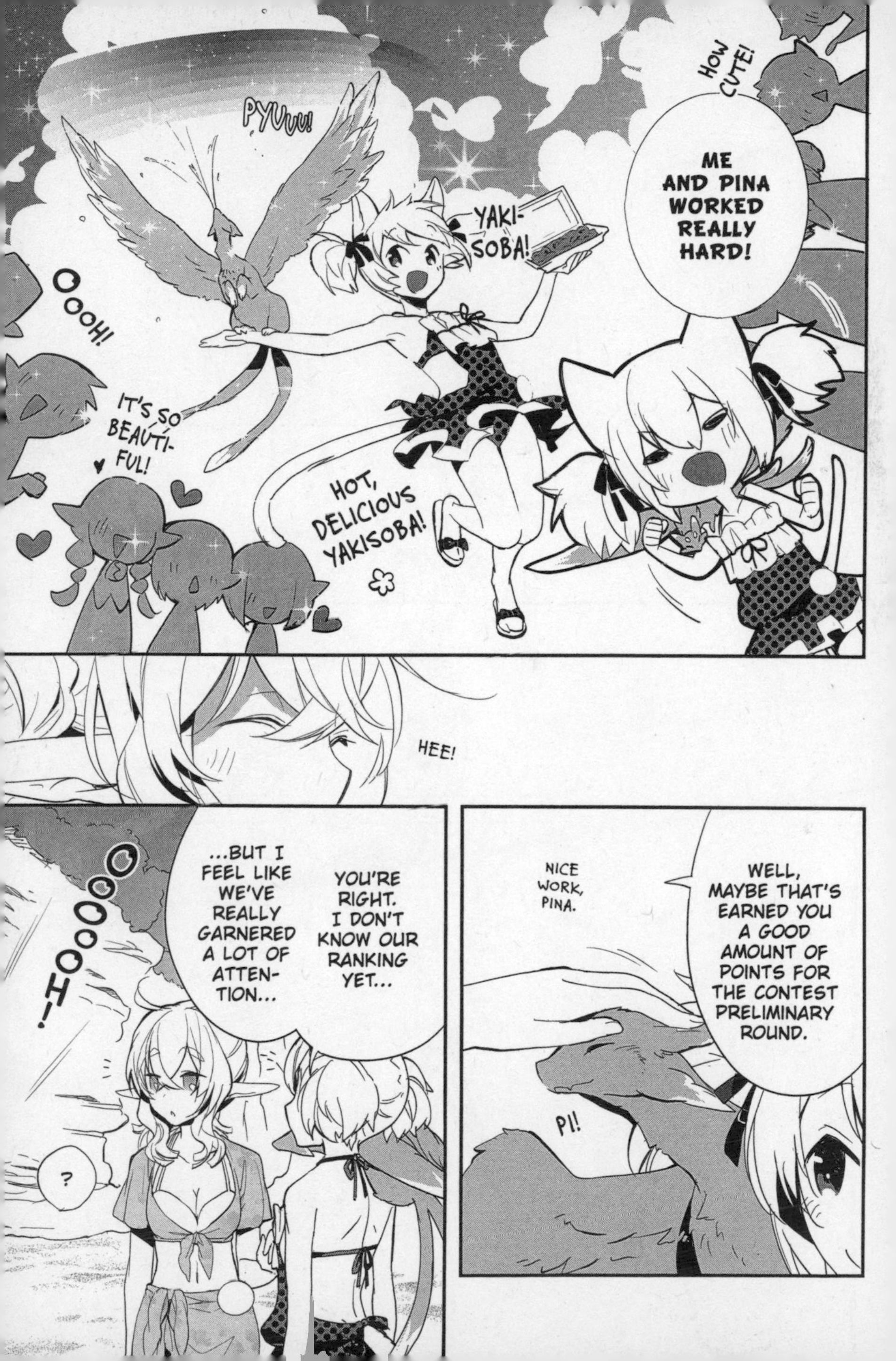
HOW CUTE!
ME AND PINA WORKED REALLY HARD!
YAKI-SOBA!
PYUUU!
OOOH!
IT'S SO BEAUTI-FUL!
HOT, DELICIOUS YAKISOBA!
HEE!
WELL, MAYBE THAT'S EARNED YOU A GOOD AMOUNT OF POINTS FOR THE CONTEST PRELIMINARY ROUND.
NICE WORK, PINA.
PI!
YOU'RE RIGHT. I DON'T KNOW OUR RANKING YET...
...BUT I FEEL LIKE WE'VE REALLY GARNERED A LOT OF ATTEN-TION...
OOOOOOH!
?

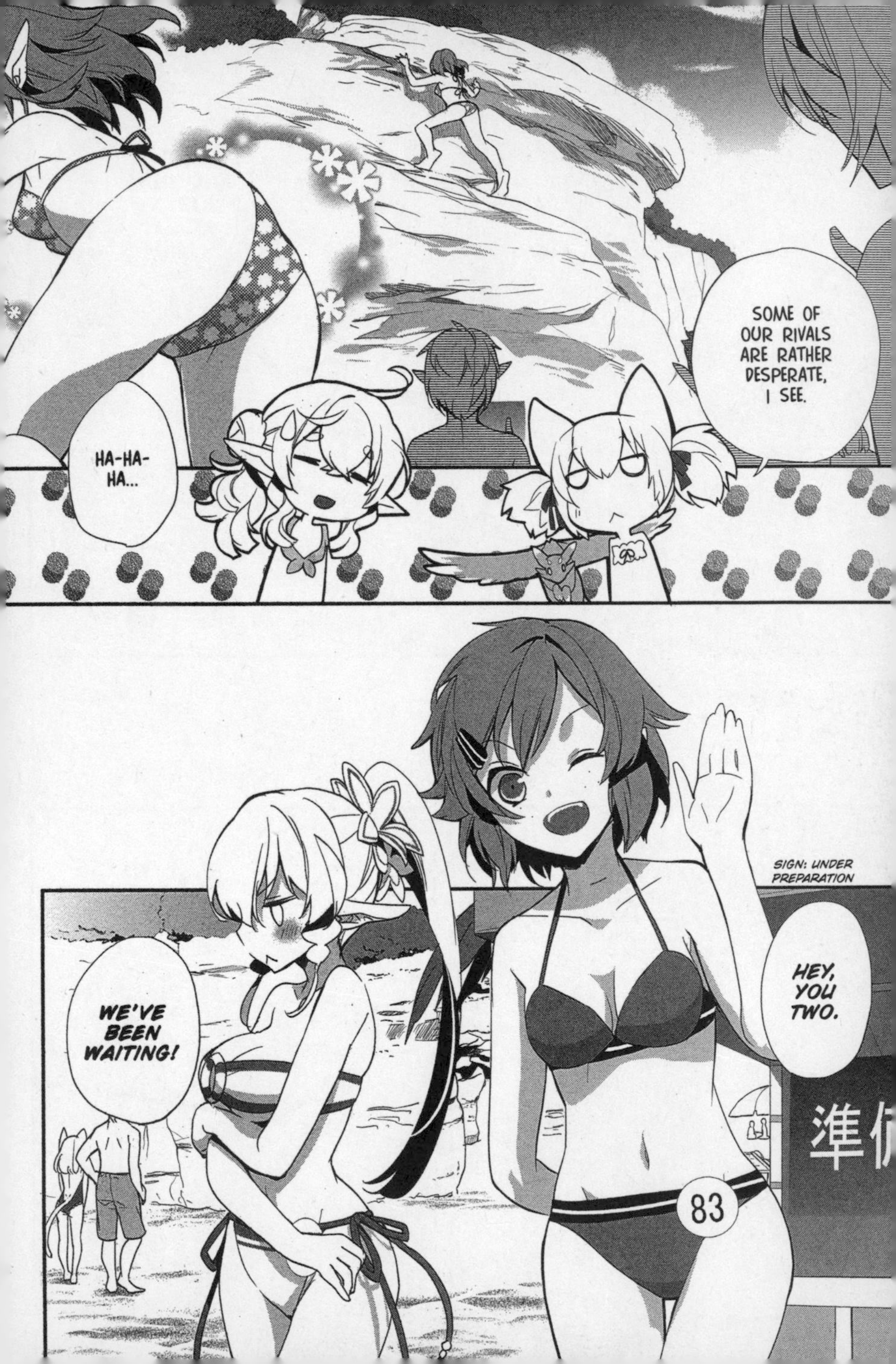
SOME OF OUR RIVALS ARE RATHER DESPERATE, I SEE.
HA-HA-HA...
SIGN: UNDER PREPARATION
準
HEY, YOU TWO.
WE'VE BEEN WAITING!
83

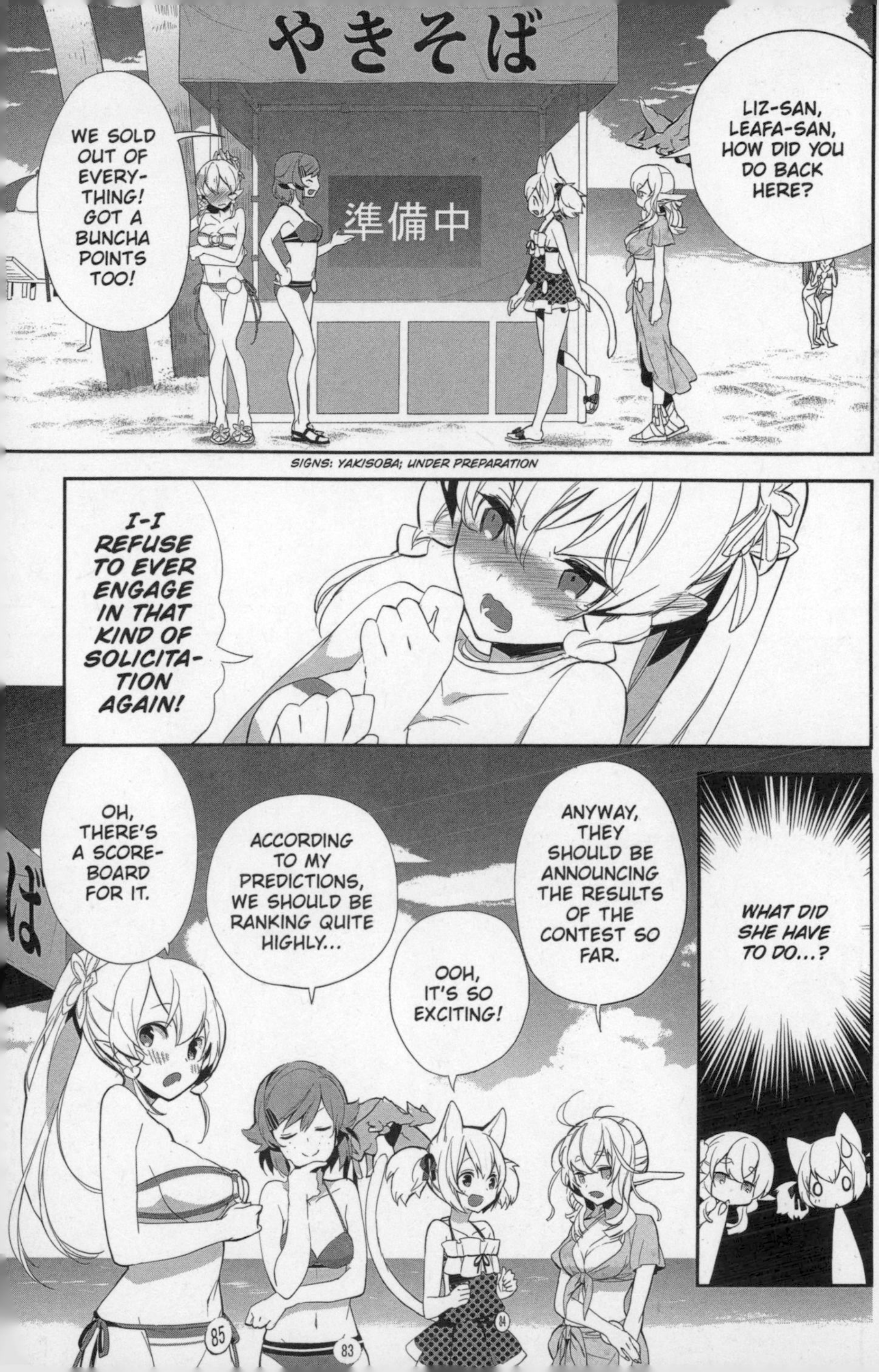

やきそば
準備中
LIZ-SAN, LEAFA-SAN, HOW DID YOU DO BACK HERE?
WE SOLD OUT OF EVERY-THING! GOT A BUNCHA POINTS TOO!
SIGNS: YAKISOBA; UNDER PREPARATION
I-I REFUSE TO EVER ENGAGE IN THAT KIND OF SOLICITA-TION AGAIN!
WHAT DID SHE HAVE TO DO...?
ANYWAY, THEY SHOULD BE ANNOUNCING THE RESULTS OF THE CONTEST SO FAR.
OOH, IT'S SO EXCITING!
ACCORDING TO MY PREDICTIONS, WE SHOULD BE RANKING QUITE HIGHLY...
OH, THERE'S A SCORE-BOARD FOR IT.
ば
85
83
84

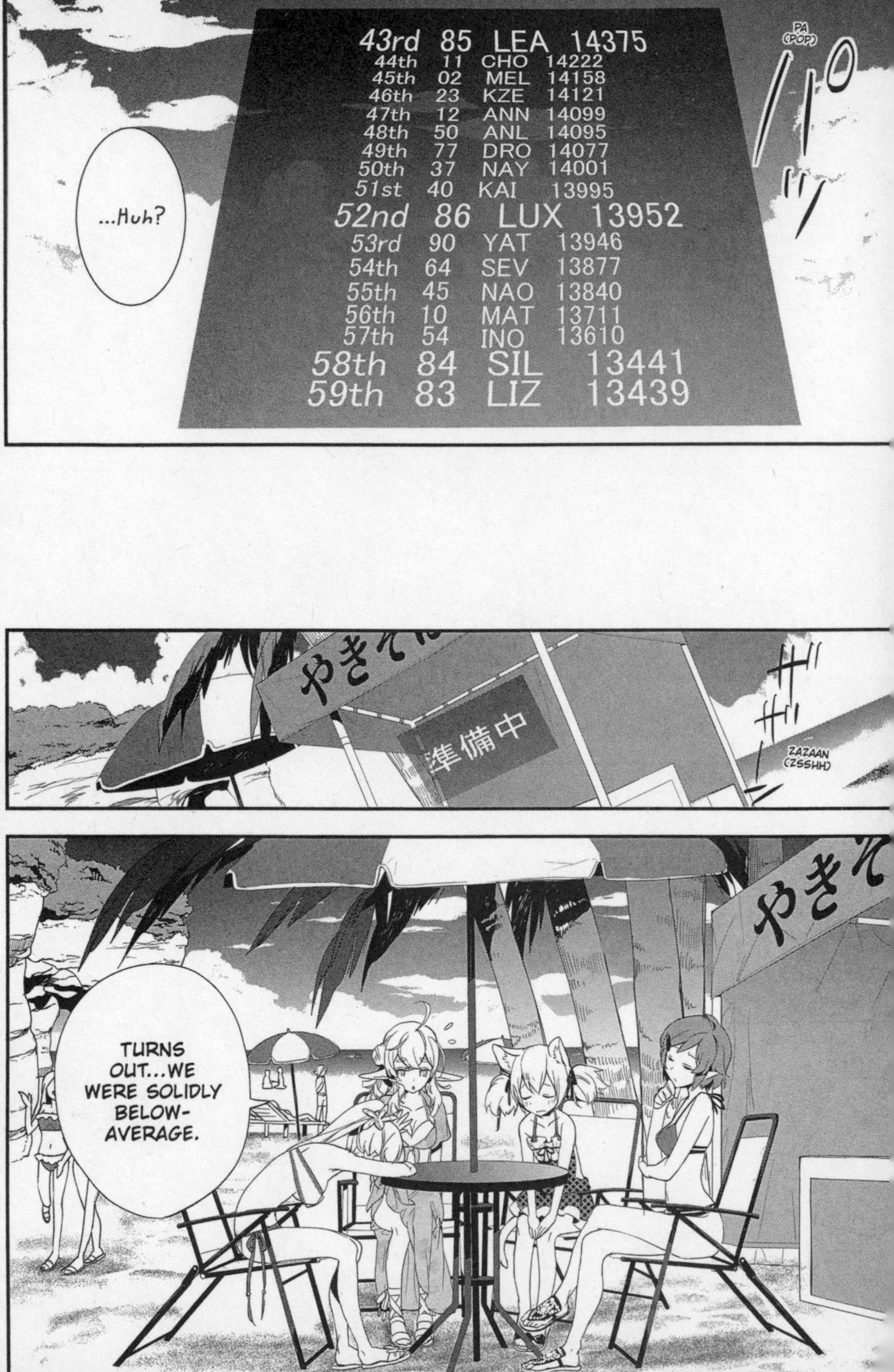

PA
(POP)
43rd 85 LEA 14375
44th 11 CHO 14222
45th 02 MEL 14158
46th 23 KZE 14121
47th 12 ANN 14099
48th 50 ANL 14095
49th 77 DRO 14077
50th 37 NAY 14001
51st 40 KAI 13995
52nd 86 LUX 13952
53rd 90 YAT 13946
54th 64 SEV 13877
55th 45 NAO 13840
56th 10 MAT 13711
57th 54 INO 13610
58th 84 SIL 13441
59th 83 LIZ 13439
...Huh?
ZAZAAN
(ZSSHH)
準備中
TURNS OUT...WE WERE SOLIDLY BELOW-AVERAGE.

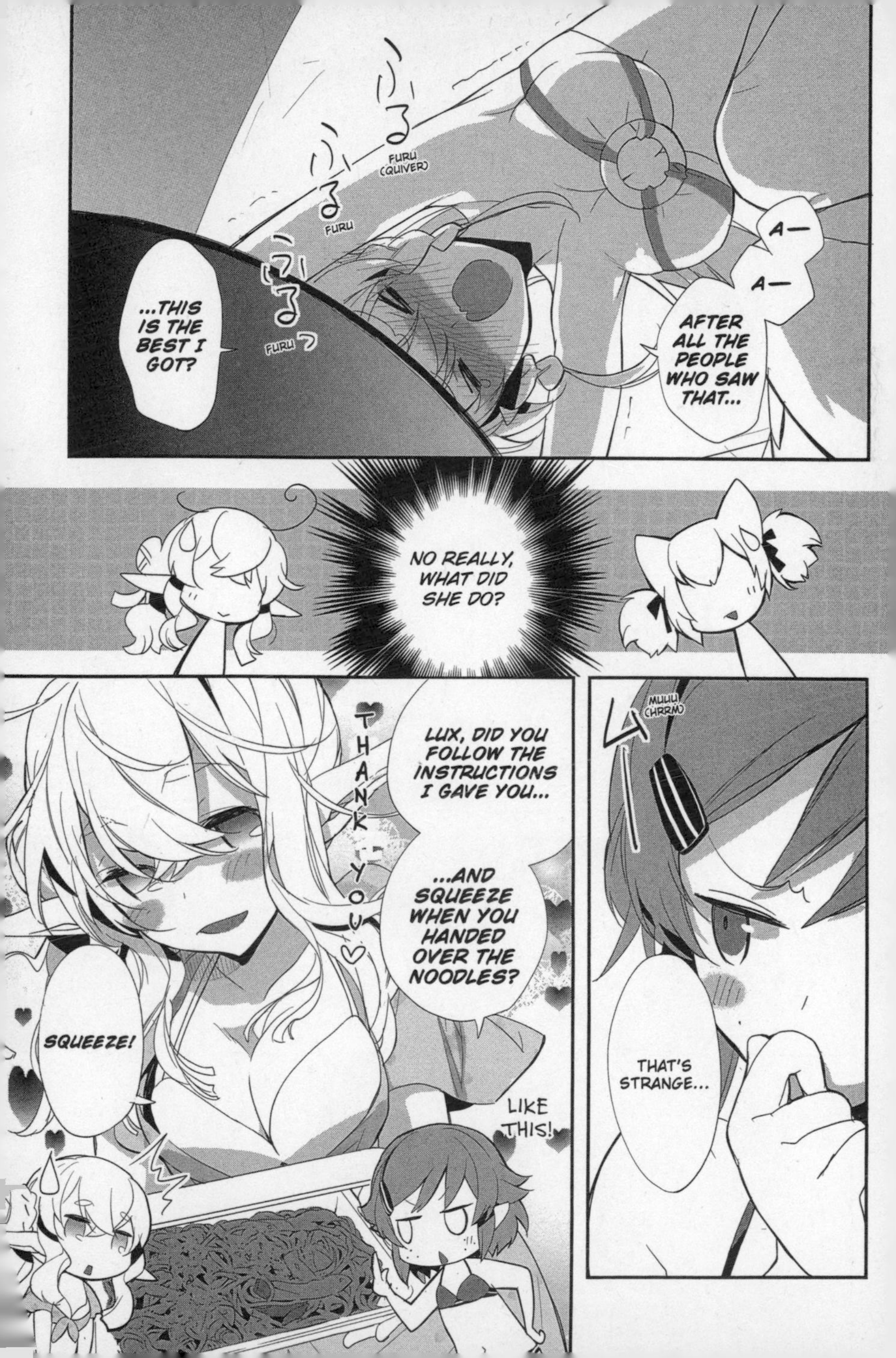
A—
A—
AFTER ALL THE PEOPLE WHO SAW THAT...
ふる
FURU (QUIVER)
ふる
FURU
ふるっ
FURU
...THIS IS THE BEST I GOT?
NO REALLY, WHAT DID SHE DO?
MUUU (HRRM)
THAT'S STRANGE...
LUX, DID YOU FOLLOW THE INSTRUCTIONS I GAVE YOU...
...AND SQUEEZE WHEN YOU HANDED OVER THE NOODLES?
THANK-YOU♡
SQUEEZE!
LIKE THIS!

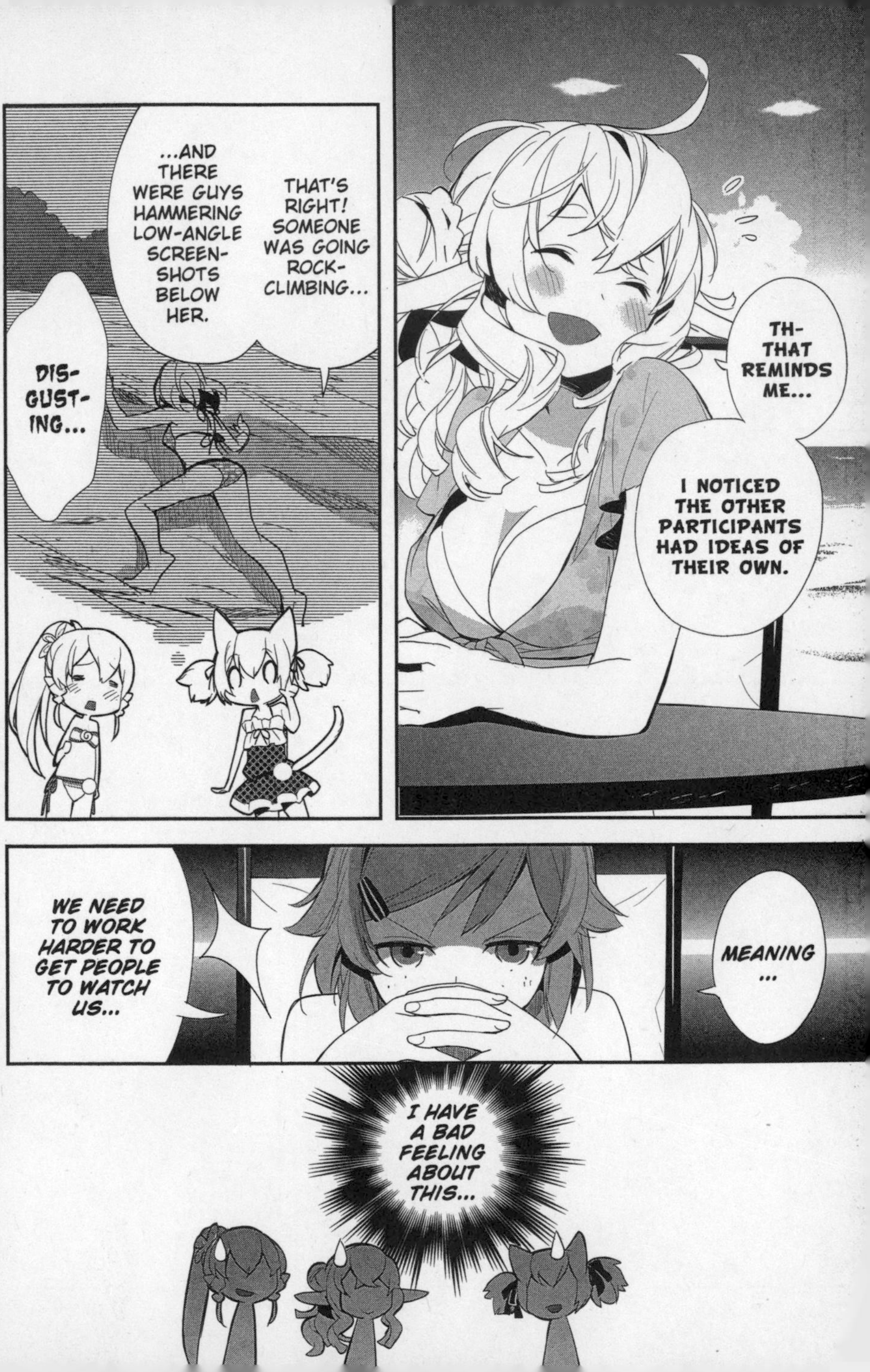
TH-THAT REMINDS ME...
I NOTICED THE OTHER PARTICIPANTS HAD IDEAS OF THEIR OWN.
THAT'S RIGHT! SOMEONE WAS GOING ROCK-CLIMBING...
...AND THERE WERE GUYS HAMMERING LOW-ANGLE SCREEN-SHOTS BELOW HER.
DIS-GUST-ING...
MEANING...
WE NEED TO WORK HARDER TO GET PEOPLE TO WATCH US...
I HAVE A BAD FEELING ABOUT THIS...

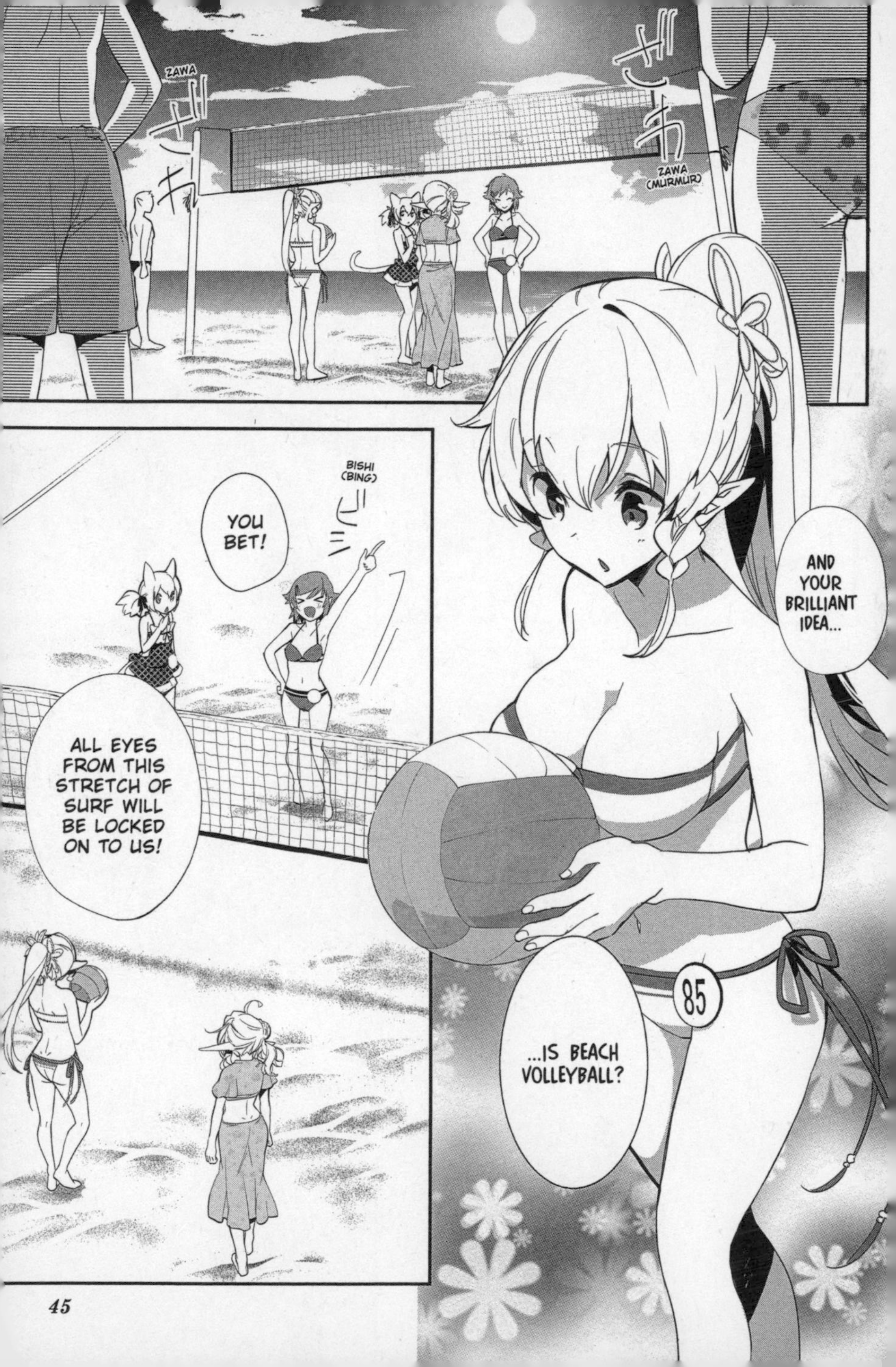
ZAWA (MURMUR)
ZAWA
AND YOUR BRILLIANT IDEA...
...IS BEACH VOLLEYBALL?
BISHI (BING)
YOU BET!
ALL EYES FROM THIS STRETCH OF SURF WILL BE LOCKED ON TO US!

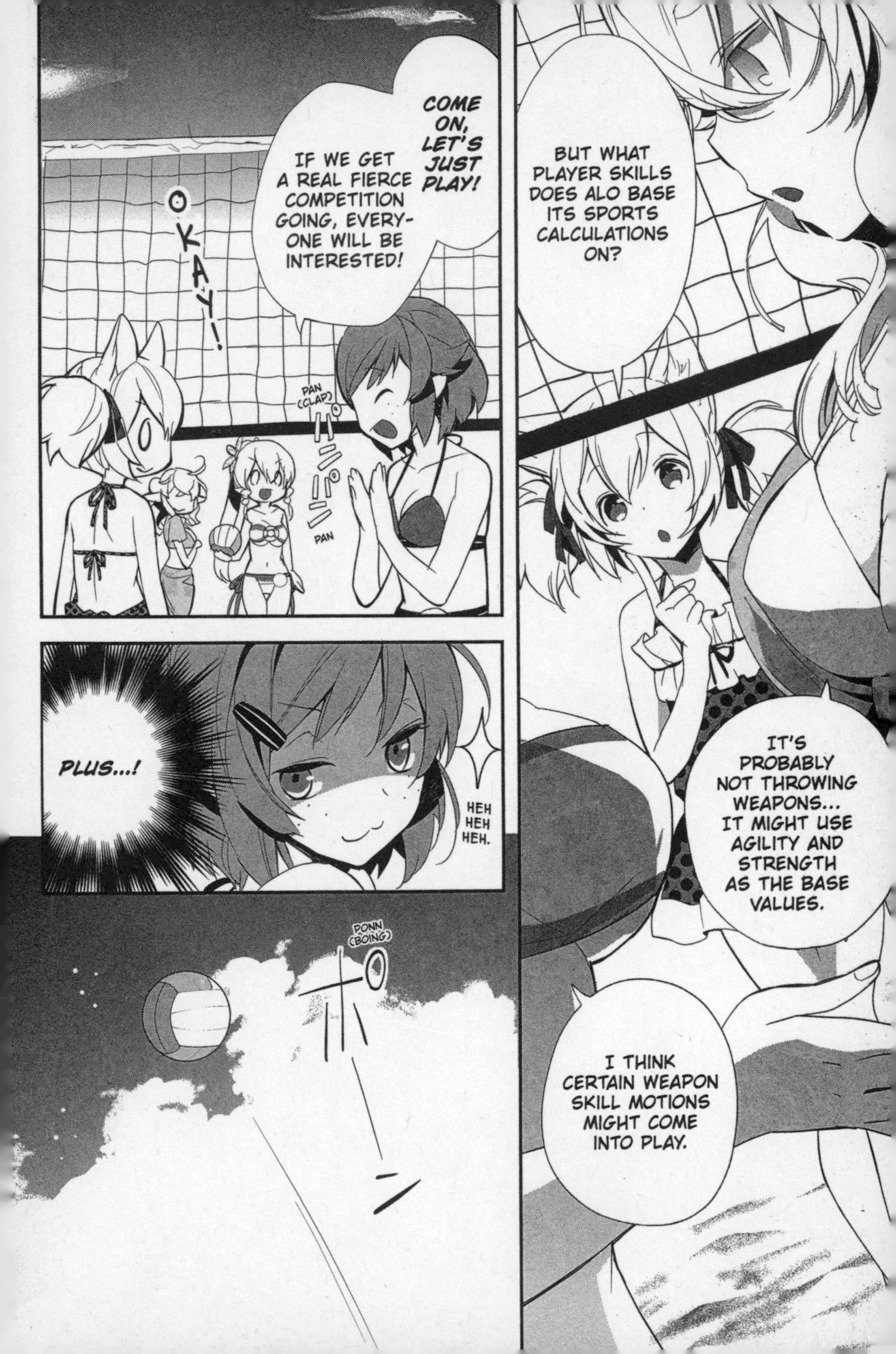
BUT WHAT PLAYER SKILLS DOES ALO BASE ITS SPORTS CALCULATIONS ON?
IT'S PROBABLY NOT THROWING WEAPONS... IT MIGHT USE AGILITY AND STRENGTH AS THE BASE VALUES.
I THINK CERTAIN WEAPON SKILL MOTIONS MIGHT COME INTO PLAY.
COME ON, LET'S JUST PLAY!
IF WE GET A REAL FIERCE COMPETITION GOING, EVERYONE WILL BE INTERESTED!
OKAY!
PAN (CLAP)
PAN
PLUS...!
HEH HEH HEH.
PONN (BOING)

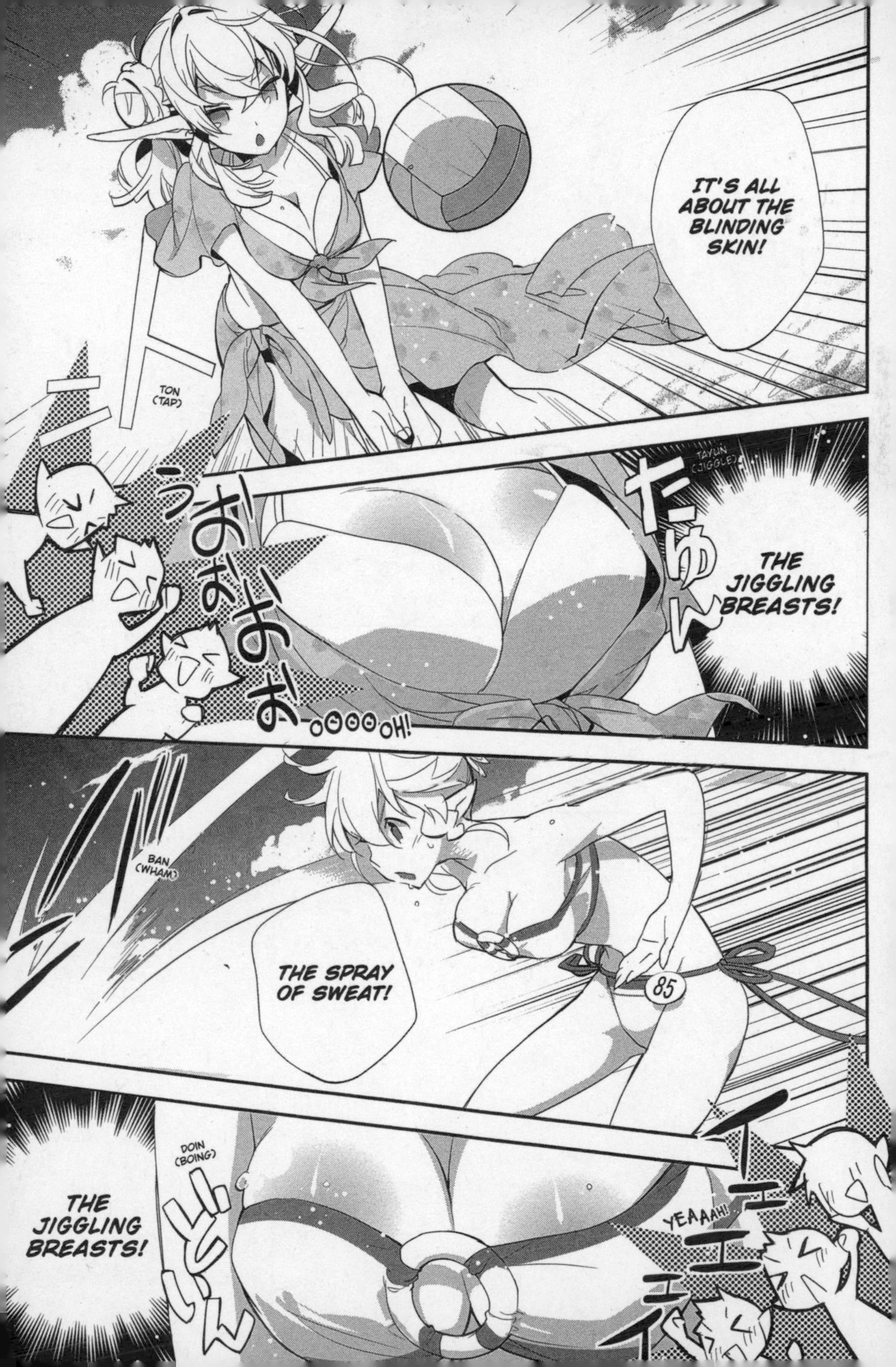
IT'S ALL ABOUT THE BLINDING SKIN!
TON (TAP)
たゆん
TAYUN (JIGGLE)
THE JIGGLING BREASTS!
うおおおお!
-OOOOOH!
BAN (WHAM)
THE SPRAY OF SWEAT!
イエエエイ
YEAAAH!
どいん
DOIN (BOING)
THE JIGGLING BREASTS!

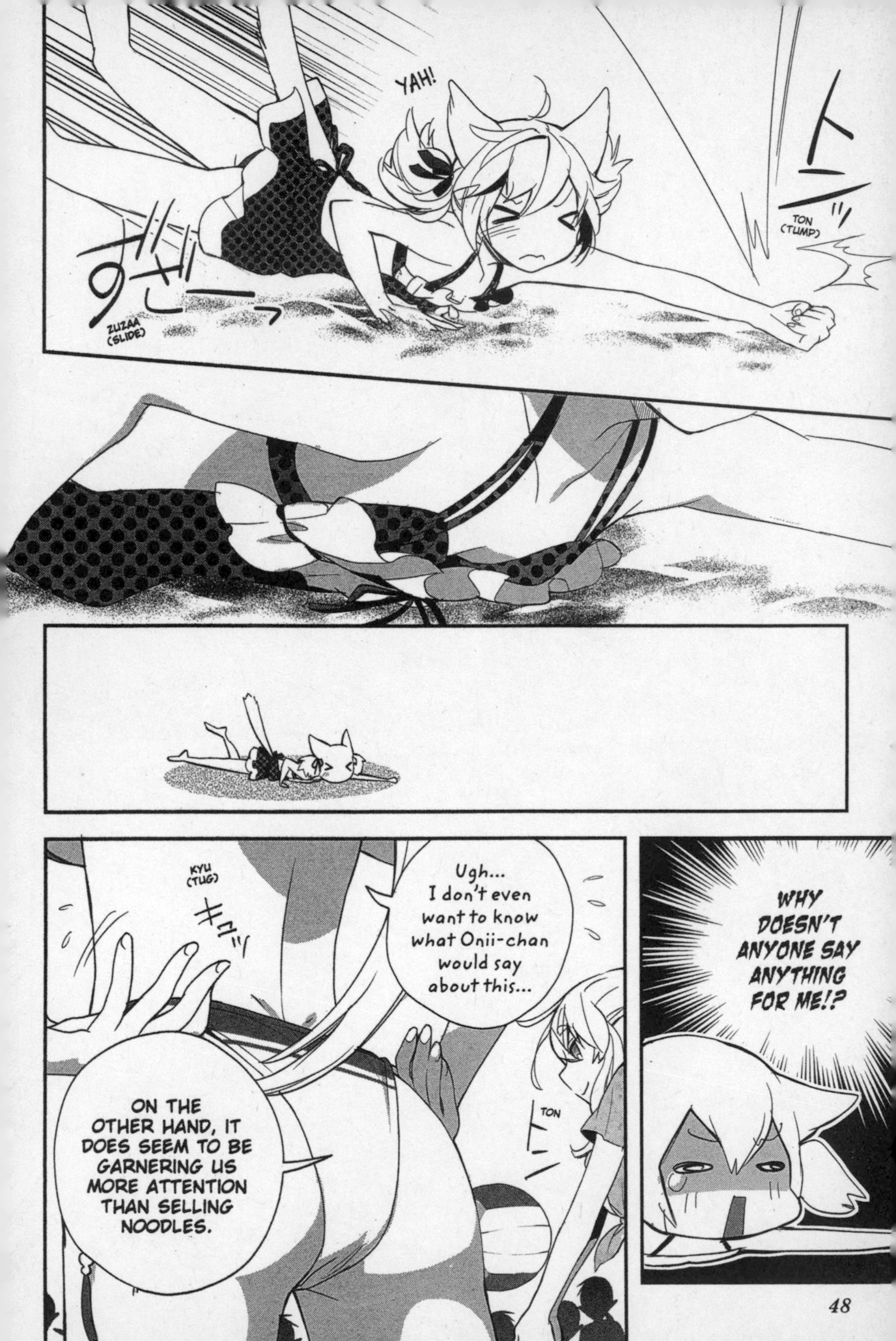
TON (TUMP)
YAH!
ZUZAA (SLIDE)
WHY DOESN'T ANYONE SAY ANYTHING FOR ME!?
Ugh... I don't even want to know what Onii-chan would say about this...
KYU (TUG)
TON
ON THE OTHER HAND, IT DOES SEEM TO BE GARNERING US MORE ATTENTION THAN SELLING NOODLES.

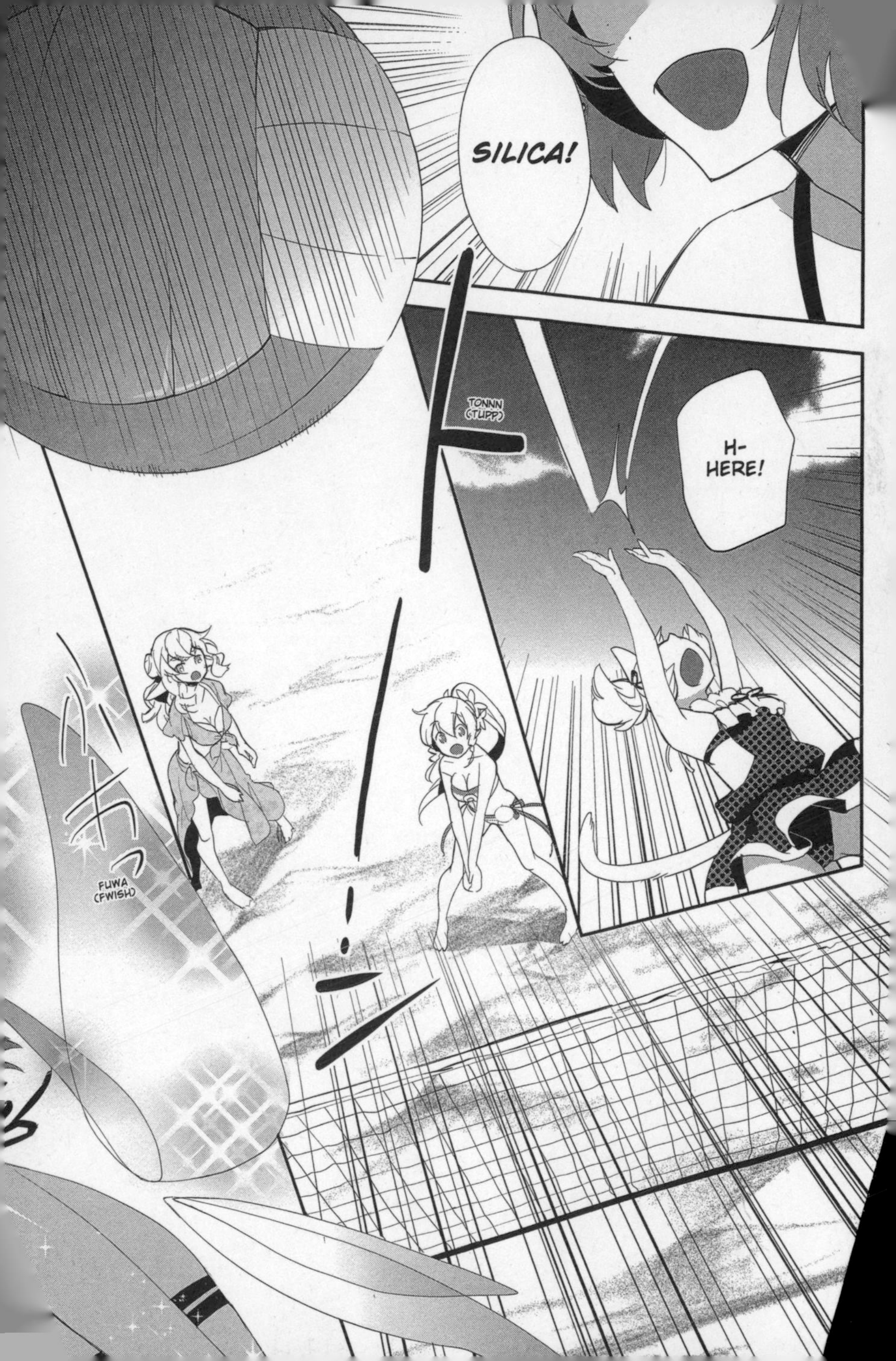
SILICA!
TONNN (TUPP)
H-HERE!
FUWA (FWISH)

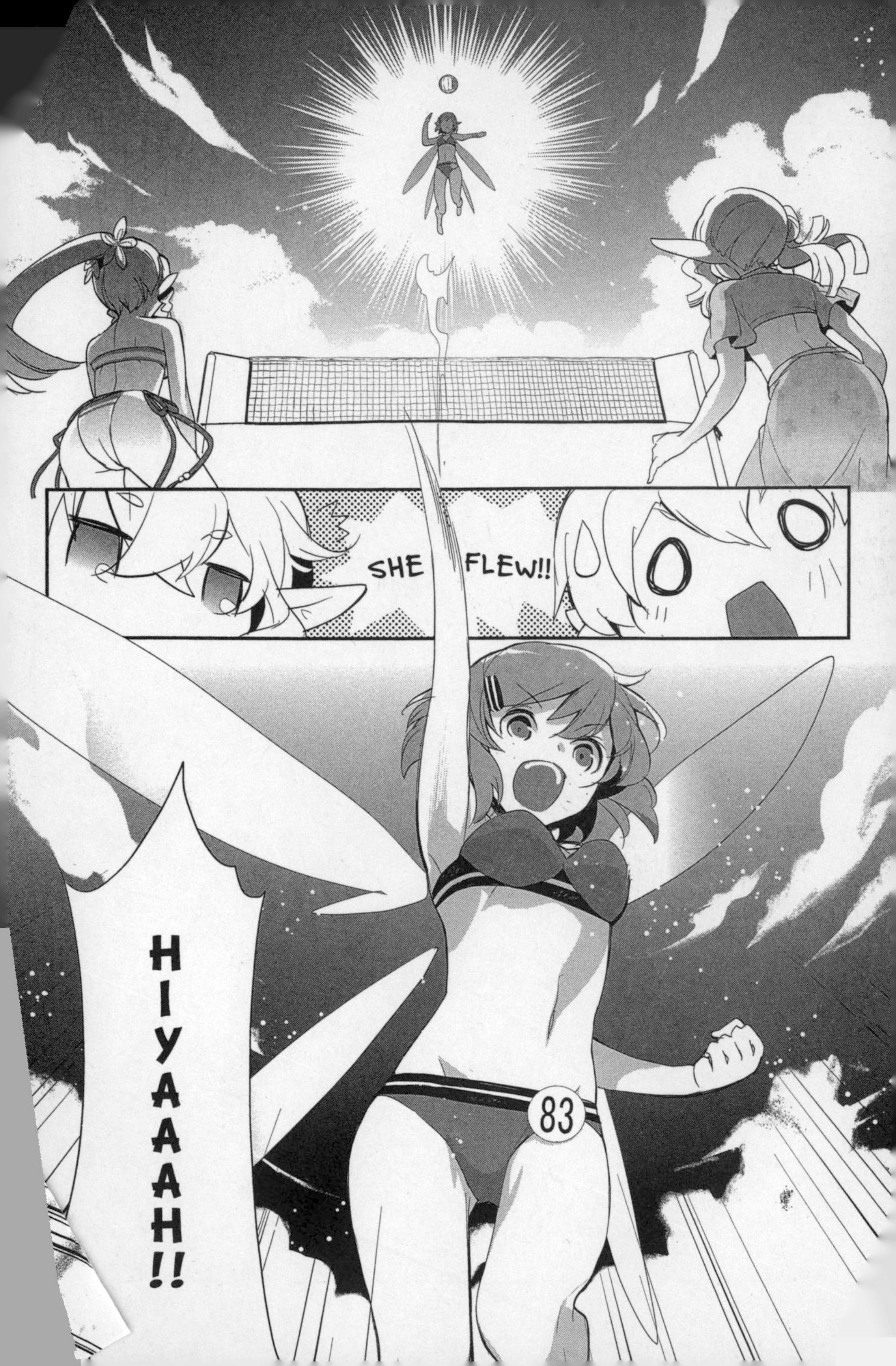
SHE FLEW!!
HIYAAAAH!!
83

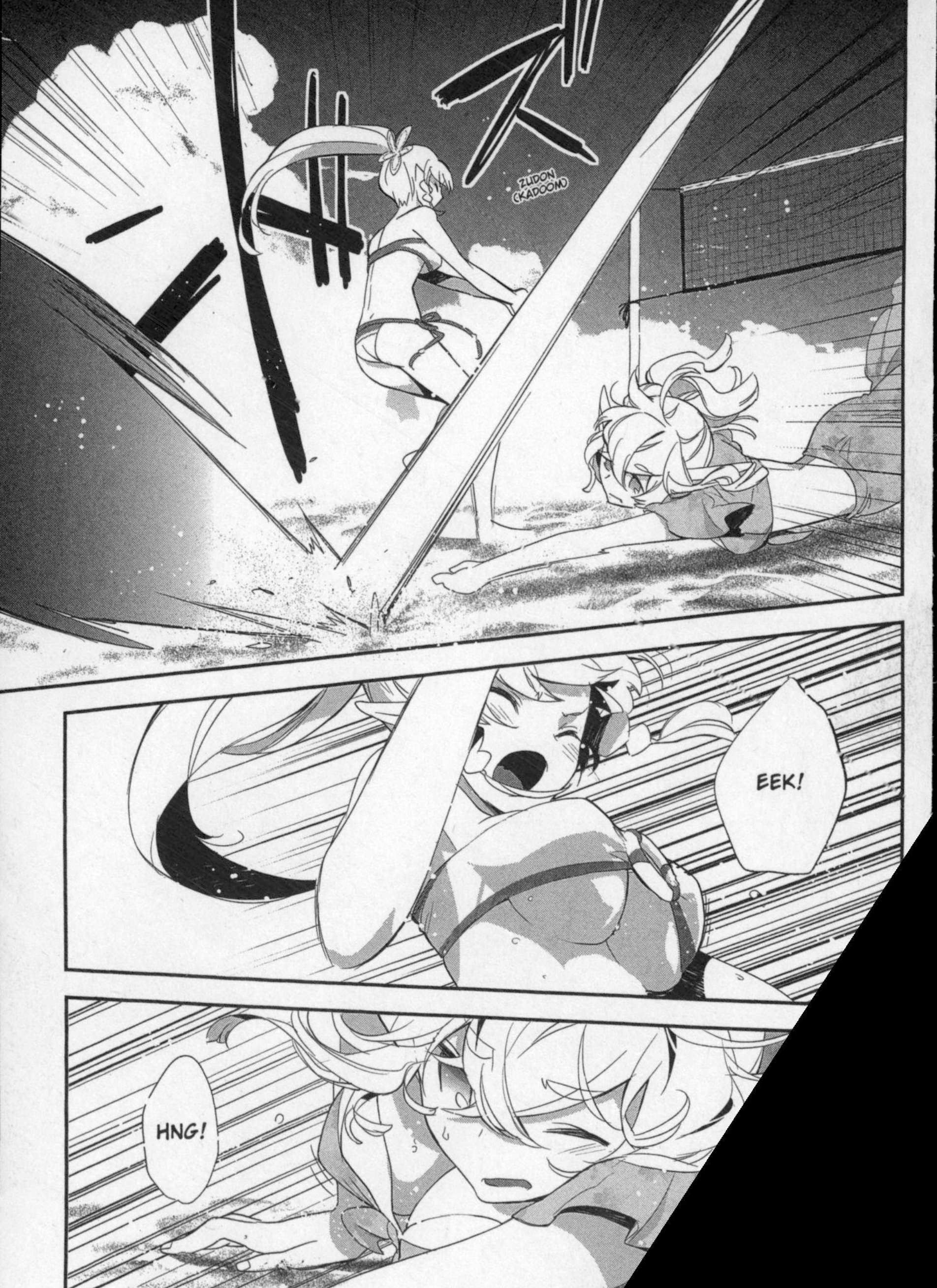
ZUDON (KADOOM)
EEK!
HNG!

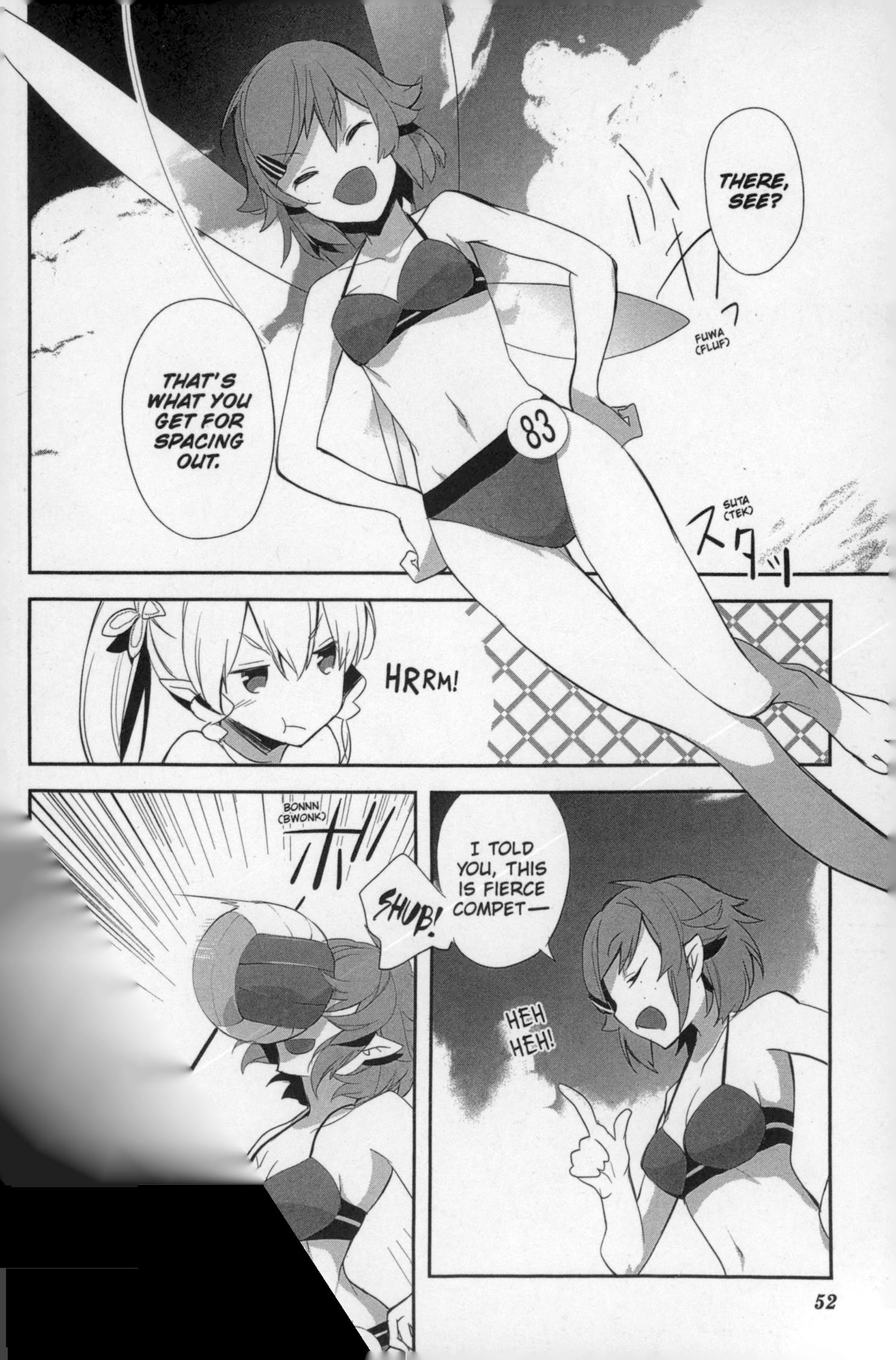
THERE, SEE?
FUWA (FLUF)
THAT'S WHAT YOU GET FOR SPACING OUT.
SUTA (TEK)
HRRM!
I TOLD YOU, THIS IS FIERCE COMPET—
HEH HEH!
SHUB!
BONNN (BWONK)

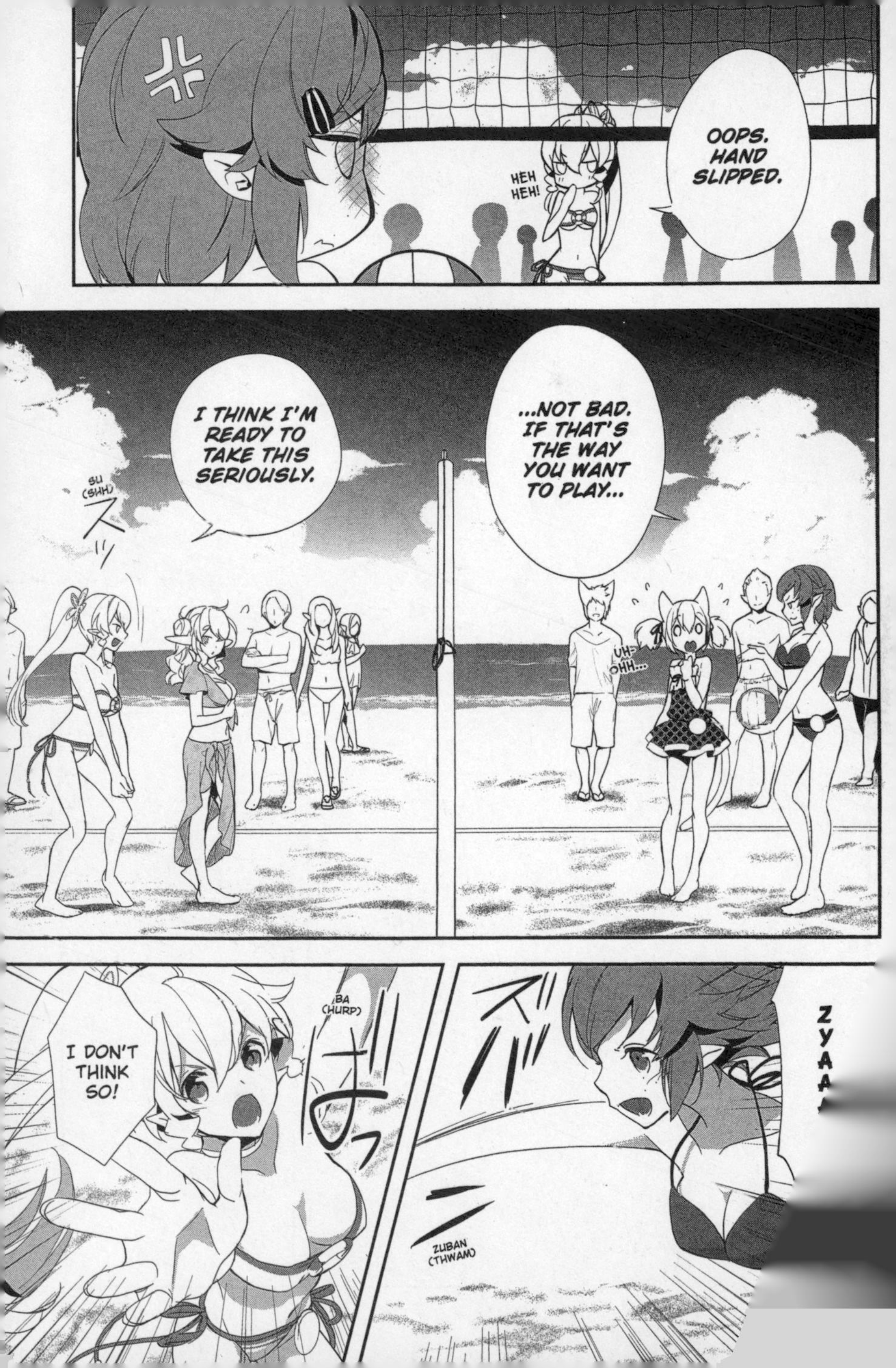
OOPS. HAND SLIPPED.
HEH HEH!
...NOT BAD. IF THAT'S THE WAY YOU WANT TO PLAY...
UH-OHH...
I THINK I'M READY TO TAKE THIS SERIOUSLY.
SU (SHH)
ZYAA
ZUBAN (THWAM)
BA (HURP)
I DON'T THINK SO!

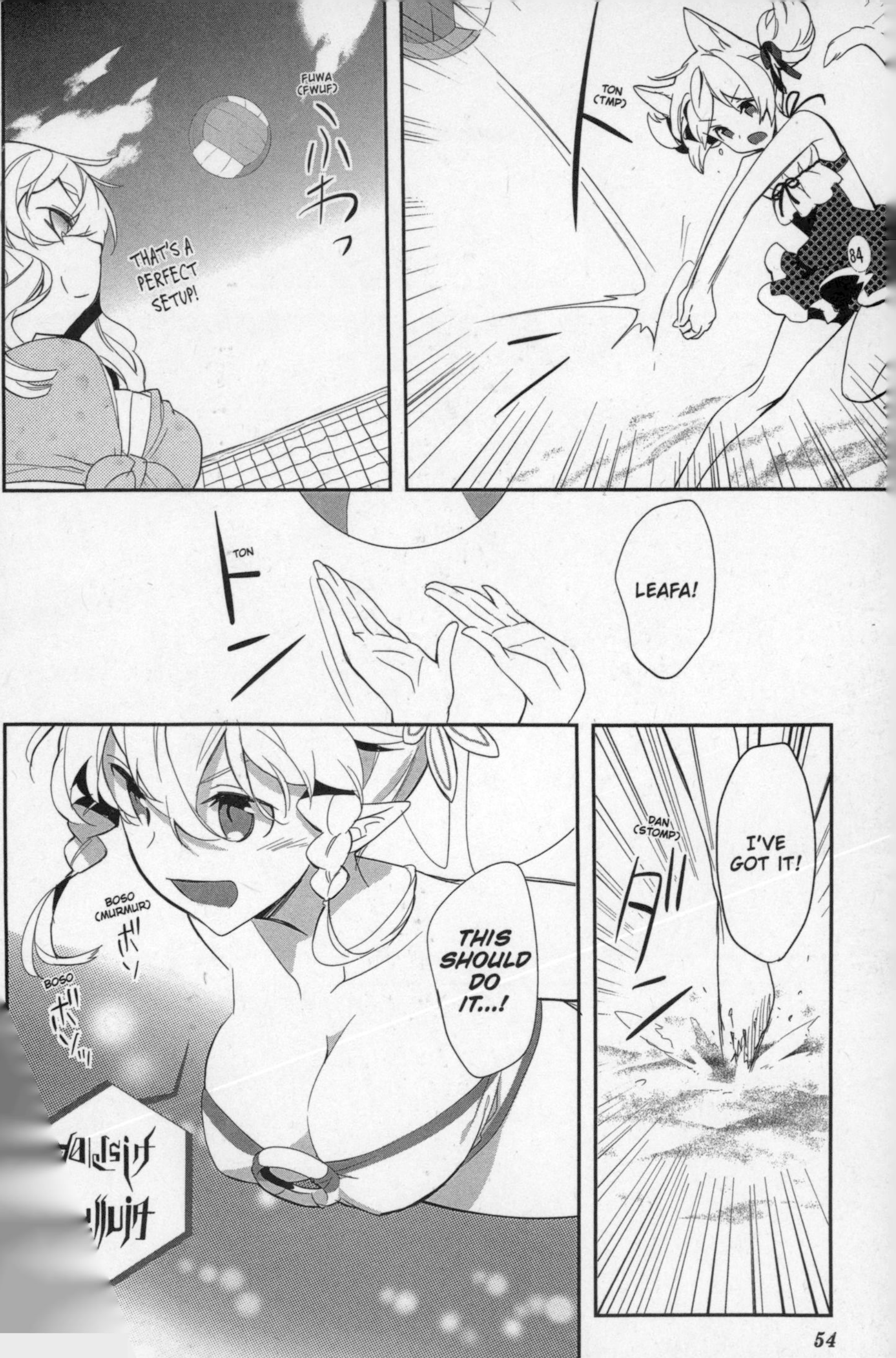
TON (TMP)
ト
FUWA (FWUF)
ふわっ
THAT'S A PERFECT SETUP!
LEAFA!
TON
ト
DAN (STOMP)
ダッ
I'VE GOT IT!
THIS SHOULD DO IT...!
BOSO (MURMUR)
ボソ
BOSO
ボソッ

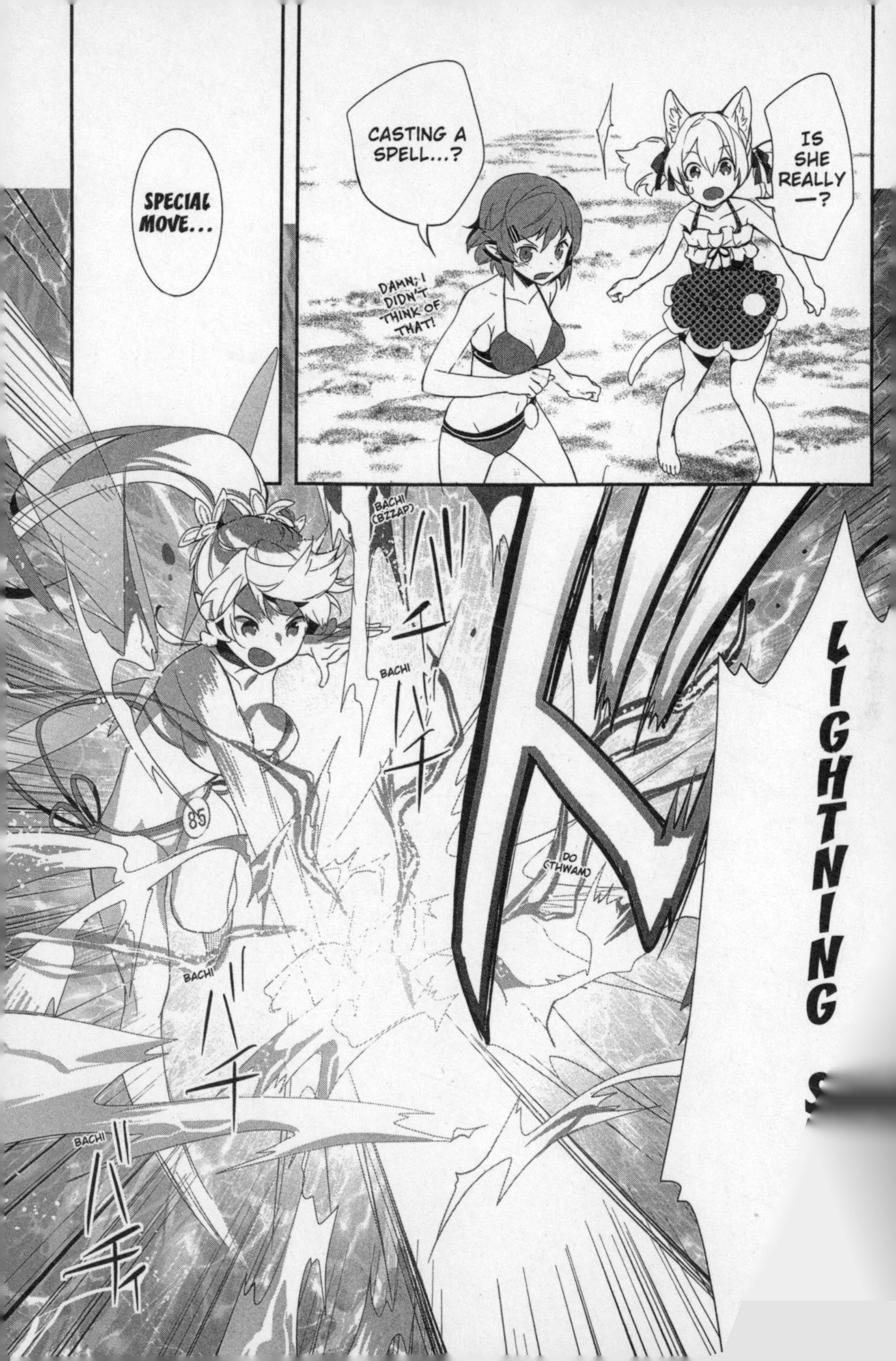
IS SHE REALLY—?
CASTING A SPELL...?
DAMN, I DIDN'T THINK OF THAT!
SPECIAL MOVE...
LIGHTNING S
BACHI (BZZAP)
BACHI
DO (THWAM)
BACHI
BACHI
85

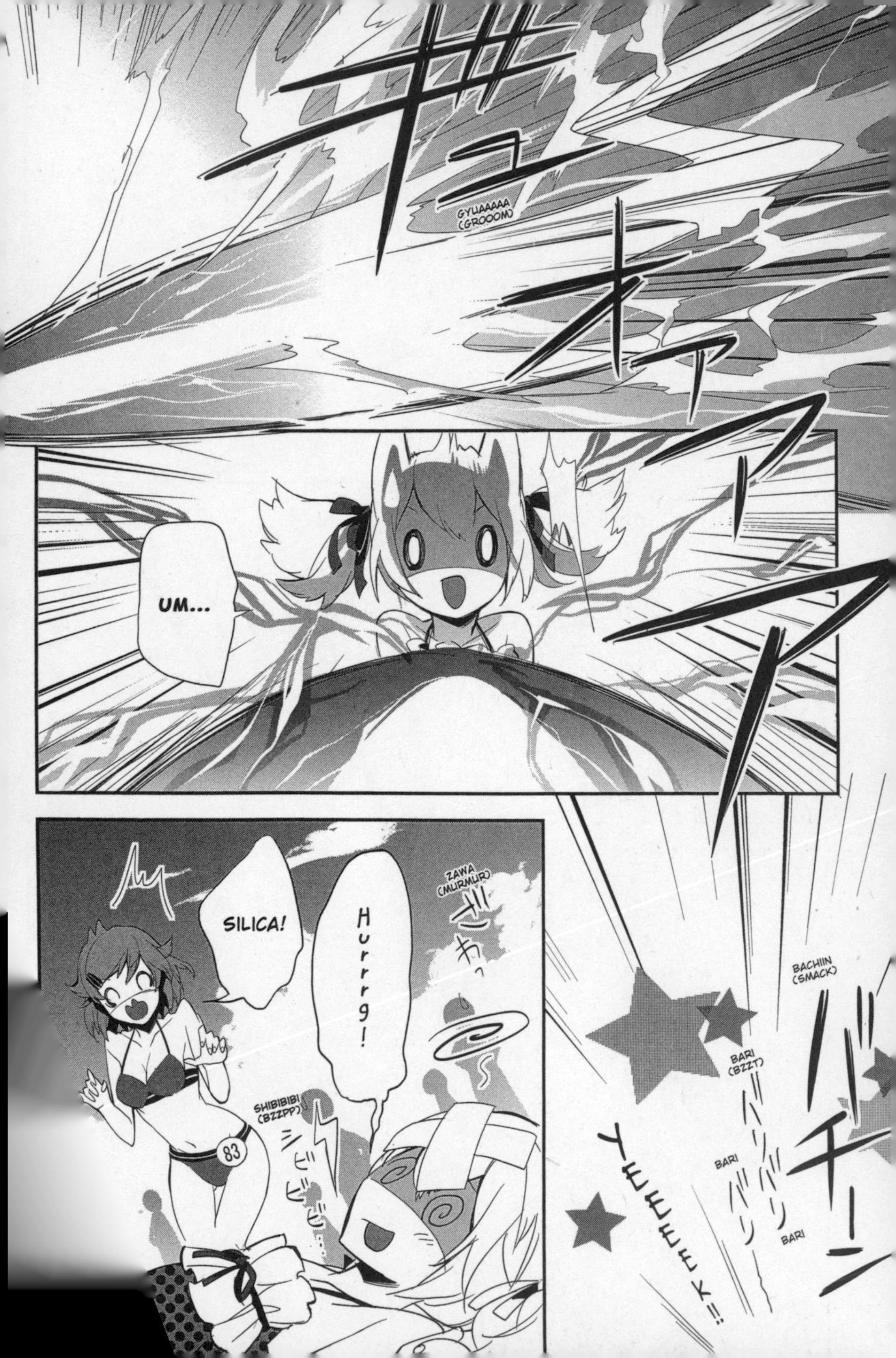
GYUAAAAA
(GROOOM)
UM...
BACHIIN
(SMACK)
BARI
(BZZT)
BARI
BARI
YEEEEEK!!
ZAWA
(MURMUR)
Hurrrg!
SILICA!
SHIBIBIBI
(BZZPP)
83

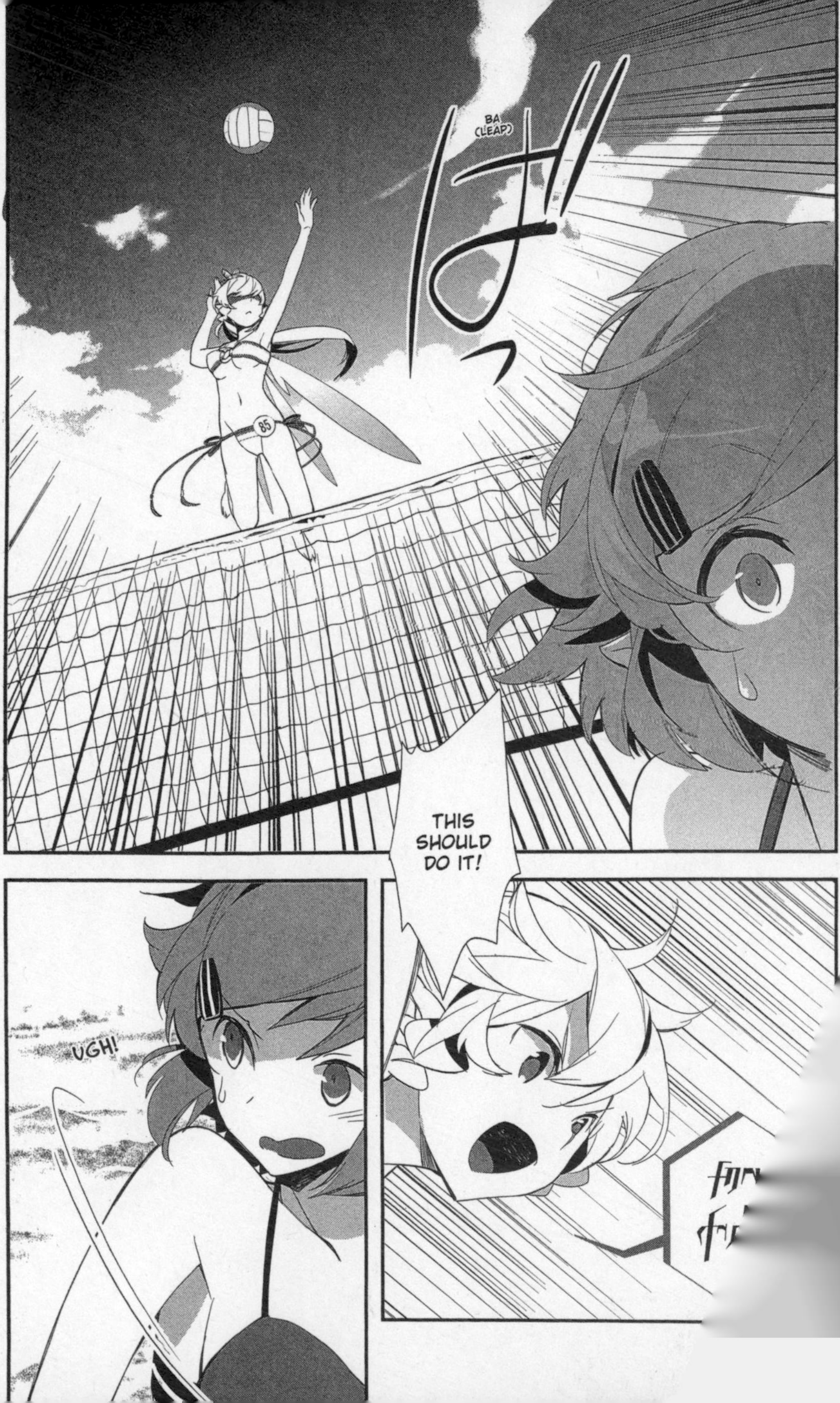
BA
(LEAP)
THIS SHOULD DO IT!
UGH!

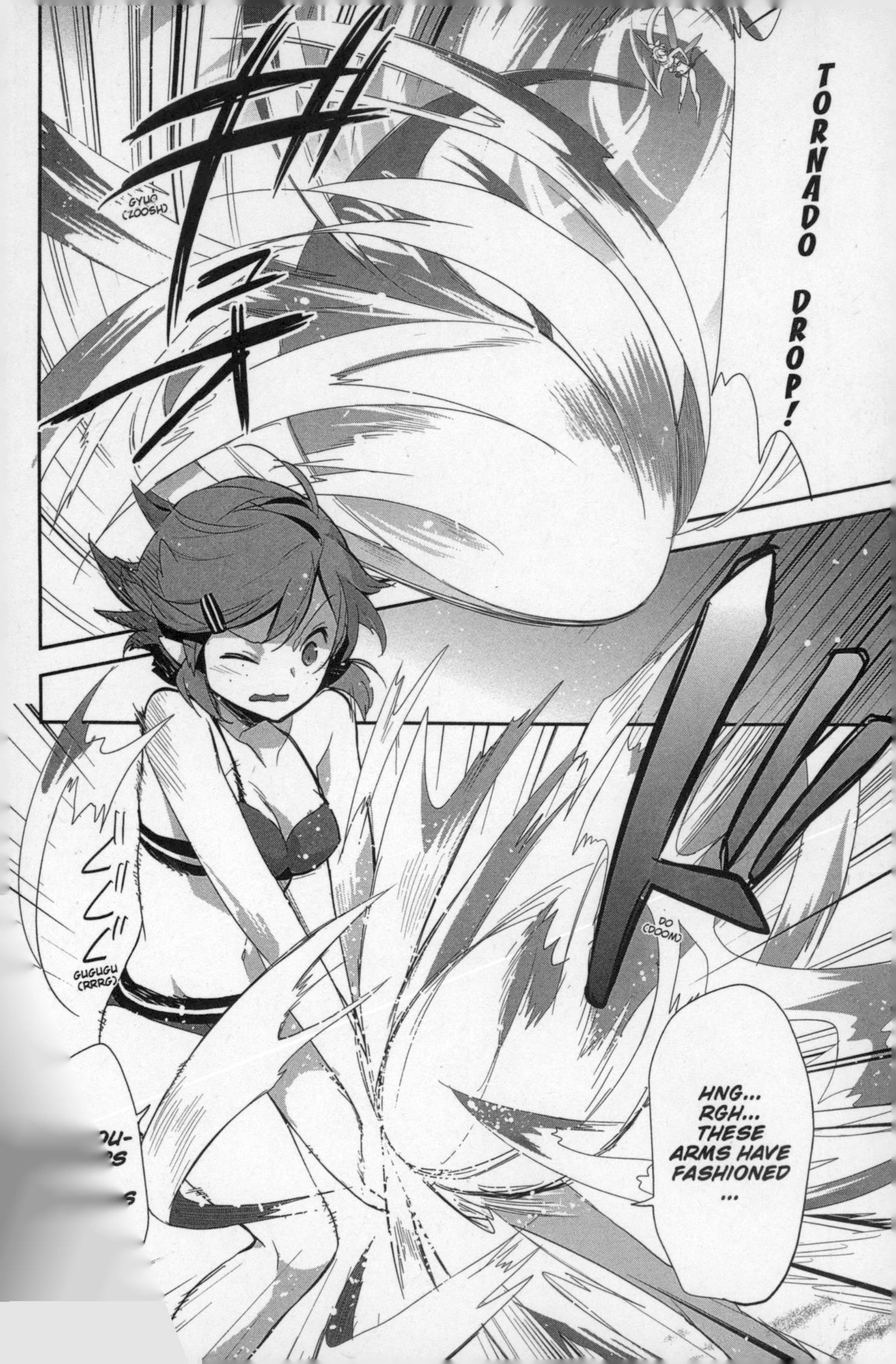
TORNADO DROP!
GYUO (ZOOSH)
DO (DOOM)
GUGUGU (RRRG)
HNG... RGH... THESE ARMS HAVE FASHIONED ...

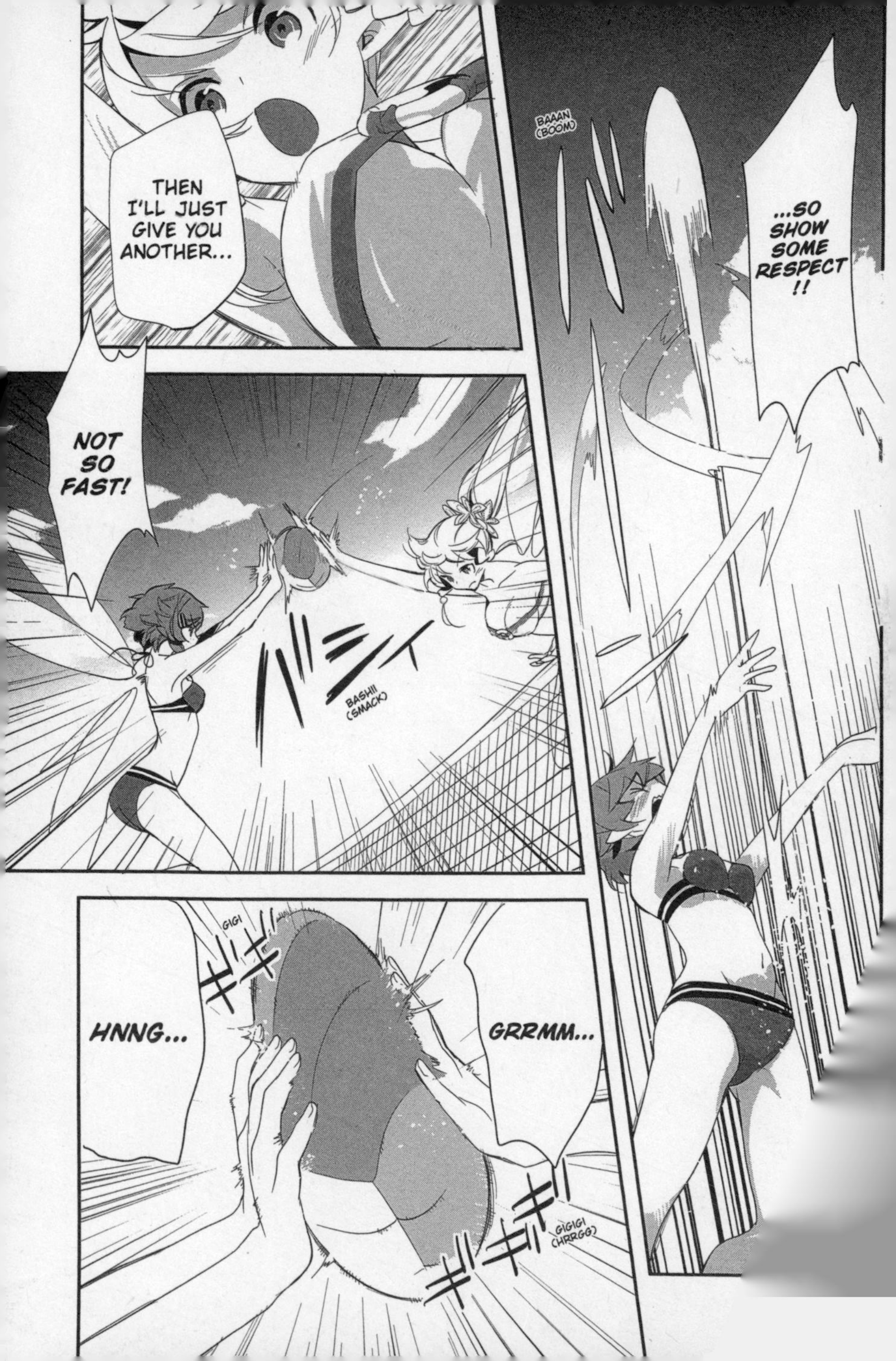

THEN I'LL JUST GIVE YOU ANOTHER...
BAAAN (BOOM)
...SO SHOW SOME RESPECT!!
NOT SO FAST!
BASHII (SMACK)
GIGI
HNNG...
GRRMM...
GIGIGI (HRRGG)

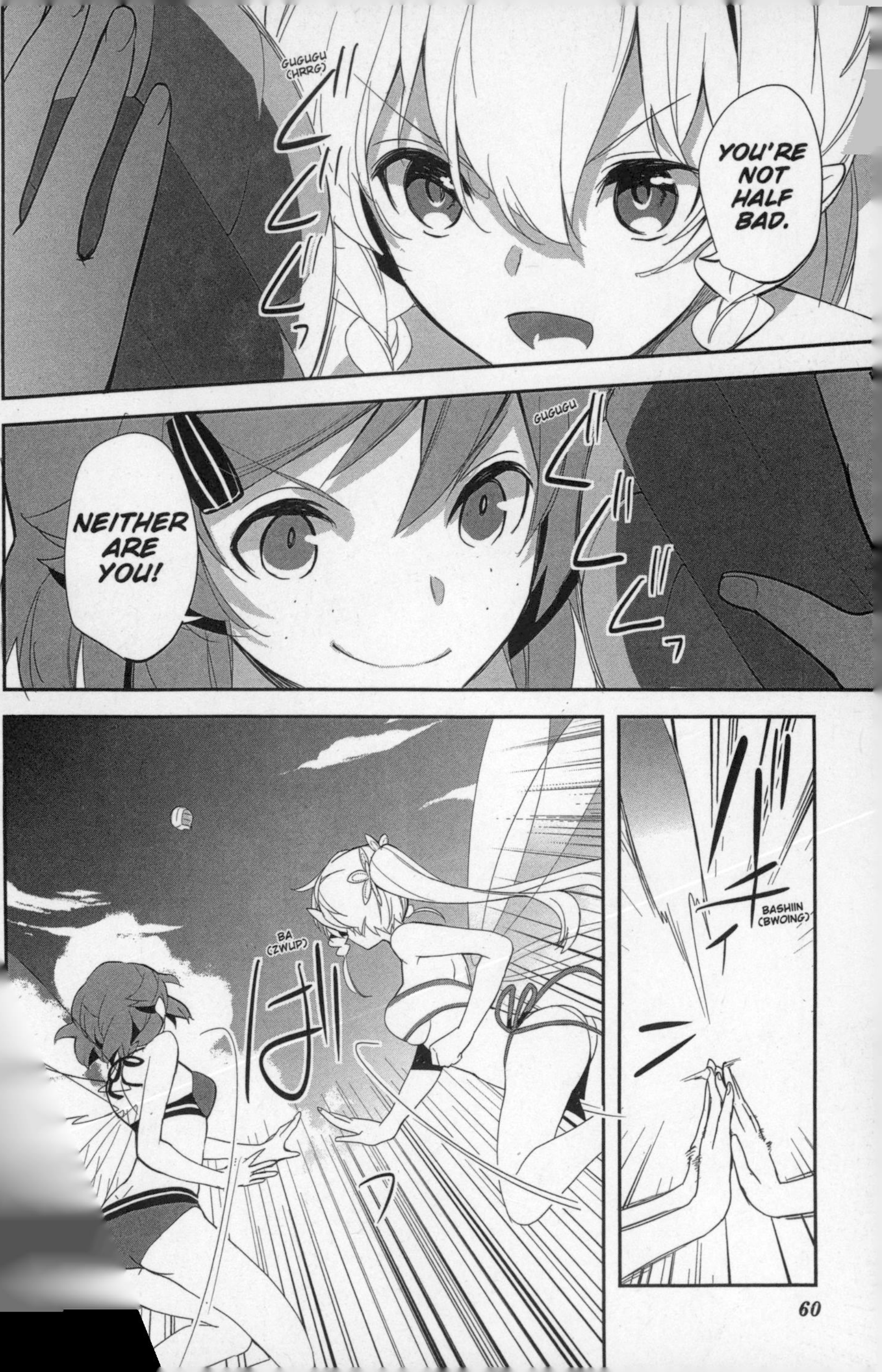
YOU'RE NOT HALF BAD.
GUGUGU (HRRG)
NEITHER ARE YOU!
GUGUGU
BASHIIN (BWOING)
BA (ZWUP)

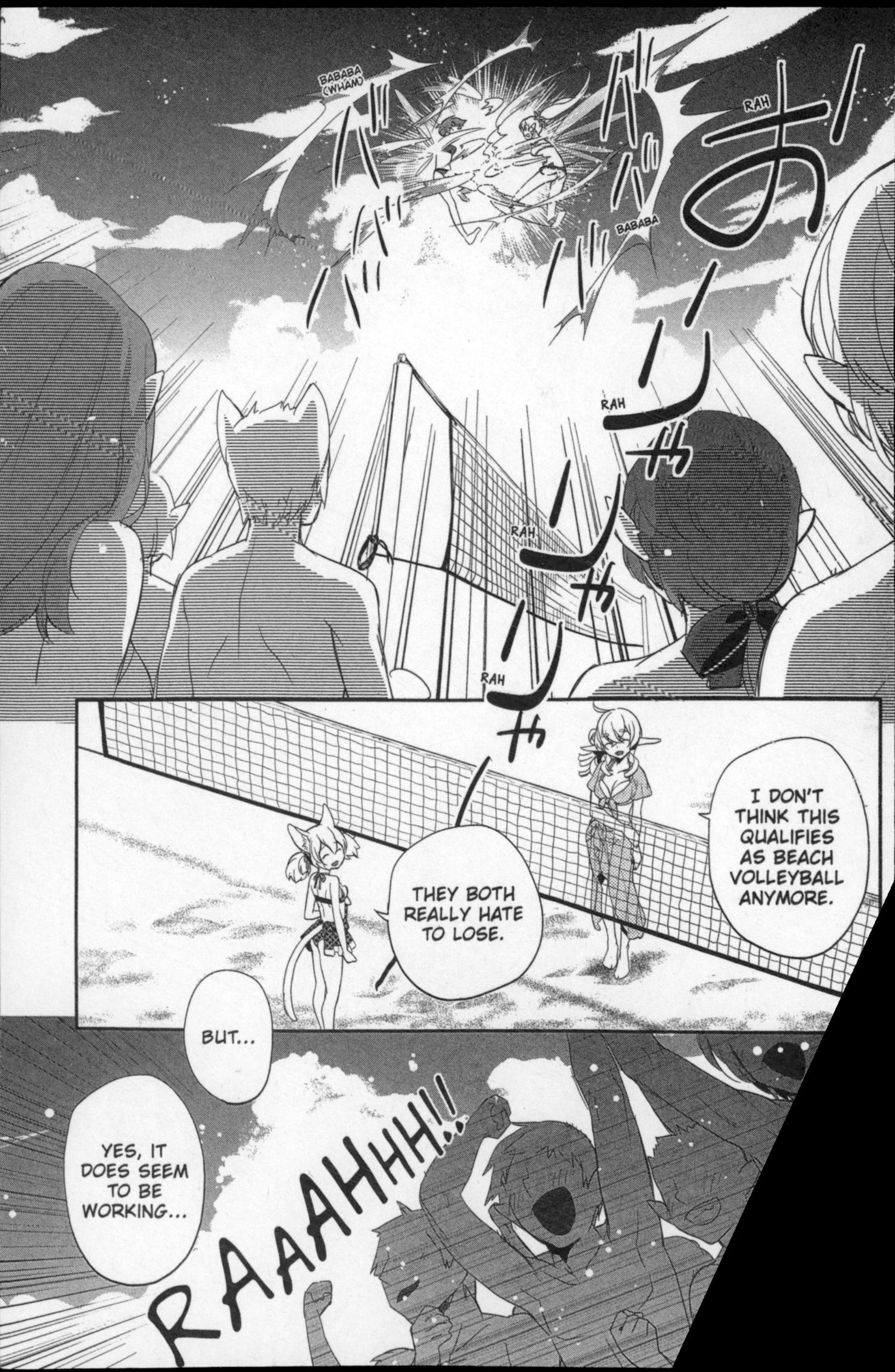
BABABA (WHAM)
BABABA
RAH
RAH
RAH
RAH
I DON'T THINK THIS QUALIFIES AS BEACH VOLLEYBALL ANYMORE.
THEY BOTH REALLY HATE TO LOSE.
BUT...
YES, IT DOES SEEM TO BE WORKING...
RAAAHHH!!

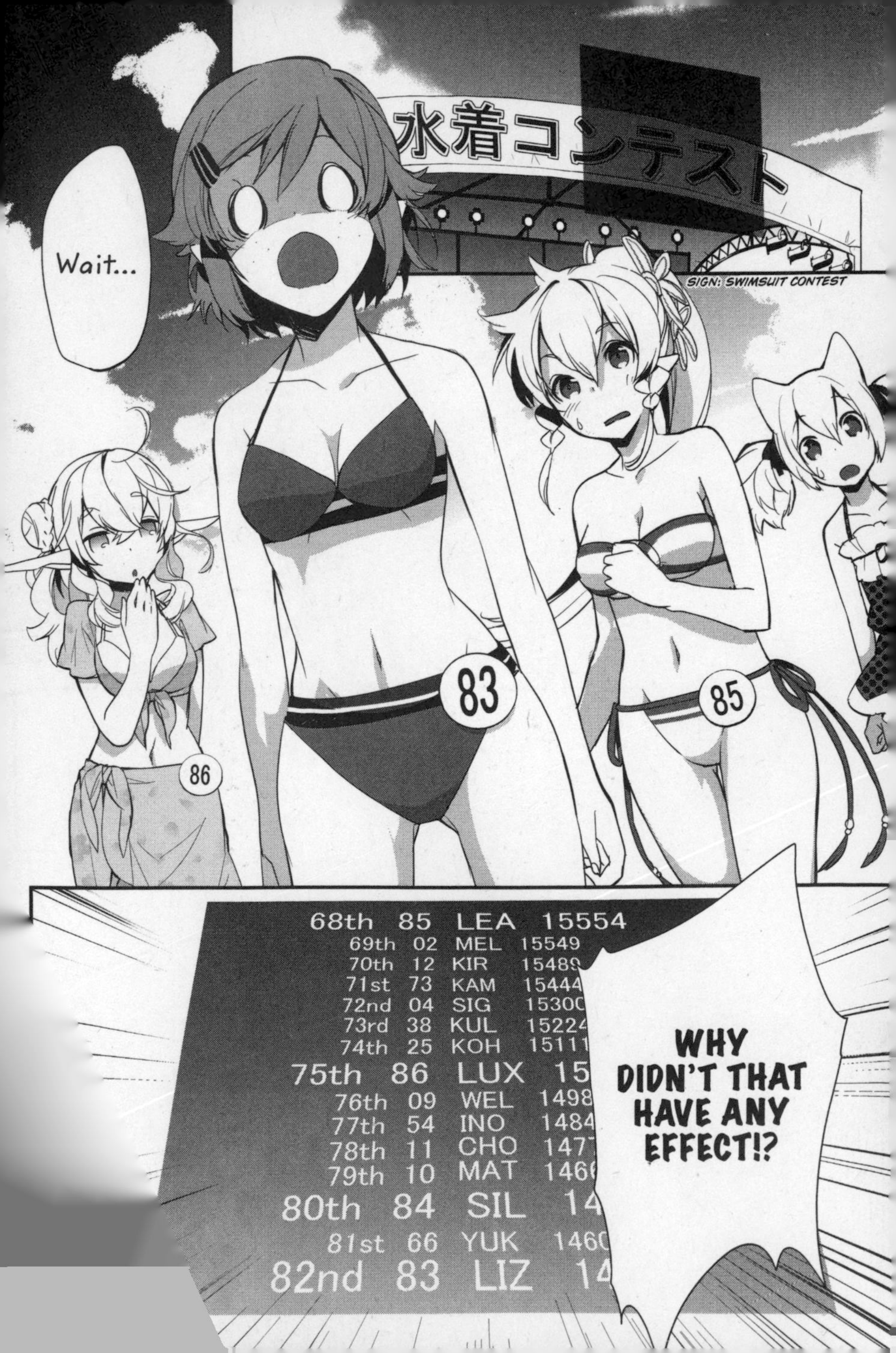
水着コンテスト
Wait...
SIGN: SWIMSUIT CONTEST
86
83
85
68th 85 LEA 15554
69th 02 MEL 15549
70th 12 KIR 15489
71st 73 KAM 15444
72nd 04 SIG 15300
73rd 38 KUL 15224
74th 25 KOH 15111
75th 86 LUX 15
76th 09 WEL 1498
77th 54 INO 1484
78th 11 CHO 1477
79th 10 MAT 1466
80th 84 SIL 14
81st 66 YUK 1460
82nd 83 LIZ 14
WHY DIDN'T THAT HAVE ANY EFFECT!?

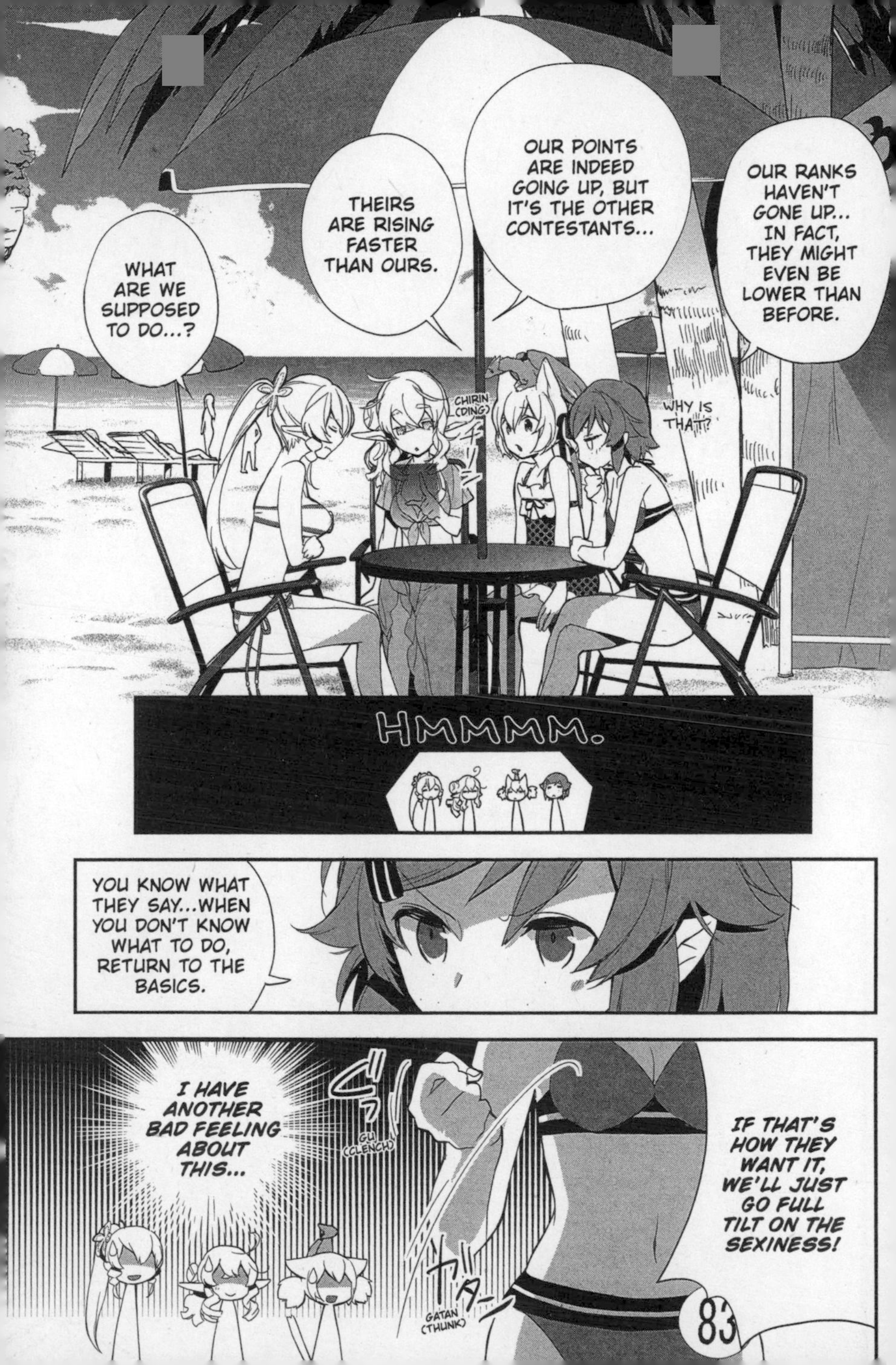

OUR RANKS HAVEN'T GONE UP... IN FACT, THEY MIGHT EVEN BE LOWER THAN BEFORE.
OUR POINTS ARE INDEED GOING UP, BUT IT'S THE OTHER CONTESTANTS...
THEIRS ARE RISING FASTER THAN OURS.
WHAT ARE WE SUPPOSED TO DO...?
WHY IS THAT?
CHIRIN (DING)
HMMMM.
YOU KNOW WHAT THEY SAY...WHEN YOU DON'T KNOW WHAT TO DO, RETURN TO THE BASICS.
IF THAT'S HOW THEY WANT IT, WE'LL JUST GO FULL TILT ON THE SEXINESS!
GATAN (THUNK)
GU (CLENCH)
I HAVE ANOTHER BAD FEELING ABOUT THIS...

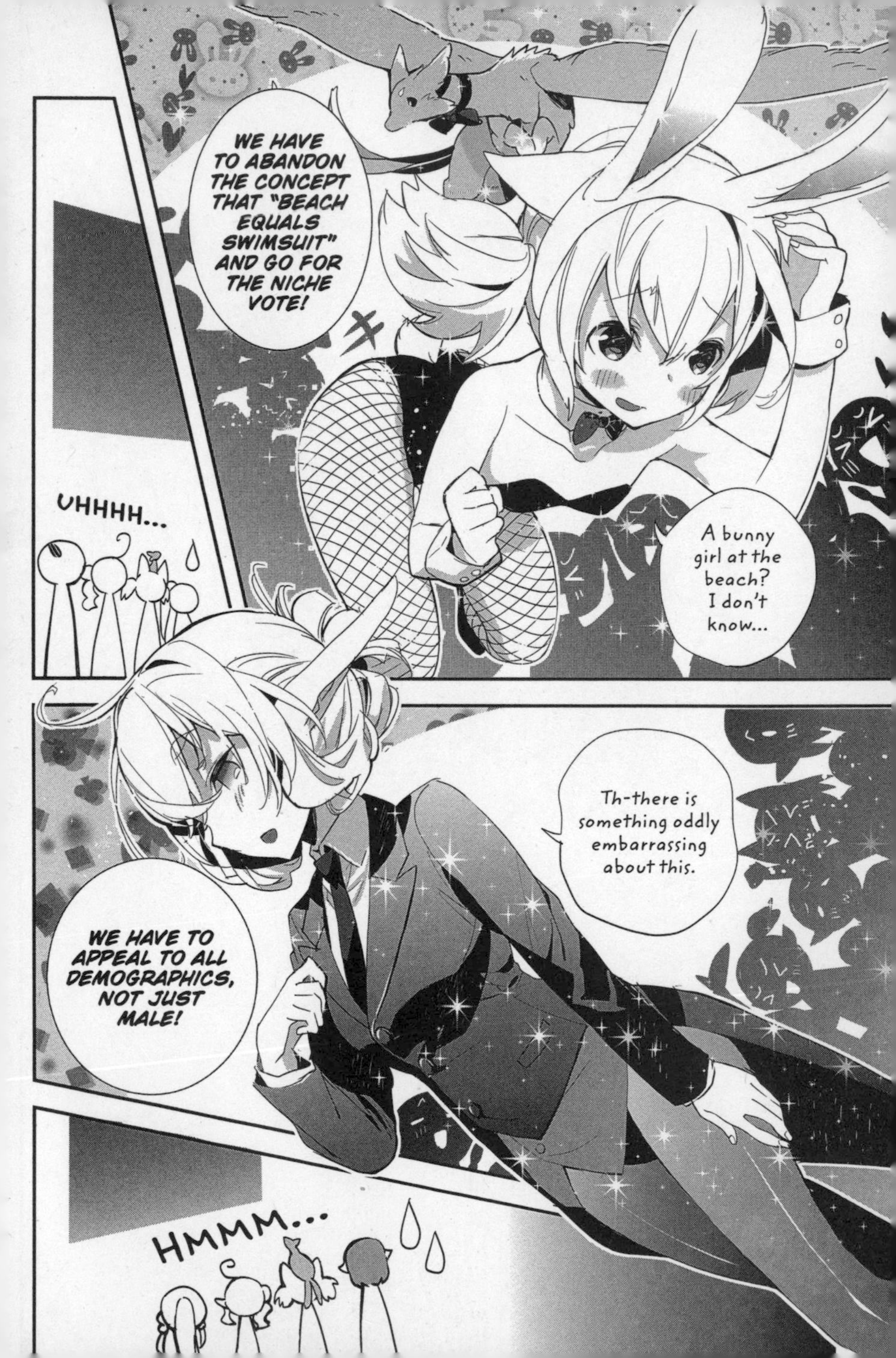
WE HAVE TO ABANDON THE CONCEPT THAT "BEACH EQUALS SWIMSUIT" AND GO FOR THE NICHE VOTE!
A bunny girl at the beach? I don't know...
UHHHH...
Th-there is something oddly embarrassing about this.
WE HAVE TO APPEAL TO ALL DEMOGRAPHICS, NOT JUST MALE!
HMMM...

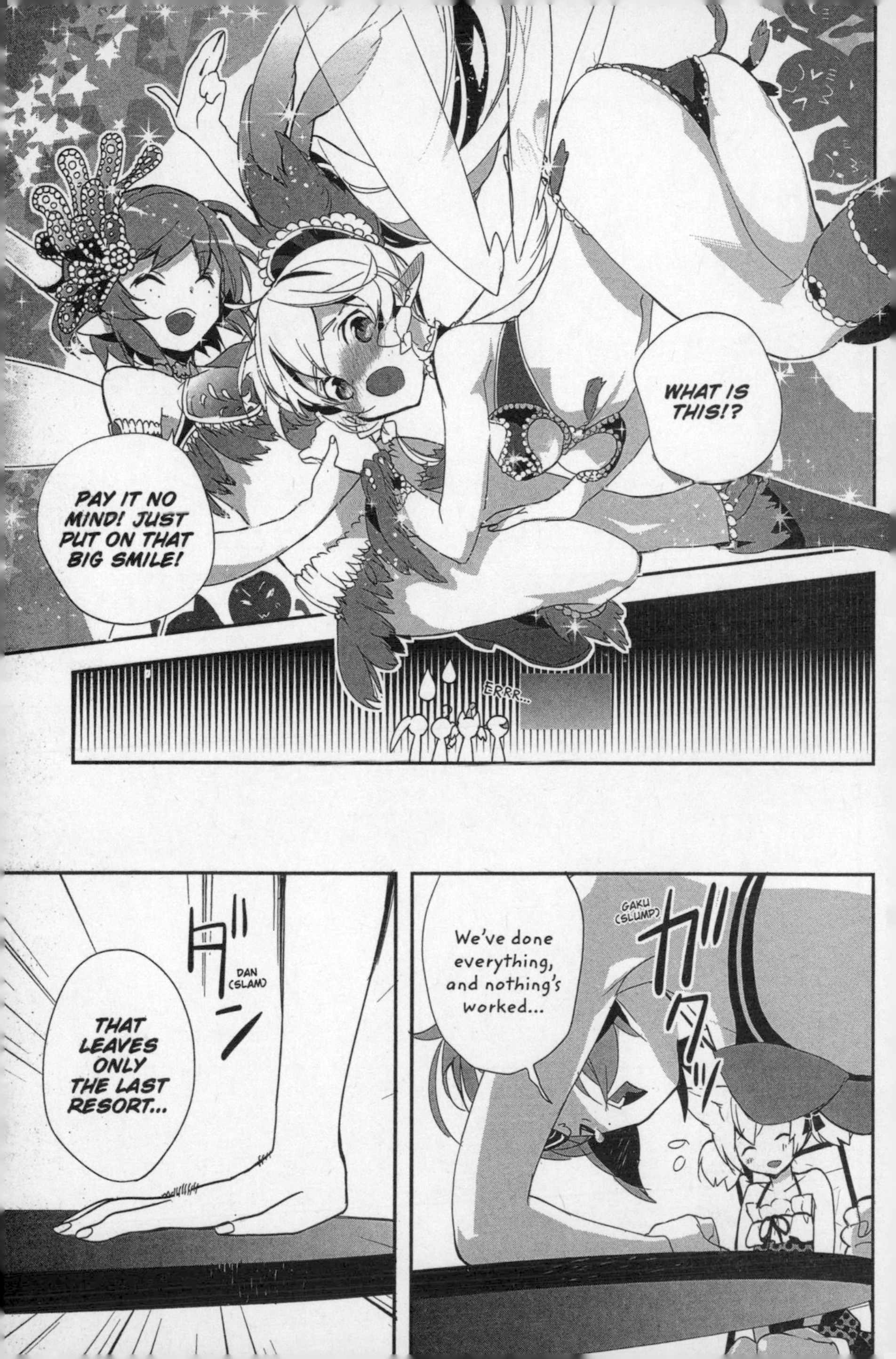
WHAT IS THIS!?
PAY IT NO MIND! JUST PUT ON THAT BIG SMILE!
ERRR...
GAKU (SLUMP)
We've done everything, and nothing's worked...
DAN (SLAM)
THAT LEAVES ONLY THE LAST RESORT...

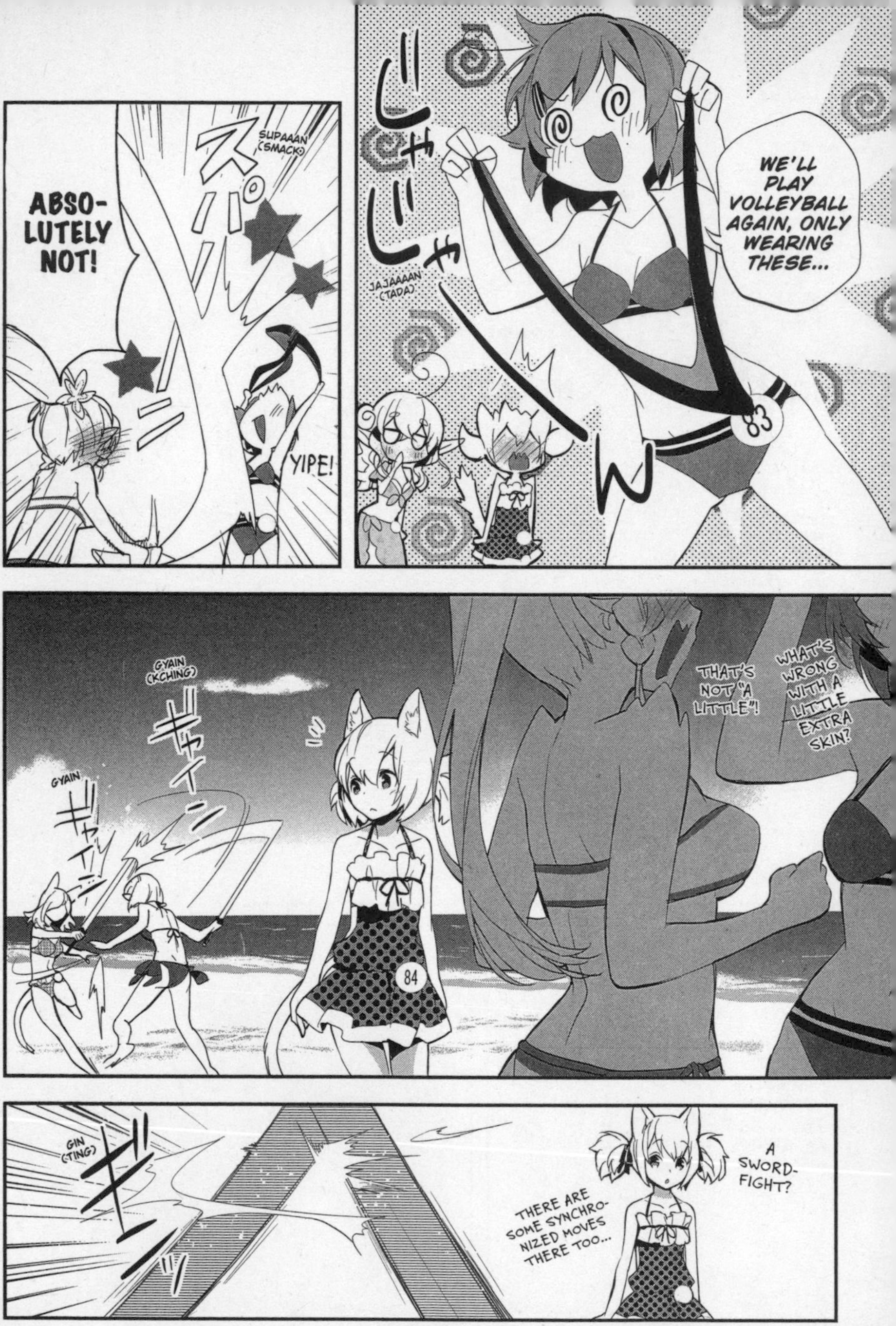
WE'LL PLAY VOLLEYBALL AGAIN, ONLY WEARING THESE...
JAJAAAAN (TADA)
SUPAAAN (SMACK)
ABSO-LUTELY NOT!
YIPE!
WHAT'S WRONG WITH A LITTLE EXTRA SKIN?
THAT'S NOT "A LITTLE"!
GYAIN (KCHING)
GYAIN
A SWORD-FIGHT?
THERE ARE SOME SYNCHRO-NIZED MOVES THERE TOO...
GIN (TING)

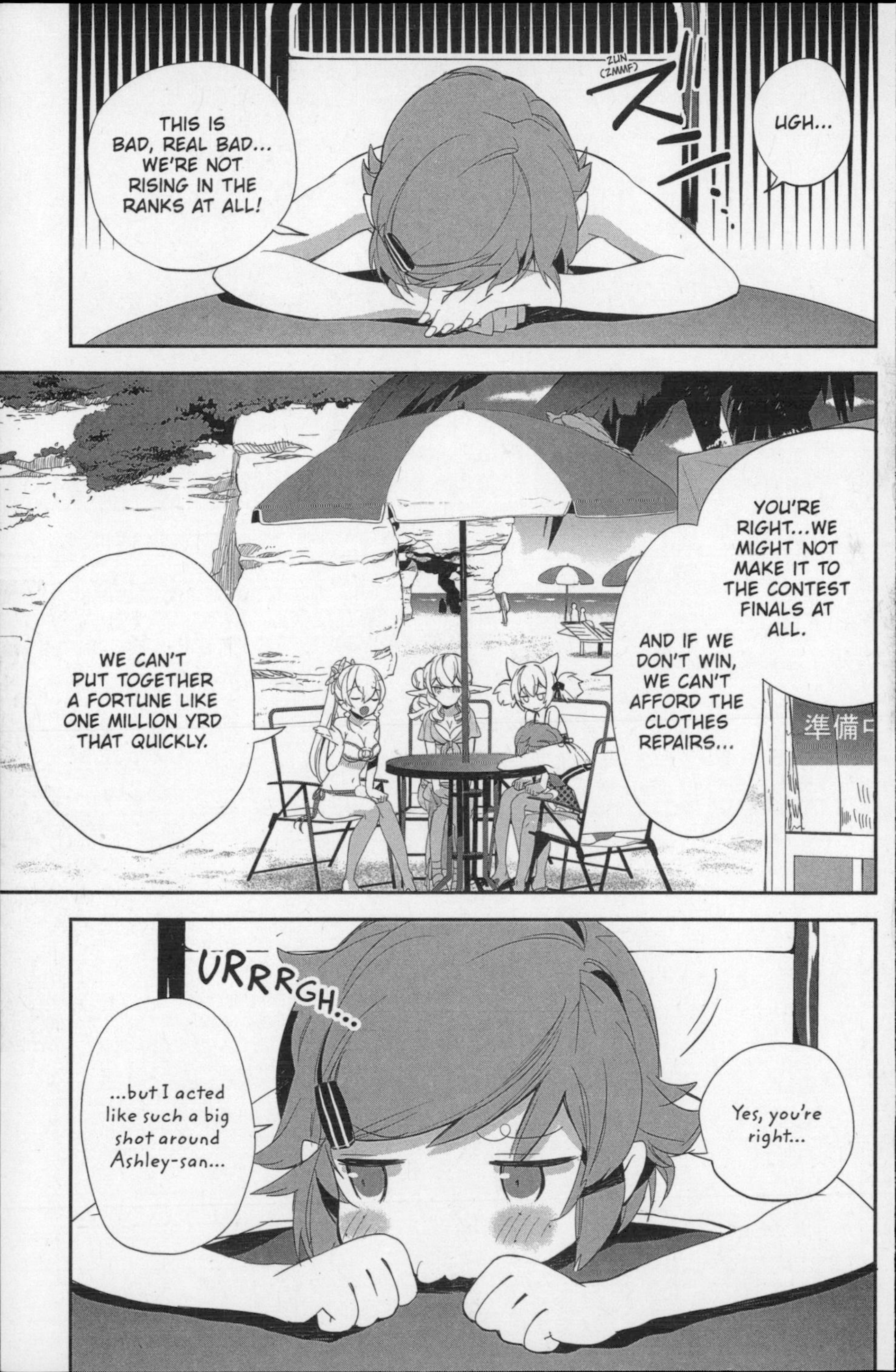
UGH...
ZUN (ZMMF)
THIS IS BAD, REAL BAD... WE'RE NOT RISING IN THE RANKS AT ALL!
YOU'RE RIGHT...WE MIGHT NOT MAKE IT TO THE CONTEST FINALS AT ALL.
AND IF WE DON'T WIN, WE CAN'T AFFORD THE CLOTHES REPAIRS...
WE CAN'T PUT TOGETHER A FORTUNE LIKE ONE MILLION YRD THAT QUICKLY.
Yes, you're right...
URRRGH...
...but I acted like such a big shot around Ashley-san...

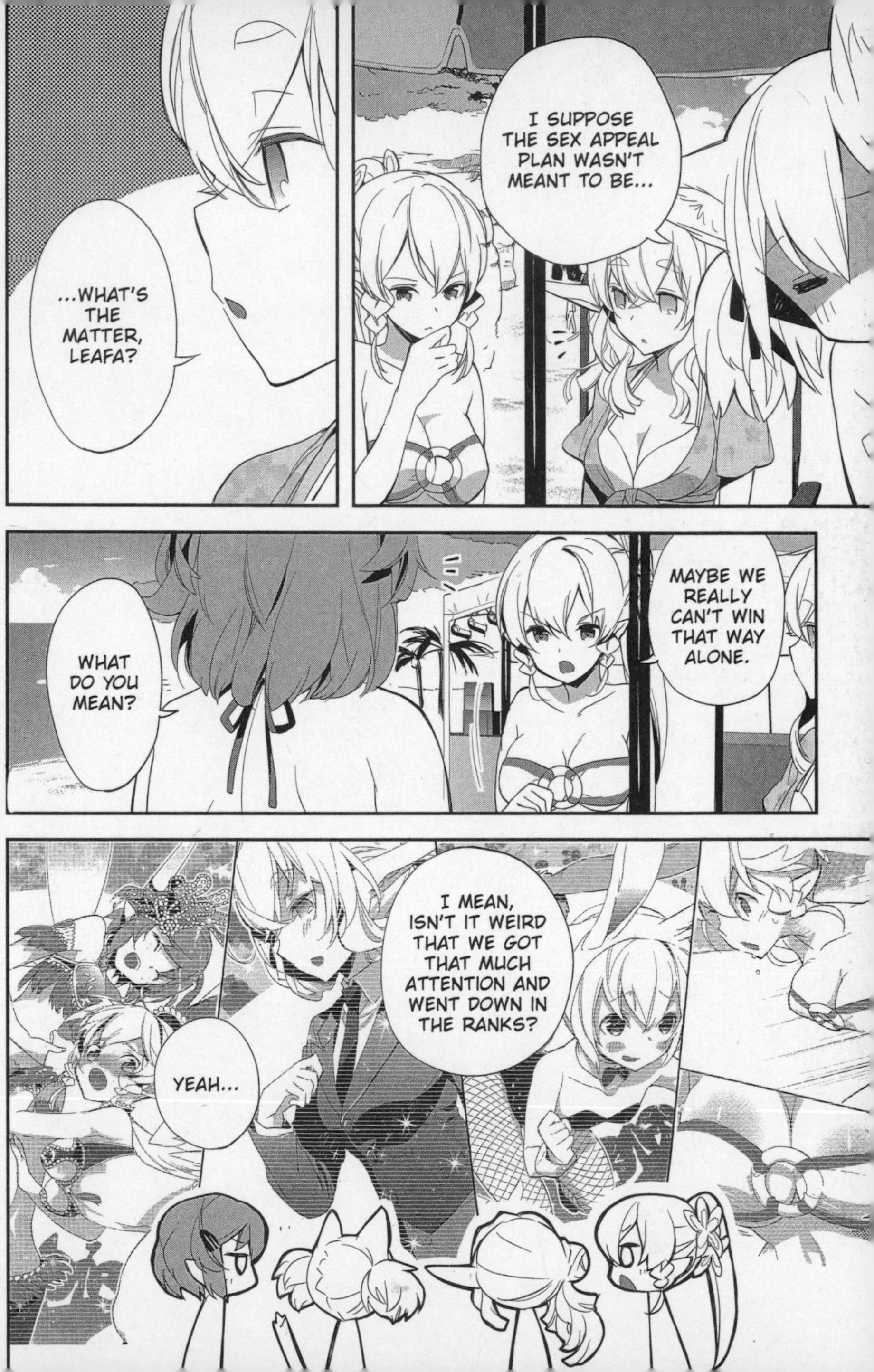
I SUPPOSE THE SEX APPEAL PLAN WASN'T MEANT TO BE...
...WHAT'S THE MATTER, LEAFA?
MAYBE WE REALLY CAN'T WIN THAT WAY ALONE.
WHAT DO YOU MEAN?
I MEAN, ISN'T IT WEIRD THAT WE GOT THAT MUCH ATTENTION AND WENT DOWN IN THE RANKS?
YEAH...

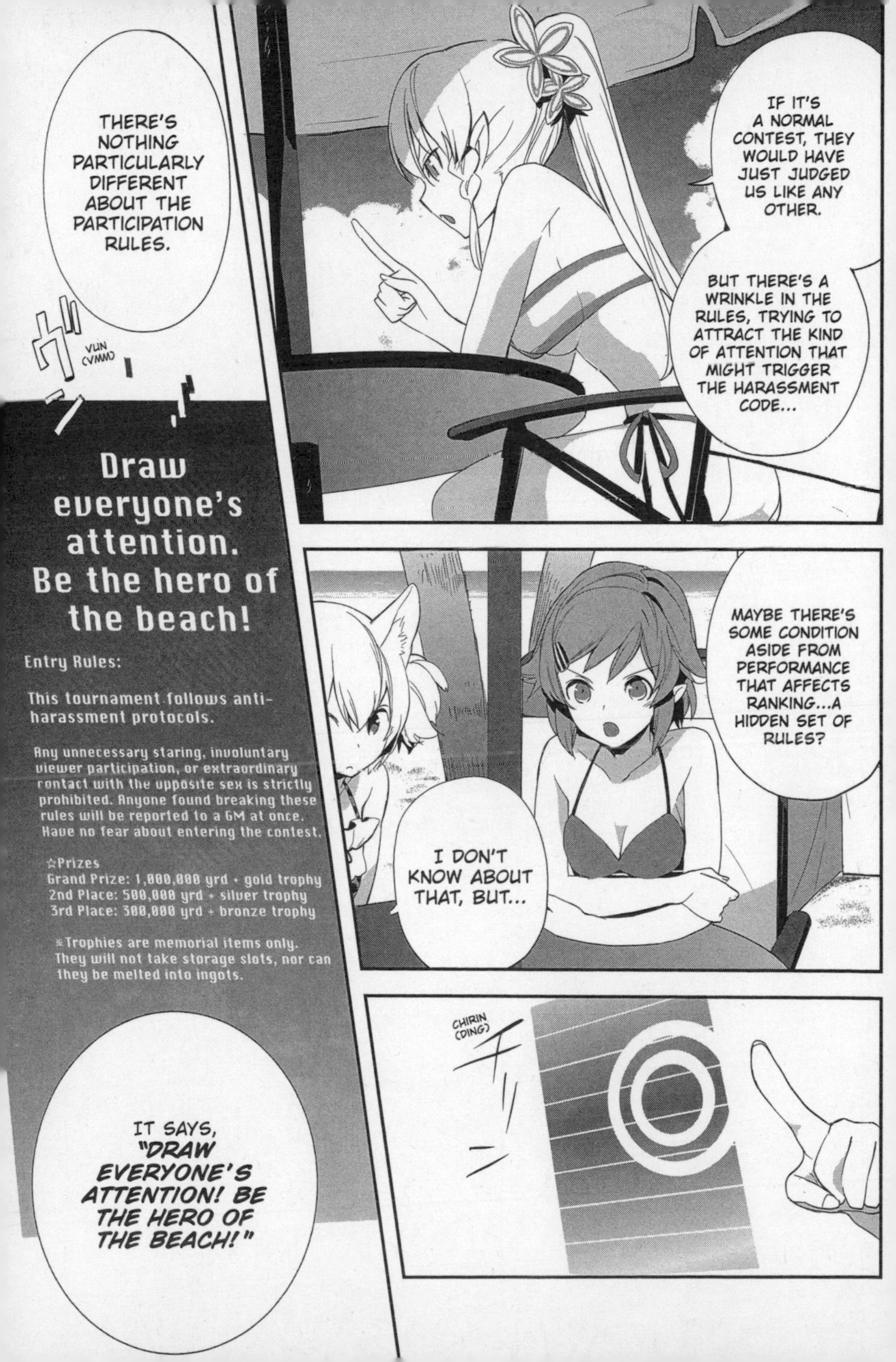
THERE'S NOTHING PARTICULARLY DIFFERENT ABOUT THE PARTICIPATION RULES.
IF IT'S A NORMAL CONTEST, THEY WOULD HAVE JUST JUDGED US LIKE ANY OTHER.
BUT THERE'S A WRINKLE IN THE RULES, TRYING TO ATTRACT THE KIND OF ATTENTION THAT MIGHT TRIGGER THE HARASSMENT CODE...
VUN (VMM)
MAYBE THERE'S SOME CONDITION ASIDE FROM PERFORMANCE THAT AFFECTS RANKING...A HIDDEN SET OF RULES?
I DON'T KNOW ABOUT THAT, BUT...
CHIRIN (DING)
Draw everyone's attention. Be the hero of the beach!
Entry Rules:
This tournament follows anti-harassment protocols.
Any unnecessary staring, involuntary viewer participation, or extraordinary contact with the opposite sex is strictly prohibited. Anyone found breaking these rules will be reported to a GM at once. Have no fear about entering the contest.
☆Prizes
Grand Prize: 1,000,000 yrd + gold trophy
2nd Place: 500,000 yrd + silver trophy
3rd Place: 300,000 yrd + bronze trophy
※Trophies are memorial items only. They will not take storage slots, nor can they be melted into ingots.
IT SAYS, "DRAW EVERYONE'S ATTENTION! BE THE HERO OF THE BEACH!"

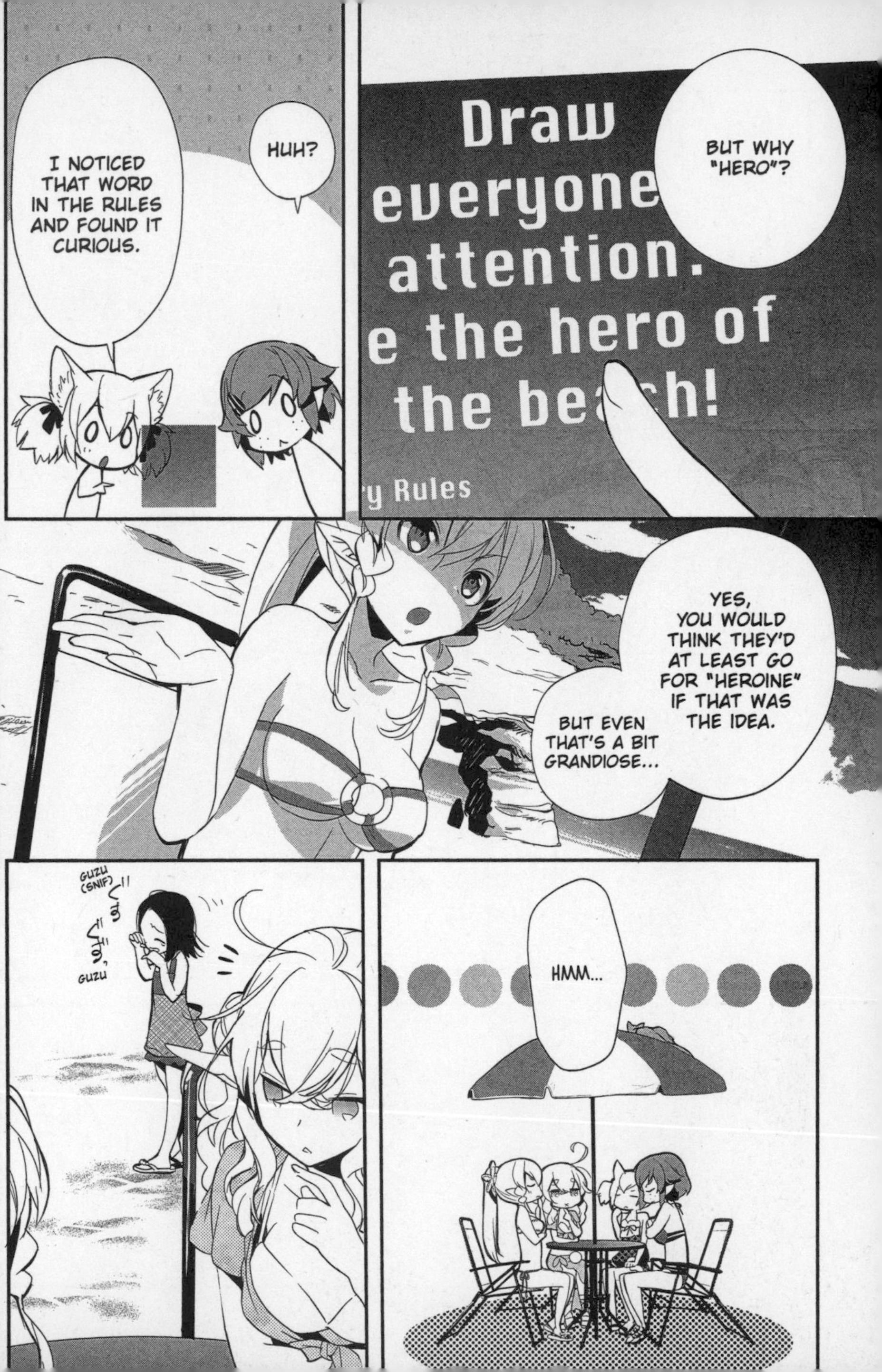
Draw everyone
attention.
e the hero of
the be h!
ry Rules
BUT WHY "HERO"?
HUH?
I NOTICED THAT WORD IN THE RULES AND FOUND IT CURIOUS.
YES, YOU WOULD THINK THEY'D AT LEAST GO FOR "HEROINE" IF THAT WAS THE IDEA.
BUT EVEN THAT'S A BIT GRANDIOSE...
HMM...
GUZU (SNIF)
GUZU

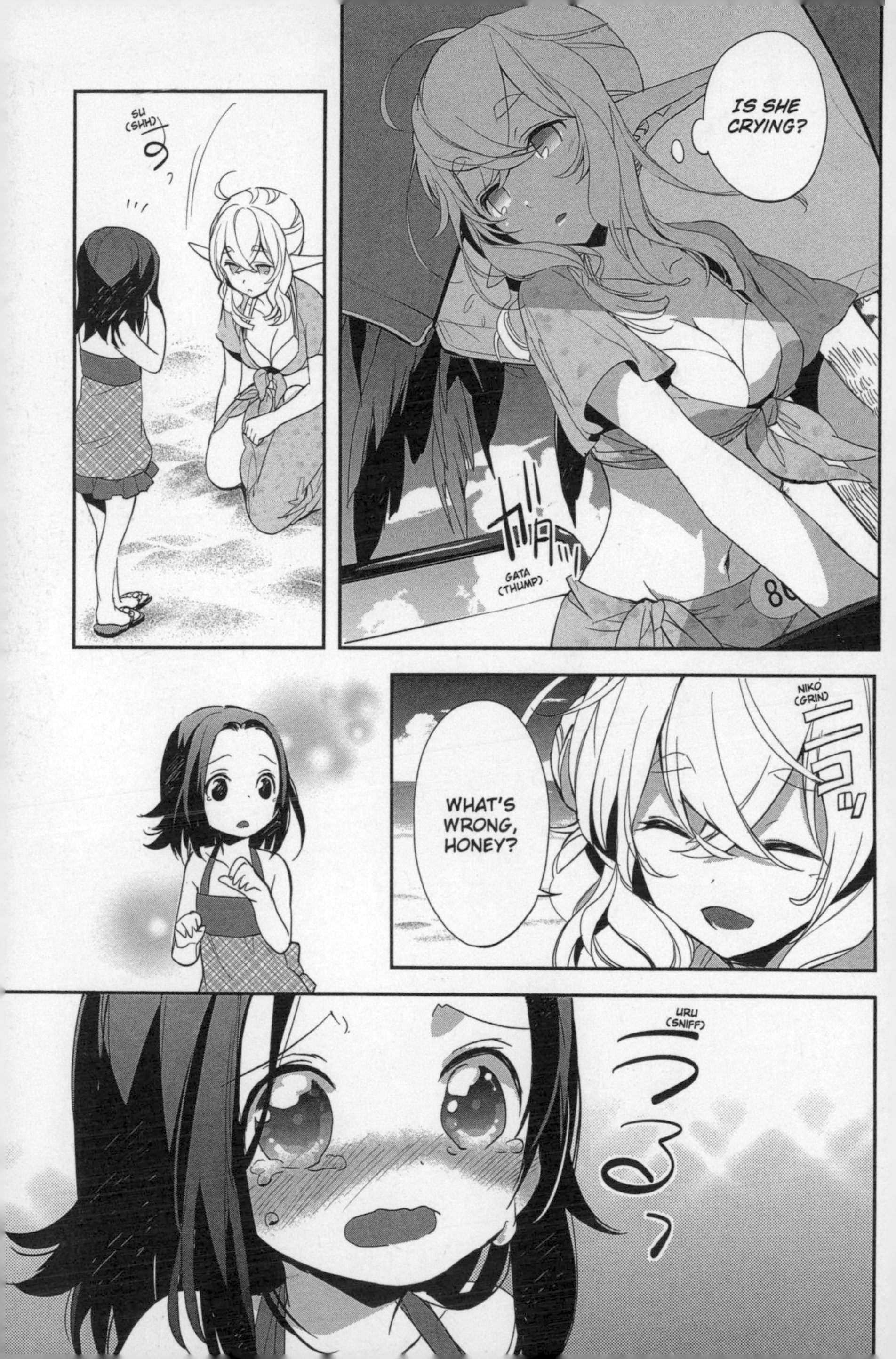
IS SHE CRYING?
GATA (THUMP)
SU (SHH)
NIKO (GRIN)
WHAT'S WRONG, HONEY?
URU (SNIFF)

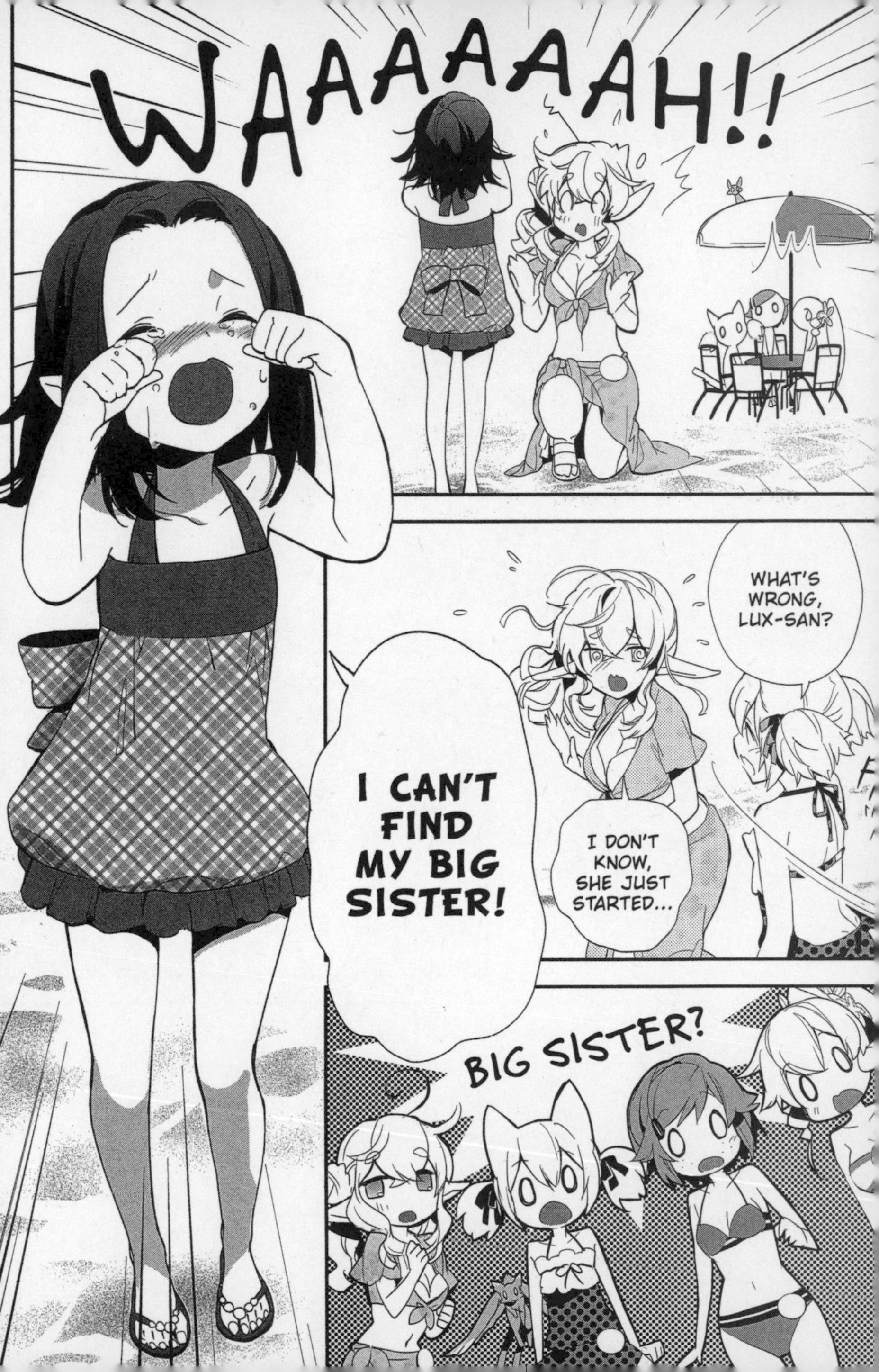
WAAAAAAAH!!
WHAT'S WRONG, LUX-SAN?
I DON'T KNOW, SHE JUST STARTED...
I CAN'T FIND MY BIG SISTER!
BIG SISTER?

SWORD ART ONLINE
GIRLS' OPS

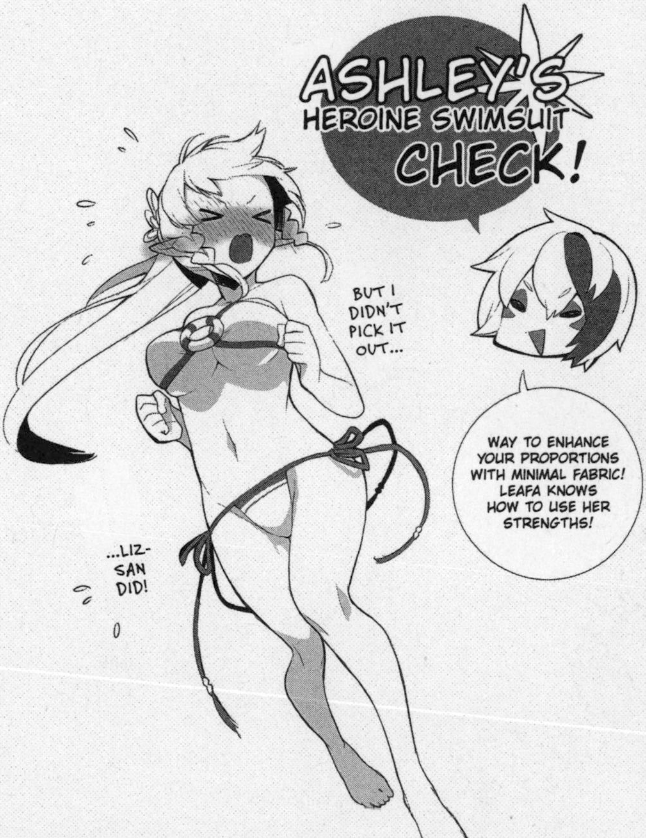
ASHLEY'S
HEROINE SWIMSUIT
CHECK!
BUT I DIDN'T PICK IT OUT...
...LIZ-SAN DID!
WAY TO ENHANCE YOUR PROPORTIONS WITH MINIMAL FABRIC! LEAFA KNOWS HOW TO USE HER STRENGTHS!

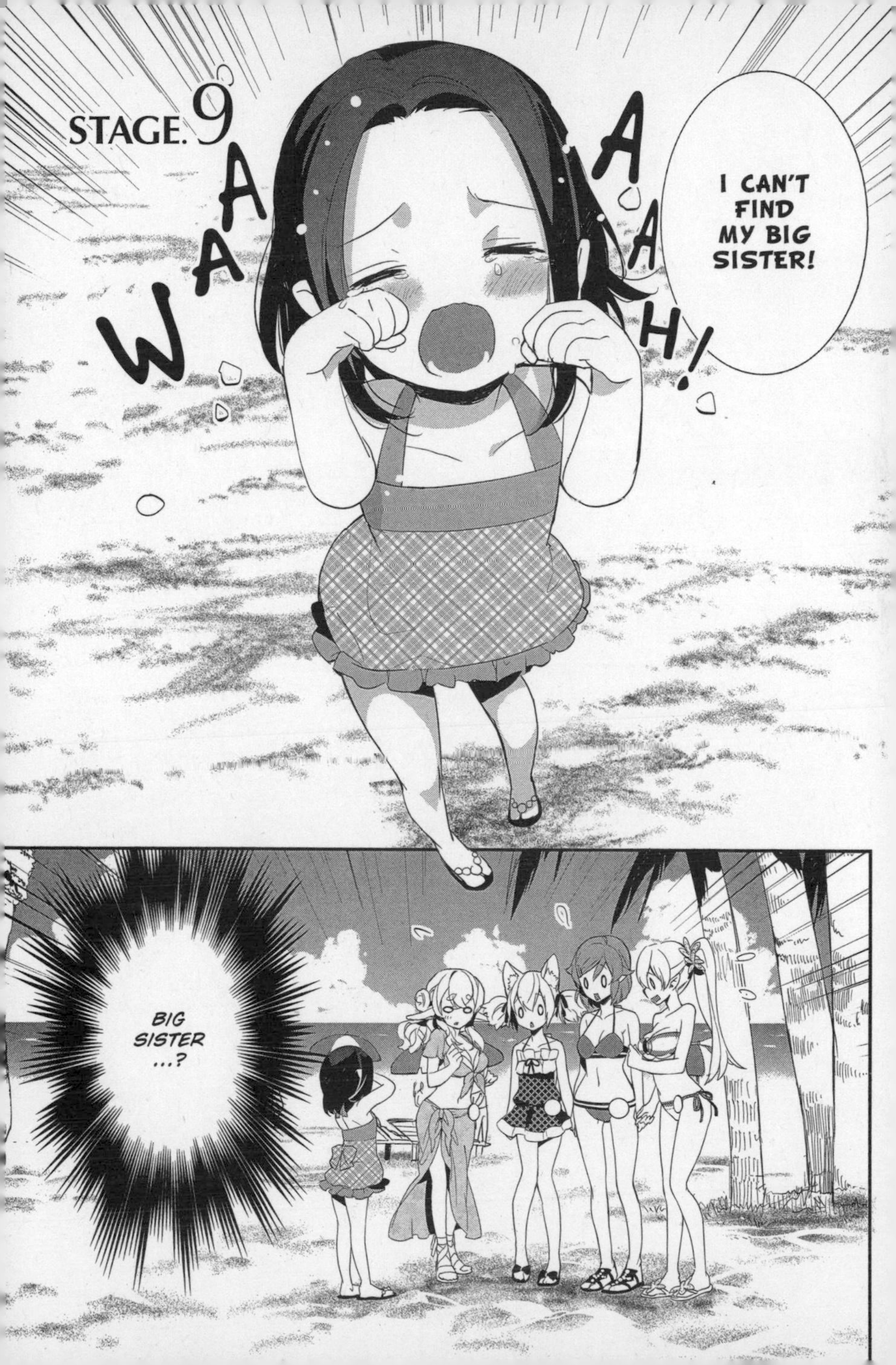
STAGE. 9
WAAAAAH!
I CAN'T FIND MY BIG SISTER!
BIG SISTER ...?

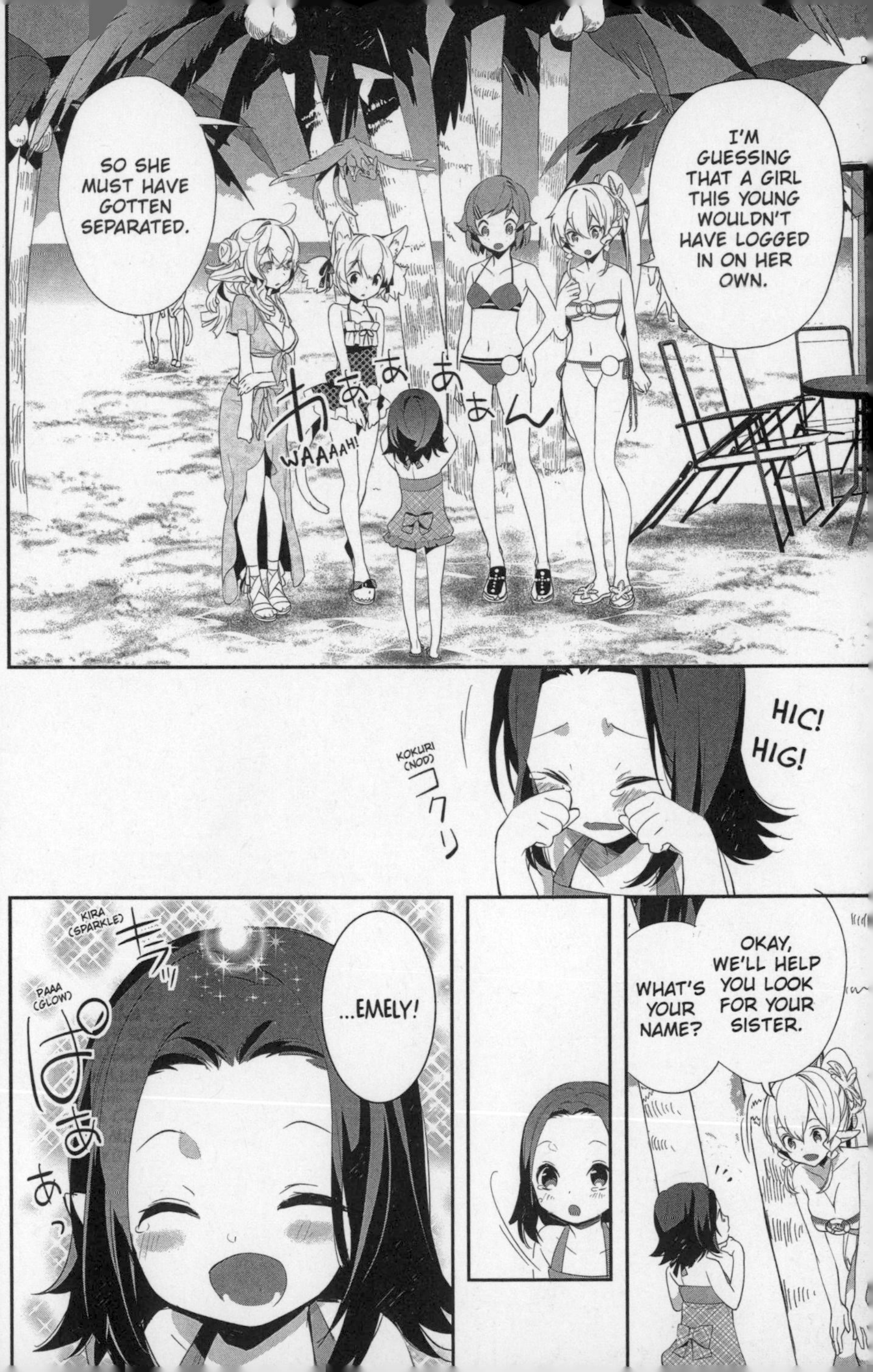
I'M GUESSING THAT A GIRL THIS YOUNG WOULDN'T HAVE LOGGED IN ON HER OWN.
SO SHE MUST HAVE GOTTEN SEPARATED.
WAAAAH!
HIC! HIG!
KOKURI (NOD)
OKAY, WE'LL HELP YOU LOOK FOR YOUR SISTER.
WHAT'S YOUR NAME?
...EMELY!
KIRA (SPARKLE)
PAAA (GLOW)

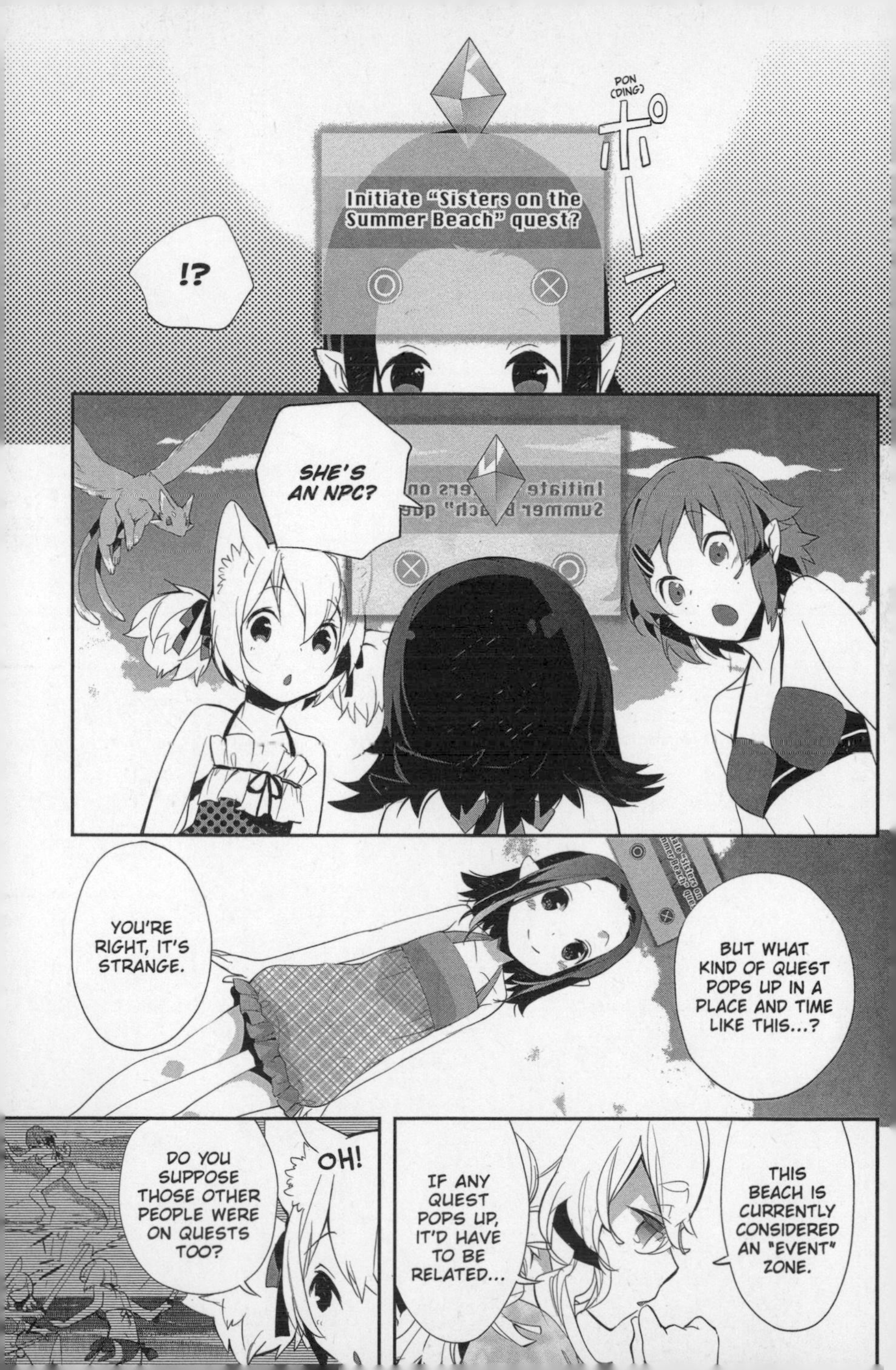
PON (DING)
Initiate "Sisters on the Summer Beach" quest?
!?
SHE'S AN NPC?
BUT WHAT KIND OF QUEST POPS UP IN A PLACE AND TIME LIKE THIS...?
YOU'RE RIGHT, IT'S STRANGE.
THIS BEACH IS CURRENTLY CONSIDERED AN "EVENT" ZONE.
IF ANY QUEST POPS UP, IT'D HAVE TO BE RELATED...
OH!
DO YOU SUPPOSE THOSE OTHER PEOPLE WERE ON QUESTS TOO?

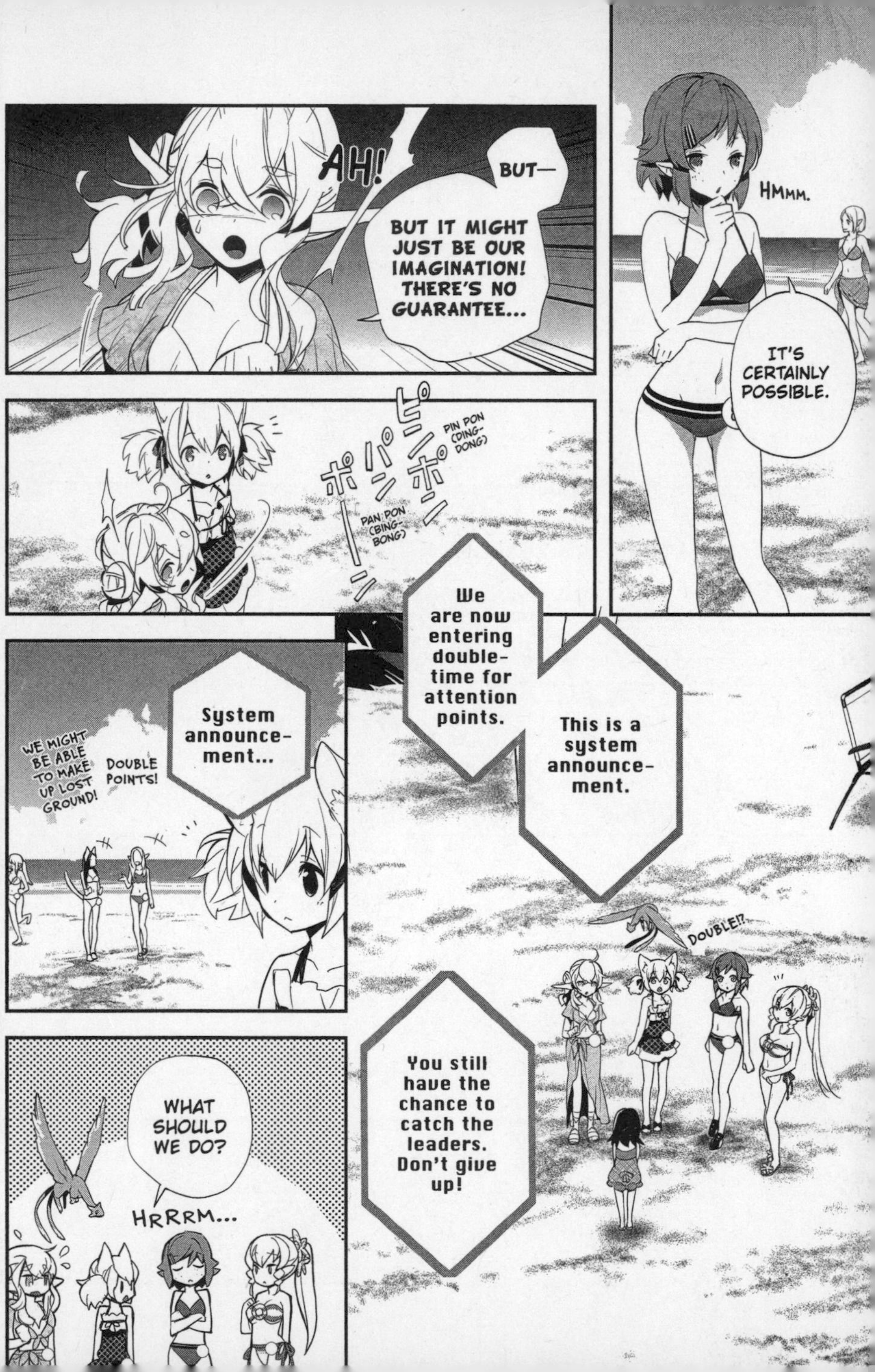
HMMM.
IT'S CERTAINLY POSSIBLE.
AH!
BUT—
BUT IT MIGHT JUST BE OUR IMAGINATION! THERE'S NO GUARANTEE...
ピンポン
PIN PON (DING-DONG)
パンポーン
PAN PON (BING-BONG)
This is a system announcement.
We are now entering double-time for attention points.
System announcement...
DOUBLE POINTS!
WE MIGHT BE ABLE TO MAKE UP LOST GROUND!
DOUBLE!?
You still have the chance to catch the leaders. Don't give up!
WHAT SHOULD WE DO?
HRRRM...

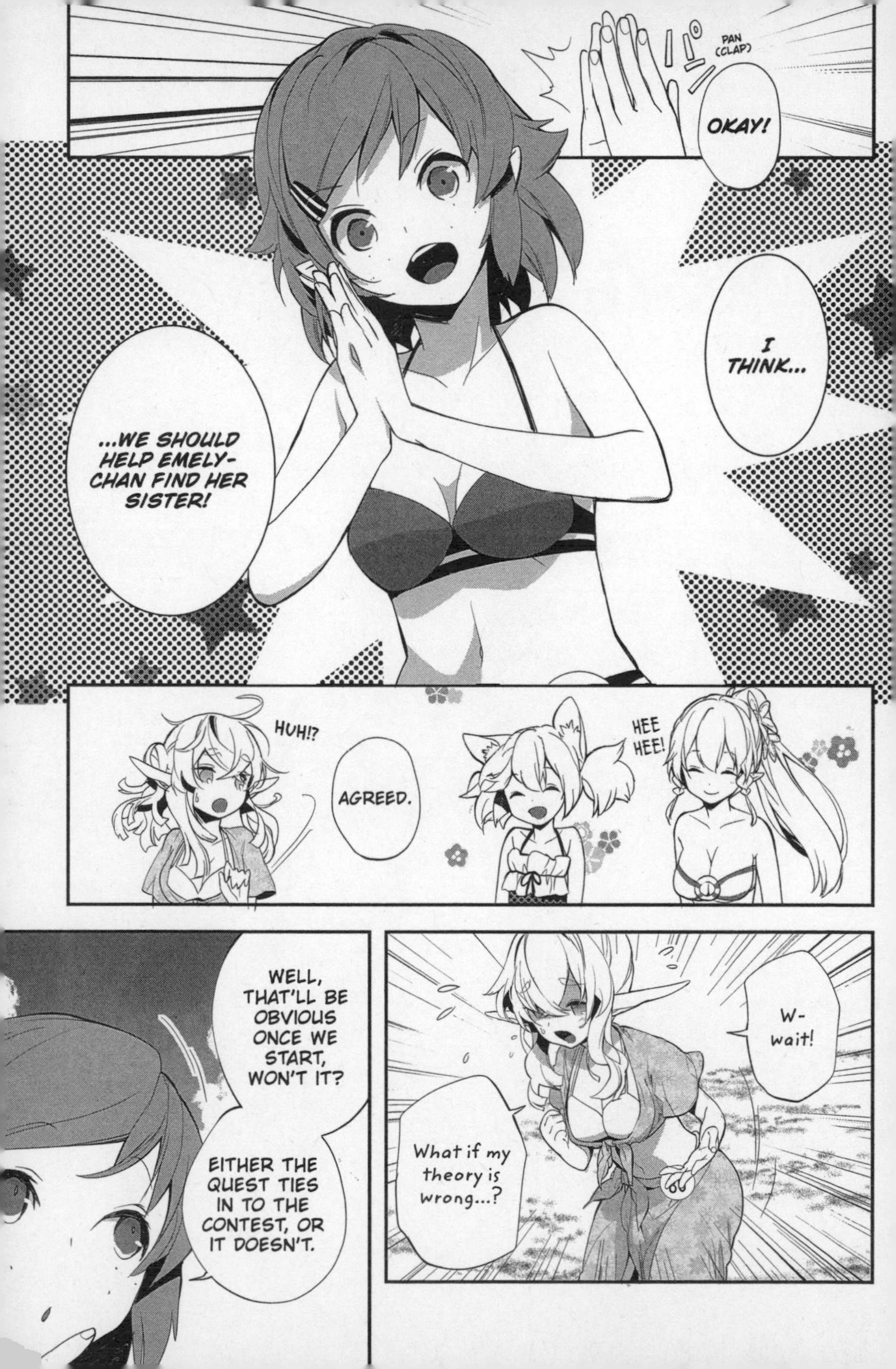
PAN (CLAP)
OKAY!
I THINK...
...WE SHOULD HELP EMELY-CHAN FIND HER SISTER!
HEE HEE!
AGREED.
HUH!?
W-wait!
What if my theory is wrong...?
WELL, THAT'LL BE OBVIOUS ONCE WE START, WON'T IT?
EITHER THE QUEST TIES IN TO THE CONTEST, OR IT DOESN'T.

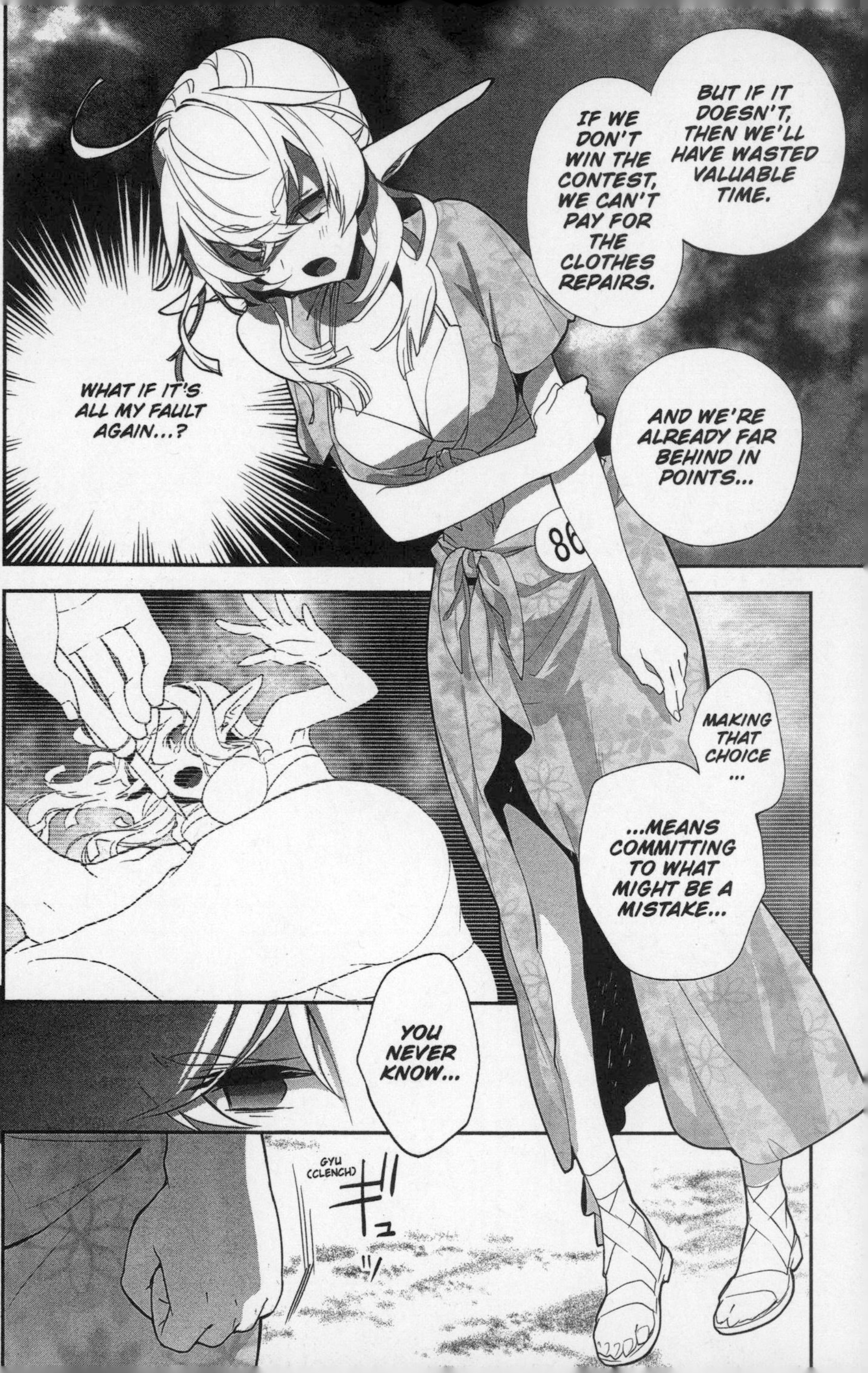
BUT IF IT DOESN'T, THEN WE'LL HAVE WASTED VALUABLE TIME.
IF WE DON'T WIN THE CONTEST, WE CAN'T PAY FOR THE CLOTHES REPAIRS.
AND WE'RE ALREADY FAR BEHIND IN POINTS...
WHAT IF IT'S ALL MY FAULT AGAIN...?
MAKING THAT CHOICE ...
...MEANS COMMITTING TO WHAT MIGHT BE A MISTAKE...
YOU NEVER KNOW...
GYU (CLENCH)

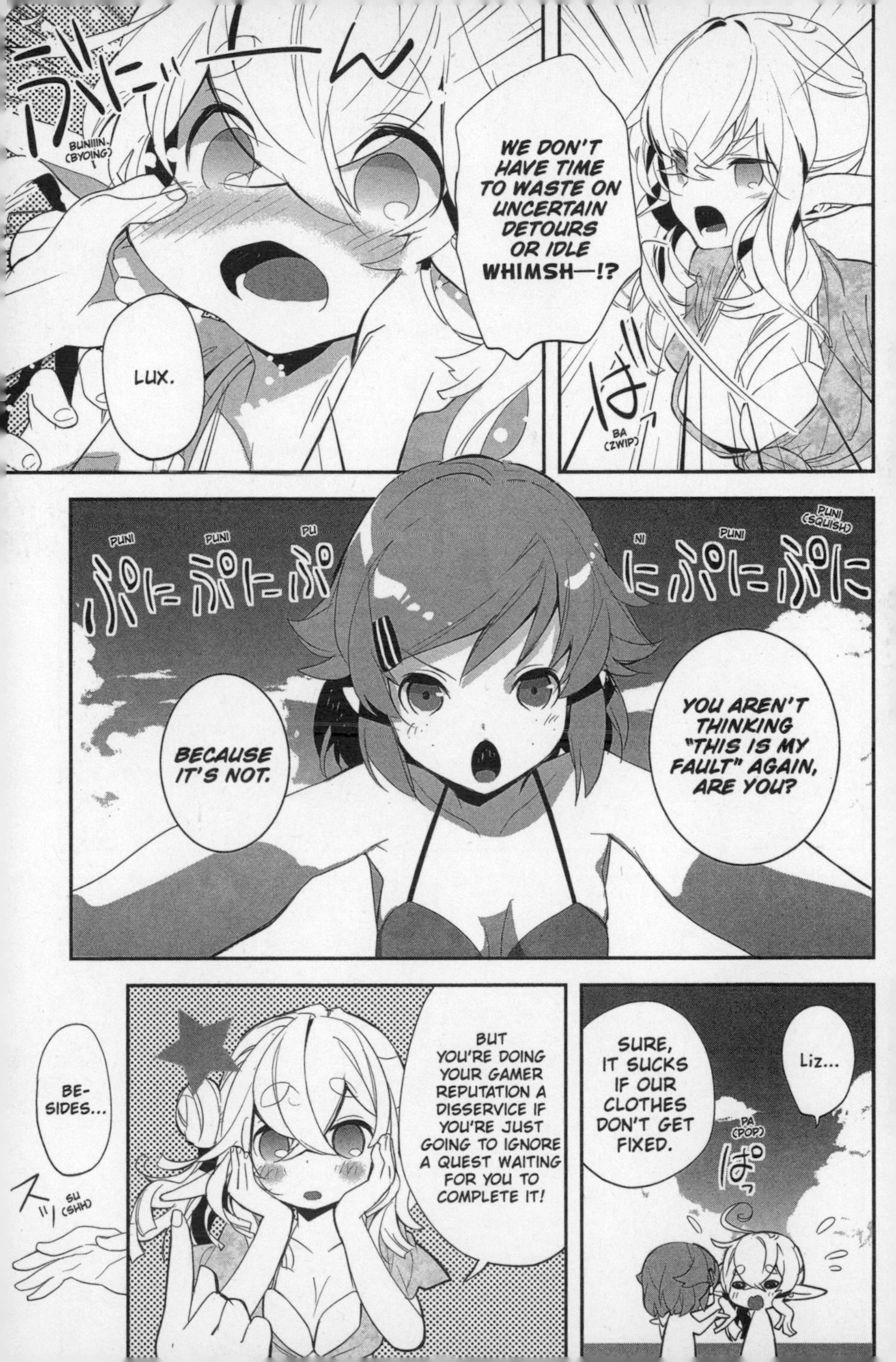
WE DON'T HAVE TIME TO WASTE ON UNCERTAIN DETOURS OR IDLE WHIMSH—!?
BA (ZWIP)
ばっ
BUNIIIN (BYOING)
LUX.
PUNI (SQUISH)
PUNI
NI
PUNI
PU
PUNI
PUNI
YOU AREN'T THINKING "THIS IS MY FAULT" AGAIN, ARE YOU?
BECAUSE IT'S NOT.
Liz...
SURE, IT SUCKS IF OUR CLOTHES DON'T GET FIXED.
PA (POP)
ぱっ
BUT YOU'RE DOING YOUR GAMER REPUTATION A DISSERVICE IF YOU'RE JUST GOING TO IGNORE A QUEST WAITING FOR YOU TO COMPLETE IT!
BE-SIDES...
SU (SHH)

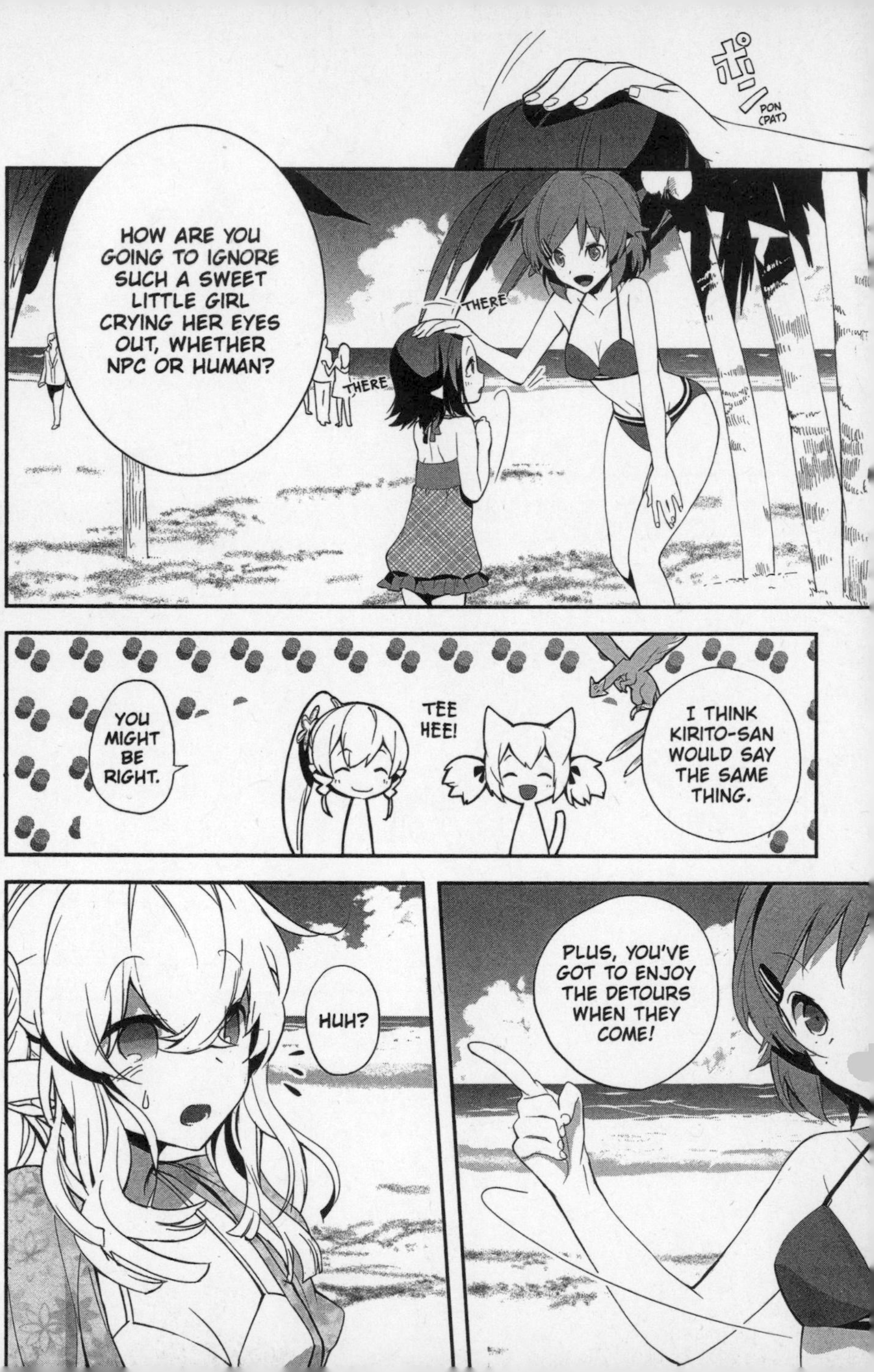
ポン
PON (PAT)
HOW ARE YOU GOING TO IGNORE SUCH A SWEET LITTLE GIRL CRYING HER EYES OUT, WHETHER NPC OR HUMAN?
THERE
THERE
I THINK KIRITO-SAN WOULD SAY THE SAME THING.
TEE HEE!
YOU MIGHT BE RIGHT.
PLUS, YOU'VE GOT TO ENJOY THE DETOURS WHEN THEY COME!
HUH?

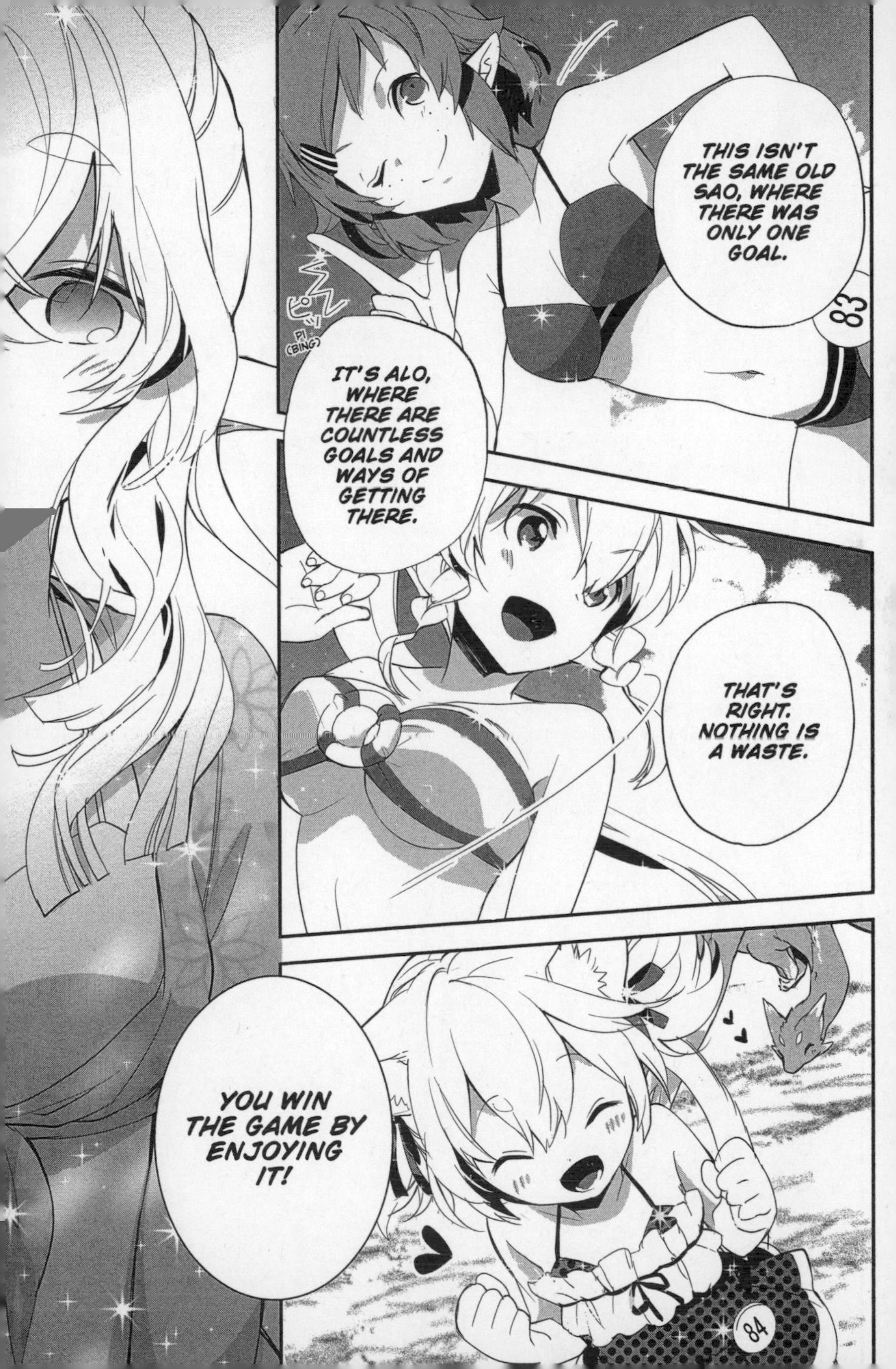
THIS ISN'T THE SAME OLD SAO, WHERE THERE WAS ONLY ONE GOAL.
PI (BING)
IT'S ALO, WHERE THERE ARE COUNTLESS GOALS AND WAYS OF GETTING THERE.
THAT'S RIGHT. NOTHING IS A WASTE.
YOU WIN THE GAME BY ENJOYING IT!
83
84

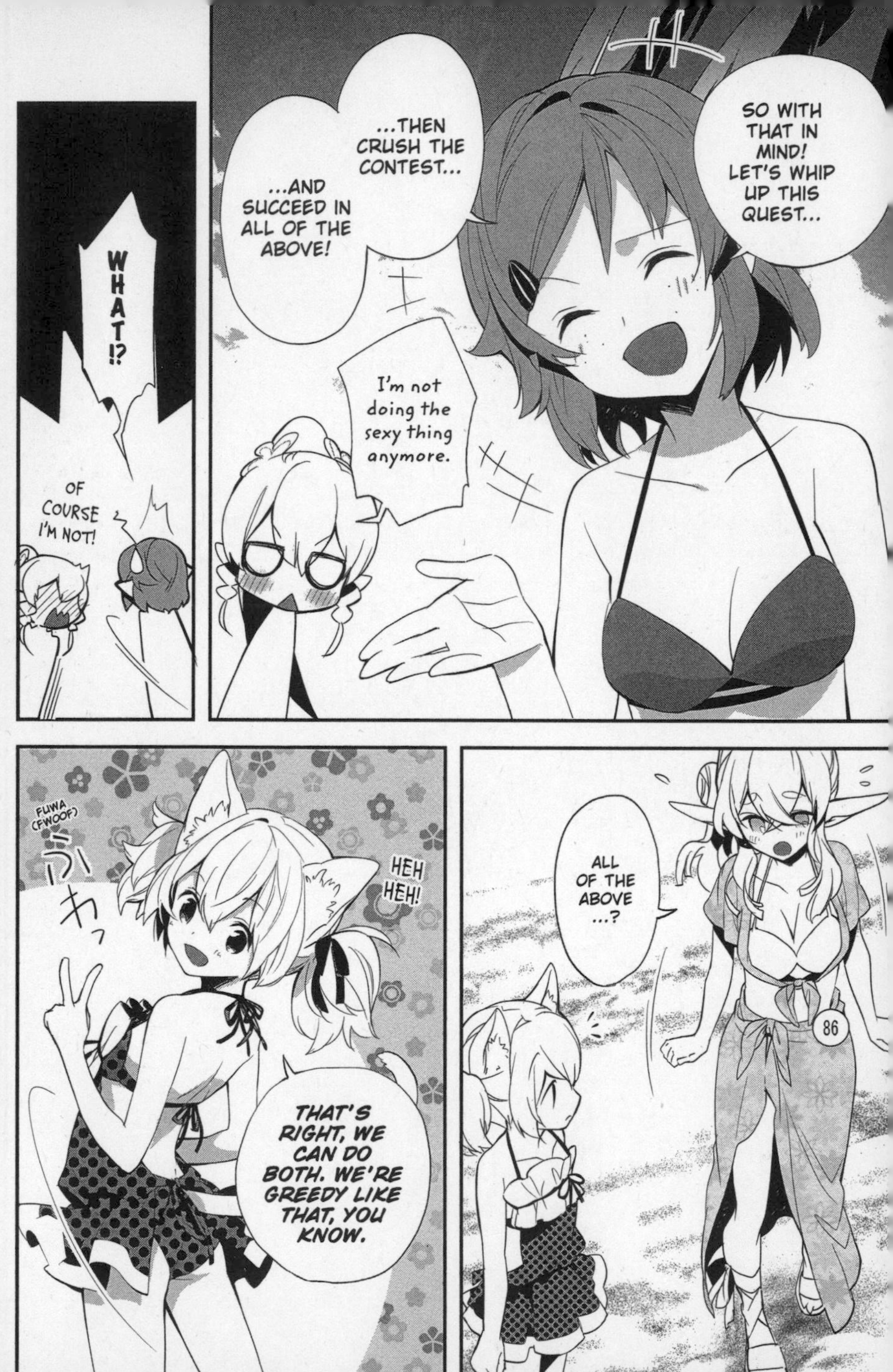

SO WITH THAT IN MIND! LET'S WHIP UP THIS QUEST...
...THEN CRUSH THE CONTEST...
...AND SUCCEED IN ALL OF THE ABOVE!
I'm not doing the sexy thing anymore.
WHAT!?
OF COURSE I'M NOT!
ALL OF THE ABOVE ...?
HEH HEH!
FUWA (FWOOF)
ふわっ
THAT'S RIGHT, WE CAN DO BOTH. WE'RE GREEDY LIKE THAT, YOU KNOW.

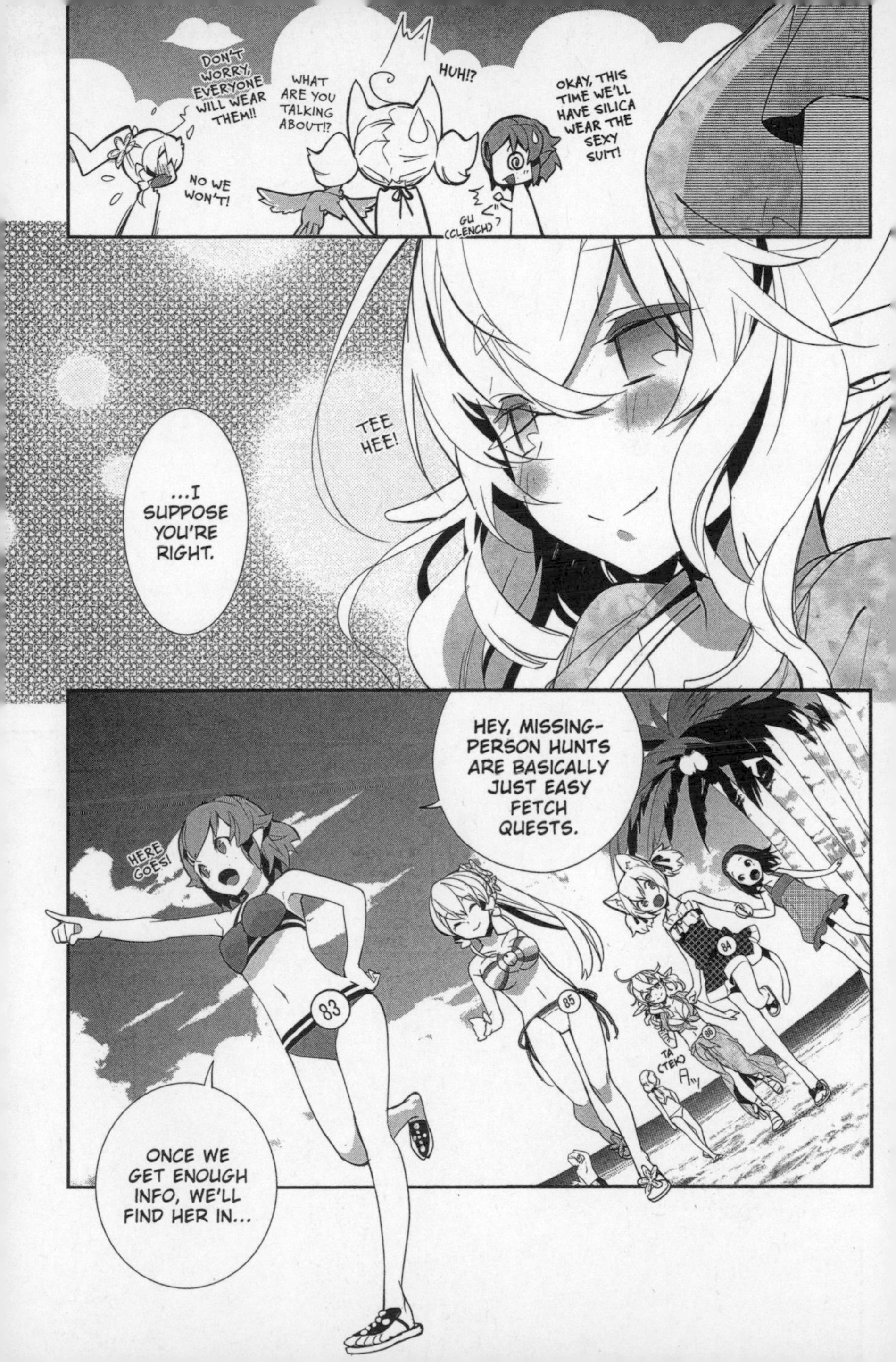
OKAY, THIS TIME WE'LL HAVE SILICA WEAR THE SEXY SUIT!
HUH!?
WHAT ARE YOU TALKING ABOUT!?
DON'T WORRY, EVERYONE WILL WEAR THEM!!
NO WE WON'T!
GU (CLENCH)
TEE HEE!
...I SUPPOSE YOU'RE RIGHT.
HEY, MISSING-PERSON HUNTS ARE BASICALLY JUST EASY FETCH QUESTS.
HERE GOES!
TA (TEK)
ONCE WE GET ENOUGH INFO, WE'LL FIND HER IN...

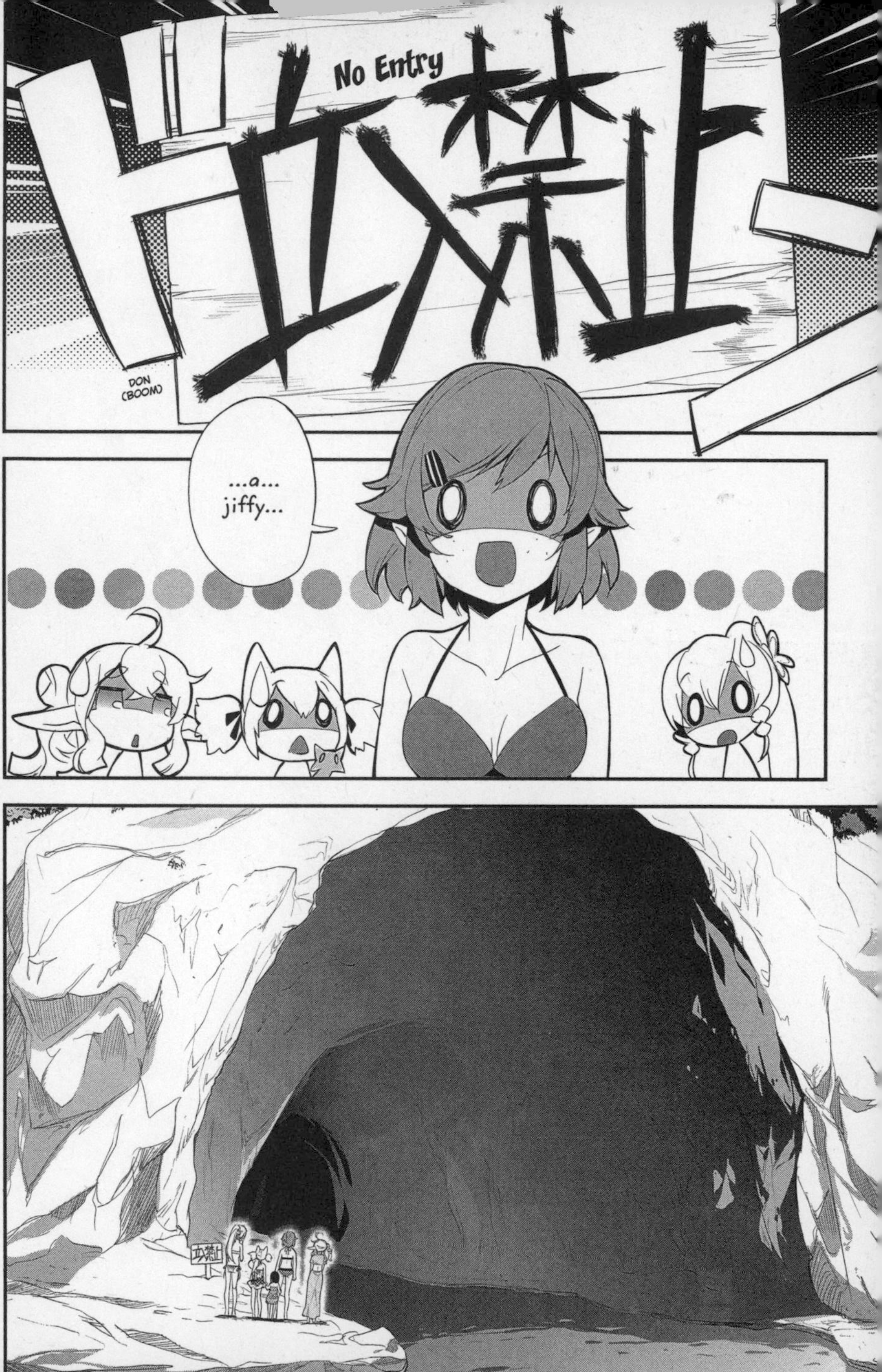
No Entry
DON (BOOM)
...a... jiffy...

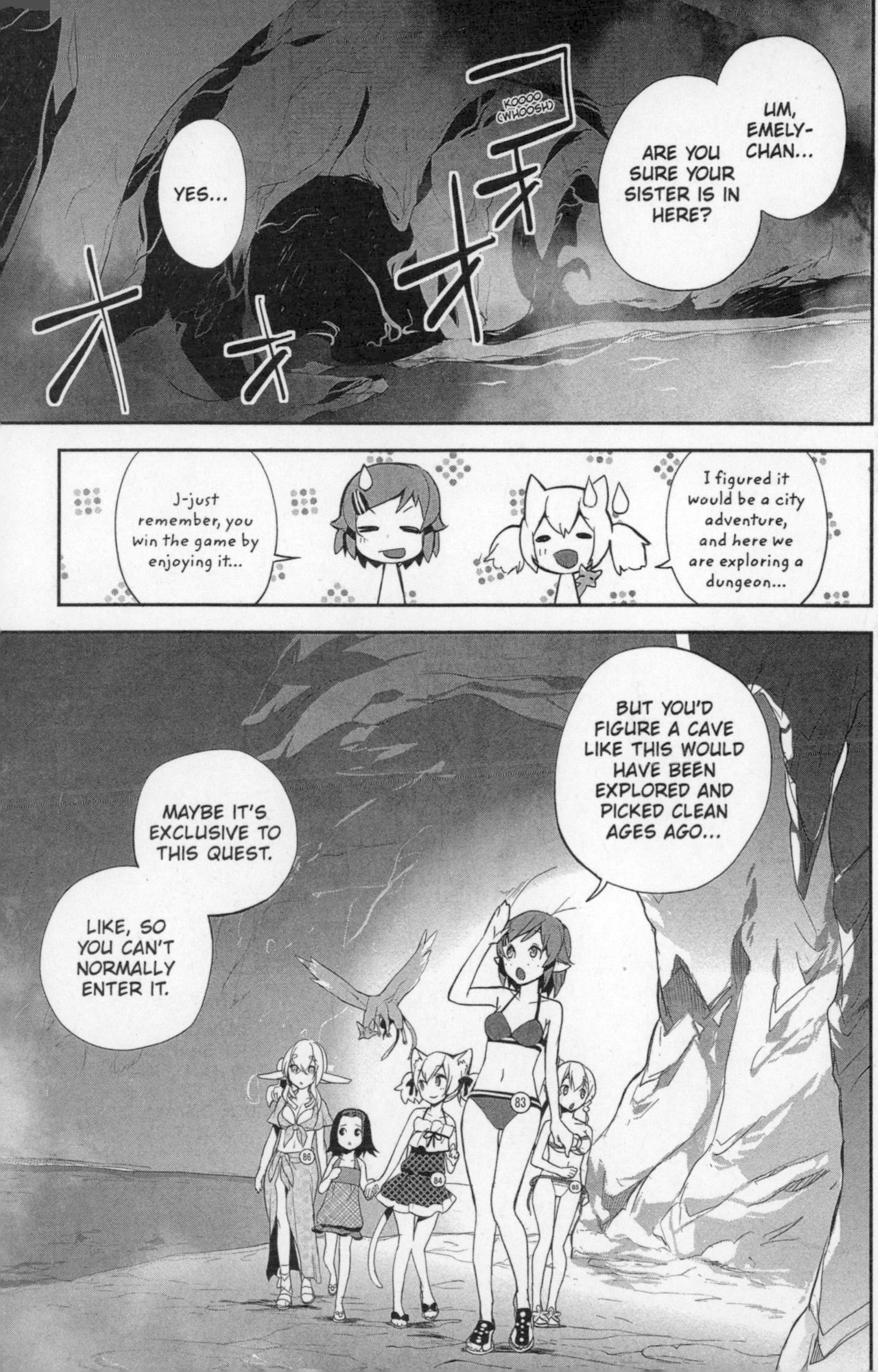
UM, EMELY-CHAN...
ARE YOU SURE YOUR SISTER IS IN HERE?
KOOOO (WHOOSH)
YES...
I figured it would be a city adventure, and here we are exploring a dungeon...
J-just remember, you win the game by enjoying it...
BUT YOU'D FIGURE A CAVE LIKE THIS WOULD HAVE BEEN EXPLORED AND PICKED CLEAN AGES AGO...
MAYBE IT'S EXCLUSIVE TO THIS QUEST.
LIKE, SO YOU CAN'T NORMALLY ENTER IT.

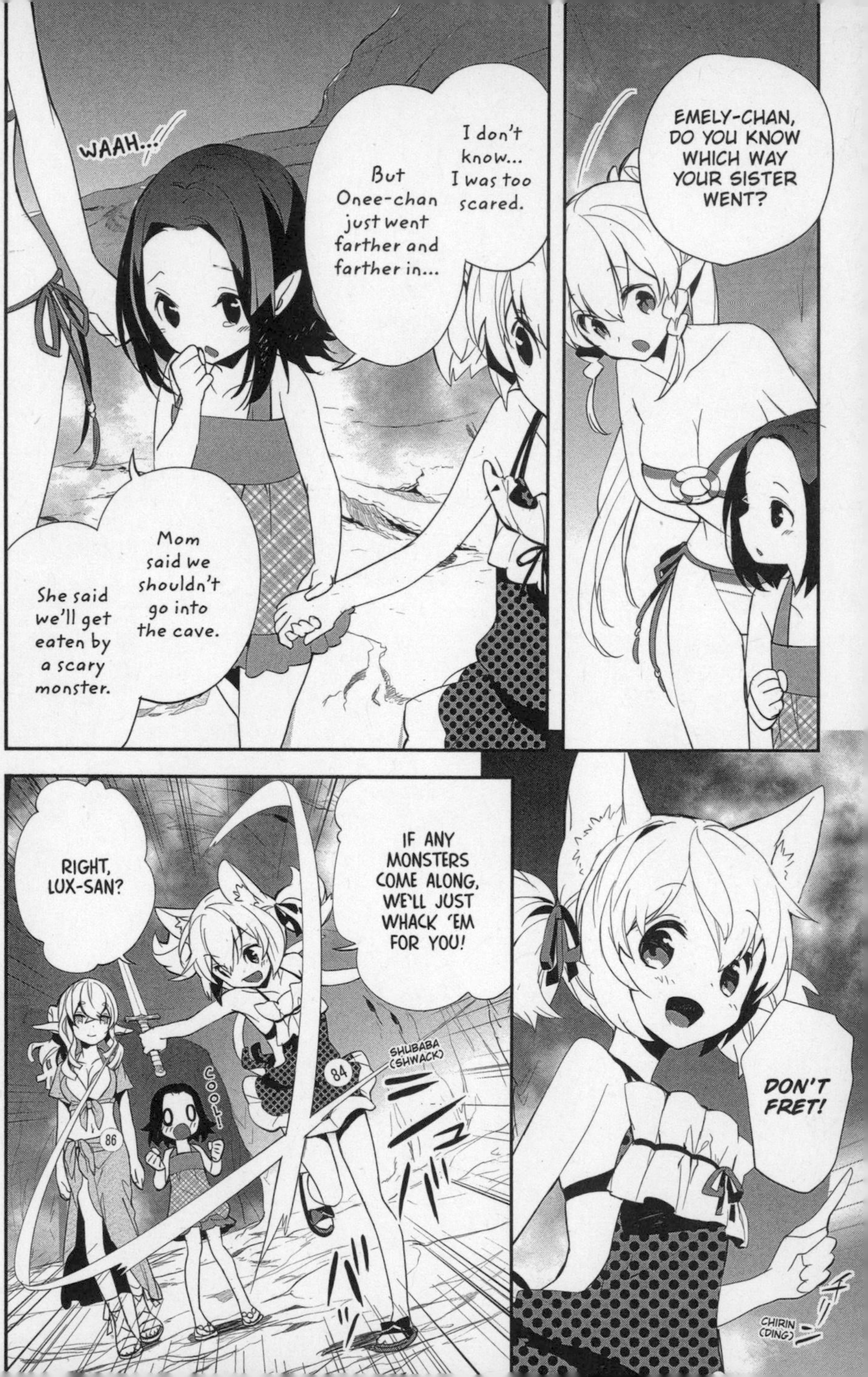
EMELY-CHAN, DO YOU KNOW WHICH WAY YOUR SISTER WENT?
I don't know... I was too scared.
But Onee-chan just went farther and farther in...
WAAH...
Mom said we shouldn't go into the cave.
She said we'll get eaten by a scary monster.
DON'T FRET!
CHIRIN (DING)
IF ANY MONSTERS COME ALONG, WE'LL JUST WHACK 'EM FOR YOU!
RIGHT, LUX-SAN?
SHUBABA (SHWACK)
84
COOL!
86

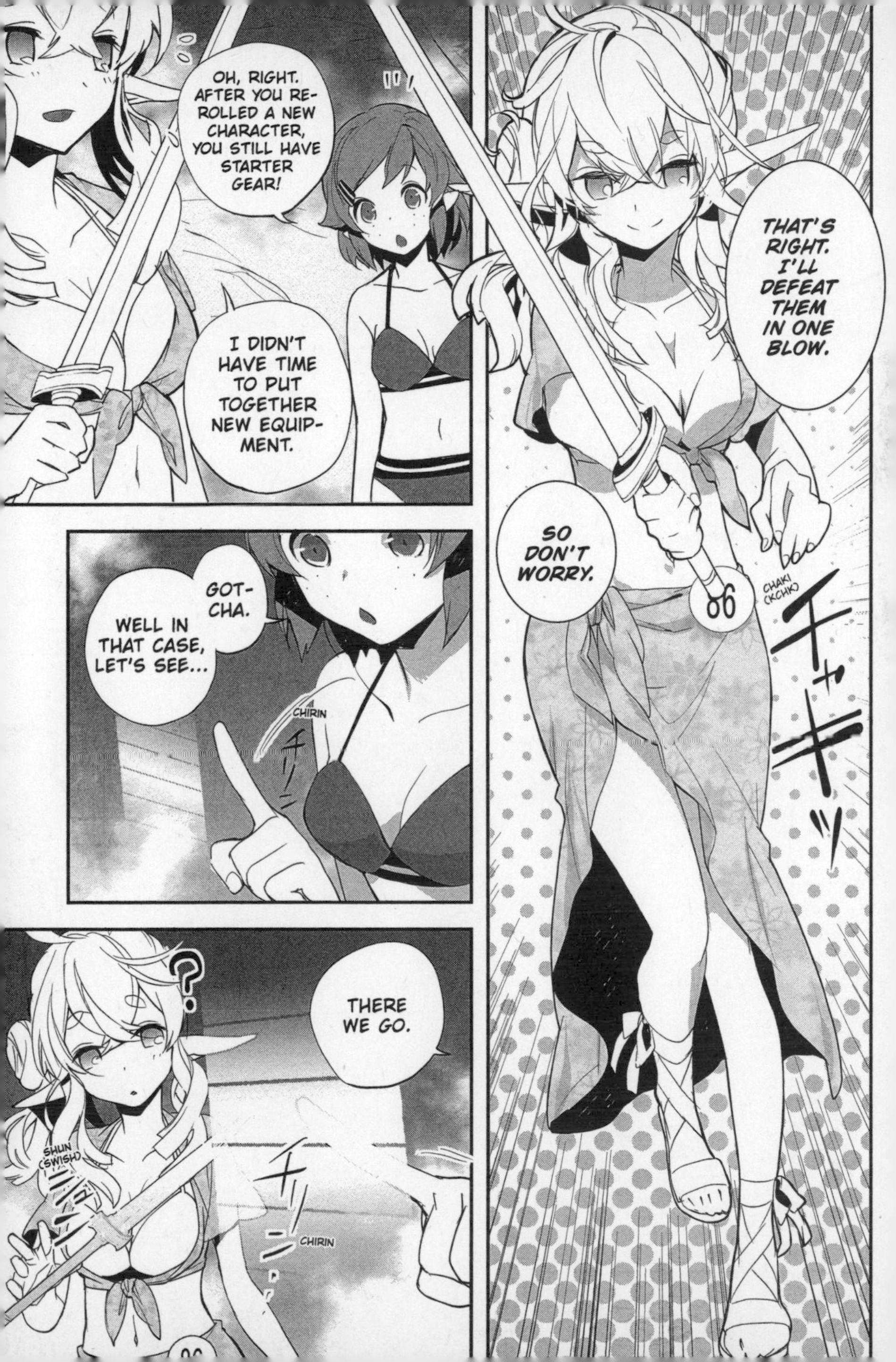
OH, RIGHT. AFTER YOU RE-ROLLED A NEW CHARACTER, YOU STILL HAVE STARTER GEAR!
I DIDN'T HAVE TIME TO PUT TOGETHER NEW EQUIP-MENT.
GOT-CHA.
WELL IN THAT CASE, LET'S SEE...
CHIRIN
THERE WE GO.
SHUN (SWISH)
CHIRIN
THAT'S RIGHT. I'LL DEFEAT THEM IN ONE BLOW.
SO DON'T WORRY.
CHAKI (KCHK)

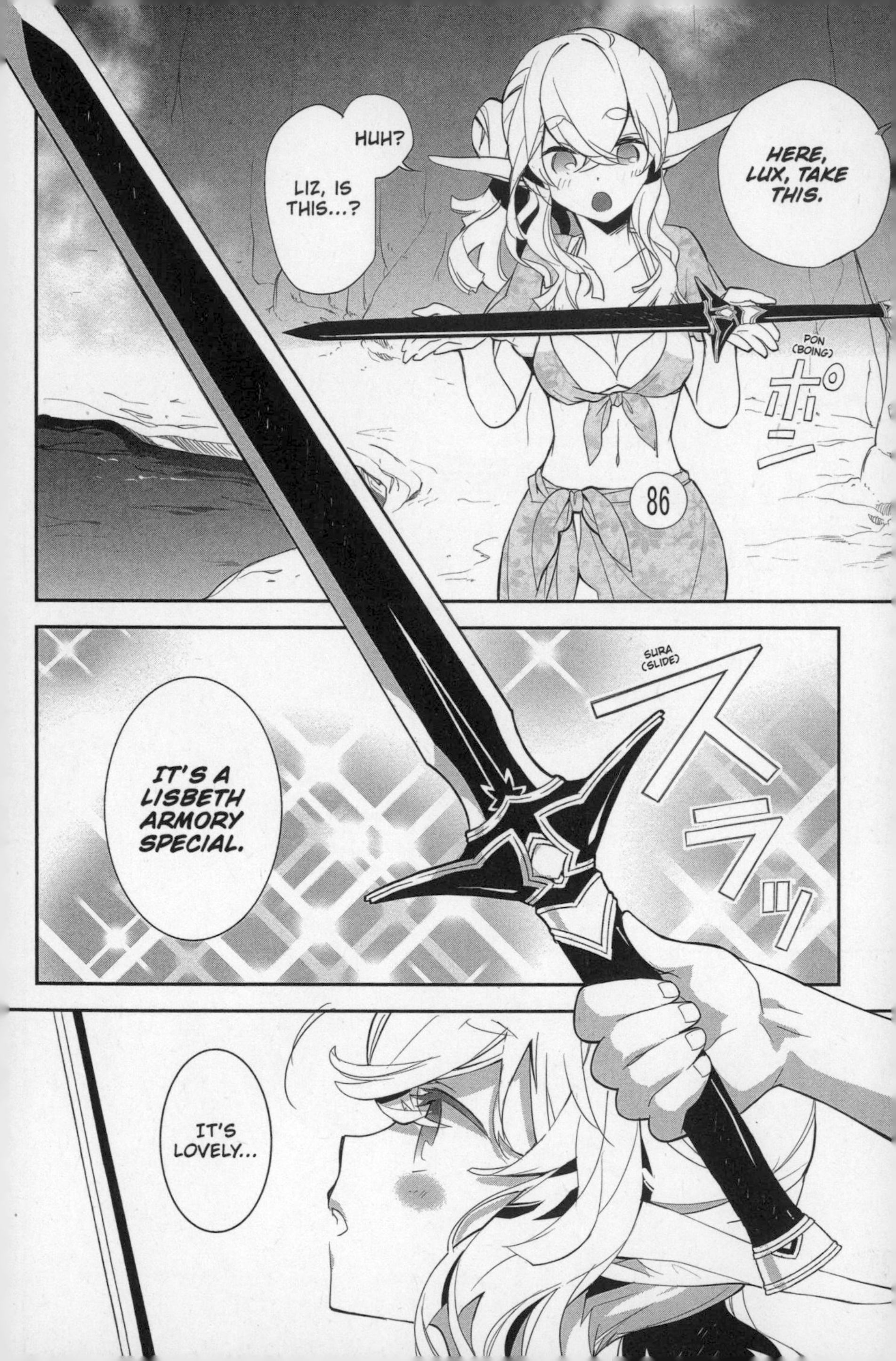
HERE, LUX, TAKE THIS.
HUH?
LIZ, IS THIS...?
PON (BOING)
ポーン
86
SURA (SLIDE)
スラッ
IT'S A LISBETH ARMORY SPECIAL.
IT'S LOVELY...

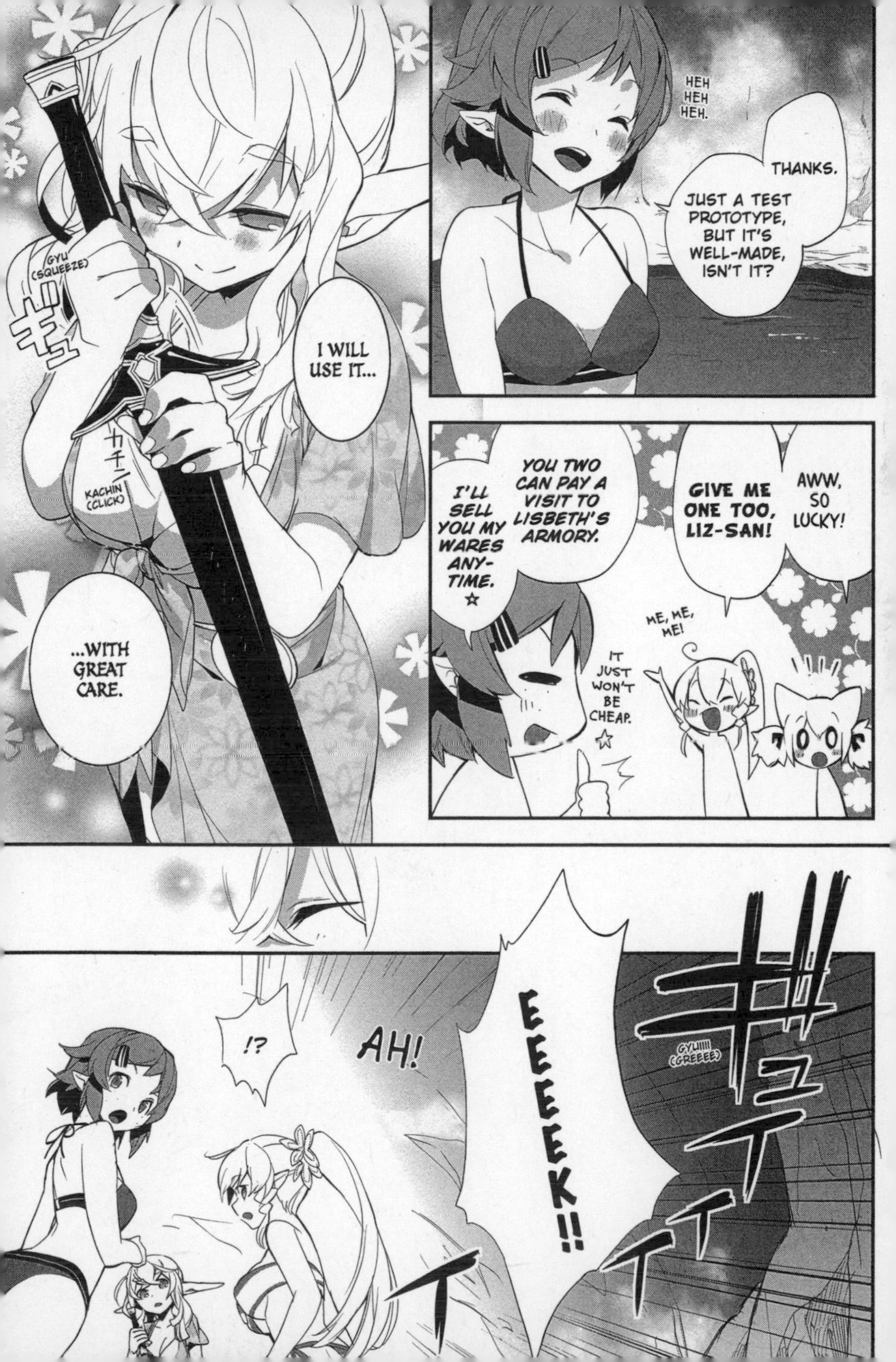
HEH HEH HEH.
THANKS.
JUST A TEST PROTOTYPE, BUT IT'S WELL-MADE, ISN'T IT?
AWW, SO LUCKY!
GIVE ME ONE TOO, LIZ-SAN!
YOU TWO CAN PAY A VISIT TO LISBETH'S ARMORY.
I'LL SELL YOU MY WARES ANY-TIME. ☆
ME, ME, ME!
IT JUST WON'T BE CHEAP. ☆
ギュ
GYU (SQUEEZE)
I WILL USE IT...
カチン
KACHIN (CLICK)
...WITH GREAT CARE.
ギュイイイ
GYUIIII (GREEEE)
EEEEEK!!
AH!
!?

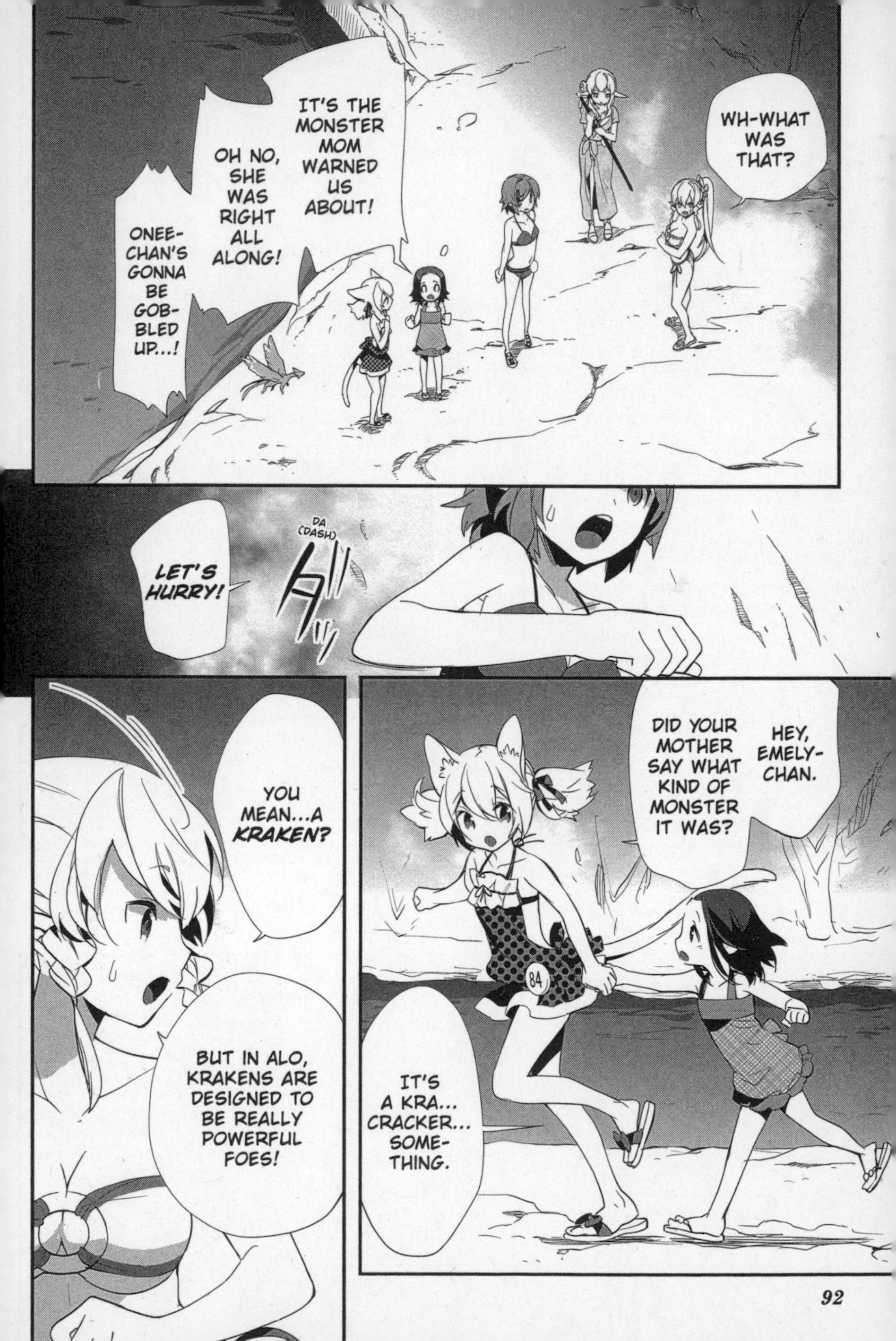
WH-WHAT WAS THAT?
IT'S THE MONSTER MOM WARNED US ABOUT!
OH NO, SHE WAS RIGHT ALL ALONG!
ONEE-CHAN'S GONNA BE GOB-BLED UP...!
DA (DASH)
LET'S HURRY!
HEY, EMELY-CHAN.
DID YOUR MOTHER SAY WHAT KIND OF MONSTER IT WAS?
IT'S A KRA... CRACKER... SOME-THING.
YOU MEAN...A *KRAKEN?*
BUT IN ALO, KRAKENS ARE DESIGNED TO BE REALLY POWERFUL FOES!

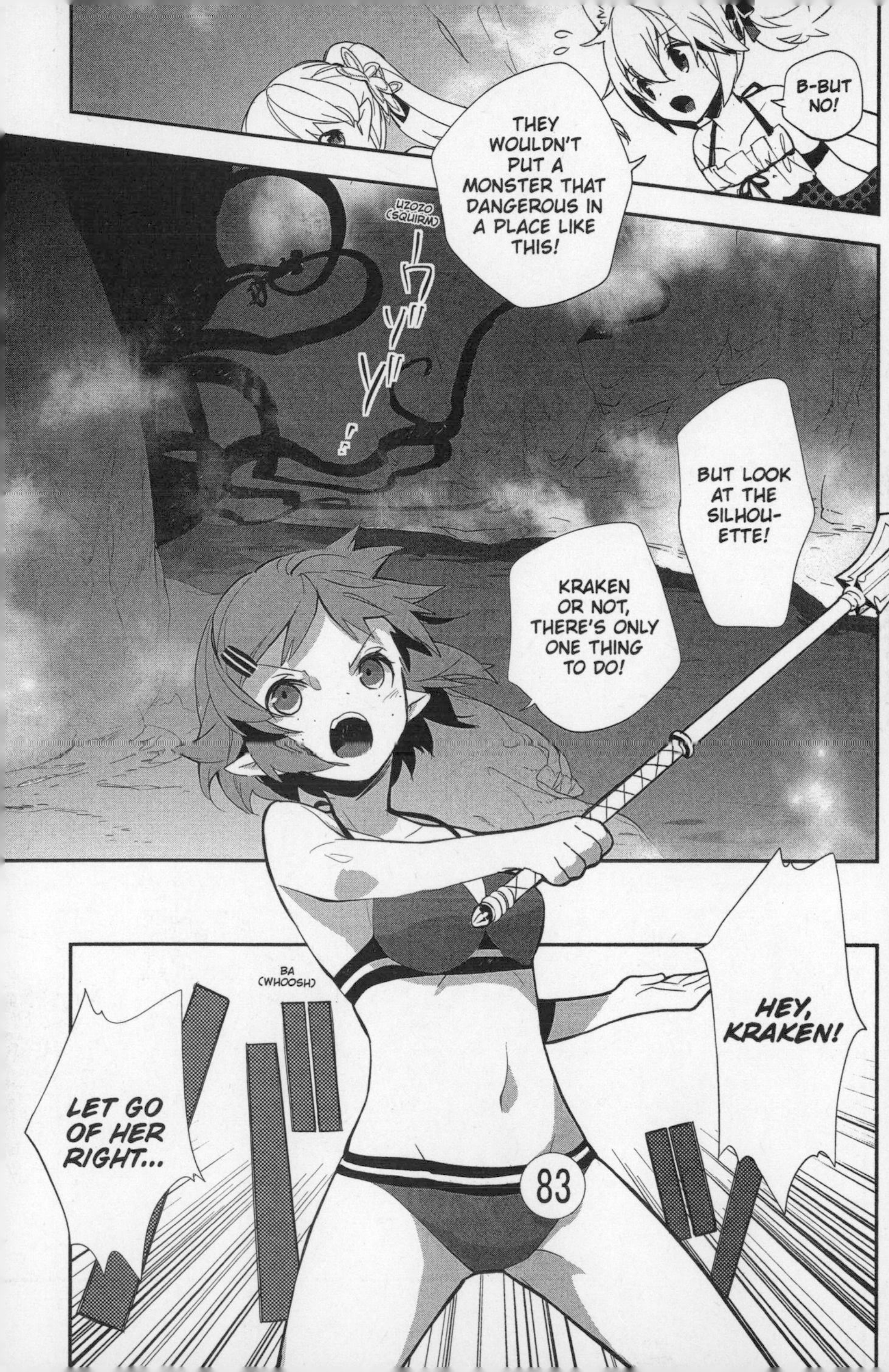
B-BUT NO!
THEY WOULDN'T PUT A MONSTER THAT DANGEROUS IN A PLACE LIKE THIS!
UZOZO (SQUIRM)
BUT LOOK AT THE SILHOU-ETTE!
KRAKEN OR NOT, THERE'S ONLY ONE THING TO DO!
BA (WHOOSH)
HEY, KRAKEN!
LET GO OF HER RIGHT...

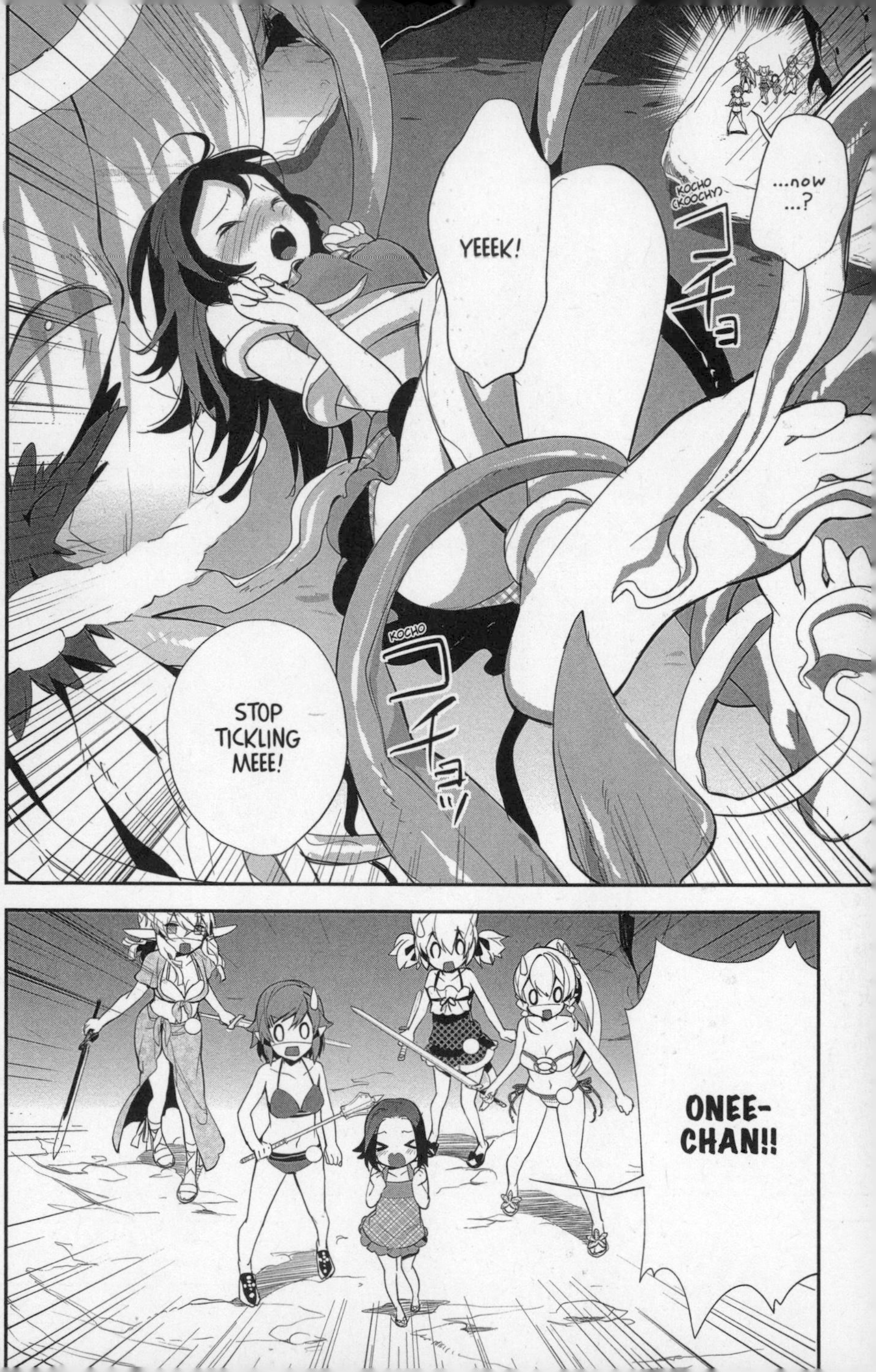
...now ...?
KOCHO (KOOCHY)
YEEEK!
KOCHO
STOP TICKLING MEEE!
ONEE-CHAN!!

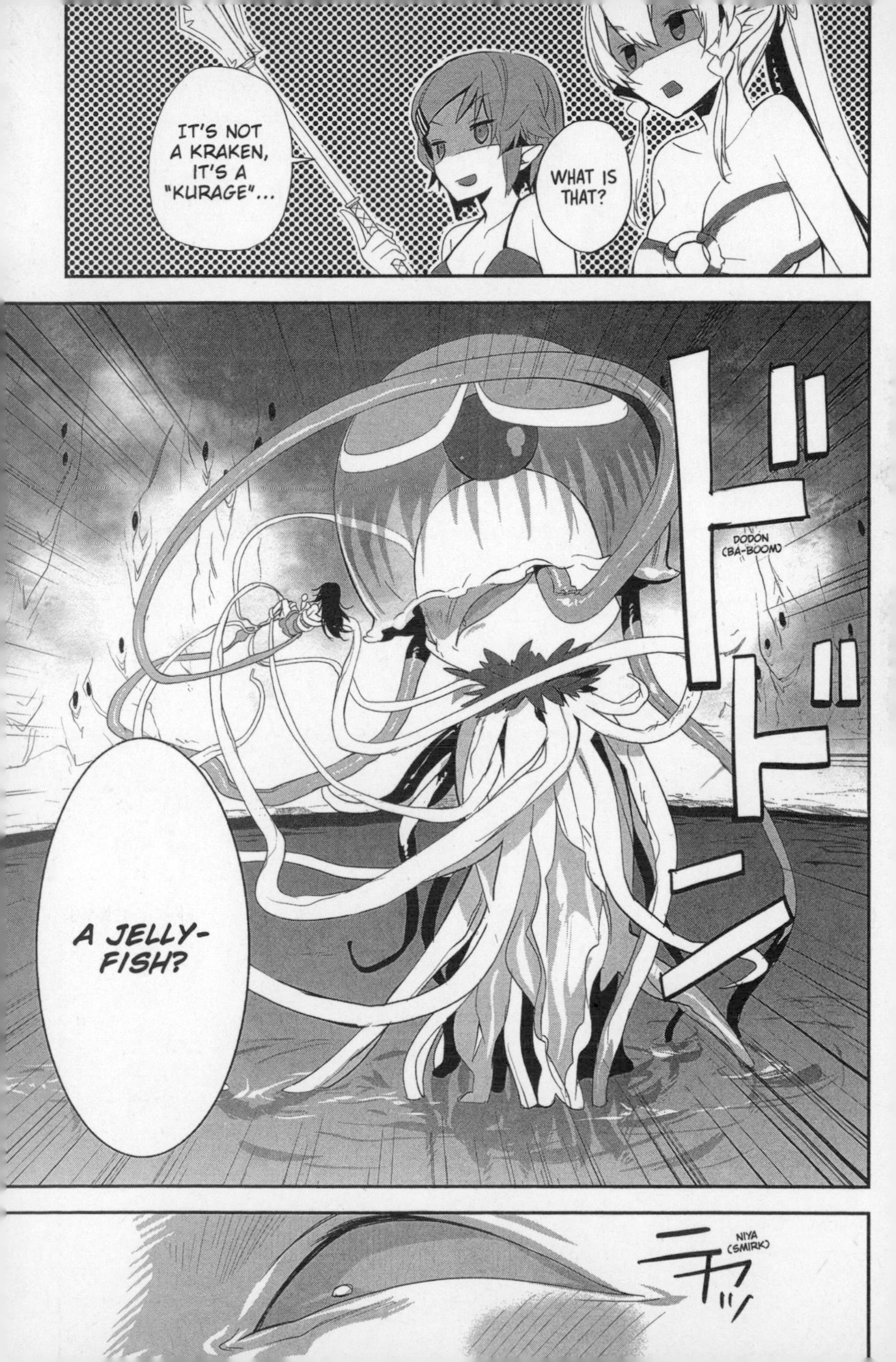
WHAT IS THAT?
IT'S NOT A KRAKEN, IT'S A "KURAGE"...
DODON (BA-BOOM)
A JELLY-FISH?
NIYA (SMIRK)

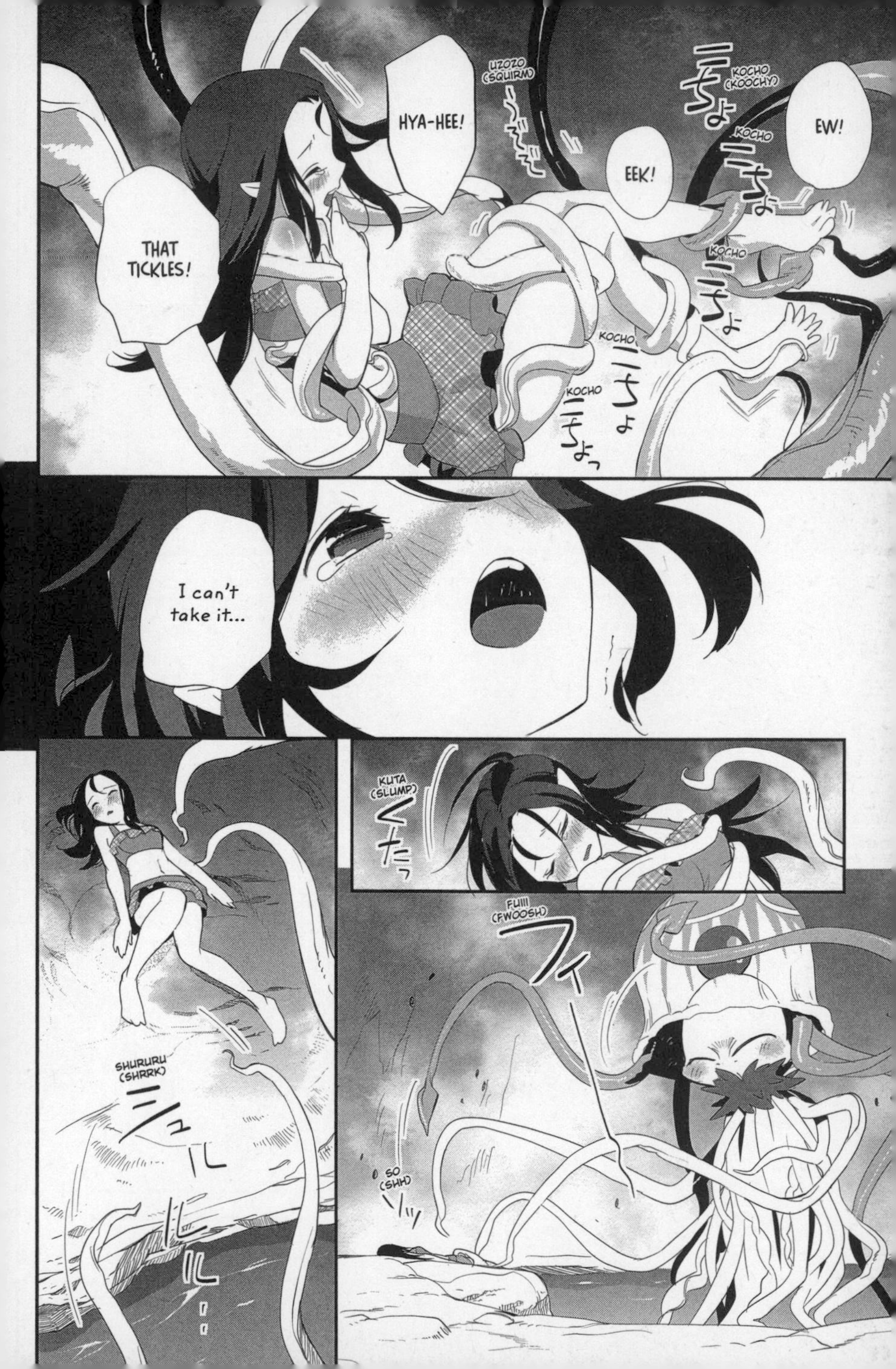
EW!
KOCHO (KOCHY)
こちょ
KOCHO
こちょ
EEK!
KOCHO
こちょ
UZOZO (SQUIRM)
うぞぞ
HYA-HEE!
THAT TICKLES!
KOCHO
こちょ
KOCHO
こちょっ
I can't take it...
KUTA (SLUMP)
くたっ
FUIII (FWOOSH)
フィー
SO (SHH)
ソッ
SHURURU (SHRRK)
シュルル...

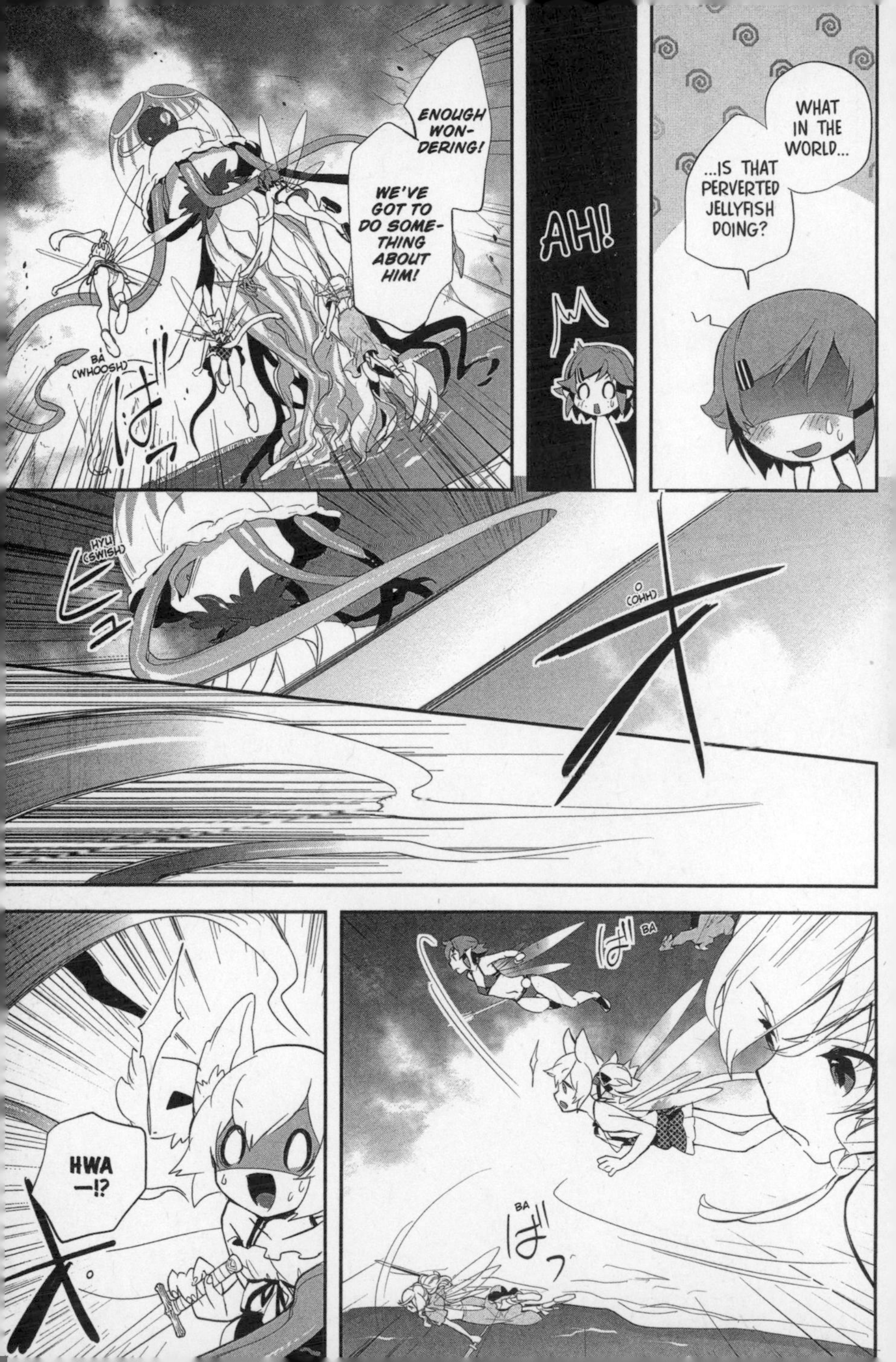
WHAT IN THE WORLD...
...IS THAT PERVERTED JELLYFISH DOING?
AH!
ENOUGH WONDERING!
WE'VE GOT TO DO SOMETHING ABOUT HIM!
BA (WHOOSH)
ばっ
HYU (SWISH)
ヒュ
O (OHH)
BA
ばっ
BA
ばっ
HWA—!?

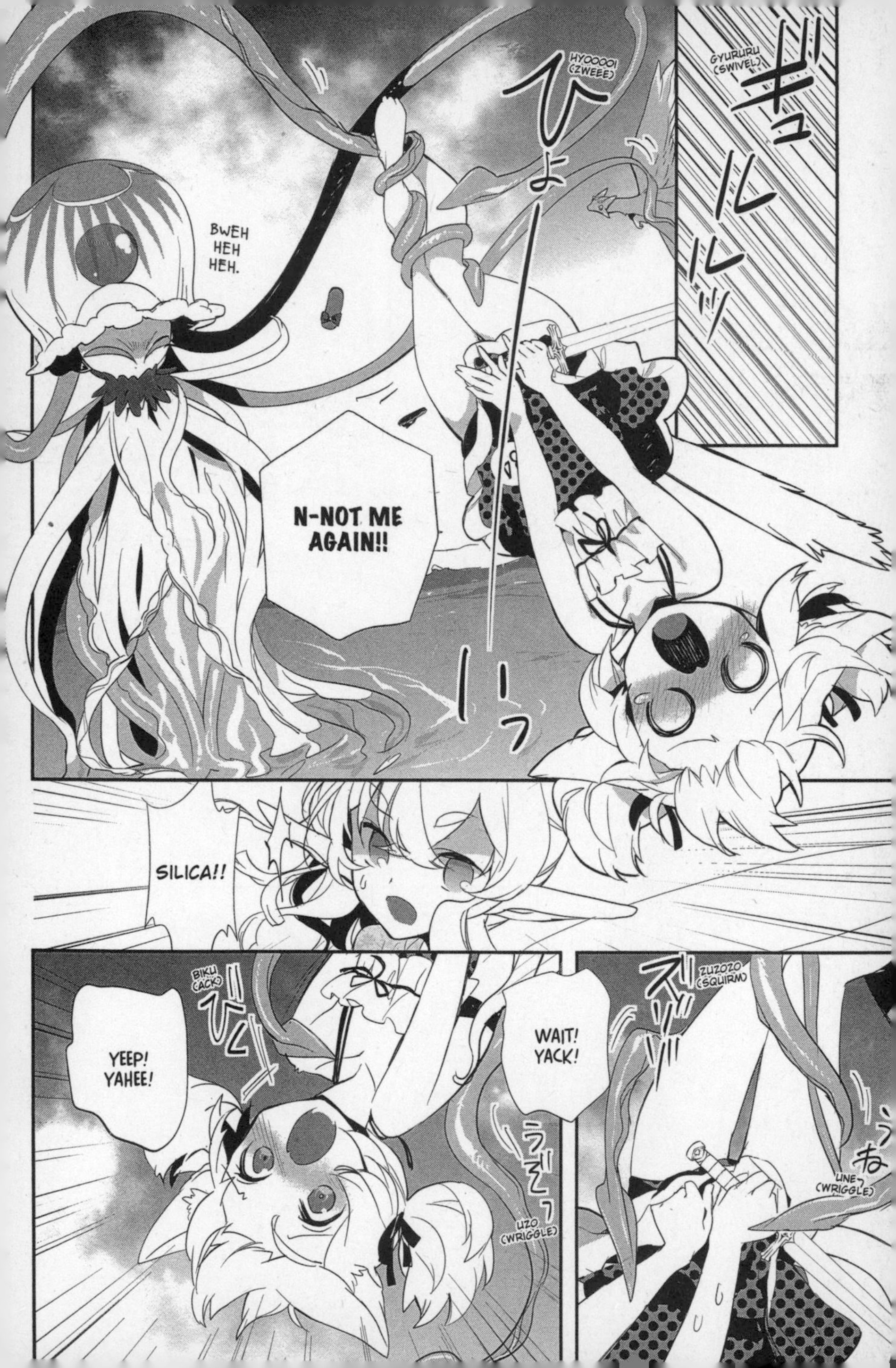

GYURURU (SWIVEL)
ギュルルルッ
HYOOOO! (ZWEEE)
ひょーーっ
BWEH HEH HEH.
N-NOT ME AGAIN!!
SILICA!!
ZUZOZO (SQUIRM)
ズゾゾ
WAIT! YACK!
BIKU (ACK)
びくっ
YEEP! YAHEE!
UNE (WRIGGLE)
うねっ
UZO (WRIGGLE)
うぞっ

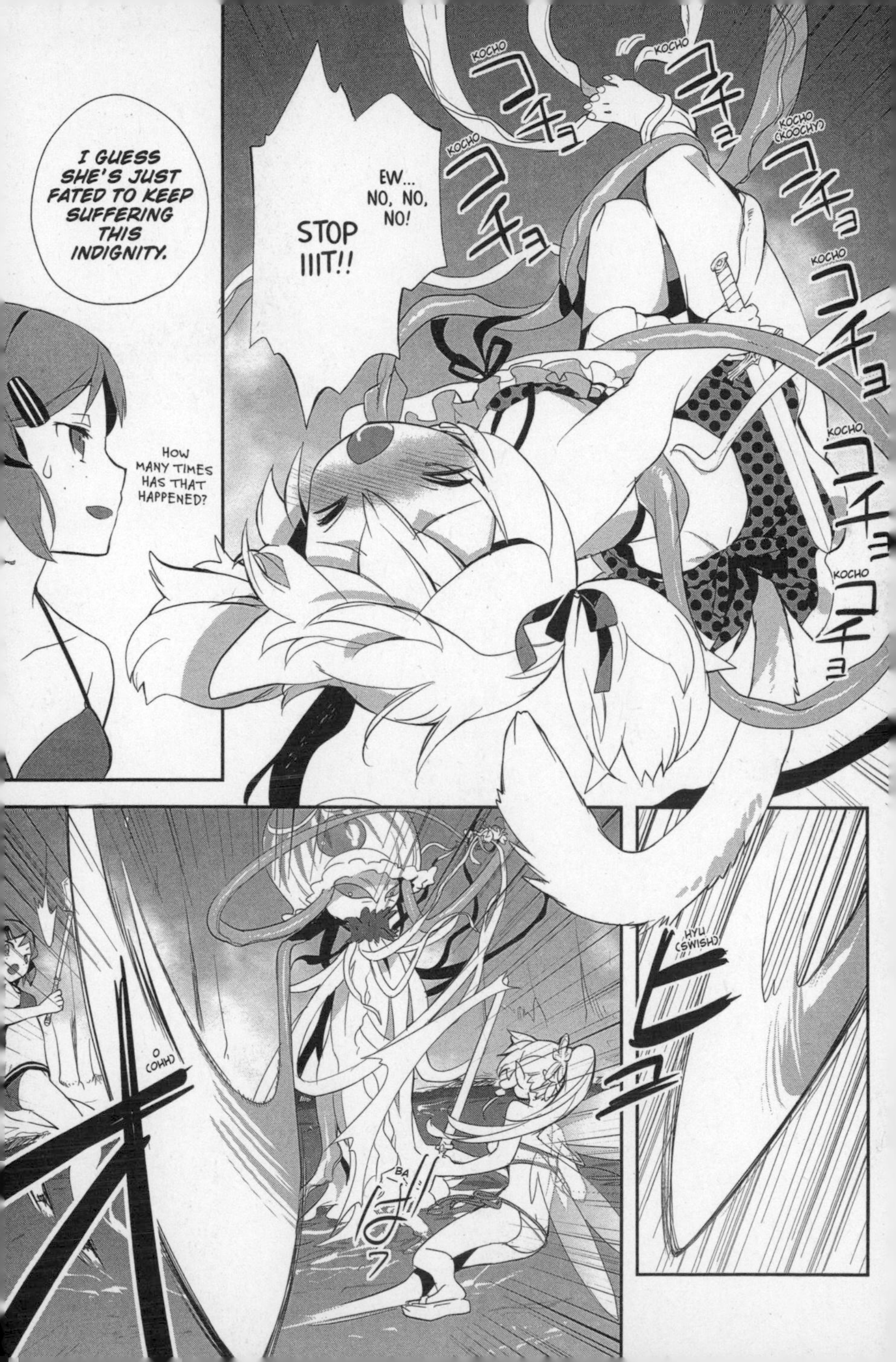

KOCHO
KOCHO (KOOCHY)
コチョコチョ
KOCHO
KOCHO
コチョコチョ
KOCHO
KOCHO
コチョコチョ
KOCHO
KOCHO
コチョコチョ
EW... NO, NO, NO!
STOP IIIT!!
I GUESS SHE'S JUST FATED TO KEEP SUFFERING THIS INDIGNITY.
HOW MANY TIMES HAS THAT HAPPENED?
HYU (SWISH)
ヒュ
BA
ばっ
O (OHH)

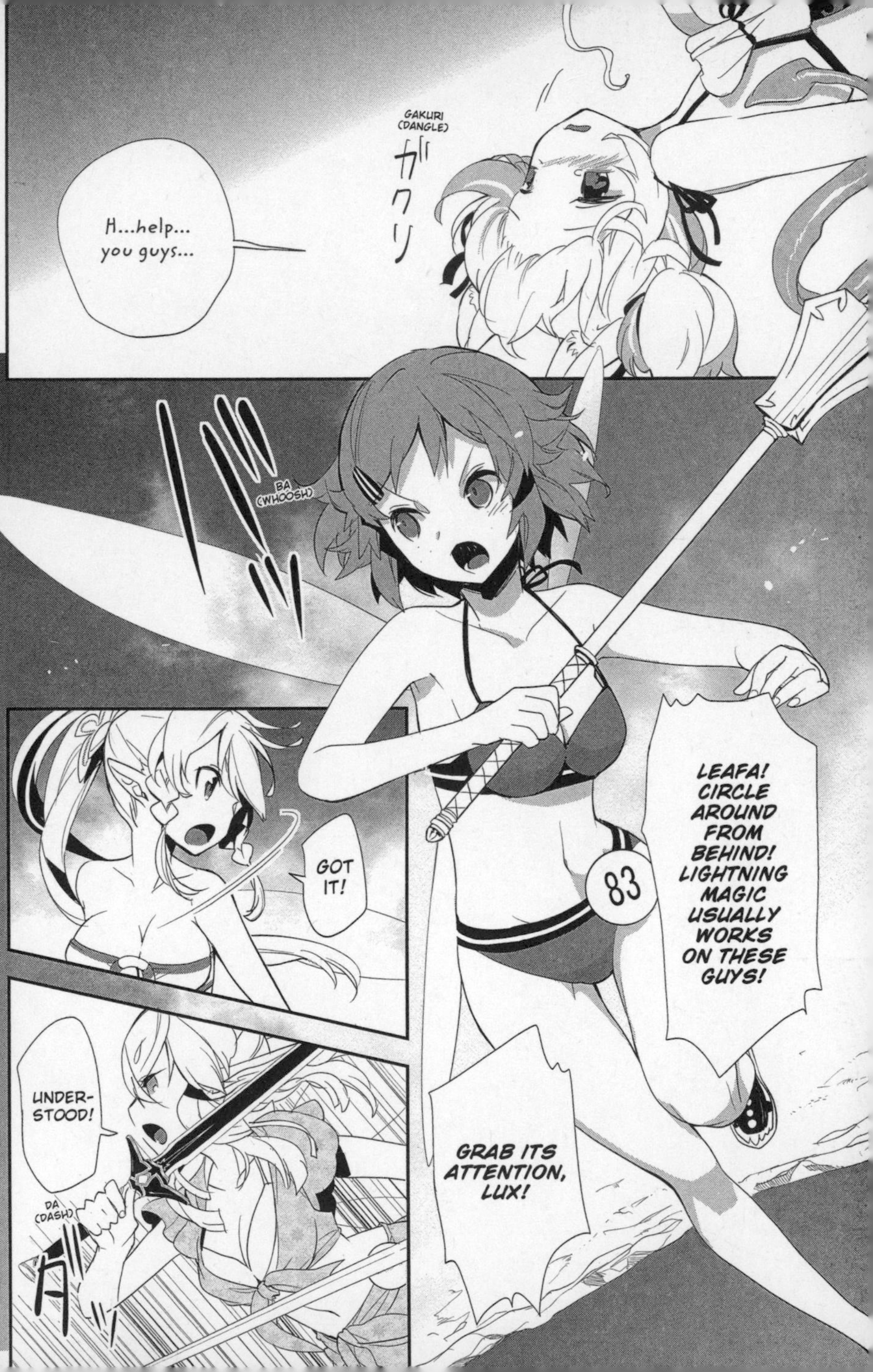
GAKURI (DANGLE)
ガクリ
H...help... you guys...
BA (WHOOSH)
LEAFA! CIRCLE AROUND FROM BEHIND! LIGHTNING MAGIC USUALLY WORKS ON THESE GUYS!
GRAB ITS ATTENTION, LUX!
GOT IT!
83
UNDER-STOOD!
DA (DASH)

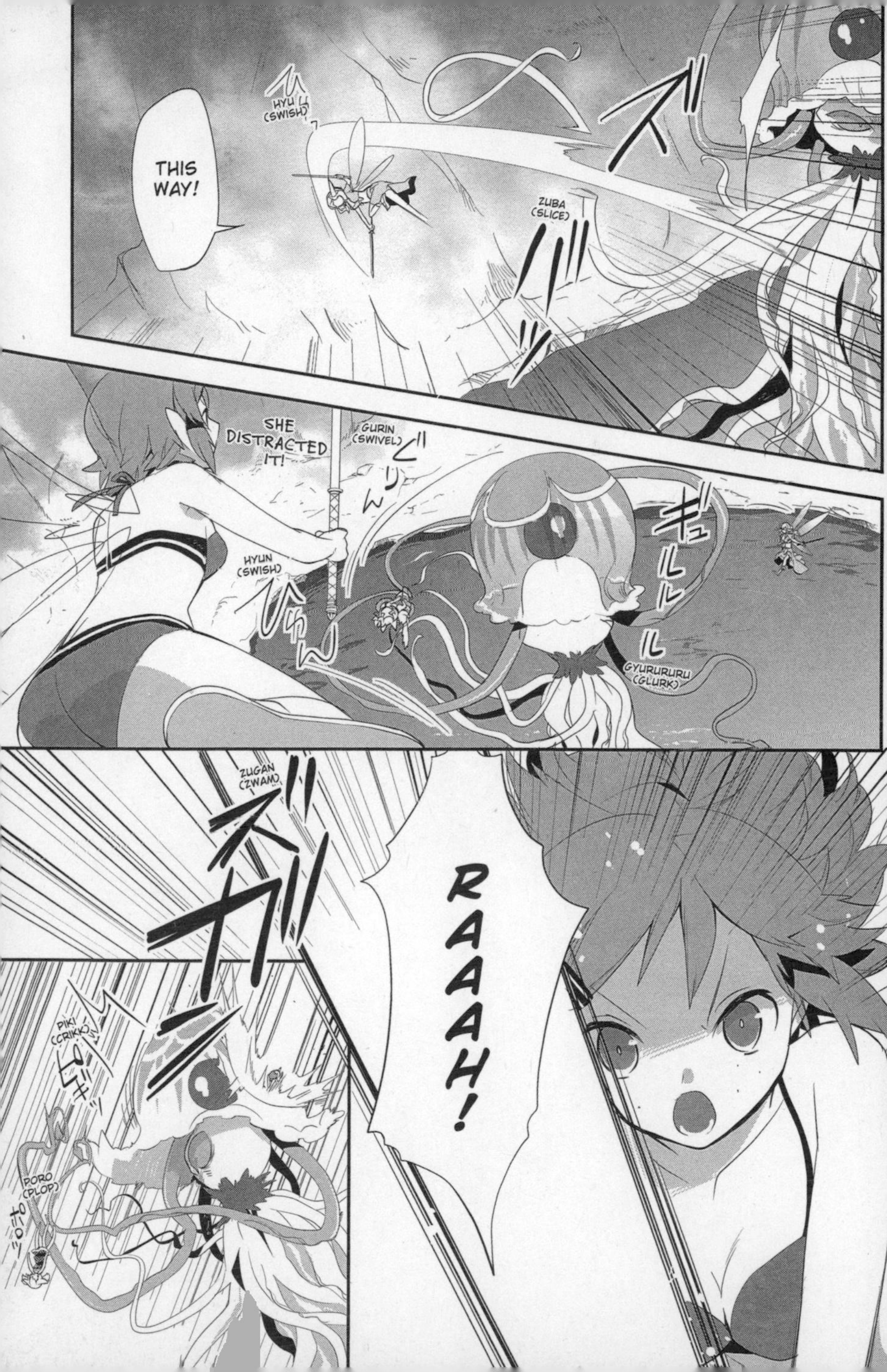
ZUBA (SLICE)
HYU (SWISH)
THIS WAY!
GURIN (SWIVEL)
SHE DISTRACTED IT!
GYURURURU (GLURK)
HYUN (SWISH)
RAAAAH!
ZUGAN (ZWAM)
PIKI (CRIKK)
PORO (PLOP)

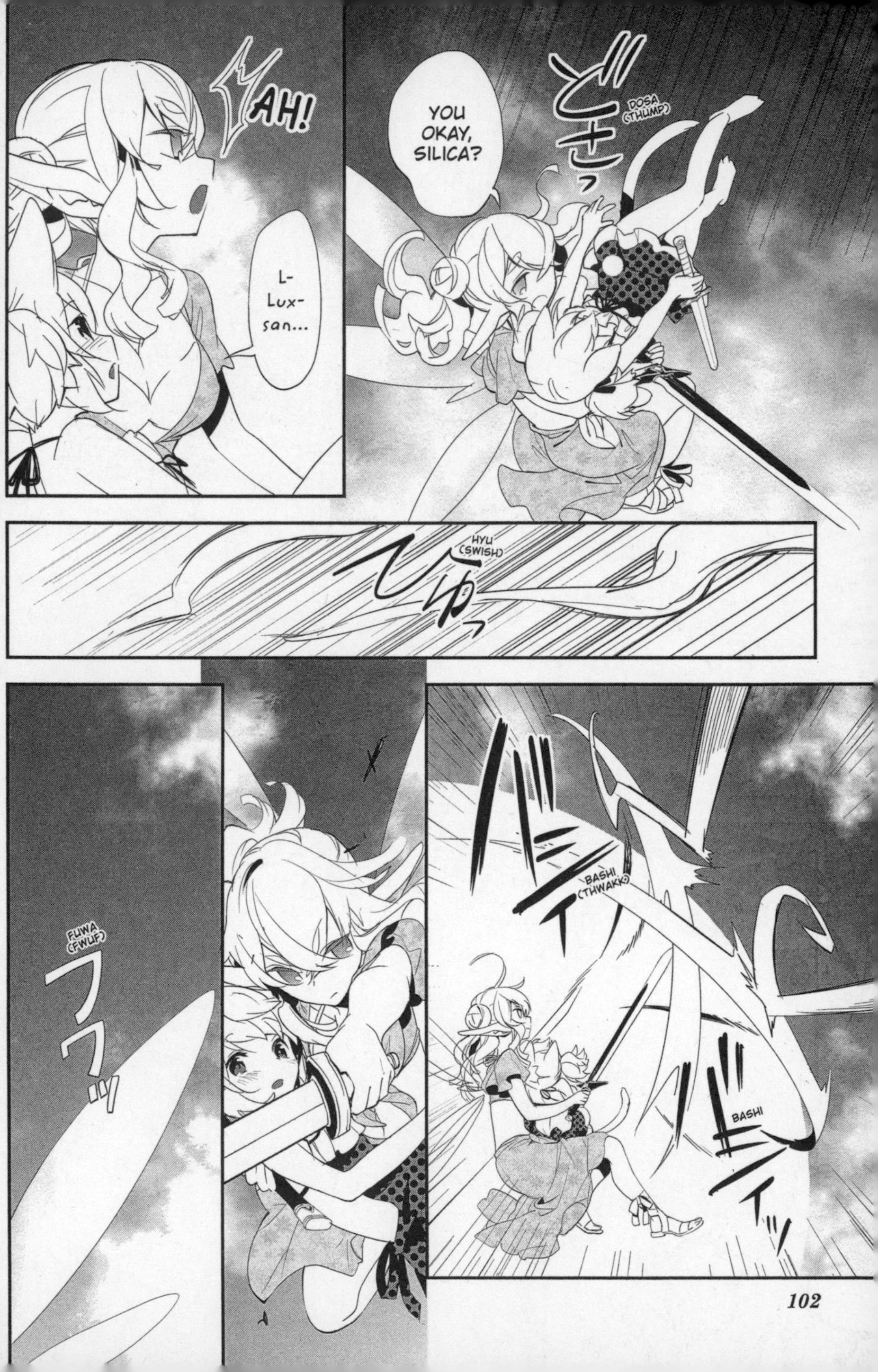

DOSA (THUMP)
YOU OKAY, SILICA?
AH!
L-Lux-san...
HYU (SWISH)
BASHI (THWAKK)
BASHI
FUWA (FWUF)

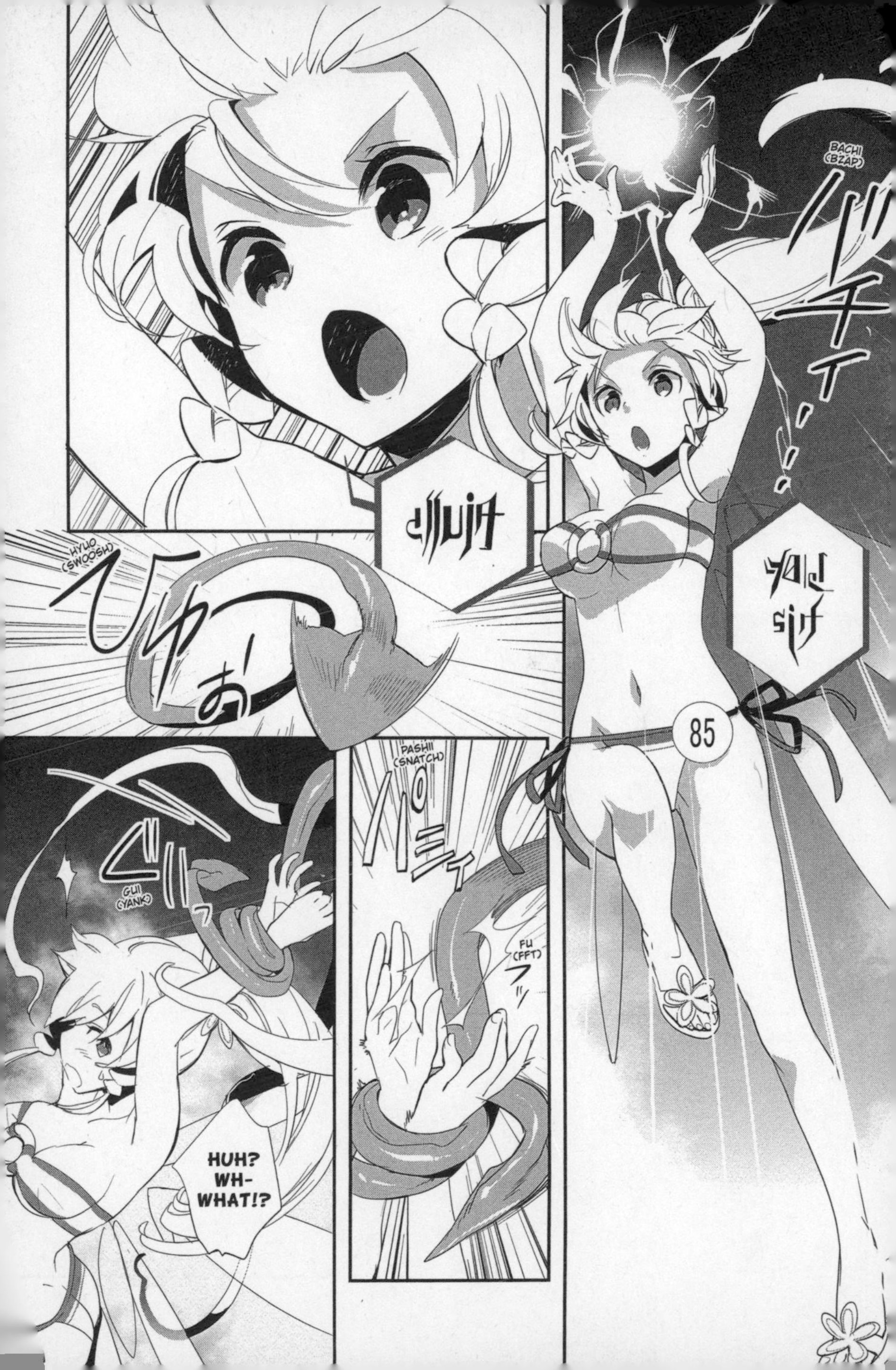
BACHI (BZAP)
HYUO (SWOOSH)
PASHII (SNATCH)
FU (FFT)
GUI (YANK)
HUH? WH-WHAT!?

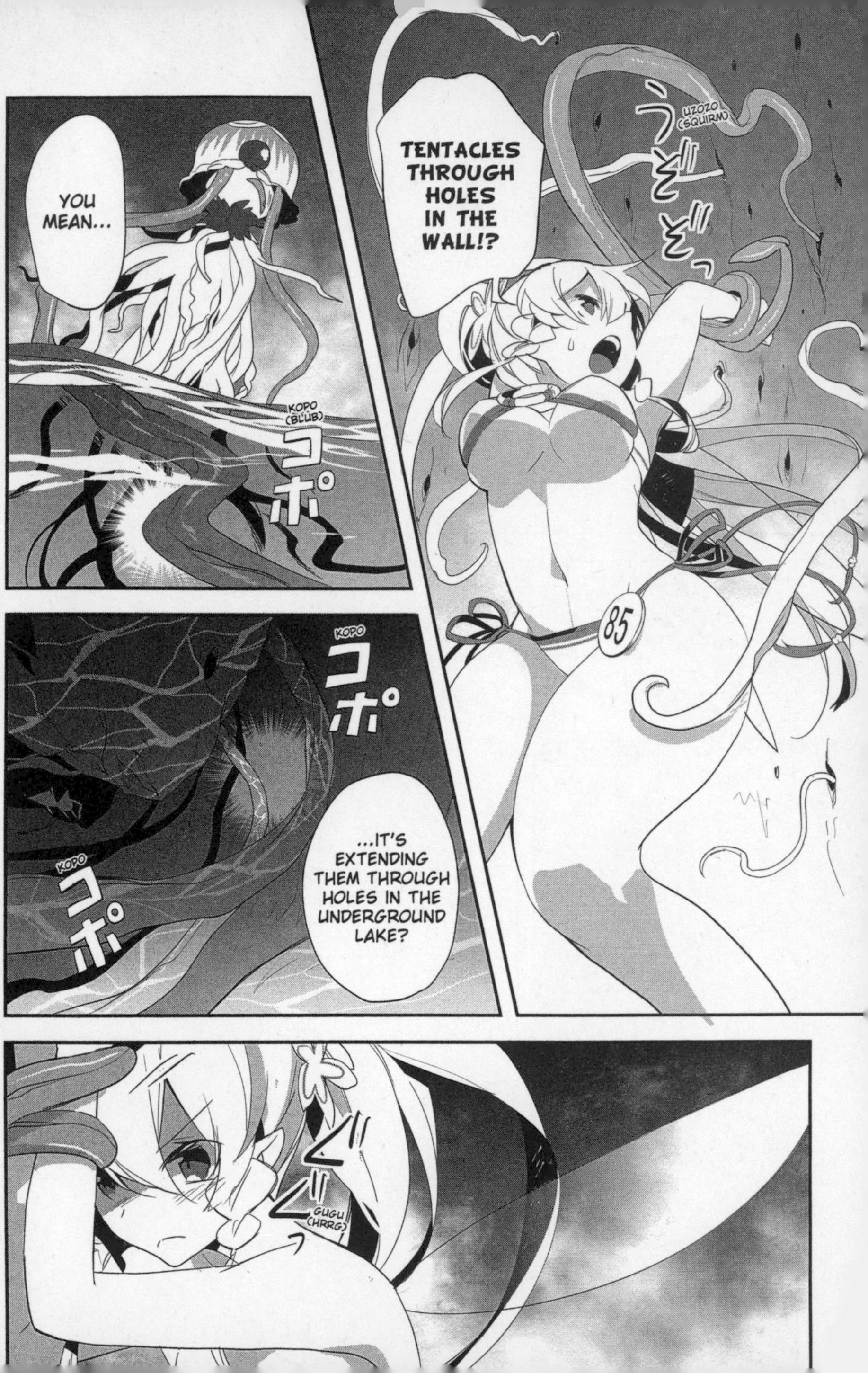
TENTACLES THROUGH HOLES IN THE WALL!?
UZOZO (SQUIRM)
うぞぞっ
YOU MEAN...
KOPO (BLUB)
コポ
KOPO
コポ
KOPO
コポ
...IT'S EXTENDING THEM THROUGH HOLES IN THE UNDERGROUND LAKE?
GUGU (HRRG)

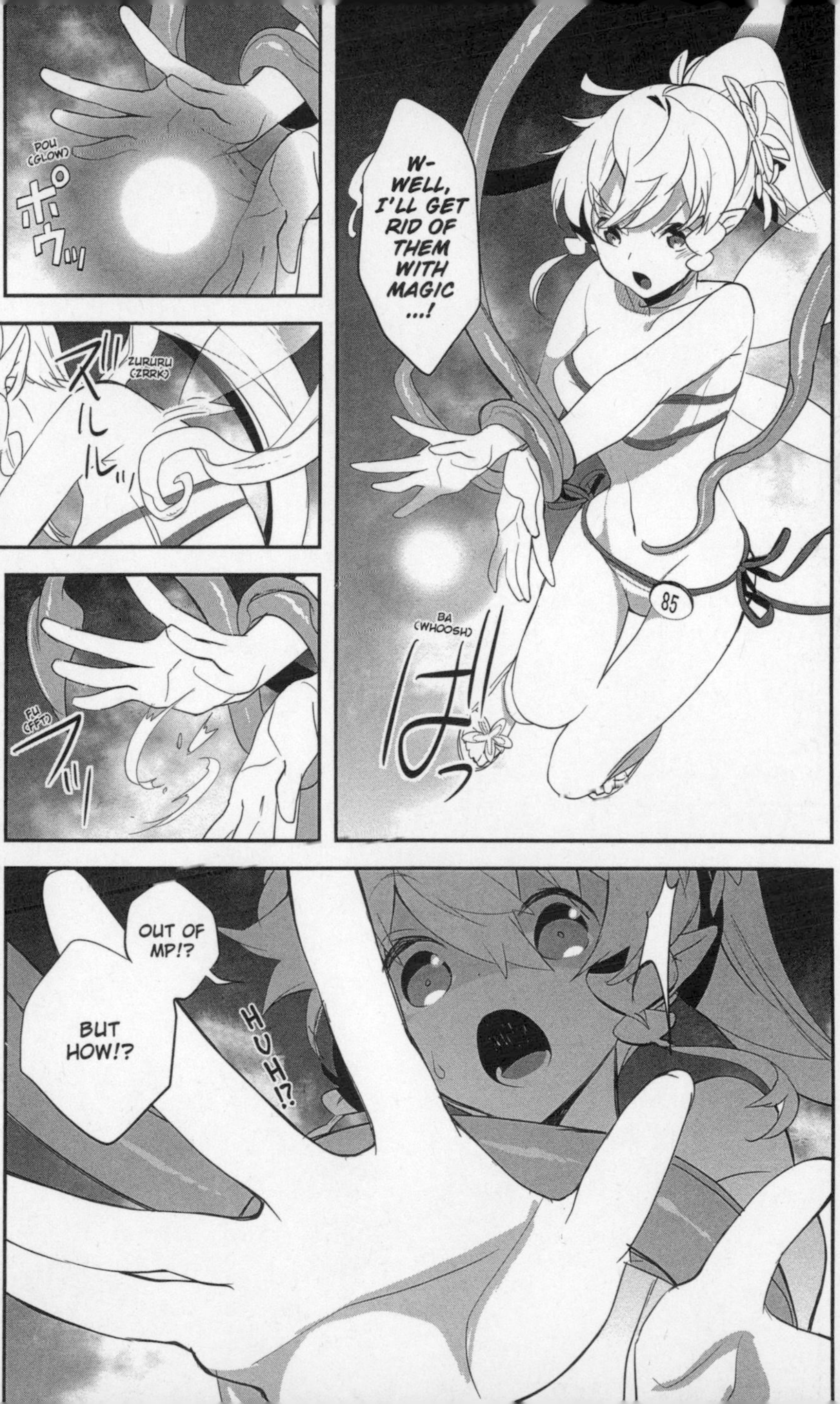
W-WELL, I'LL GET RID OF THEM WITH MAGIC...!
BA (WHOOSH)
ばっ
POU (GLOW)
ポウッ
ZURURU (ZRRK)
ズルルッ
FU (FFT)
フッ
HUH!?
OUT OF MP!?
BUT HOW!?

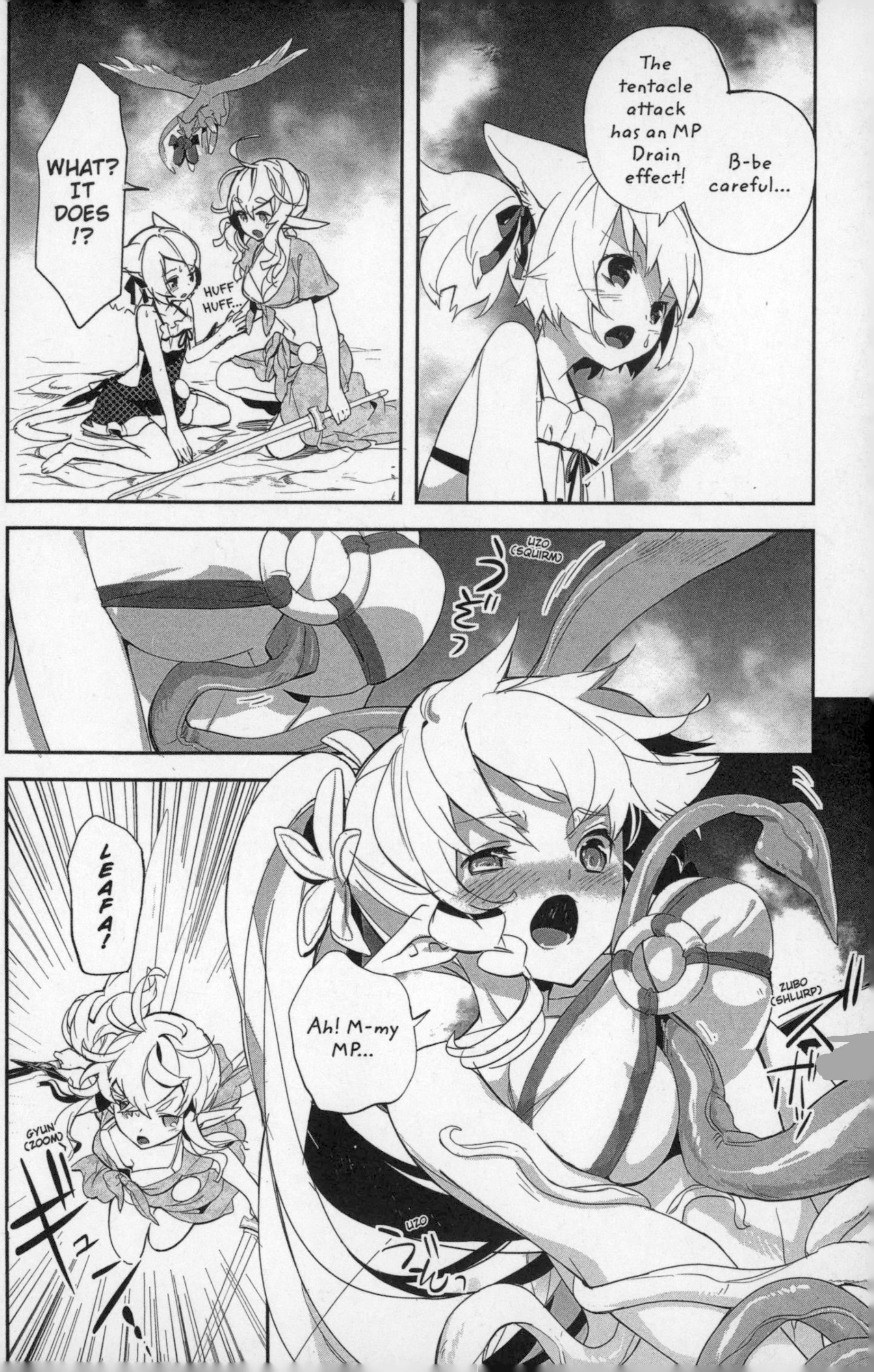

The tentacle attack has an MP Drain effect!
B-be careful...
WHAT? IT DOES!?
HUFF HUFF...
UZO (SQUIRM)
Ah! M-my MP...
ZUBO (SHLURP)
UZO
LEAFA!
GYUN (ZOOM)

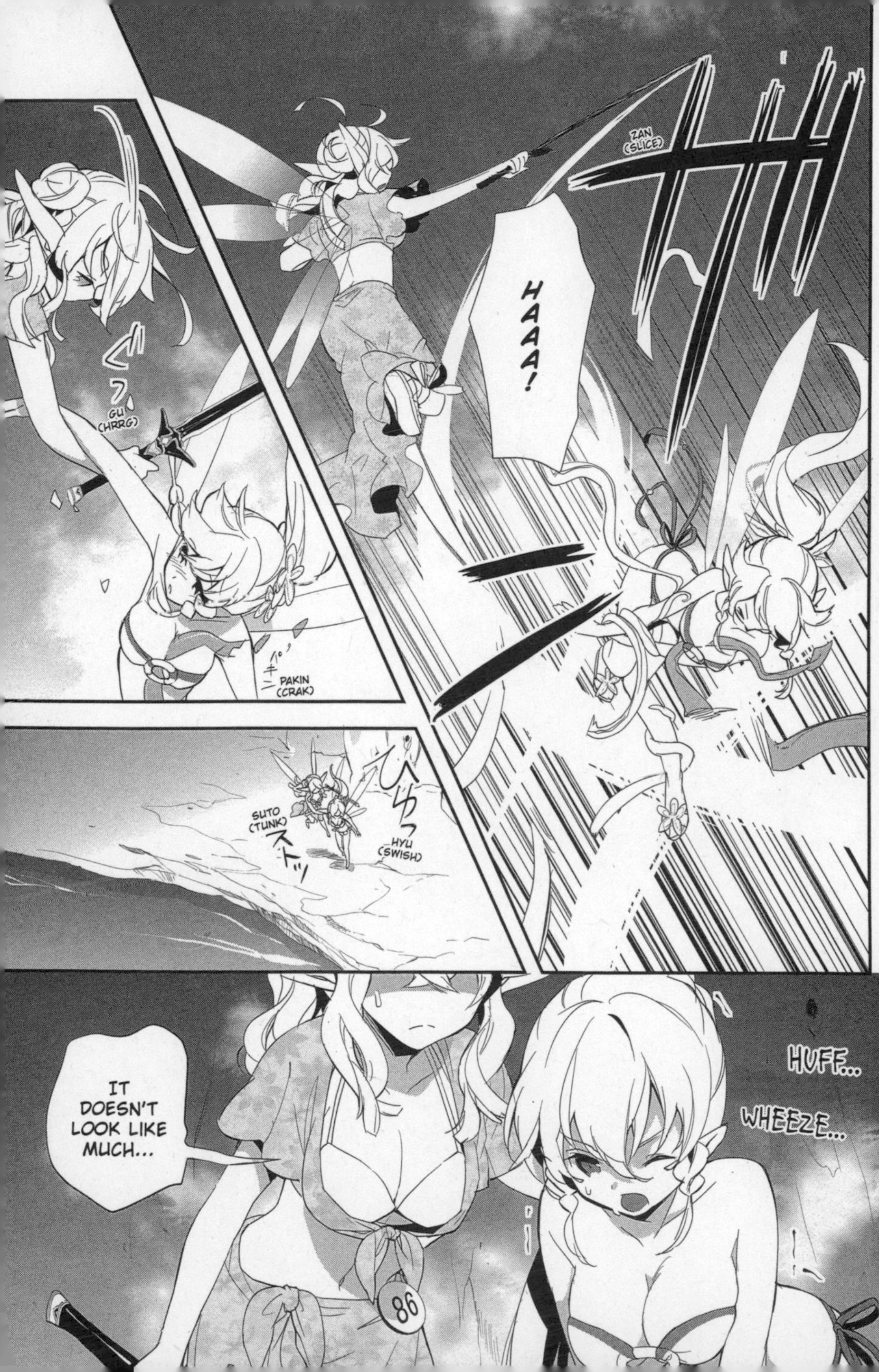
ZAN (SLICE)
HAAAA!
GU (HRRG)
PAKIN (CRAK)
HYU (SWISH)
SUTO (TUNK)
HUFF...
WHEEZE...
IT DOESN'T LOOK LIKE MUCH...

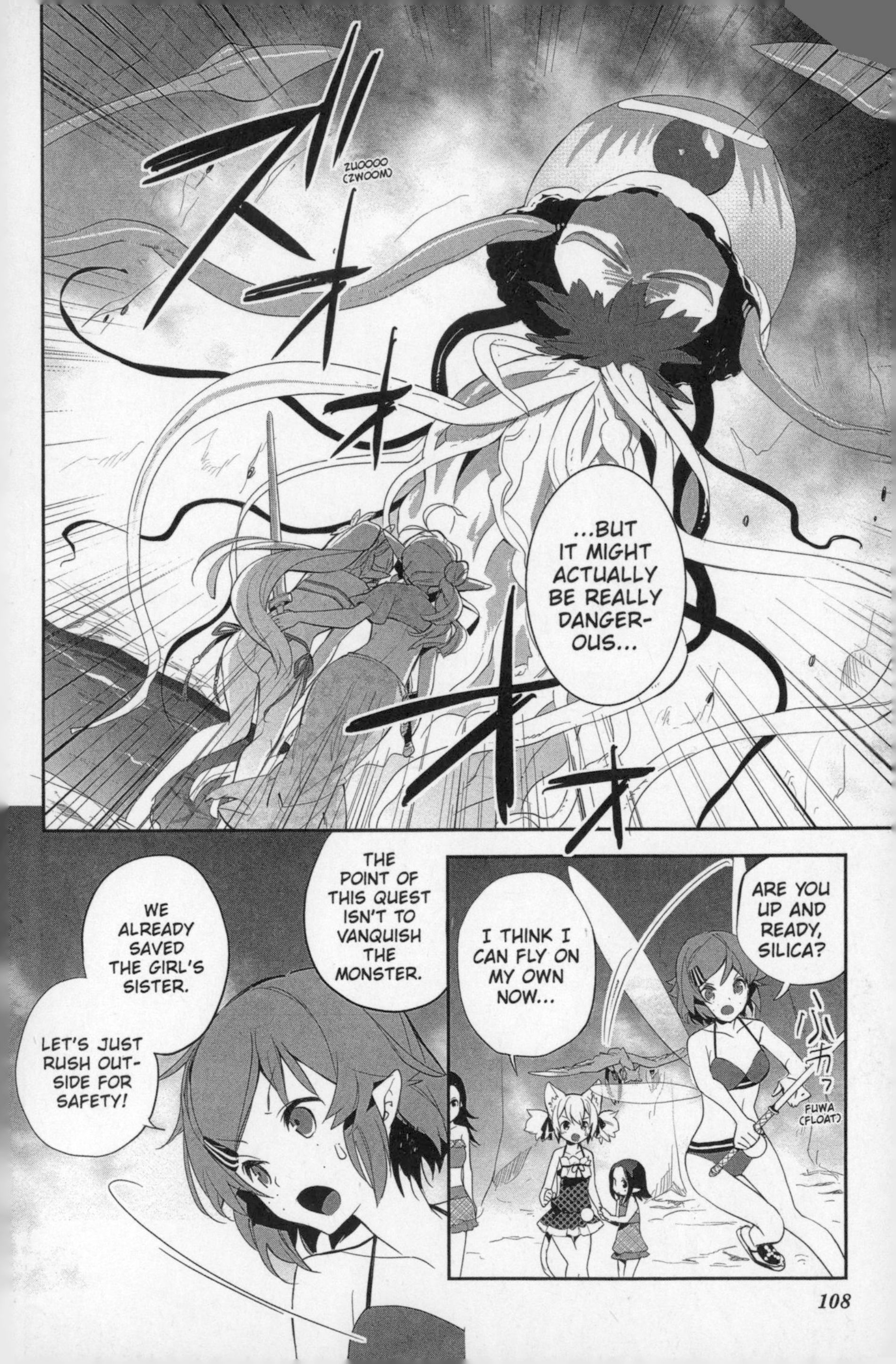
ZUOOOO (ZWOOOM)
...BUT IT MIGHT ACTUALLY BE REALLY DANGER-OUS...
ARE YOU UP AND READY, SILICA?
FUWA (FLOAT)
I THINK I CAN FLY ON MY OWN NOW...
THE POINT OF THIS QUEST ISN'T TO VANQUISH THE MONSTER.
WE ALREADY SAVED THE GIRL'S SISTER.
LET'S JUST RUSH OUT-SIDE FOR SAFETY!

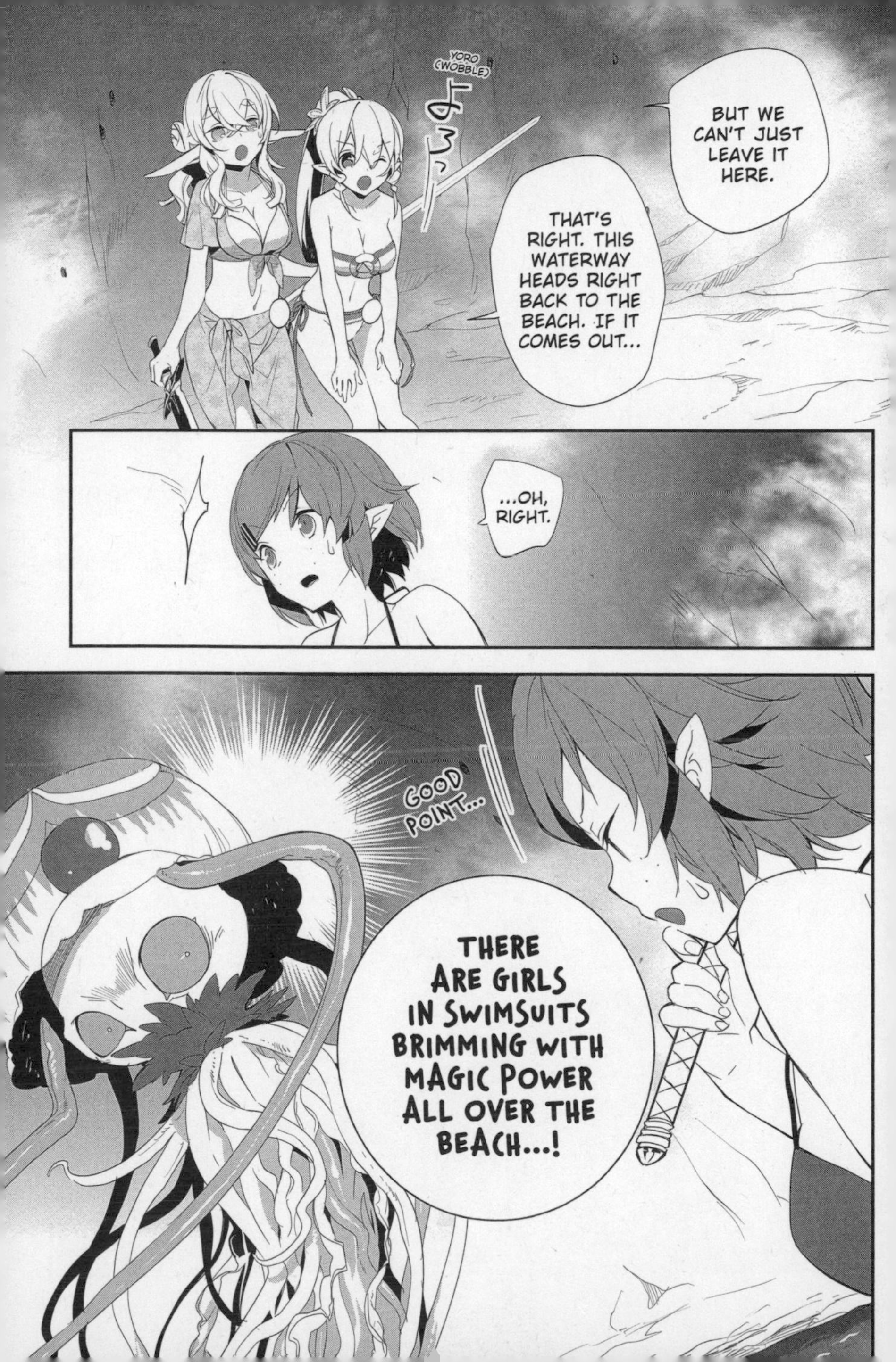
BUT WE CAN'T JUST LEAVE IT HERE.
YORO (WOBBLE)
よろっ
THAT'S RIGHT. THIS WATERWAY HEADS RIGHT BACK TO THE BEACH. IF IT COMES OUT...
...OH, RIGHT.
GOOD POINT...
THERE ARE GIRLS IN SWIMSUITS BRIMMING WITH MAGIC POWER ALL OVER THE BEACH...!

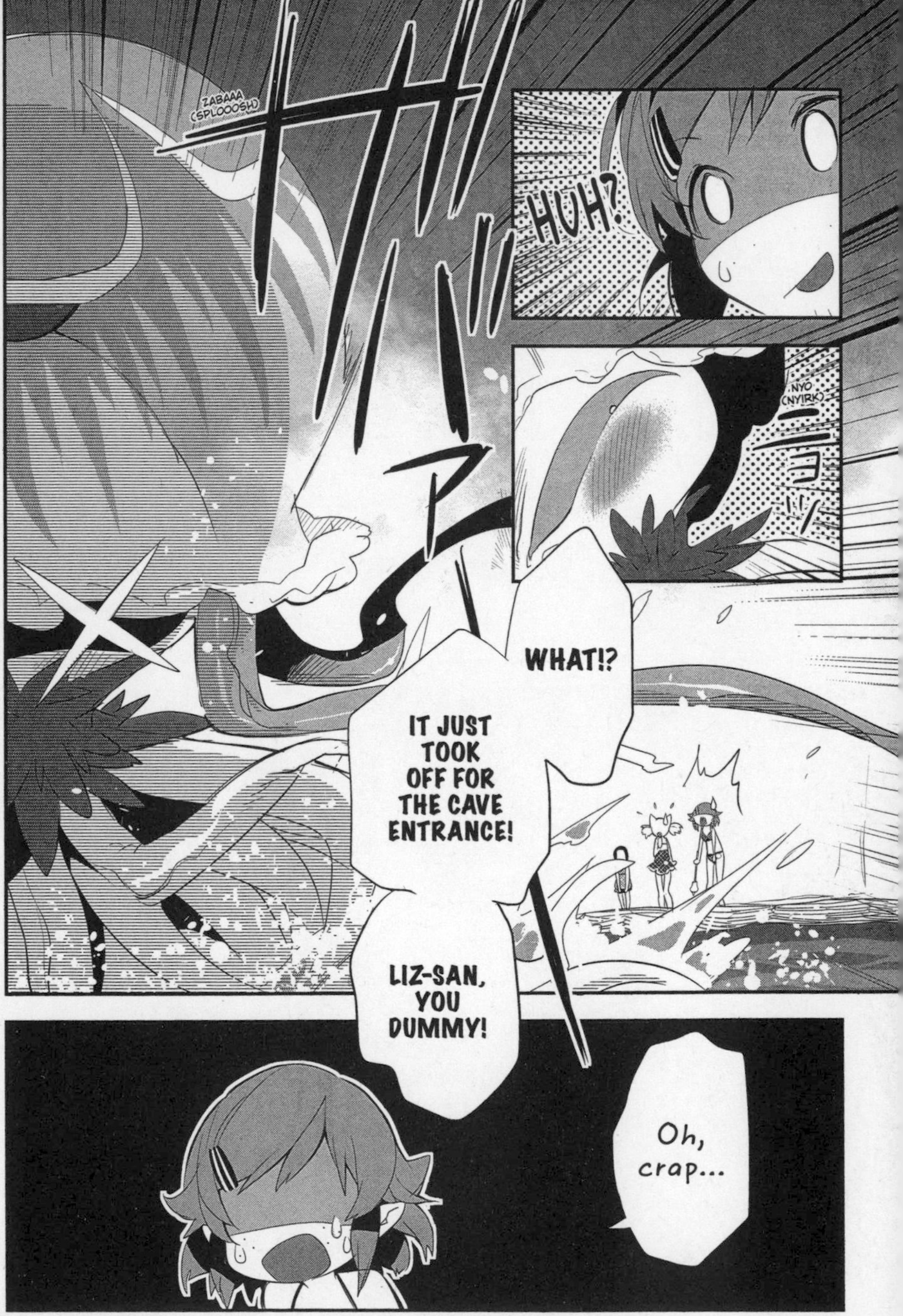

HUH?
ZABAAA (SPLOOOSH)
NYO (NYIRK)
WHAT!?
IT JUST TOOK OFF FOR THE CAVE ENTRANCE!
LIZ-SAN, YOU DUMMY!
Oh, crap...

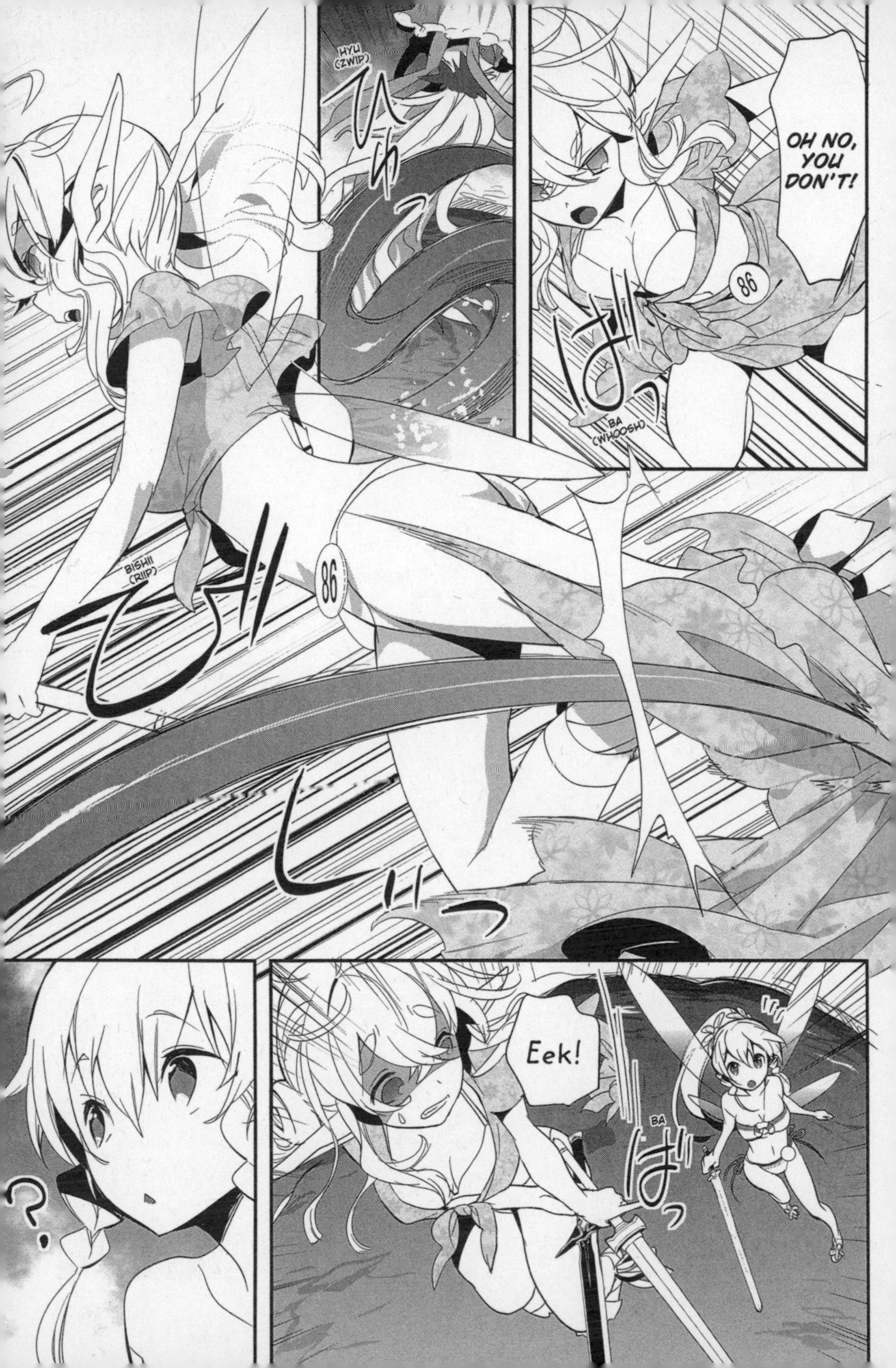
OH NO, YOU DON'T!
ばっ
BA (WHOOSH)
ひゅっ
HYU (ZWIP)
98
98
びしぃっ
BISHII (RIIP)
Eek!
ばっ
BA
?

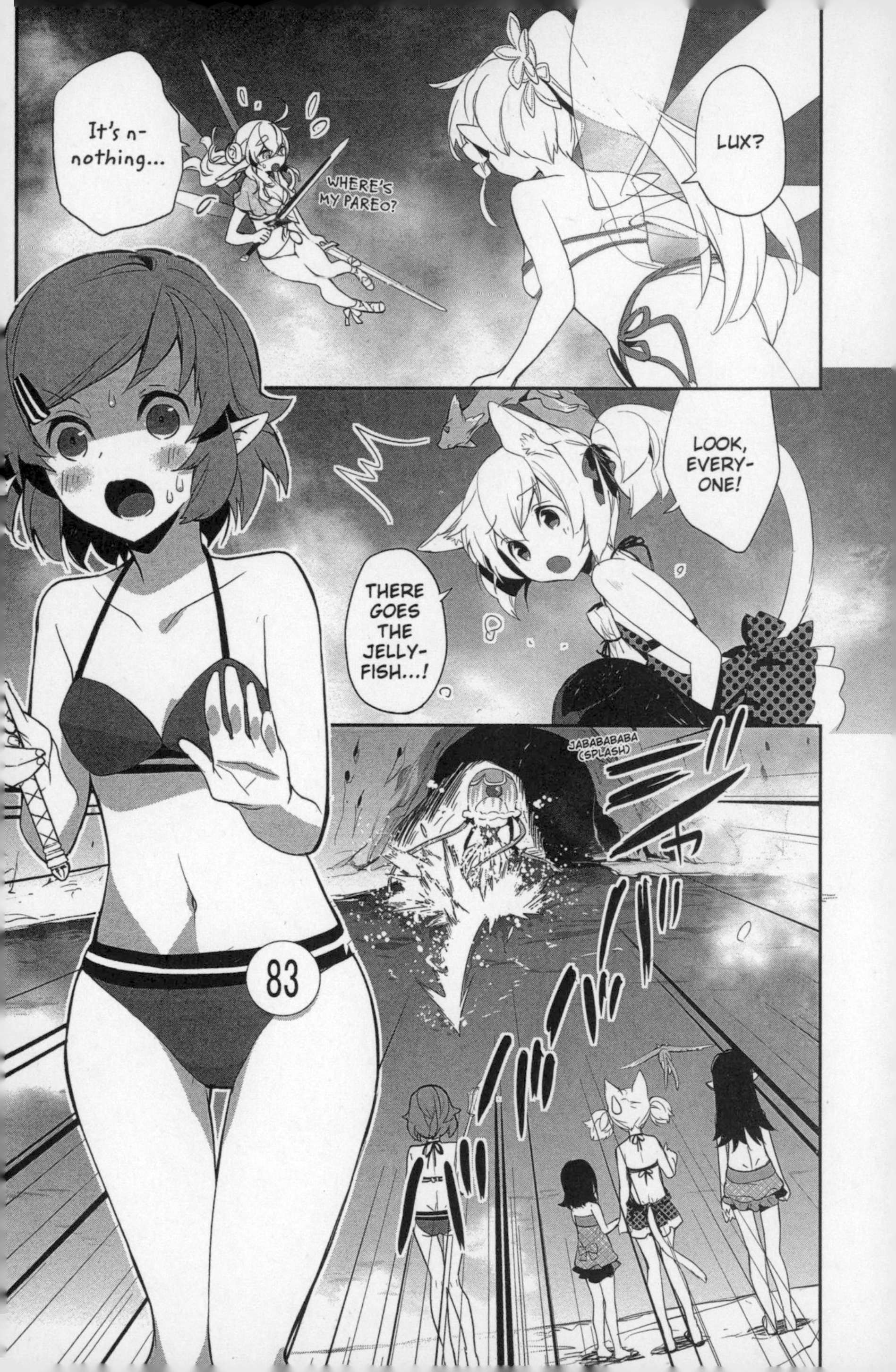
LUX?
It's n-
nothing...
WHERE'S
MY PAREO?
LOOK,
EVERY-
ONE!
THERE
GOES
THE
JELLY-
FISH...!
JABABABABA
(SPLASH)
83

SWORD ART ONLINE
GIRLS' OPS

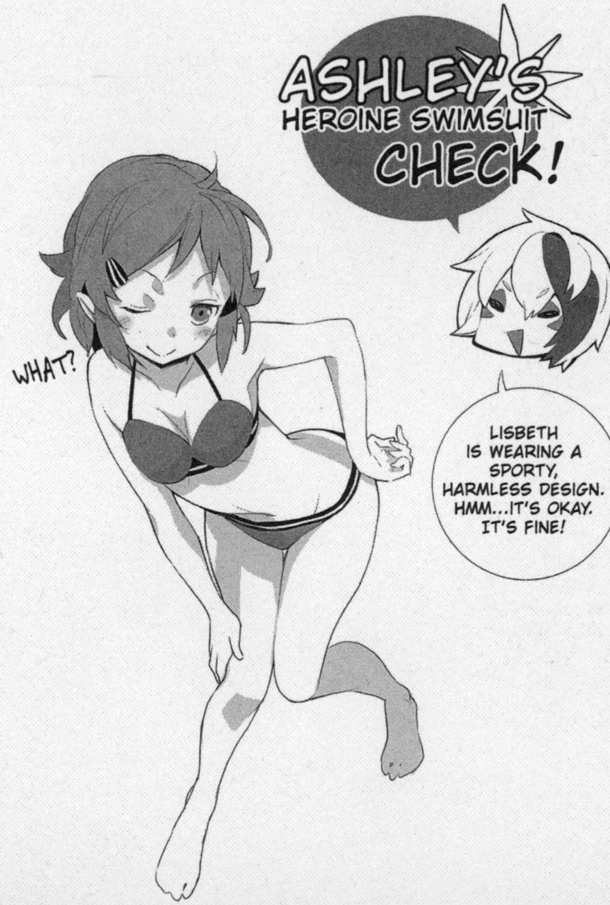
ASHLEY'S
HEROINE SWIMSUIT
CHECK!
LISBETH IS WEARING A SPORTY, HARMLESS DESIGN. HMM...IT'S OKAY. IT'S FINE!
WHAT?

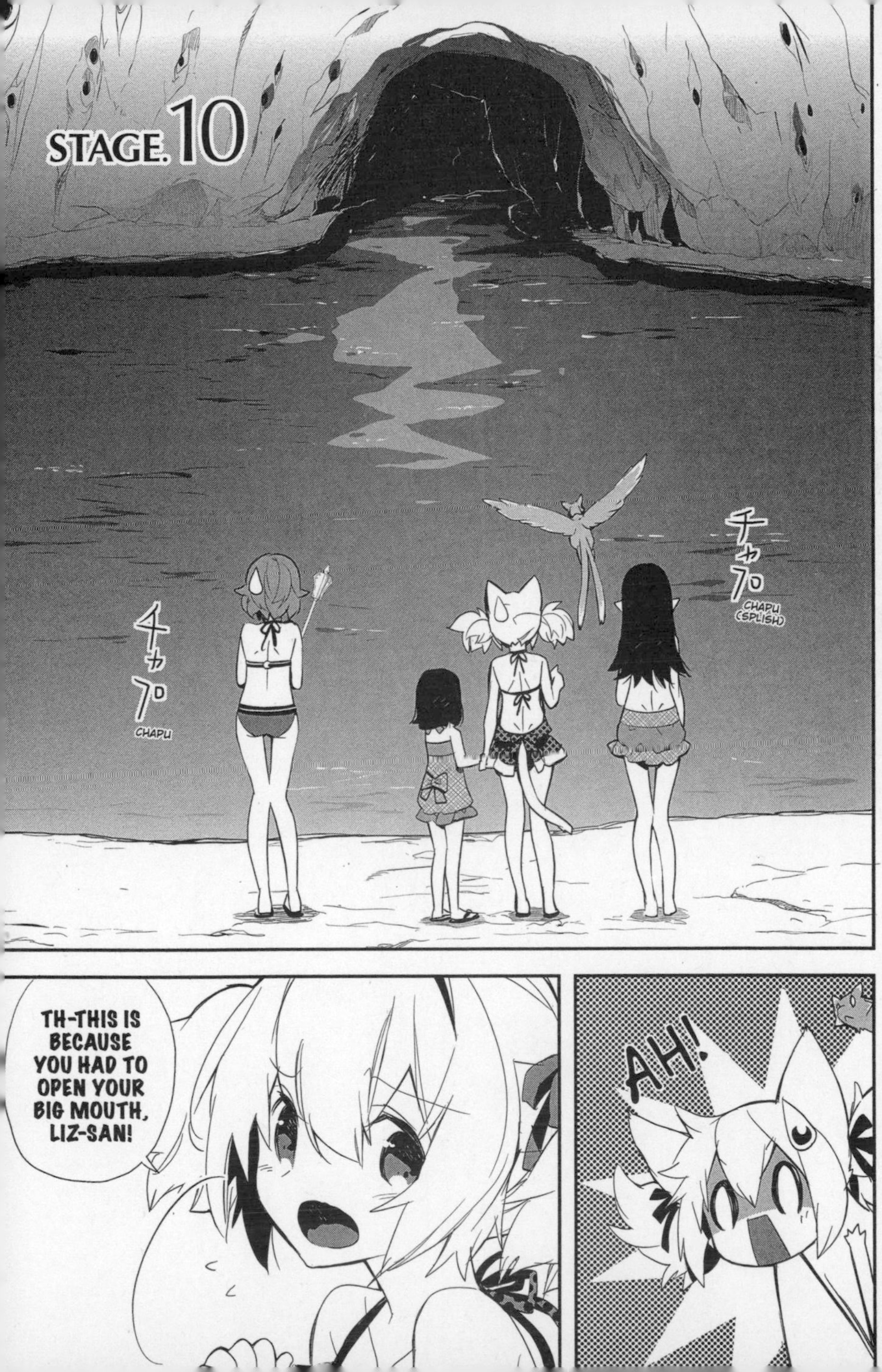
STAGE. 10
チャプ
CHAPU (SPLISH)
チャプ
CHAPU
AH!
TH-THIS IS BECAUSE YOU HAD TO OPEN YOUR BIG MOUTH, LIZ-SAN!

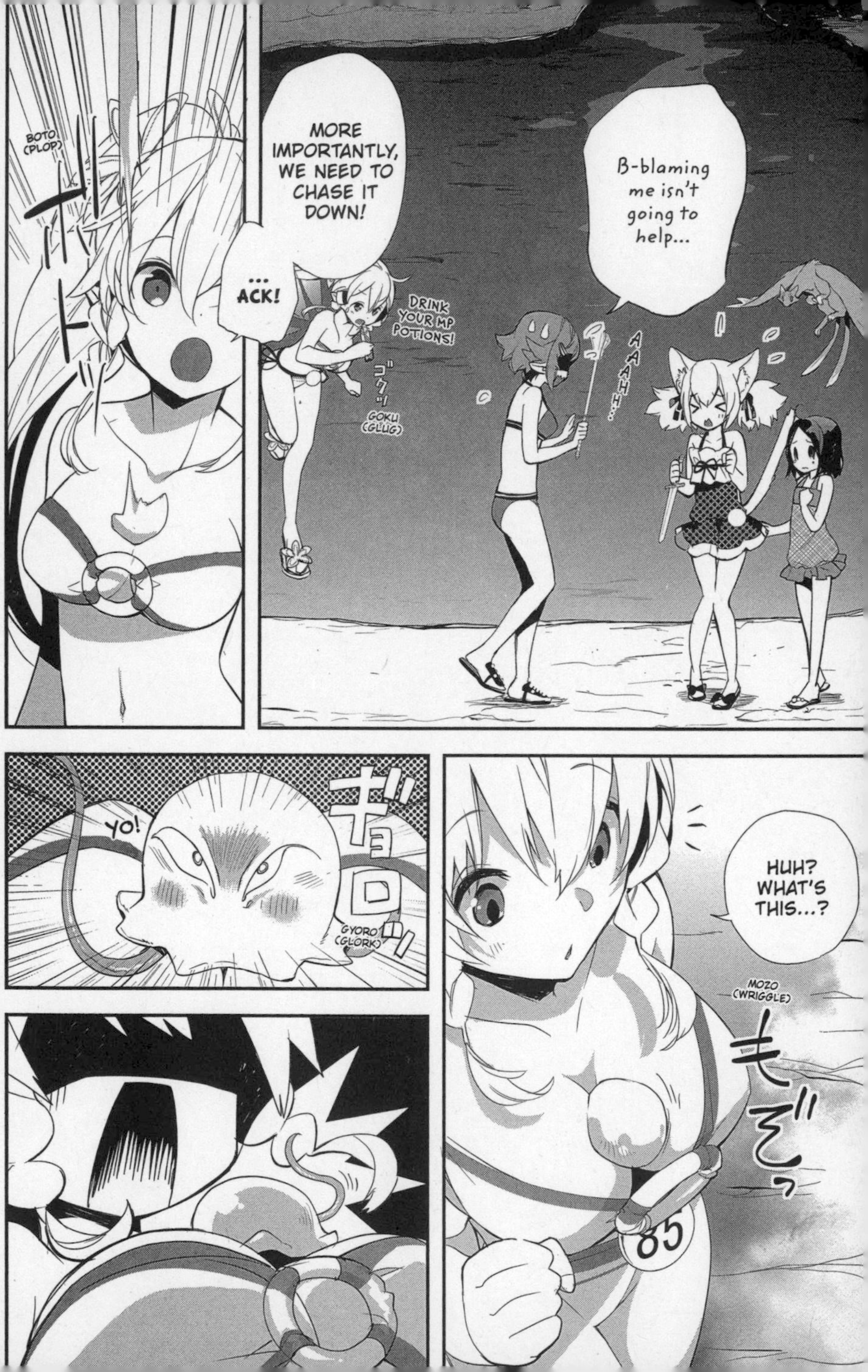
B-blaming me isn't going to help...
AAAAHH...!
MORE IMPORTANTLY, WE NEED TO CHASE IT DOWN!
DRINK YOUR MP POTIONS!
GOKU (GLUG)
...ACK!
BOTO (PLOP)
HUH? WHAT'S THIS...?
MOZO (WRIGGLE)
GYORO (GLORK)
YO!
85

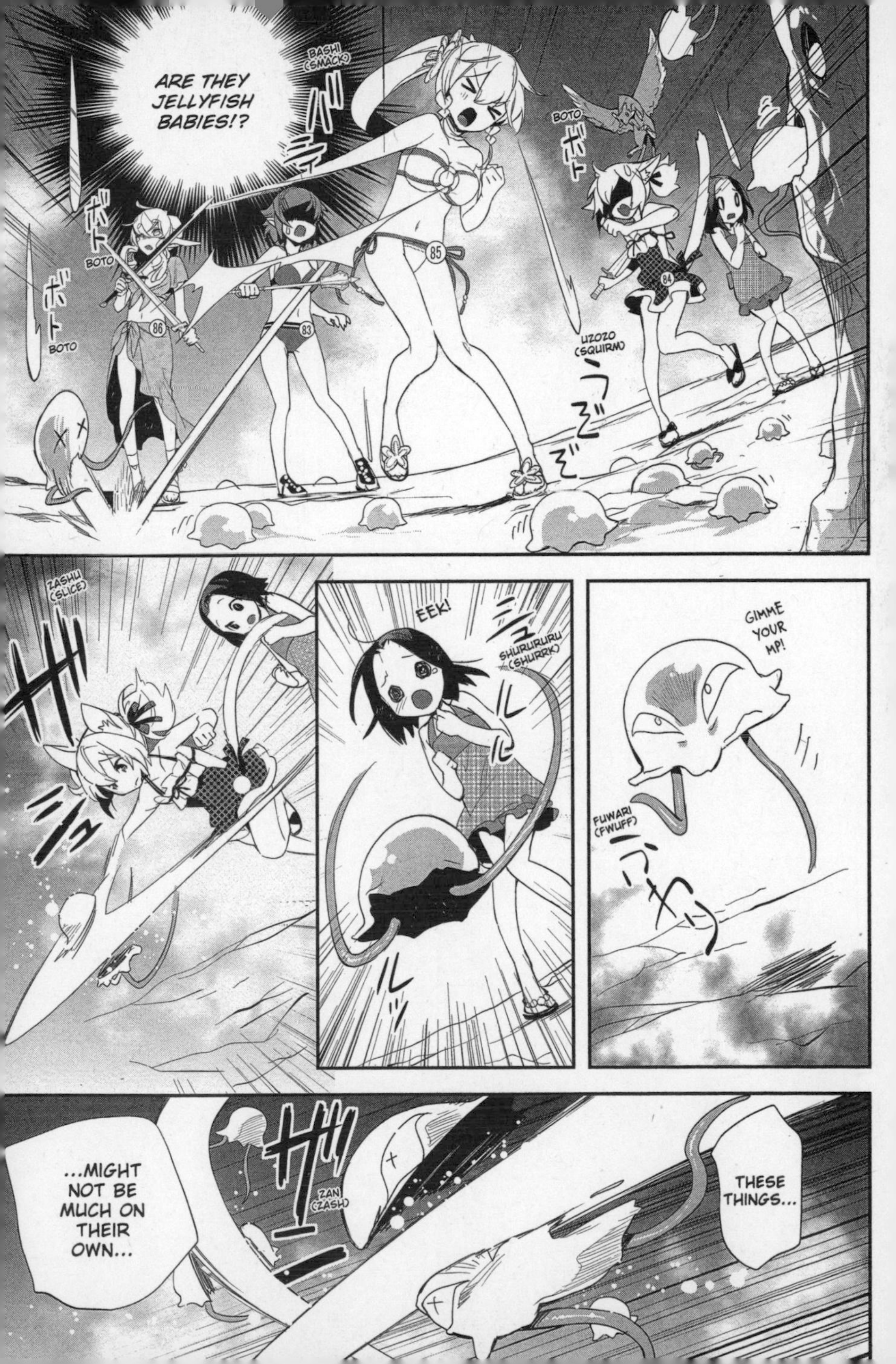
BOTO
BASHI (SMACK)
ARE THEY JELLYFISH BABIES!?
BOTO
BOTO
UZOZO (SQUIRM)
GIMME YOUR MP!
FUWARI (FWUFF)
EEK!
SHURURURU (SHURRK)
ZASHU (SLICE)
THESE THINGS...
ZAN (ZASH)
...MIGHT NOT BE MUCH ON THEIR OWN...

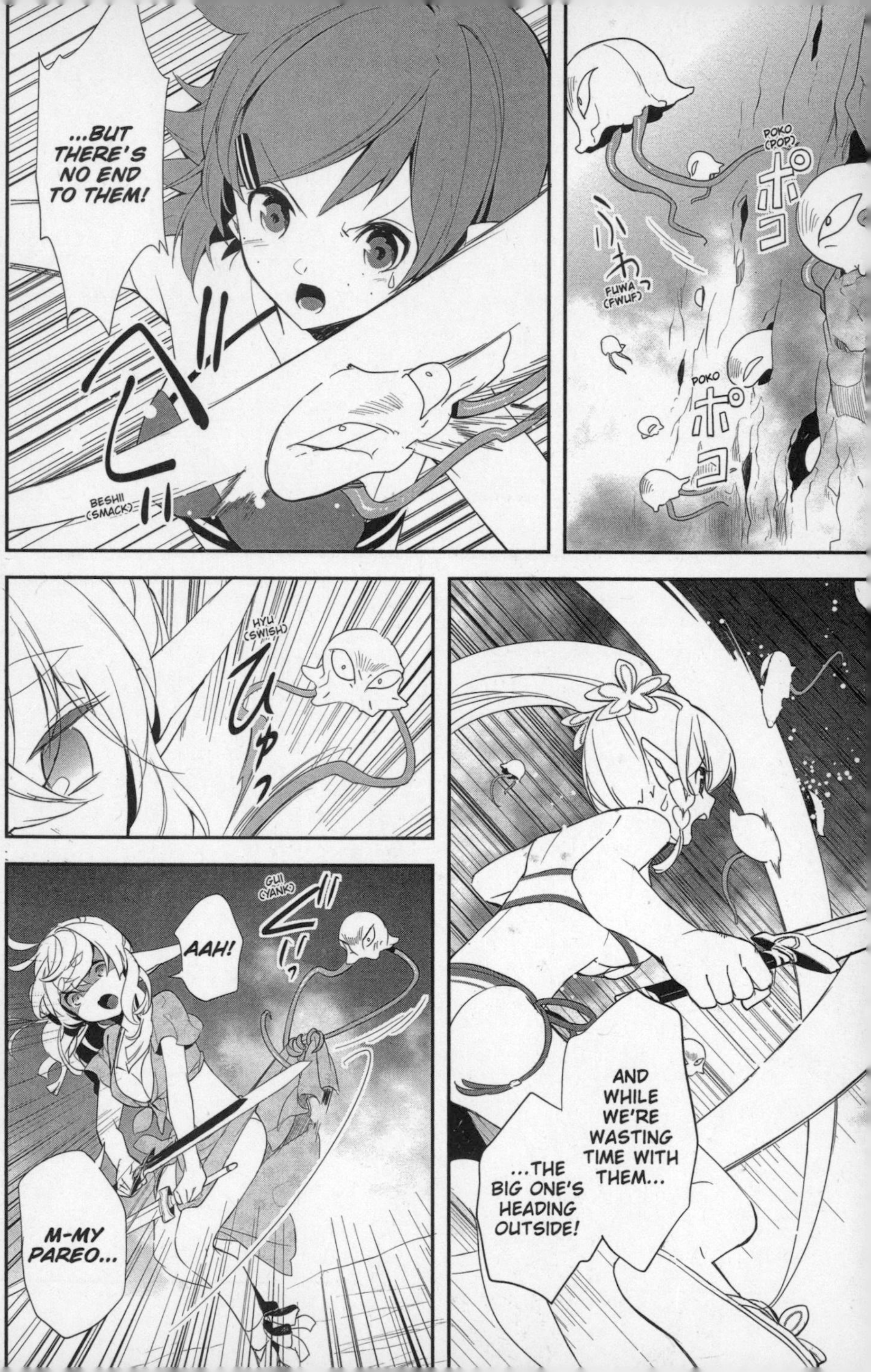

POKO (POP)
ポコ
FUWA (FWUF)
ふわっ
POKO
ポコ
...BUT THERE'S NO END TO THEM!
BESHII (SMACK)
HYU (SWISH)
ひゅっ
AND WHILE WE'RE WASTING TIME WITH THEM...
...THE BIG ONE'S HEADING OUTSIDE!
GUI (YANK)
ぐいっ
AAH!
M-MY PAREO...

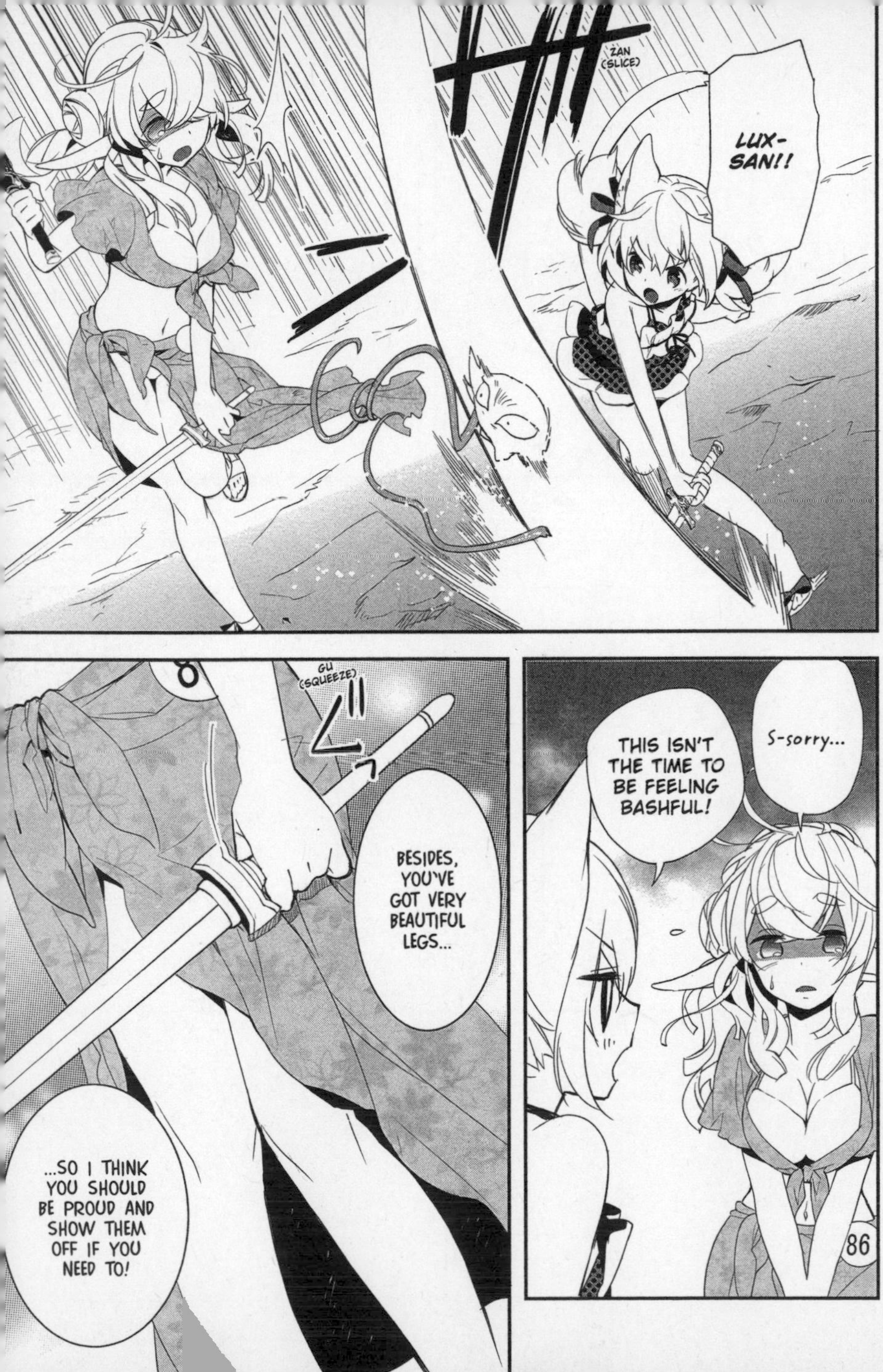
ZAN
(SLICE)
LUX-SAN!!
THIS ISN'T THE TIME TO BE FEELING BASHFUL!
S-sorry...
GU
(SQUEEZE)
BESIDES, YOU'VE GOT VERY BEAUTIFUL LEGS...
...SO I THINK YOU SHOULD BE PROUD AND SHOW THEM OFF IF YOU NEED TO!

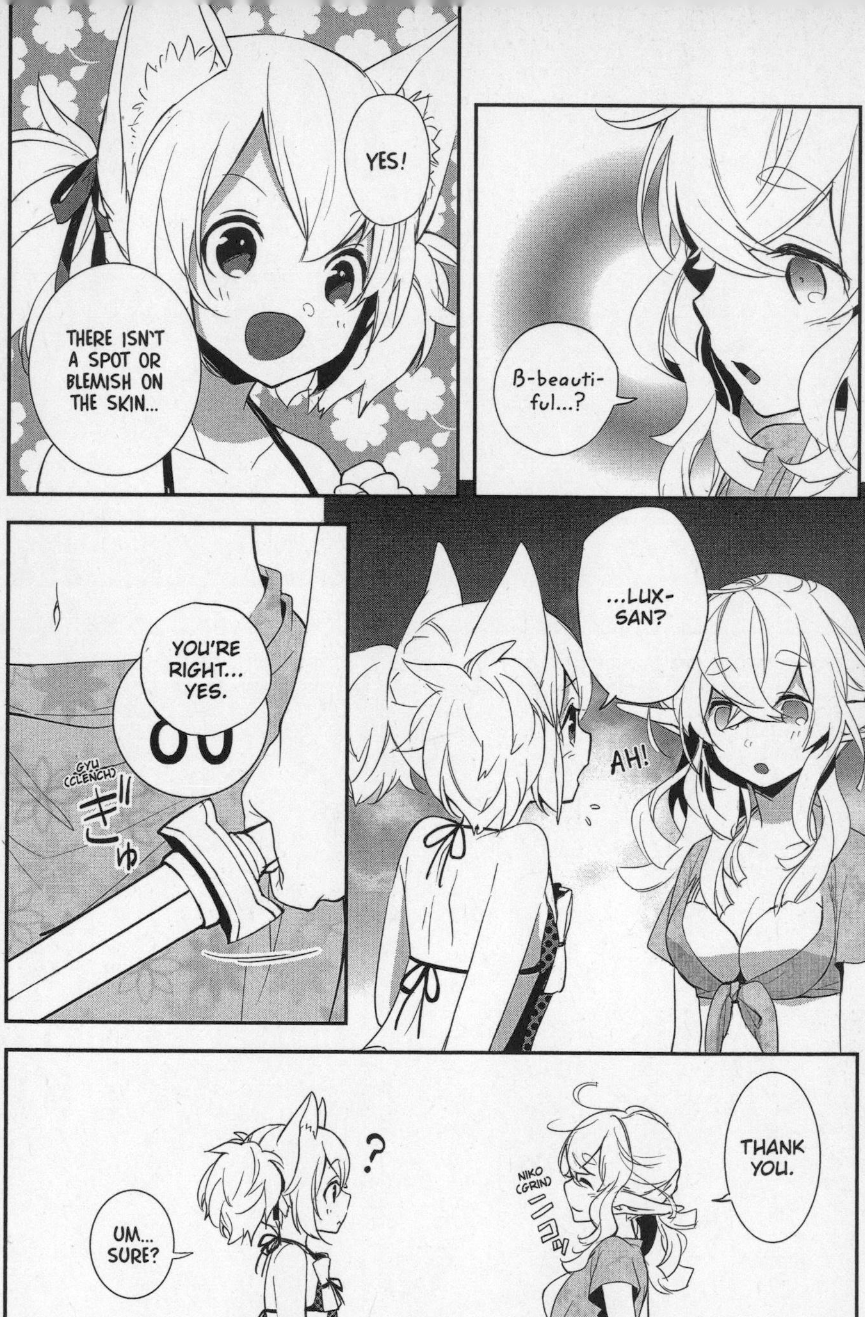
B-beauti-ful...?
YES!
THERE ISN'T A SPOT OR BLEMISH ON THE SKIN...
...LUX-SAN?
AH!
YOU'RE RIGHT... YES.
GYU (CLENCH)
ぎゅ
THANK YOU.
NIKO (GRIN)
ニコッ
?
UM... SURE?

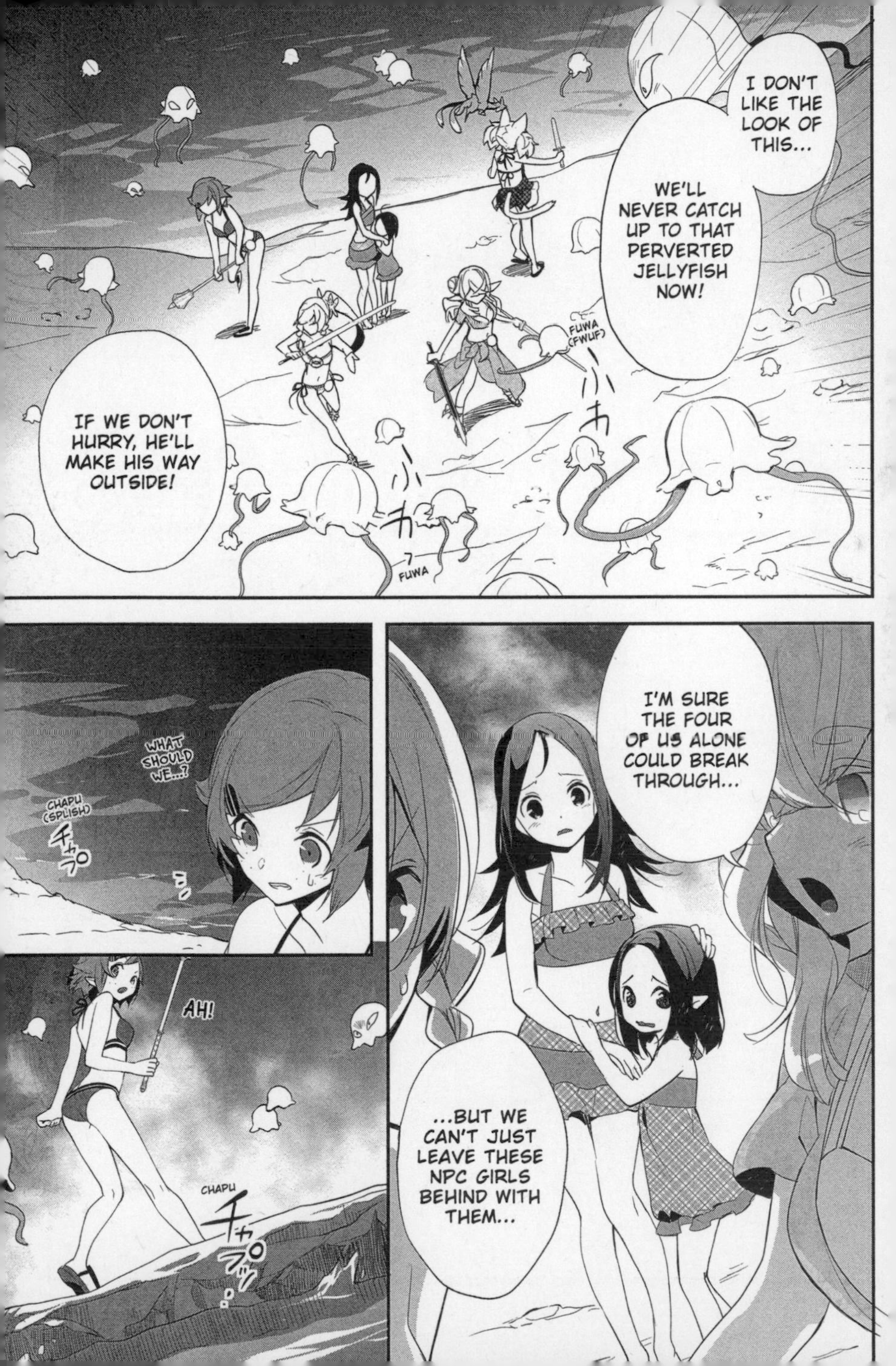
I DON'T LIKE THE LOOK OF THIS...
WE'LL NEVER CATCH UP TO THAT PERVERTED JELLYFISH NOW!
FUWA (FWUF)
ふわ
ふわ
FUWA
IF WE DON'T HURRY, HE'LL MAKE HIS WAY OUTSIDE!
I'M SURE THE FOUR OF US ALONE COULD BREAK THROUGH...
...BUT WE CAN'T JUST LEAVE THESE NPC GIRLS BEHIND WITH THEM...
WHAT SHOULD WE...?
CHAPU (SPLISH)
チャプ
AH!
CHAPU
チャプッ

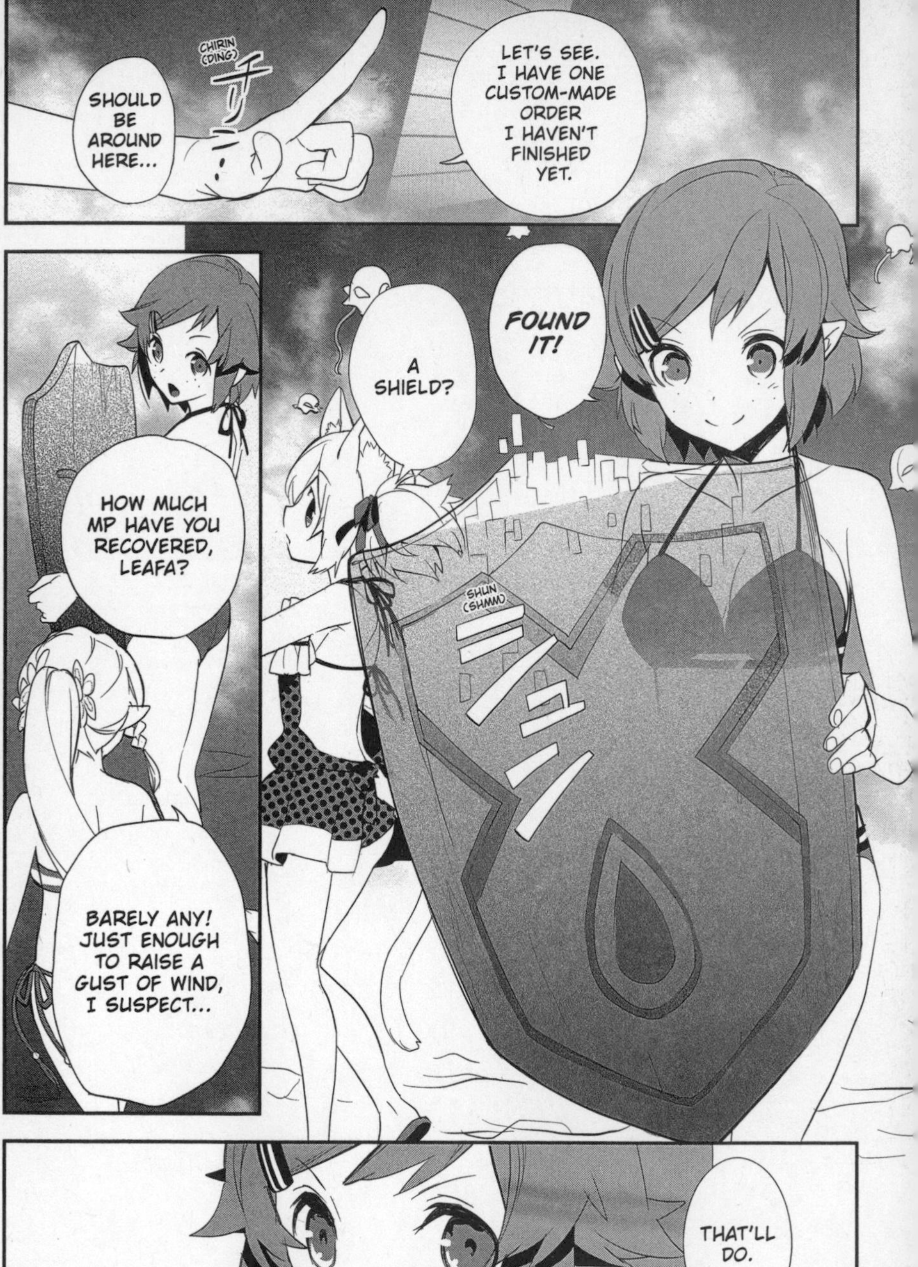
LET'S SEE. I HAVE ONE CUSTOM-MADE ORDER I HAVEN'T FINISHED YET.
CHIRIN (DING)
SHOULD BE AROUND HERE...
FOUND IT!
SHUN (SHMM)
A SHIELD?
HOW MUCH MP HAVE YOU RECOVERED, LEAFA?
BARELY ANY! JUST ENOUGH TO RAISE A GUST OF WIND, I SUSPECT...
THAT'LL DO.

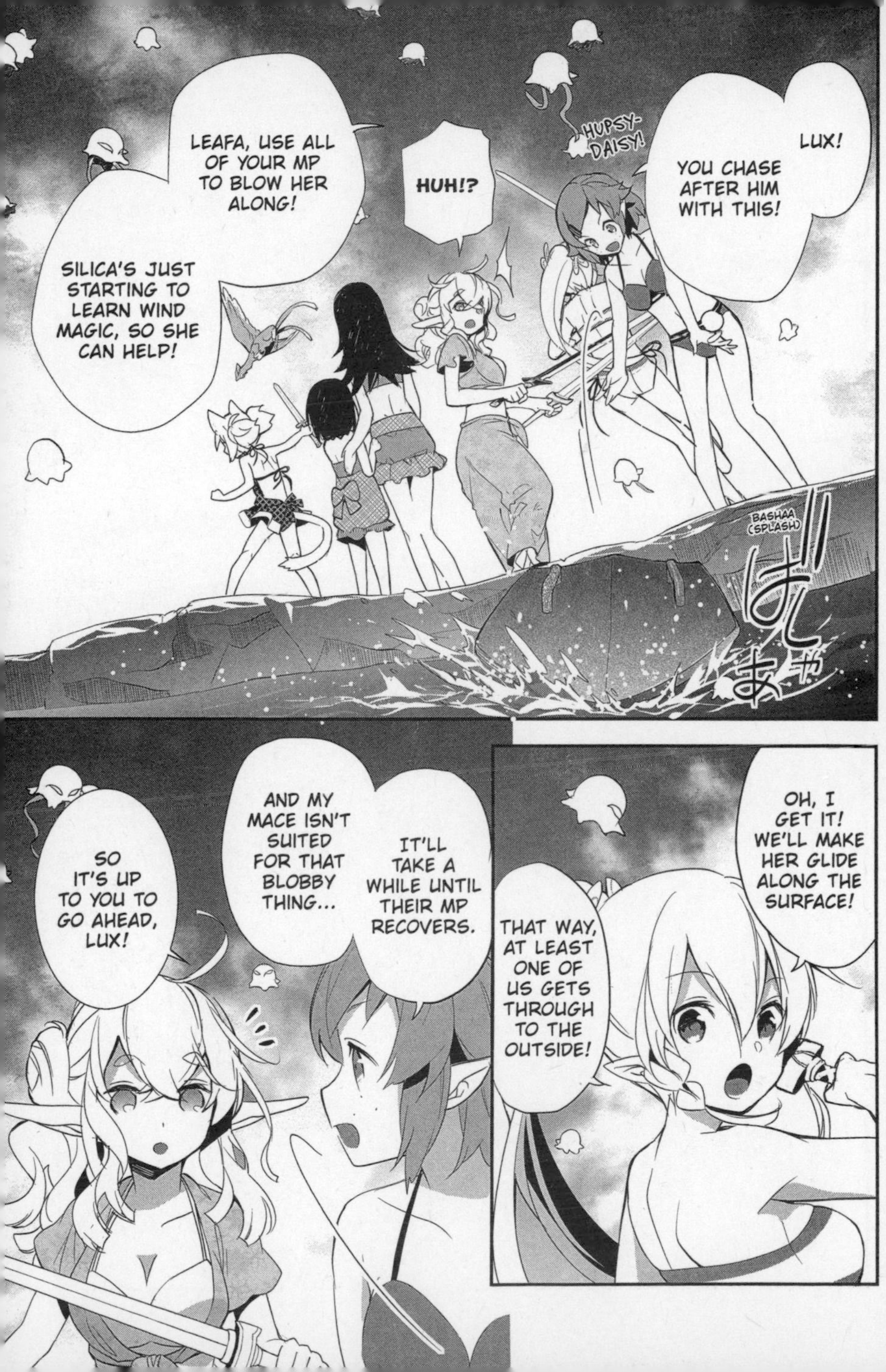
LUX!
YOU CHASE AFTER HIM WITH THIS!
HUPSY-DAISY!
HUH!?
LEAFA, USE ALL OF YOUR MP TO BLOW HER ALONG!
SILICA'S JUST STARTING TO LEARN WIND MAGIC, SO SHE CAN HELP!
BASHAA (SPLASH)
ばしゃあ
OH, I GET IT! WE'LL MAKE HER GLIDE ALONG THE SURFACE!
THAT WAY, AT LEAST ONE OF US GETS THROUGH TO THE OUTSIDE!
IT'LL TAKE A WHILE UNTIL THEIR MP RECOVERS.
AND MY MACE ISN'T SUITED FOR THAT BLOBBY THING...
SO IT'S UP TO YOU TO GO AHEAD, LUX!

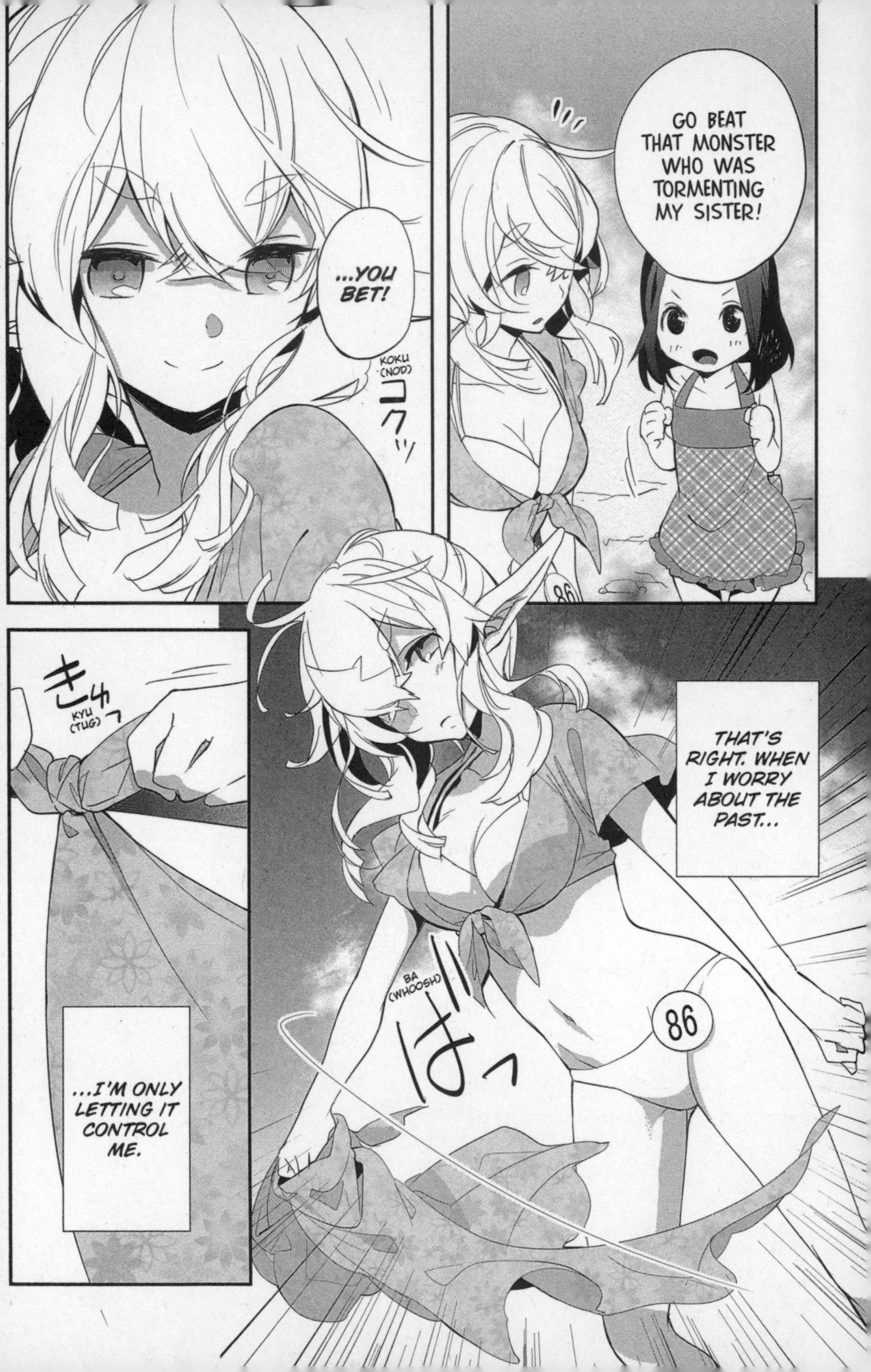
GO BEAT THAT MONSTER WHO WAS TORMENTING MY SISTER!
...YOU BET!
KOKU (NOD)
コクッ
THAT'S RIGHT. WHEN I WORRY ABOUT THE PAST...
BA (WHOOSH)
ばっ
86
KYU (TUG)
きゅっ
...I'M ONLY LETTING IT CONTROL ME.

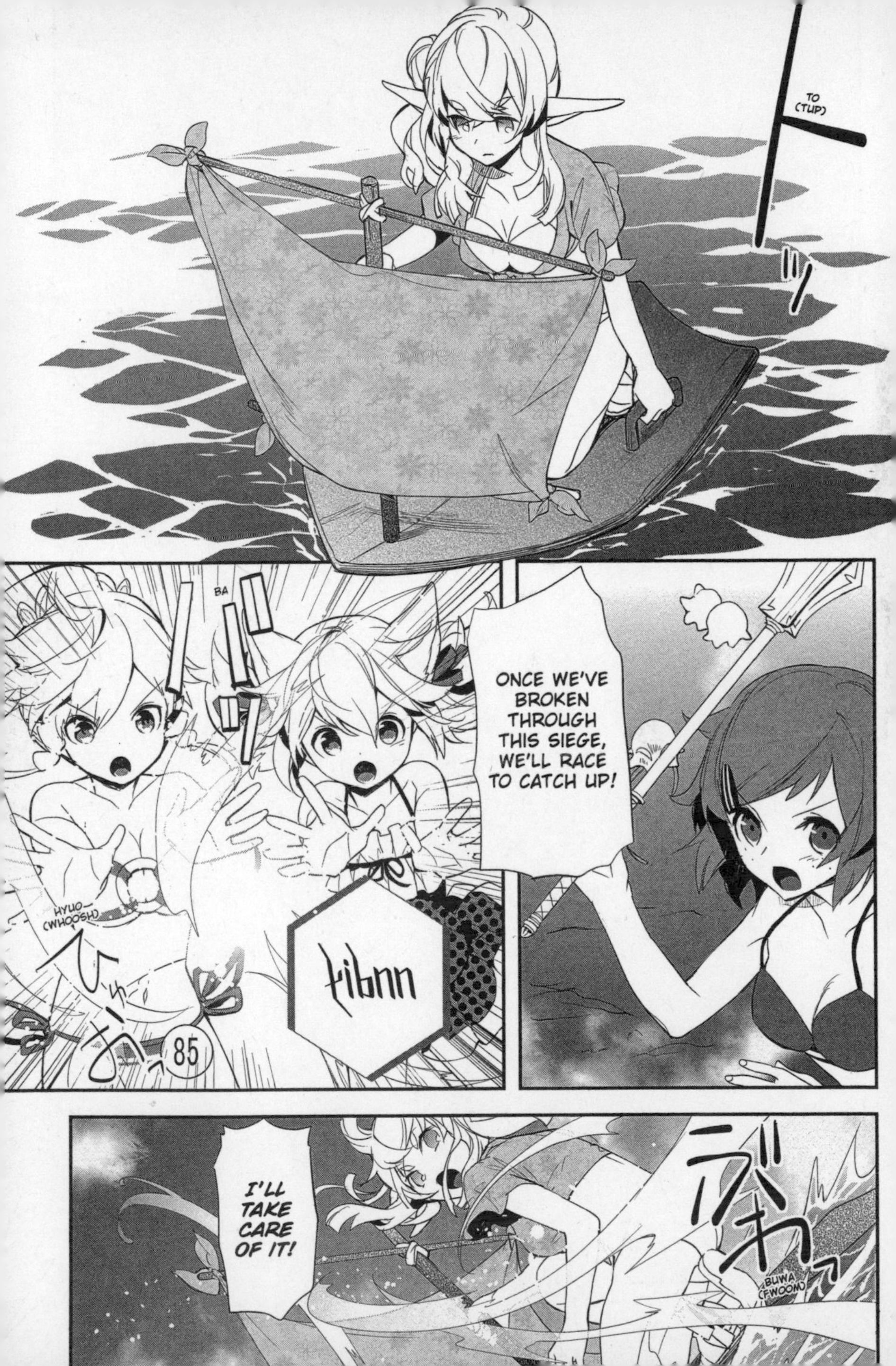
TO
(TUP)
BA
ONCE WE'VE BROKEN THROUGH THIS SIEGE, WE'LL RACE TO CATCH UP!
HYUO
(WHOOSH)
I'LL TAKE CARE OF IT!
BUWA
(FWOOM)

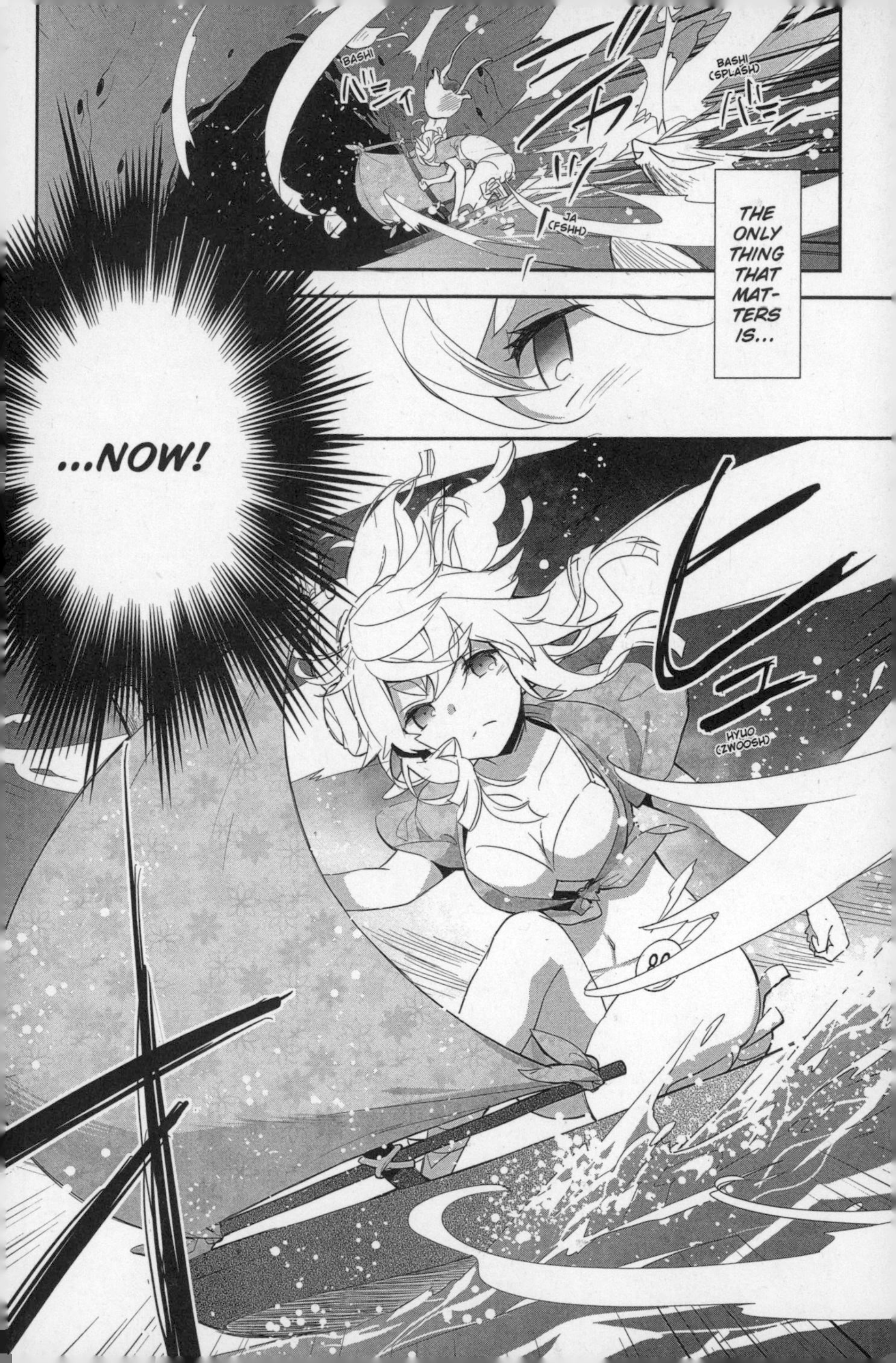

BASHI
BASHI (SPLASH)
JA (FSHH)
THE ONLY THING THAT MAT-TERS IS...
...NOW!
HYUO (ZWOOSH)

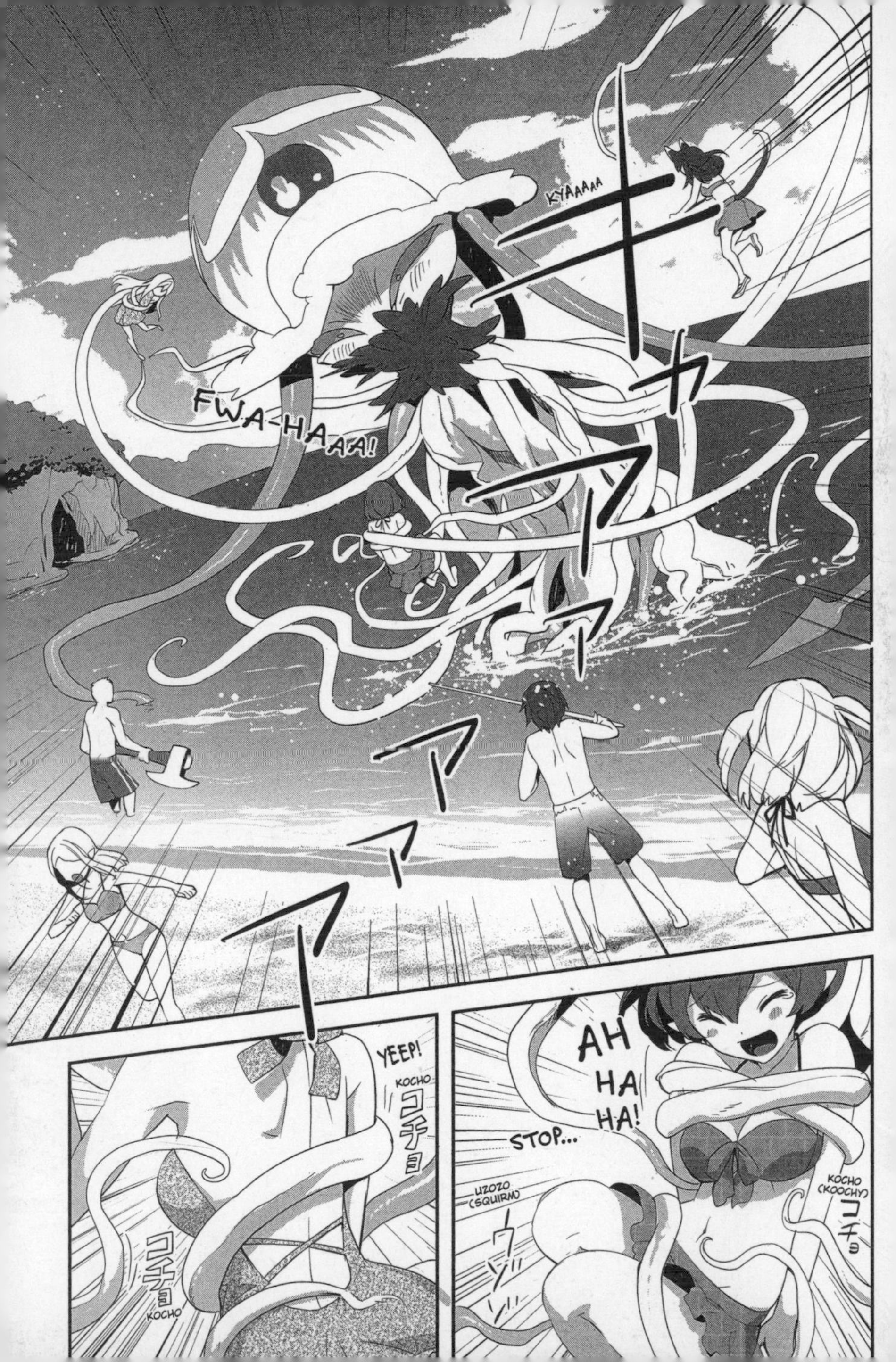
KYAAAAA
FWA-HAAAA!
AH HA HA!
STOP...
KOCHO (KOOCHY)
コチョ
UZOZO (SQUIRM)
ウゾゾ
YEEP!
KOCHO
コチョ
コチョ
KOCHO

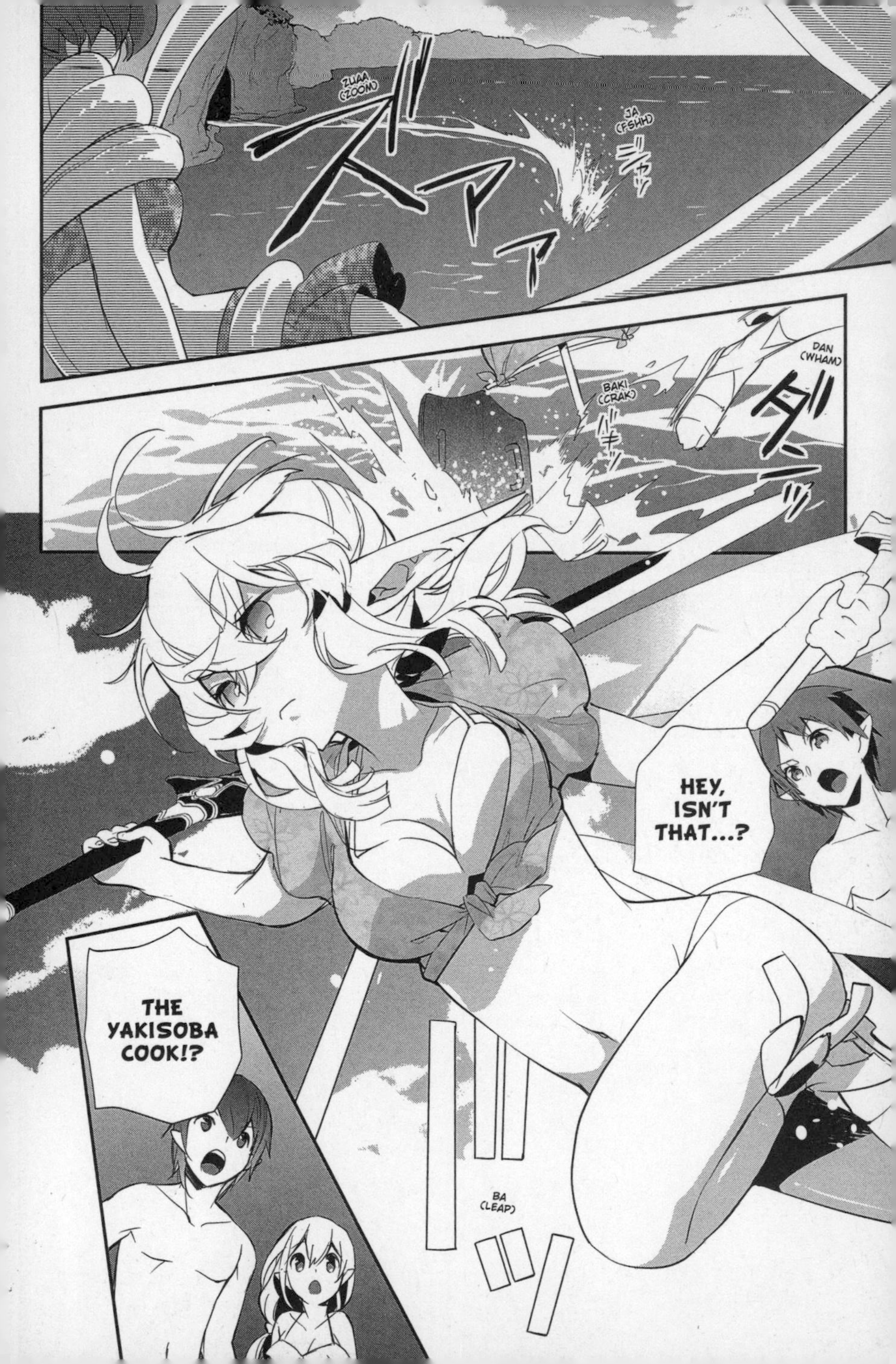
ZUAA (ZOOM)
ズァアア
JA (FSHH)
ジャッ
DAN (WHAM)
ダンッ
BAKI (CRAK)
バキッ
HEY, ISN'T THAT...?
THE YAKISOBA COOK!?
BA (LEAP)

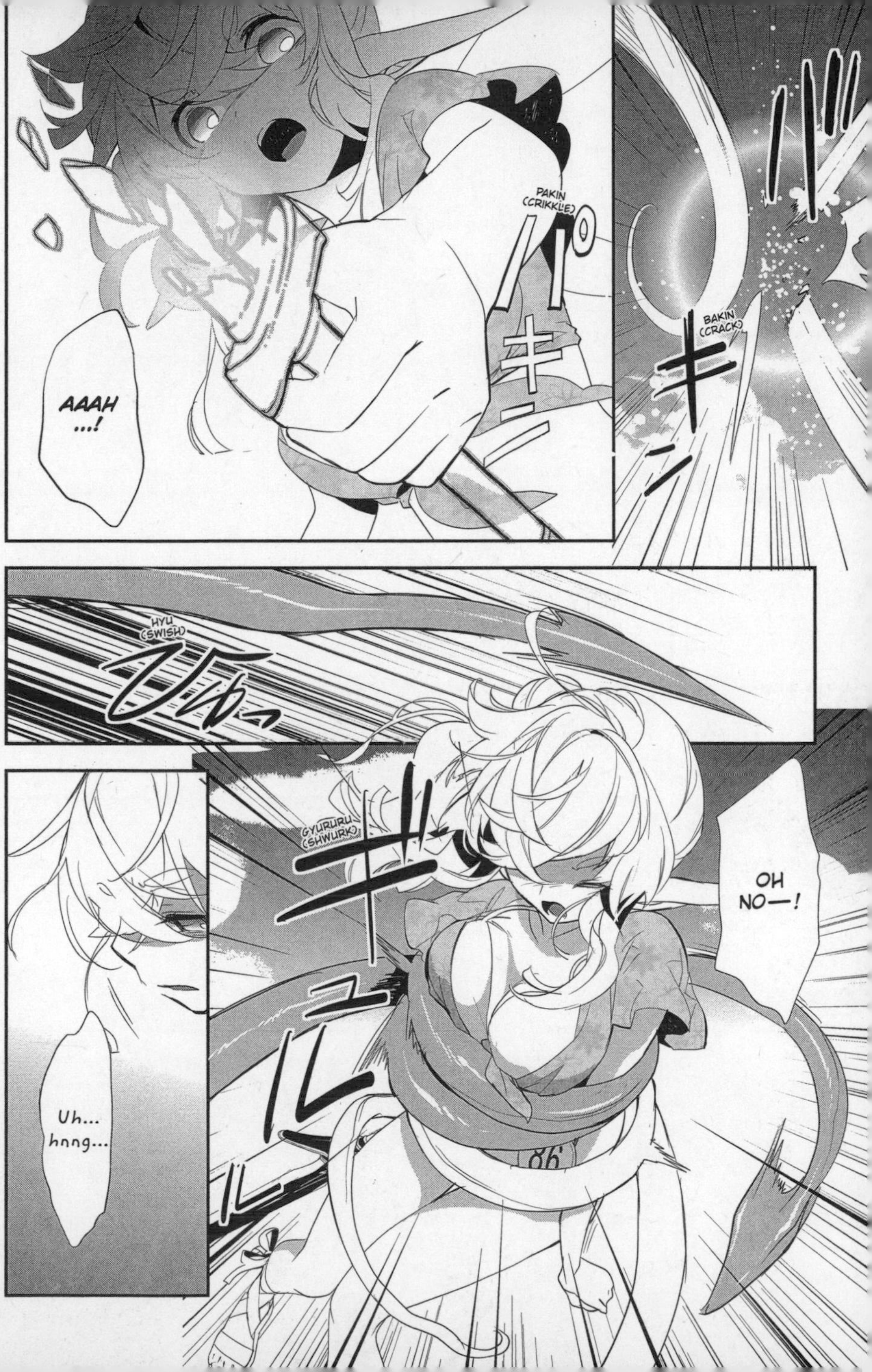
BAKIN (CRACK)
PAKIN (CRIKKLE)
AAAH ...!
HYU (SWISH)
GYURURU (SHWURK)
OH NO—!
Uh... hnng...

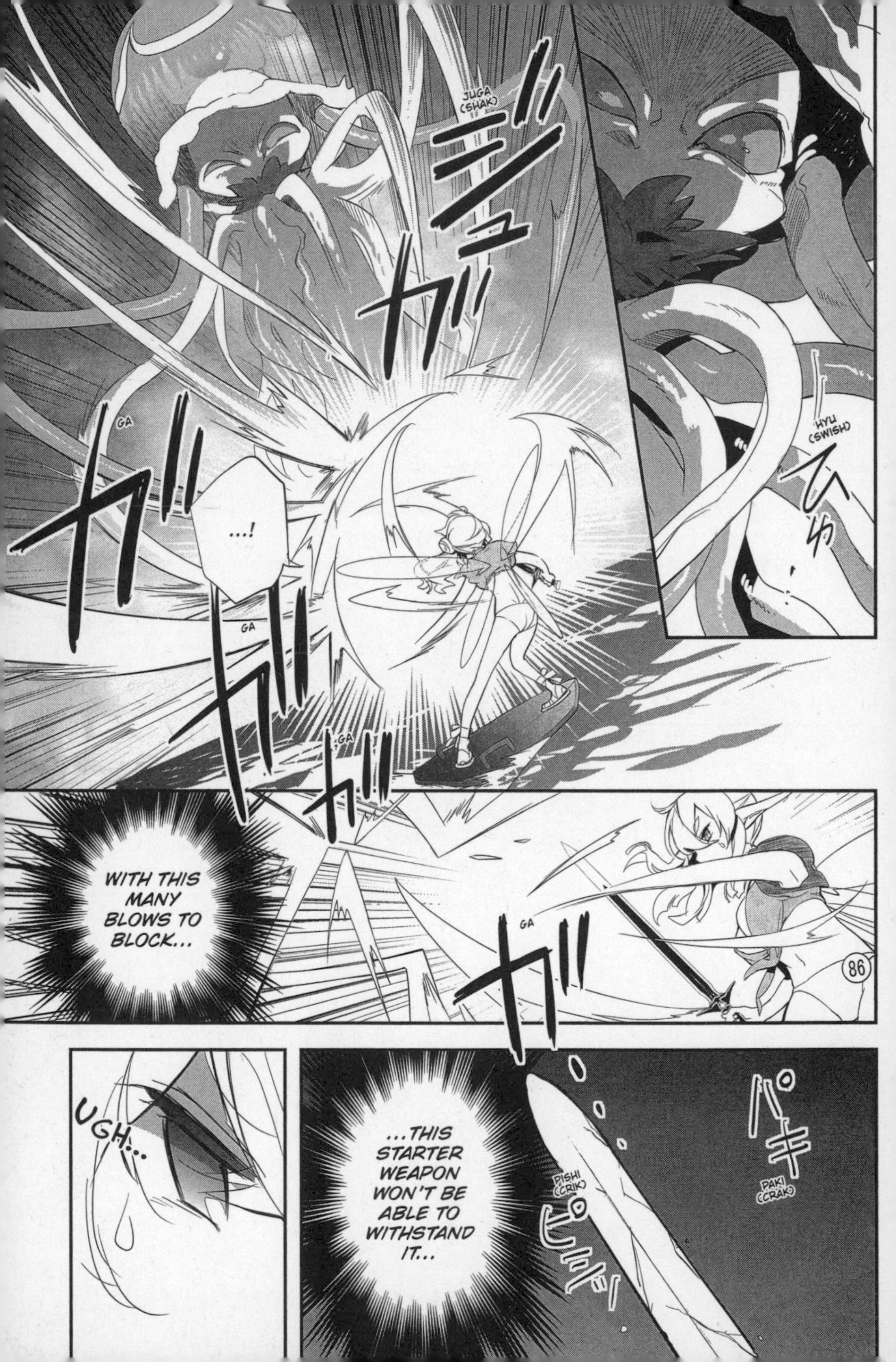

JUGA (SHAK)
HYU (SWISH)
GA
...!
GA
GA
WITH THIS MANY BLOWS TO BLOCK...
GA
UGH...
PAKI (CRAK)
PISHI (CRIK)
...THIS STARTER WEAPON WON'T BE ABLE TO WITHSTAND IT...

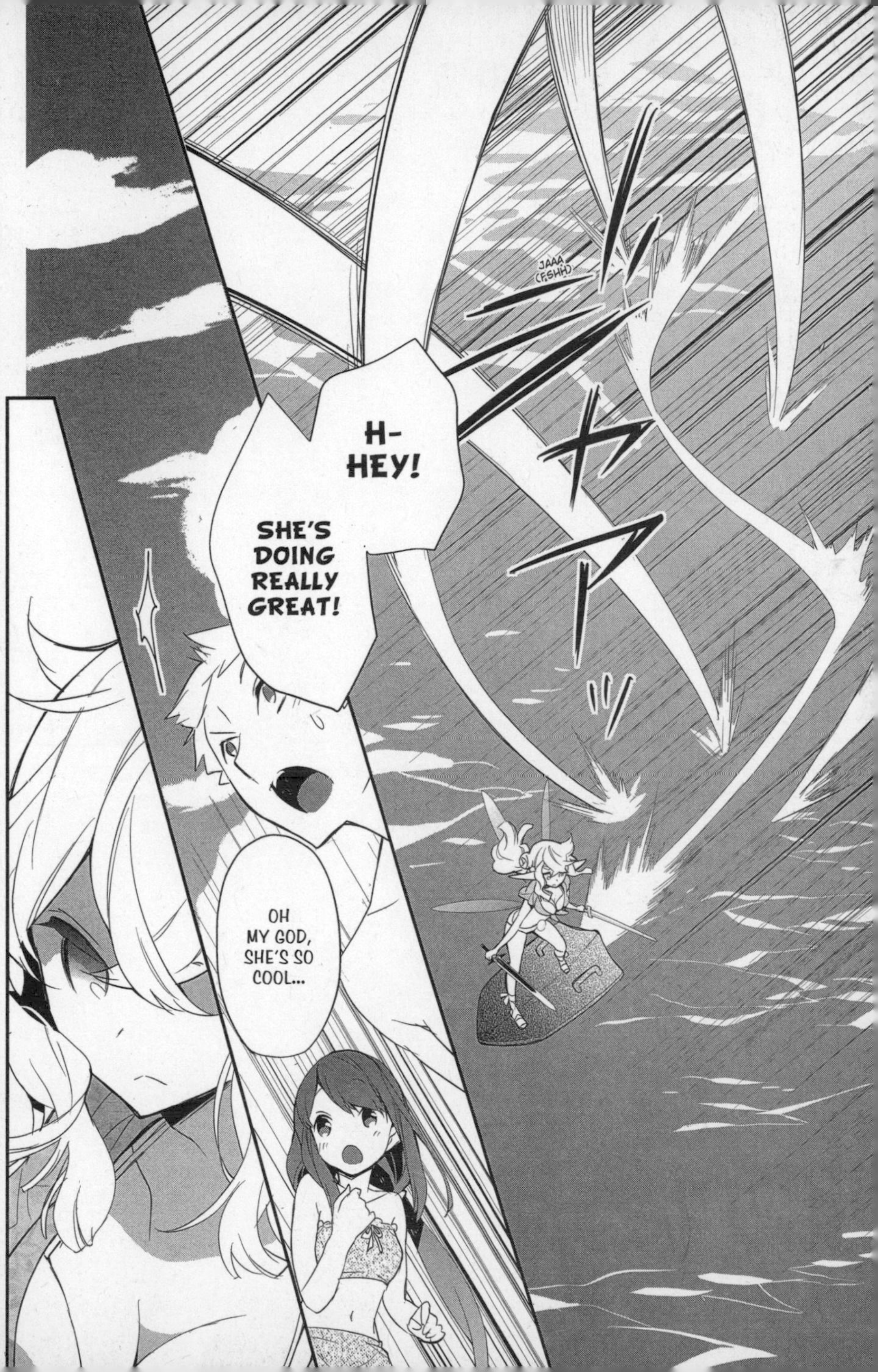
JAAA (FSHH)
H-HEY!
SHE'S DOING REALLY GREAT!
OH MY GOD, SHE'S SO COOL...

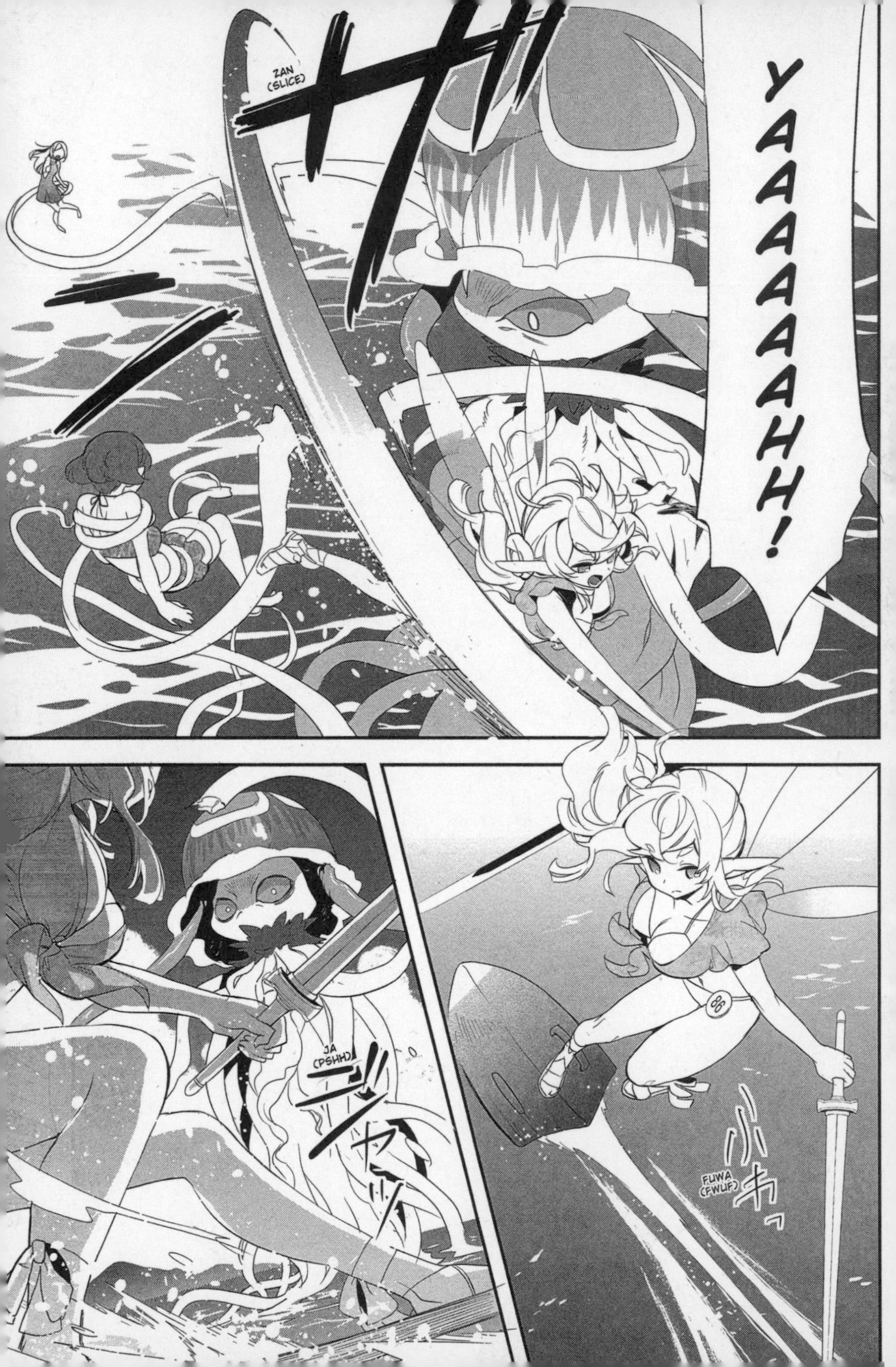
YAAAAAAAHH!
ZAN (SLICE)
JA (PSHH)
FUWA (FWUF)

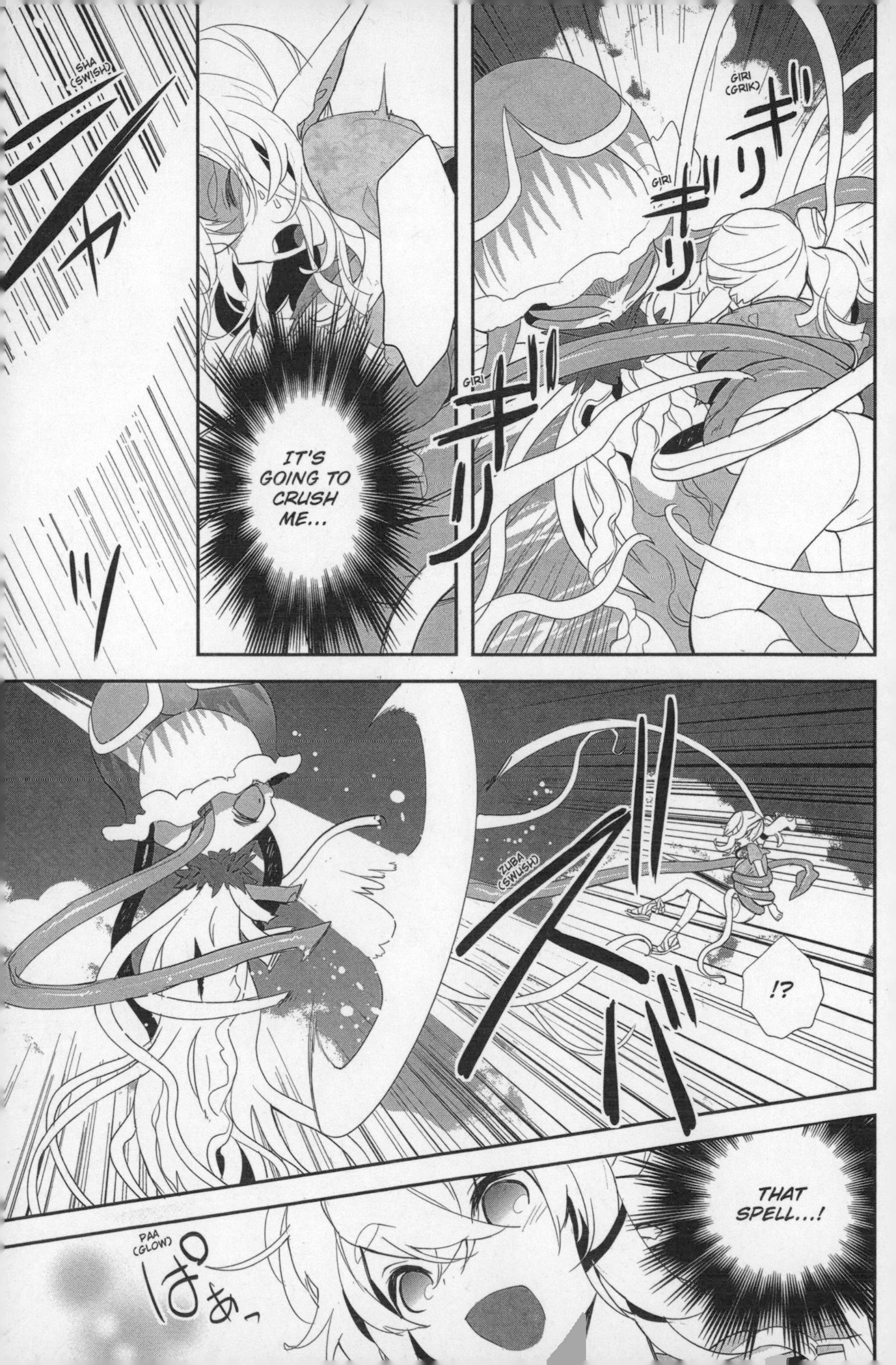
GIRI (GRIK)
GIRI
GIRI
IT'S GOING TO CRUSH ME...
SHA (SWISH)
!?
ZUBA (SWISH)
THAT SPELL...!
PAA (GLOW)

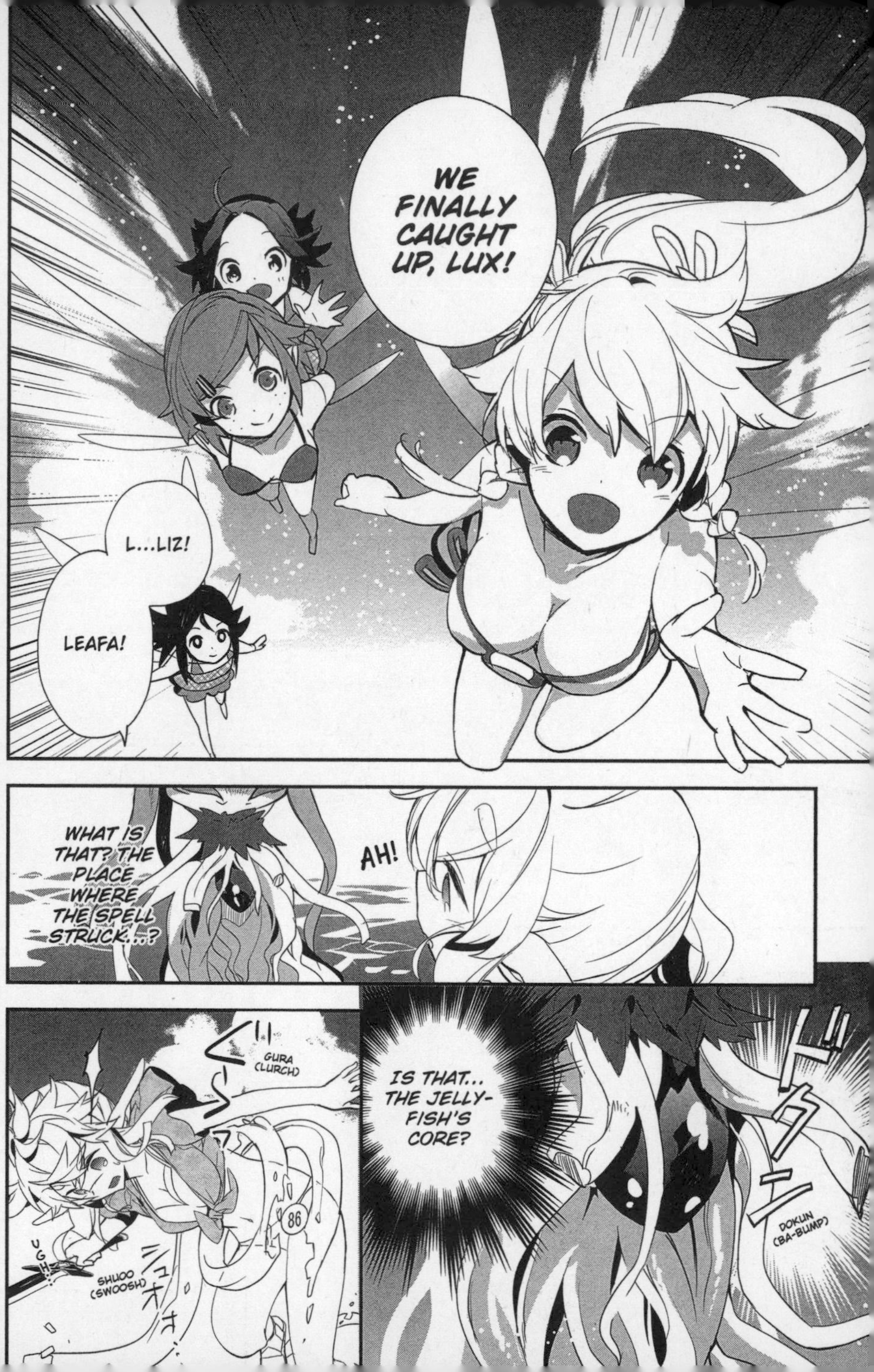
WE FINALLY CAUGHT UP, LUX!
L...LIZ!
LEAFA!
AH!
WHAT IS THAT? THE PLACE WHERE THE SPELL STRUCK...?
DOKUN (BA-BUMP)
IS THAT... THE JELLY-FISH'S CORE?
GURA (LURCH)
SHUOO (SWOOSH)
UGH...

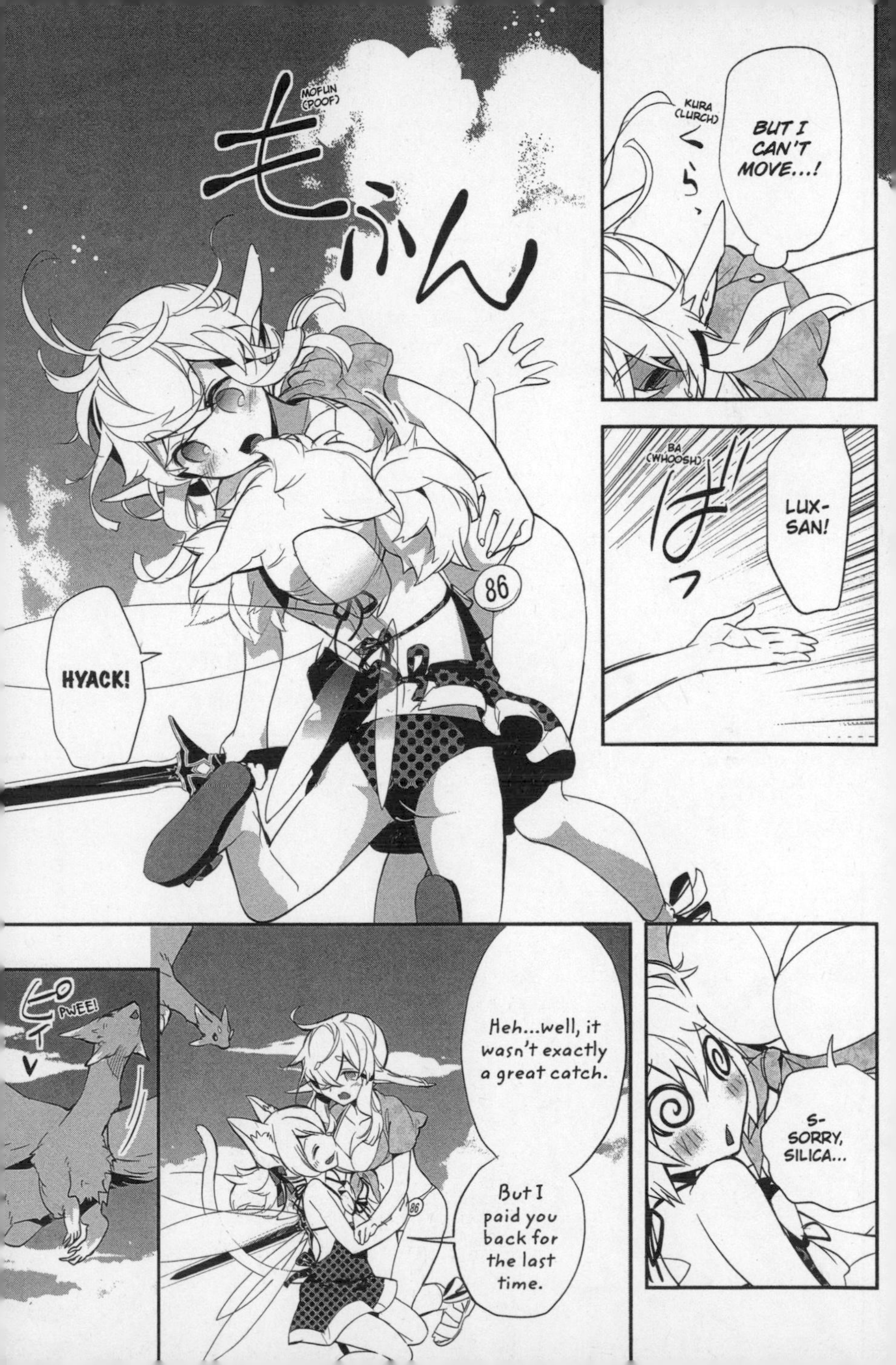
KURA (LURCH)
くら、
BUT I CAN'T MOVE...!
MOFUN (POOF)
もふん
BA (WHOOSH)
ばっ
LUX-SAN!
HYACK!
86
S-SORRY, SILICA...
Heh...well, it wasn't exactly a great catch.
But I paid you back for the last time.
86
ピィ
PWEE!

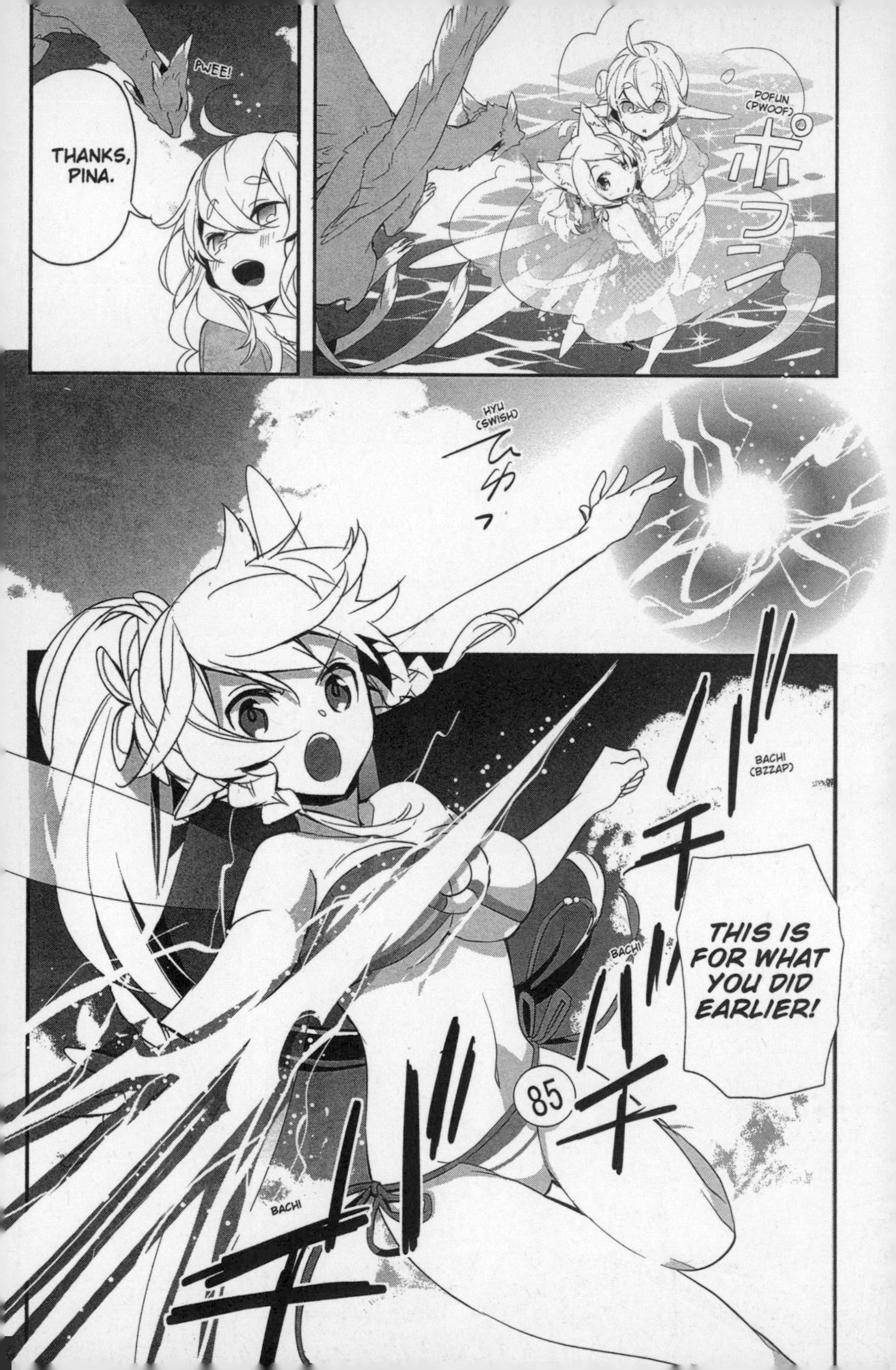
POFUN (PWOOF)
ポフン
PWEE!
THANKS, PINA.
HYU (SWISH)
ひゅっ
BACHI (BZZAP)
THIS IS FOR WHAT YOU DID EARLIER!
BACHI
BACHI

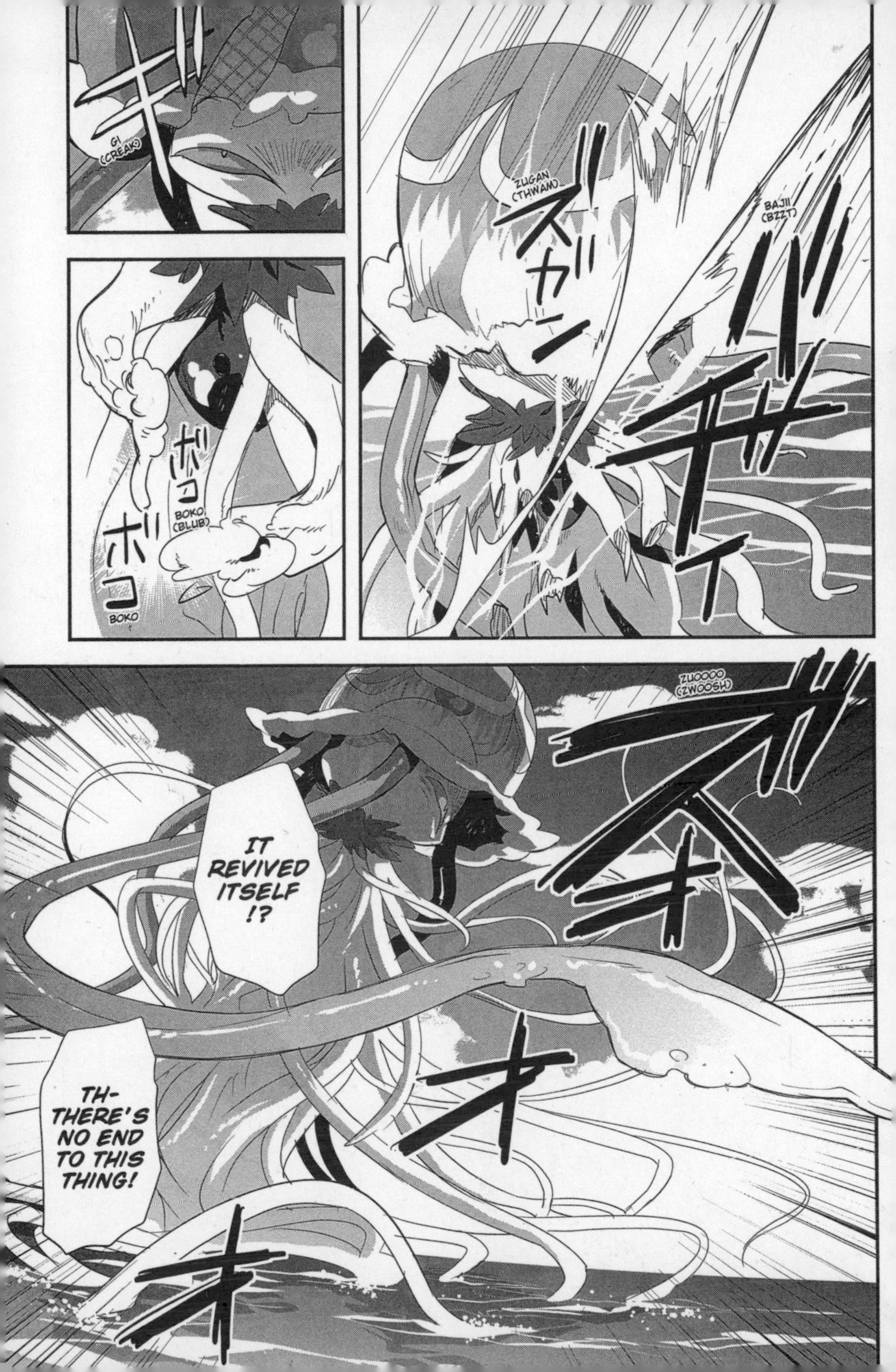
BAJII (BZZT)
ZUGAN (THWAM)
GI (CREAK)
BOKO (BLUB)
BOKO
ZUOOOO (ZWOOSH)
IT REVIVED ITSELF!?
TH-THERE'S NO END TO THIS THING!

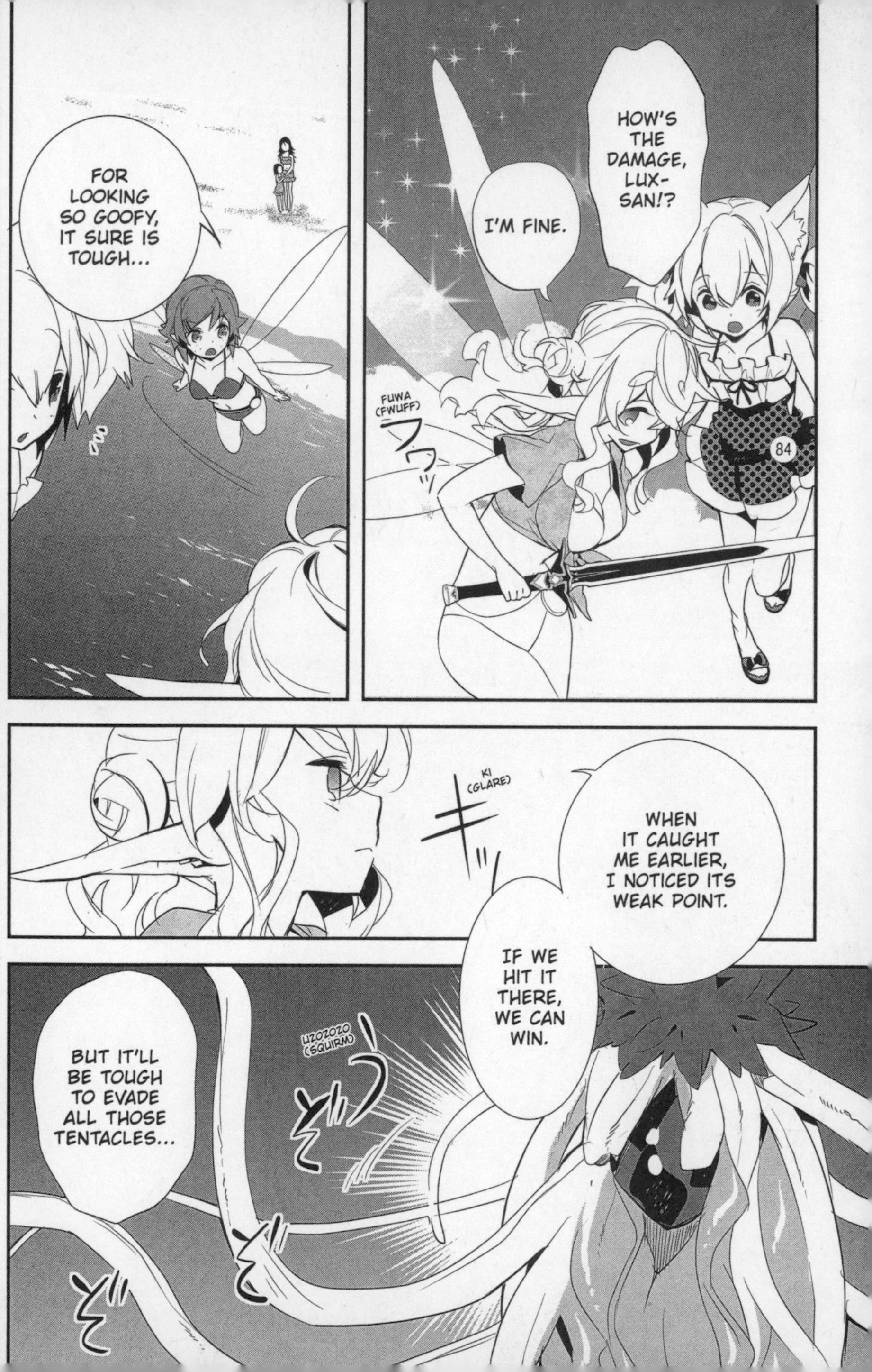
HOW'S THE DAMAGE, LUX-SAN!?
I'M FINE.
84
FUWA (FWUFF)
FOR LOOKING SO GOOFY, IT SURE IS TOUGH...
KI (GLARE)
WHEN IT CAUGHT ME EARLIER, I NOTICED ITS WEAK POINT.
IF WE HIT IT THERE, WE CAN WIN.
UZOZOZO (SQUIRM)
BUT IT'LL BE TOUGH TO EVADE ALL THOSE TENTACLES...

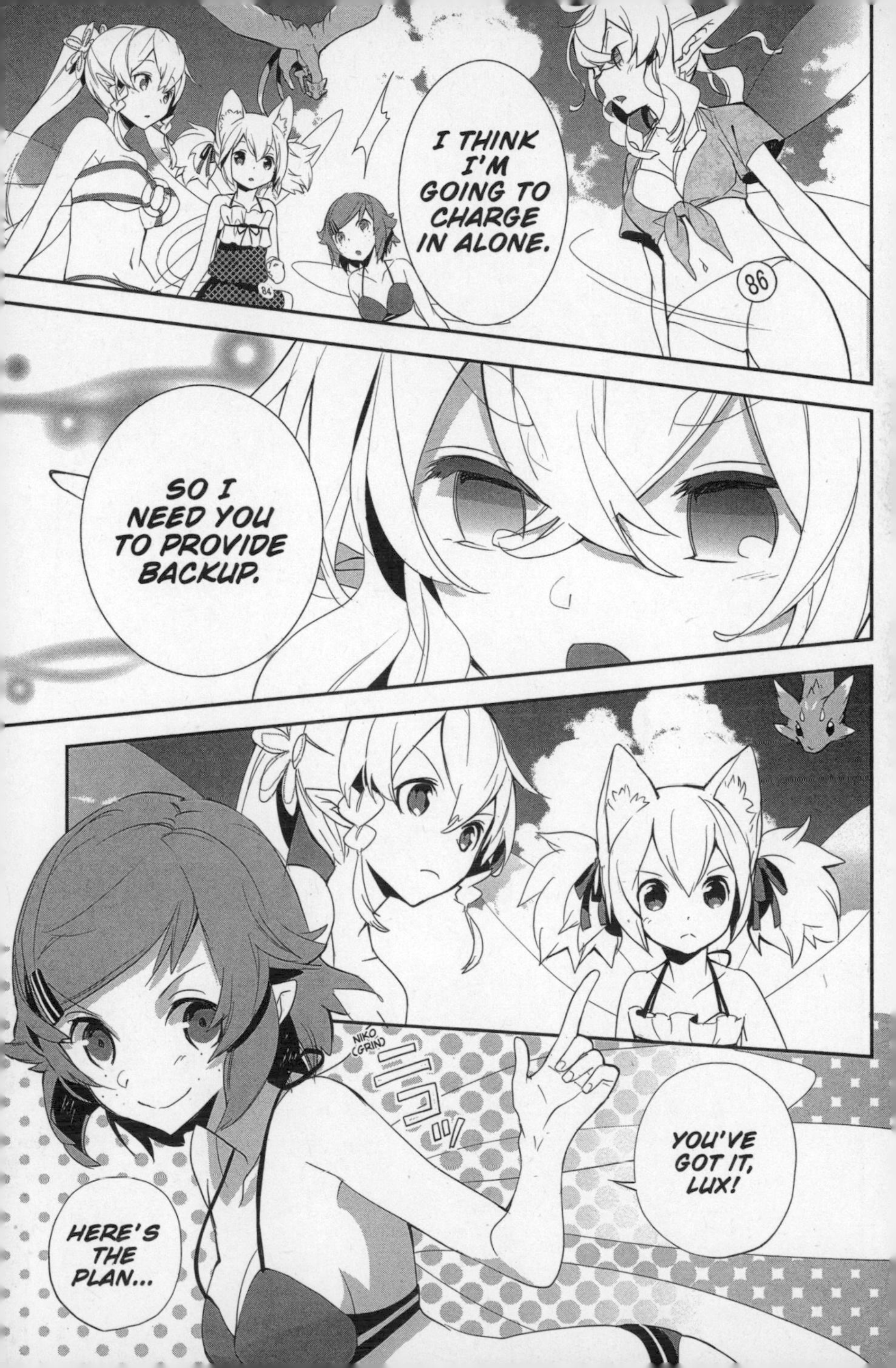
I THINK I'M GOING TO CHARGE IN ALONE.
SO I NEED YOU TO PROVIDE BACKUP.
YOU'VE GOT IT, LUX!
NIKO (GRIN)
HERE'S THE PLAN...

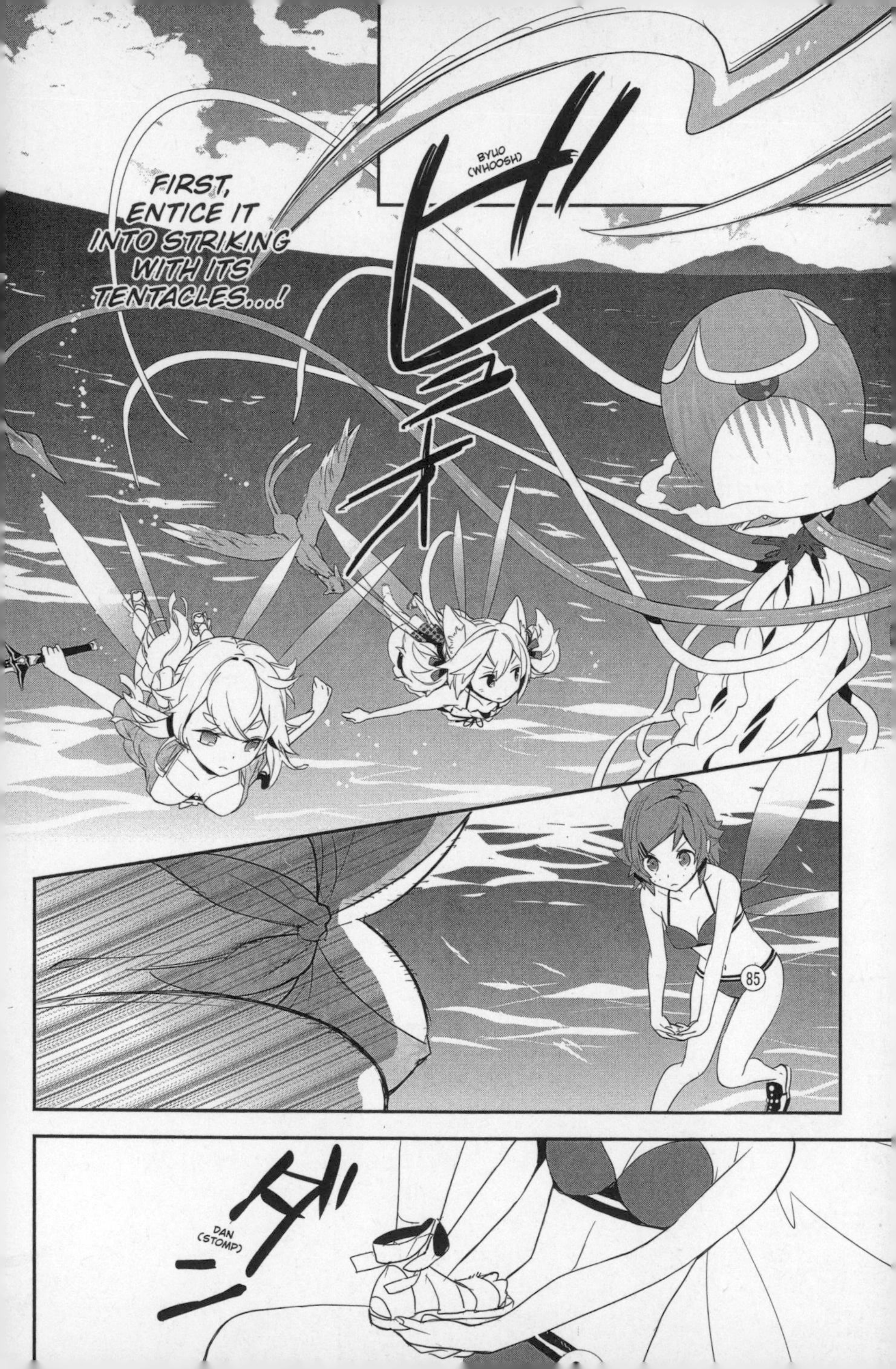

FIRST, ENTICE IT INTO STRIKING WITH ITS TENTACLES...!
BYUO (WHOOSH)
DAN (STOMP)

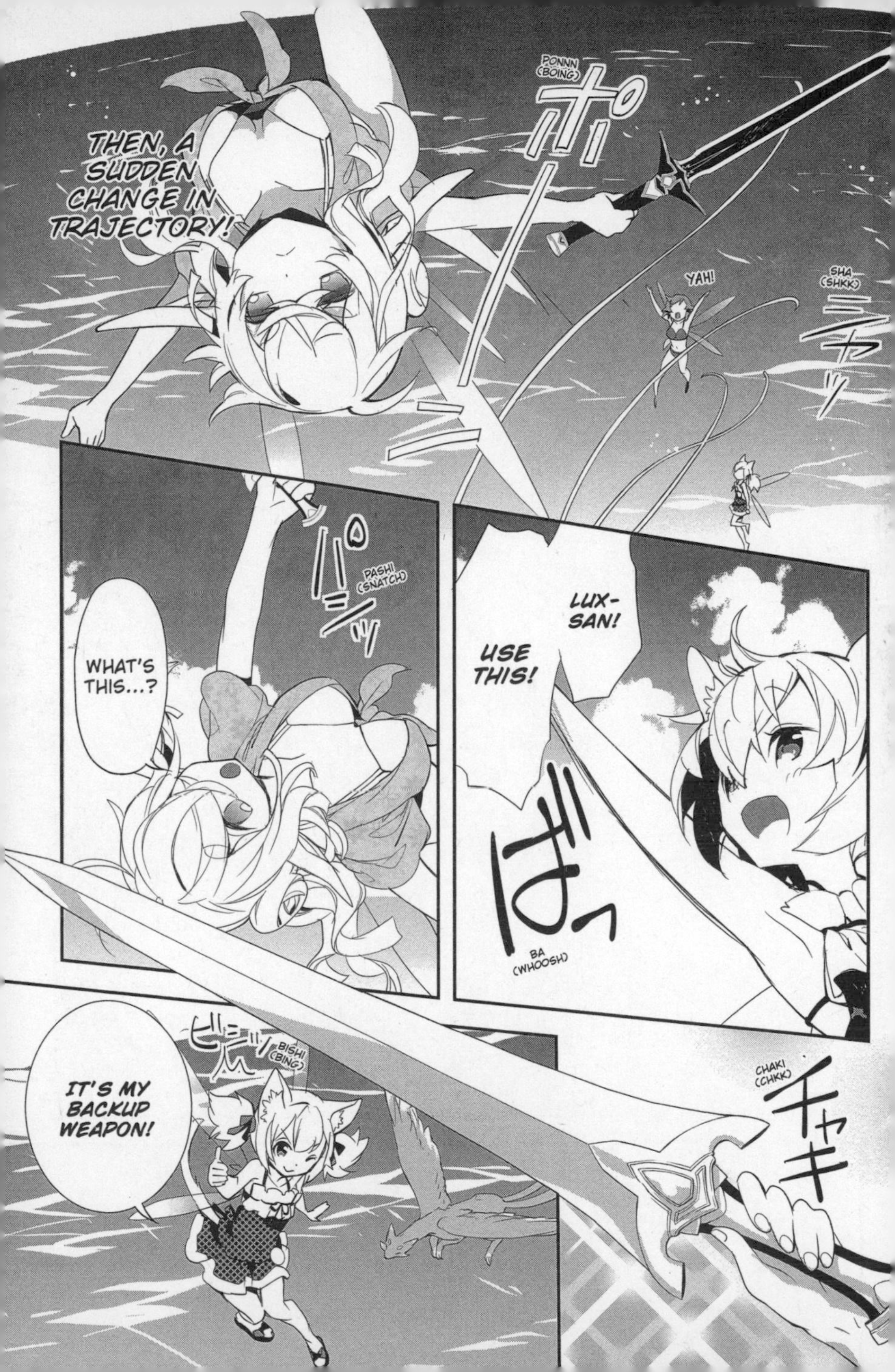
SHA (SHKK)
YAH!
PONNN (BOING)
THEN, A SUDDEN CHANGE IN TRAJECTORY!
LUX-SAN!
USE THIS!
BA (WHOOSH)
PASHI (SNATCH)
WHAT'S THIS...?
CHAKI (CHKK)
BISHI (BING)
IT'S MY BACKUP WEAPON!

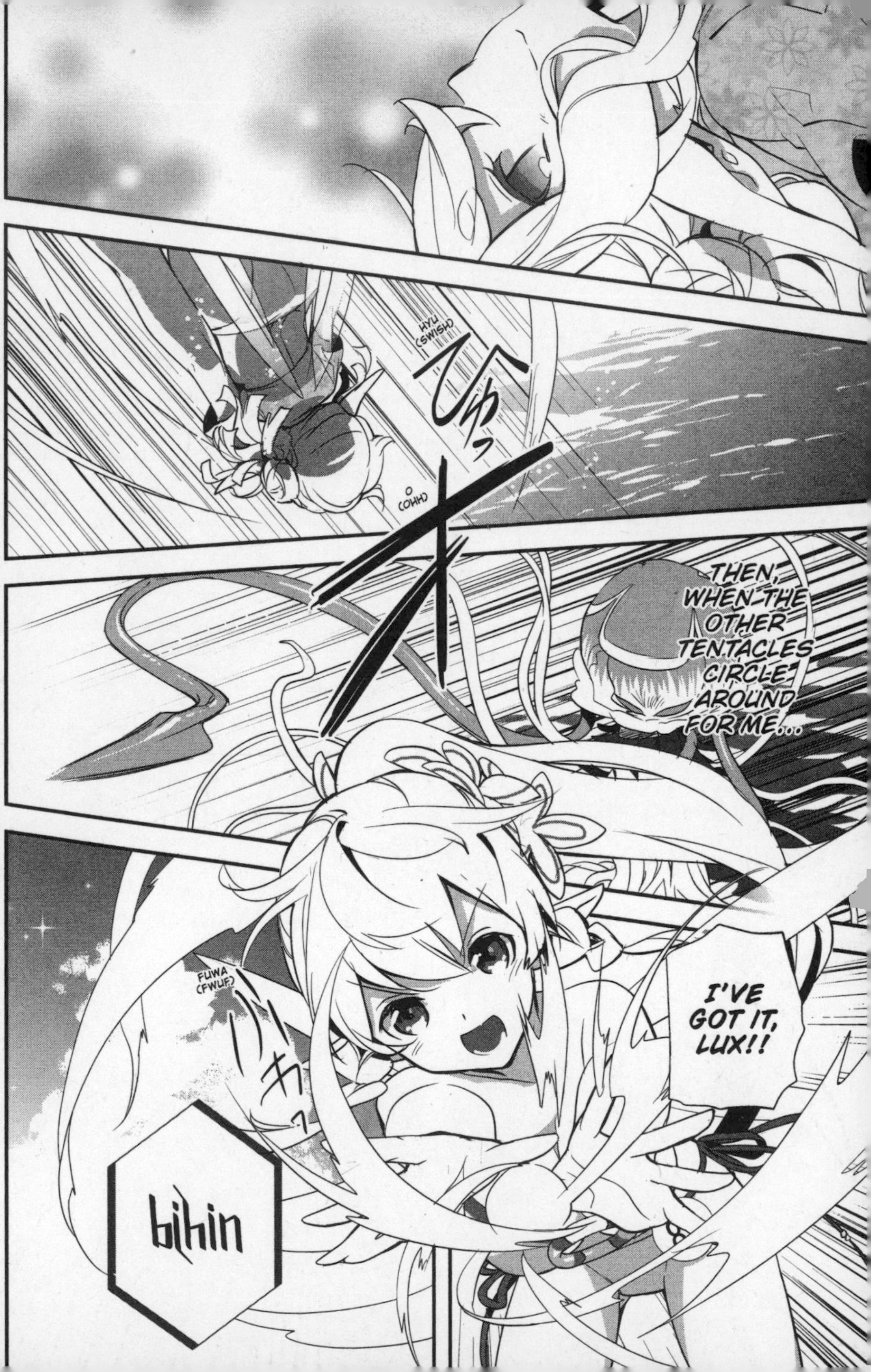
HYU (SWISH)
O (OHH)
THEN, WHEN THE OTHER TENTACLES CIRCLE AROUND FOR ME...
I'VE GOT IT, LUX!!
FUWA (FWUF)
bihin

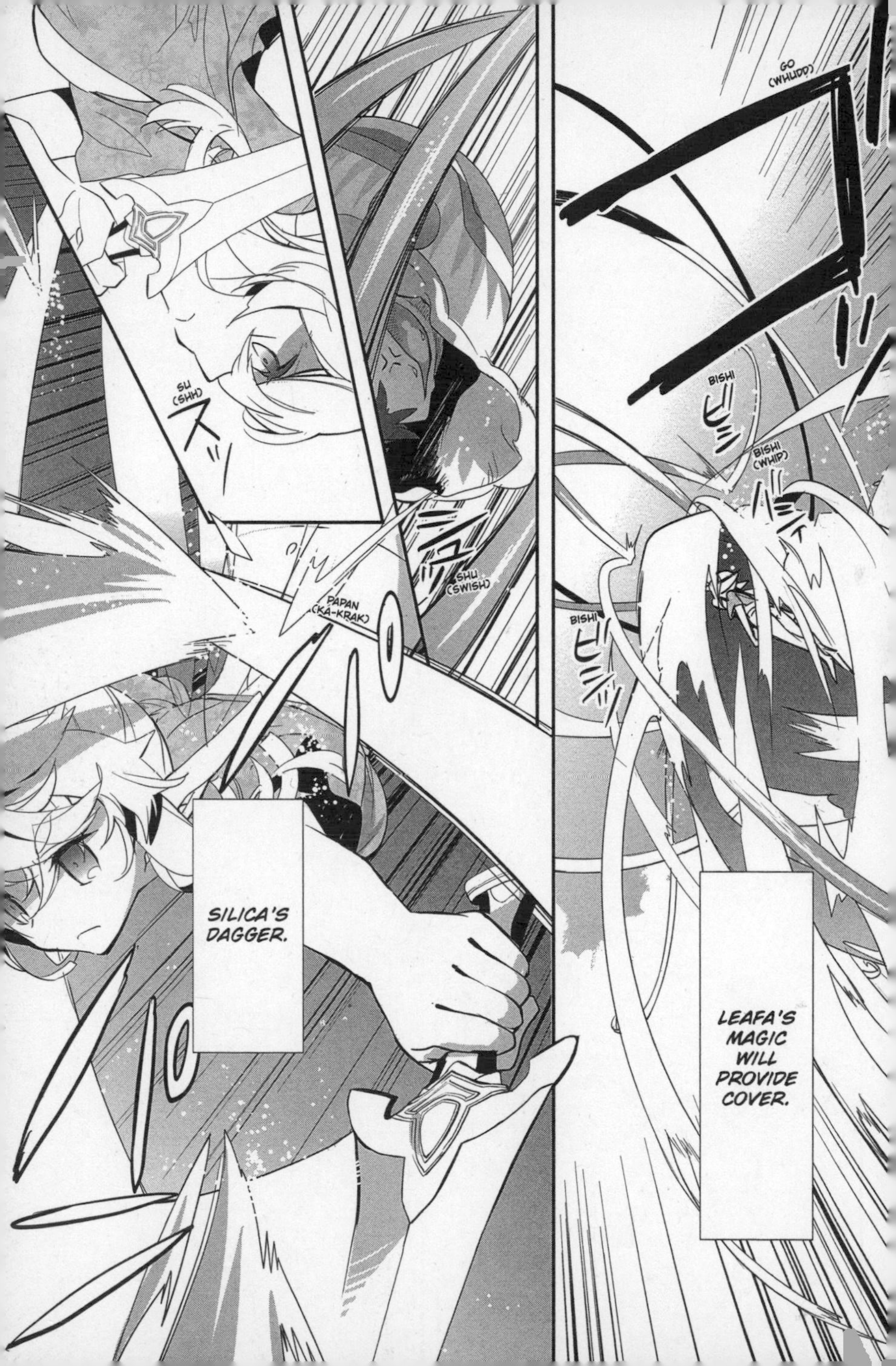
GO (WHUDD)
BISHI
BISHI (WHIP)
BISHI
LEAFA'S MAGIC WILL PROVIDE COVER.
SU (SHH)
SHU (SWISH)
PAPAN (KA-KRAK)
SILICA'S DAGGER.

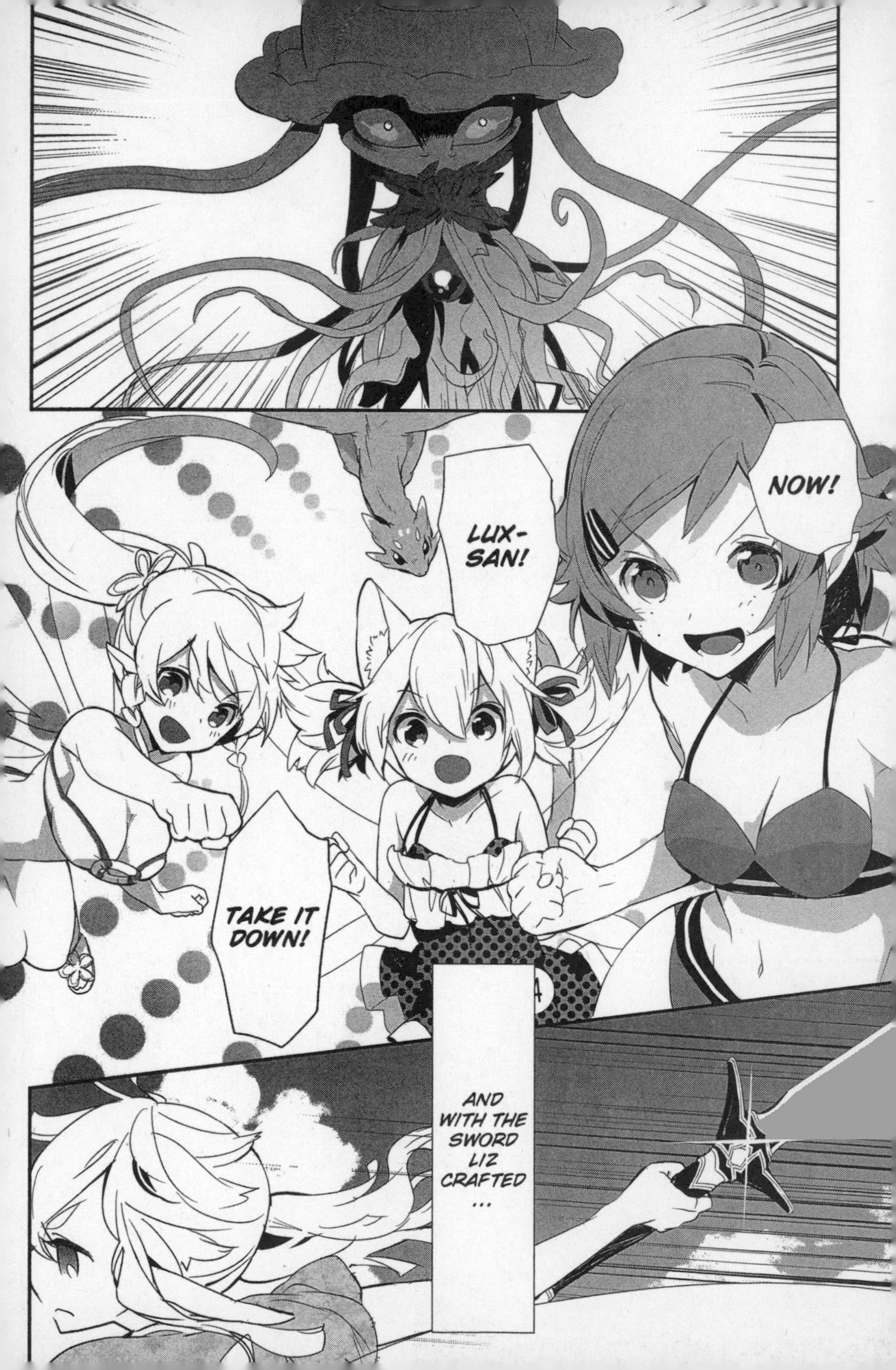
NOW!
LUX-SAN!
TAKE IT DOWN!
AND WITH THE SWORD LIZ CRAFTED...

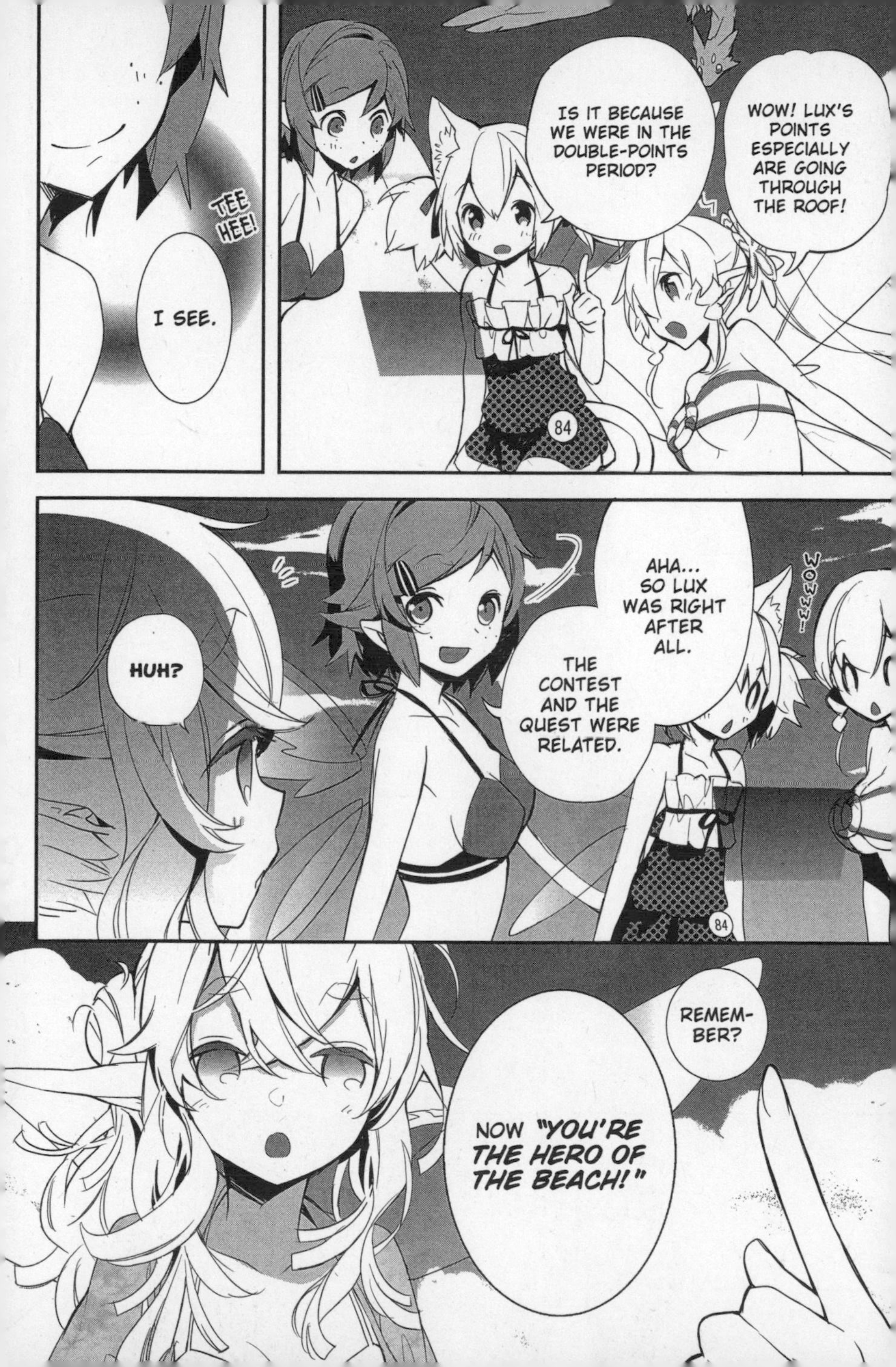
WOW! LUX'S POINTS ESPECIALLY ARE GOING THROUGH THE ROOF!
IS IT BECAUSE WE WERE IN THE DOUBLE-POINTS PERIOD?
84
TEE HEE!
I SEE.
WOWWW!
AHA... SO LUX WAS RIGHT AFTER ALL.
THE CONTEST AND THE QUEST WERE RELATED.
84
HUH?
REMEMBER?
NOW "YOU'RE THE HERO OF THE BEACH!"

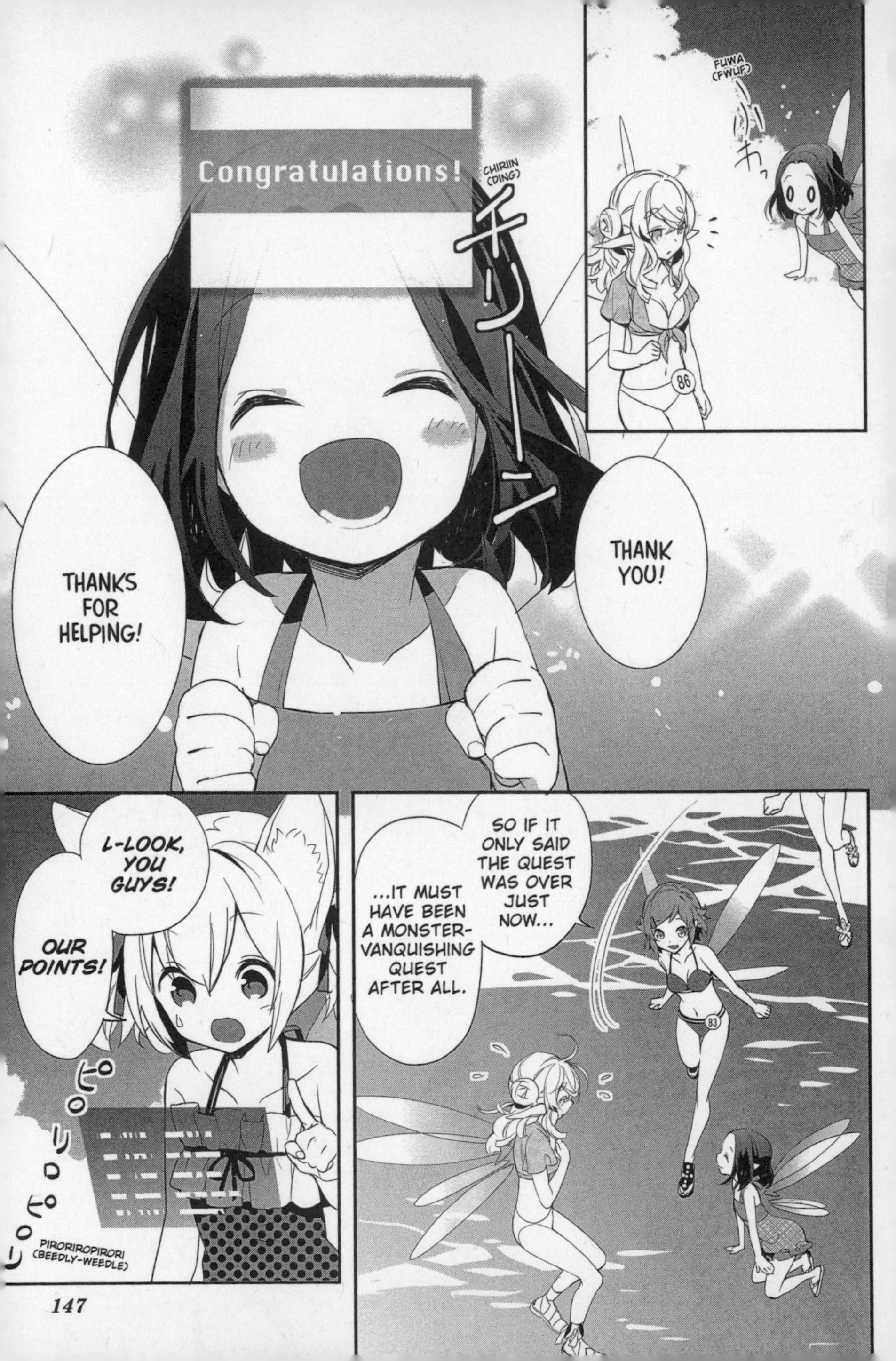
FUWA (FWUF)
Congratulations!
CHIRIIN (DING)
THANK YOU!
THANKS FOR HELPING!
SO IF IT ONLY SAID THE QUEST WAS OVER JUST NOW...
...IT MUST HAVE BEEN A MONSTER-VANQUISHING QUEST AFTER ALL.
L-LOOK, YOU GUYS!
OUR POINTS!
PIRORIROPIRORI (BEEDLY-WEEDLE)

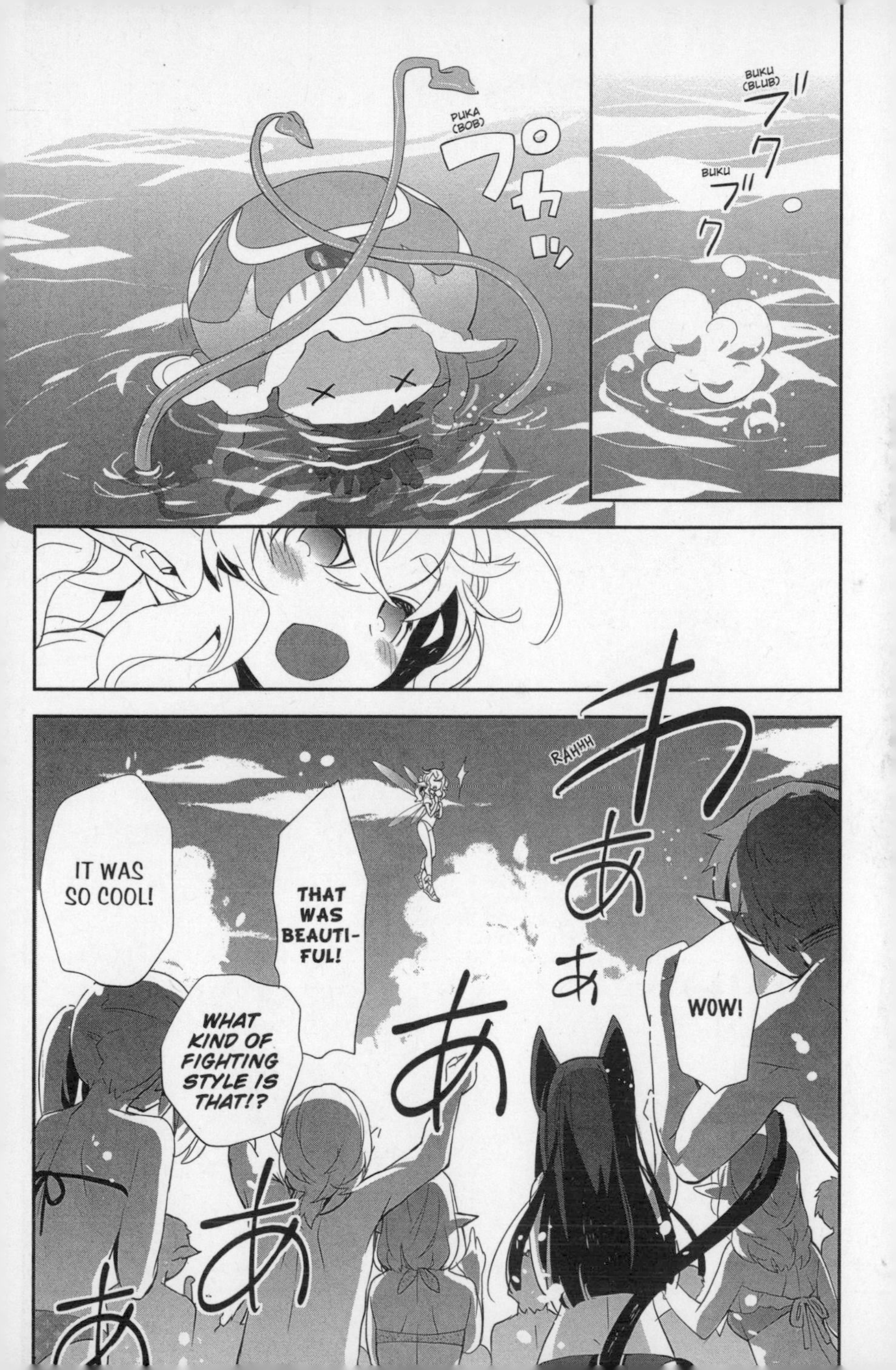
BUKU (BLUB)
ブク
BUKU
ブク
PUKA (BOB)
プカッ
RAHHH
わあああ
WOW!
THAT WAS BEAUTI- FUL!
IT WAS SO COOL!
WHAT KIND OF FIGHTING STYLE IS THAT!?

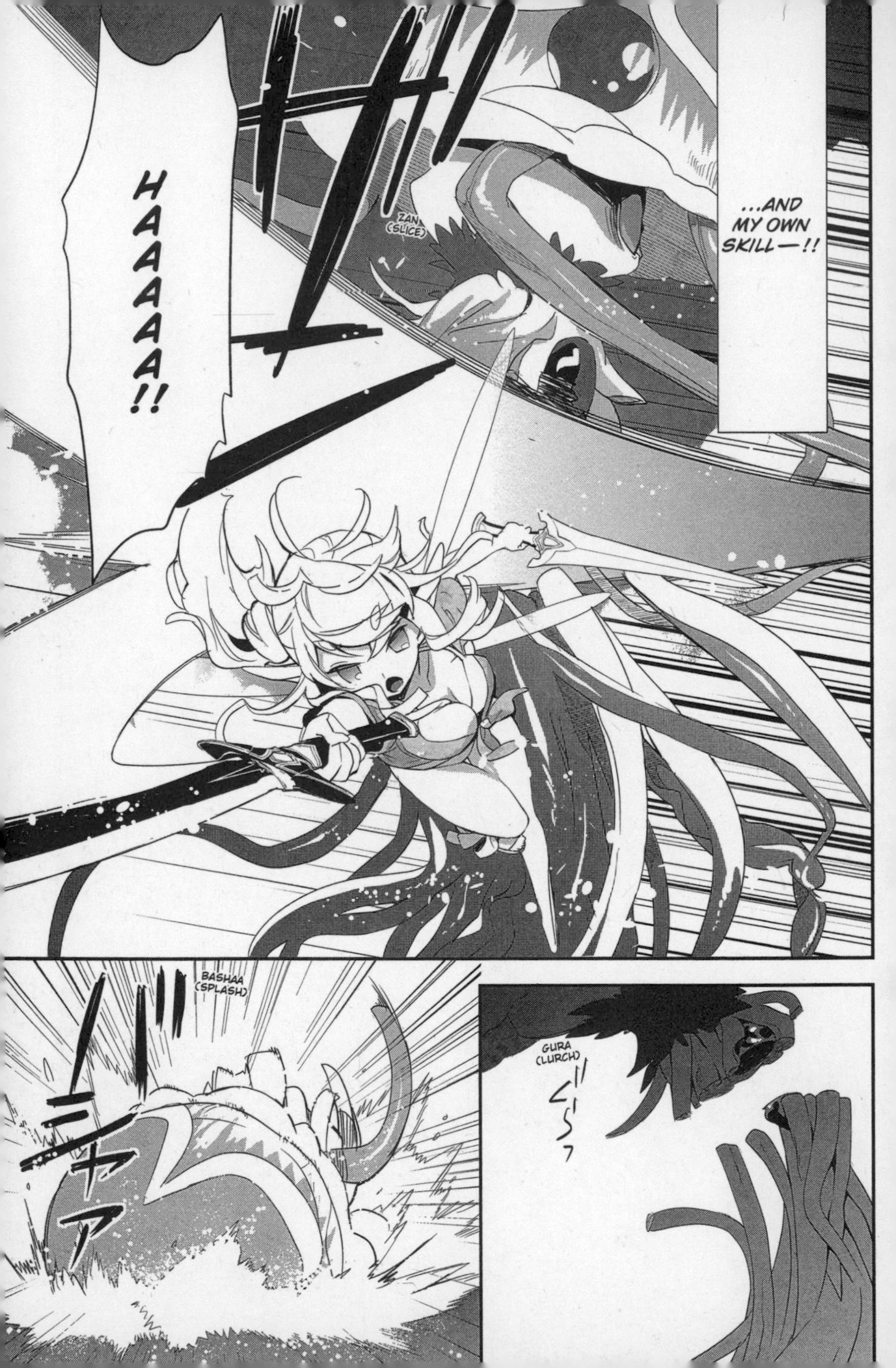
...AND MY OWN SKILL—!!
ZAN (SLICE)
HAAAAAA!!
GURA (LURCH)
BASHAA (SPLASH)

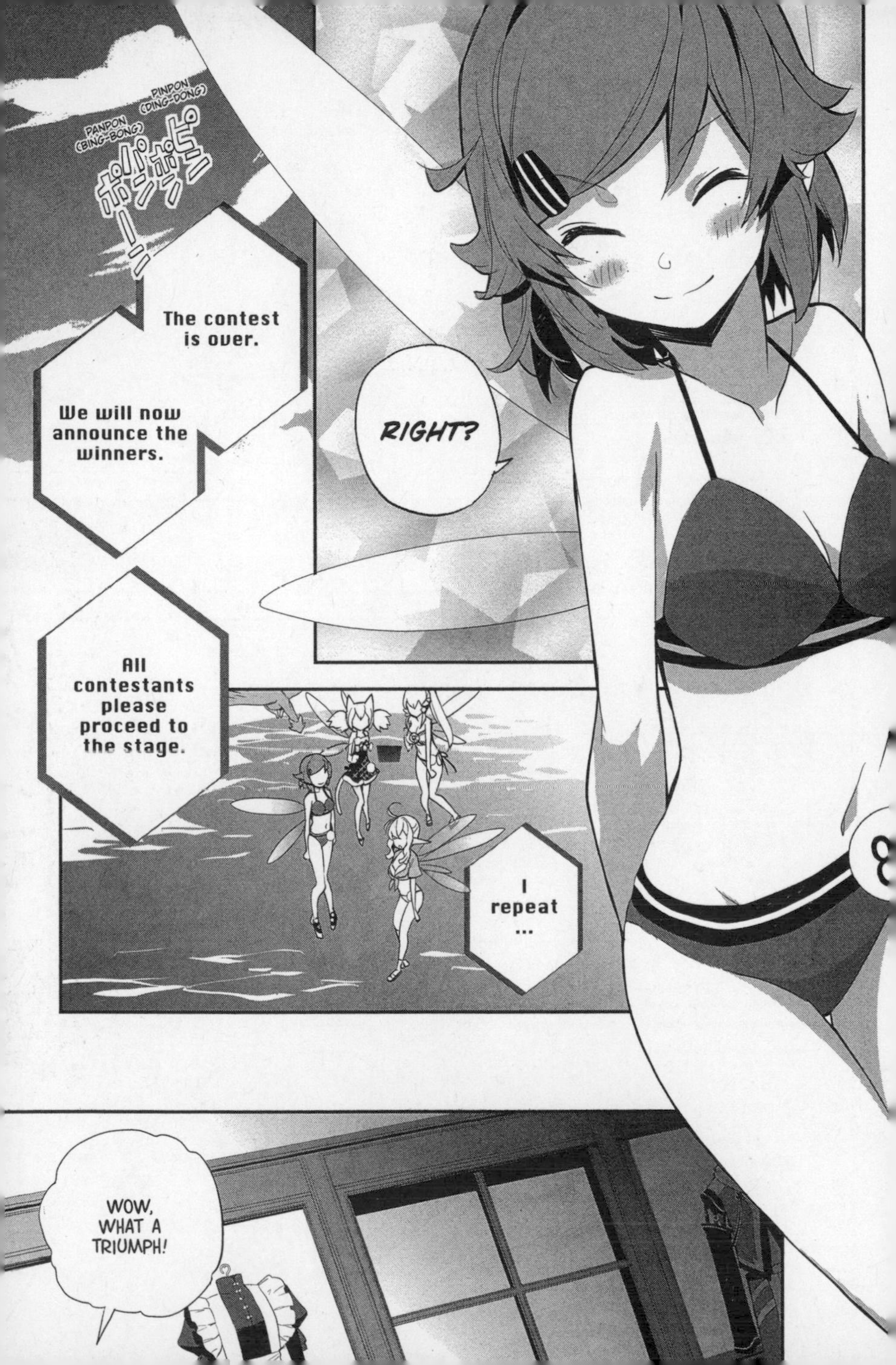
RIGHT?
PANPON (BING-BONG)
PINPON (DING-DONG)
The contest is over.
We will now announce the winners.
All contestants please proceed to the stage.
I repeat ...
WOW, WHAT A TRIUMPH!

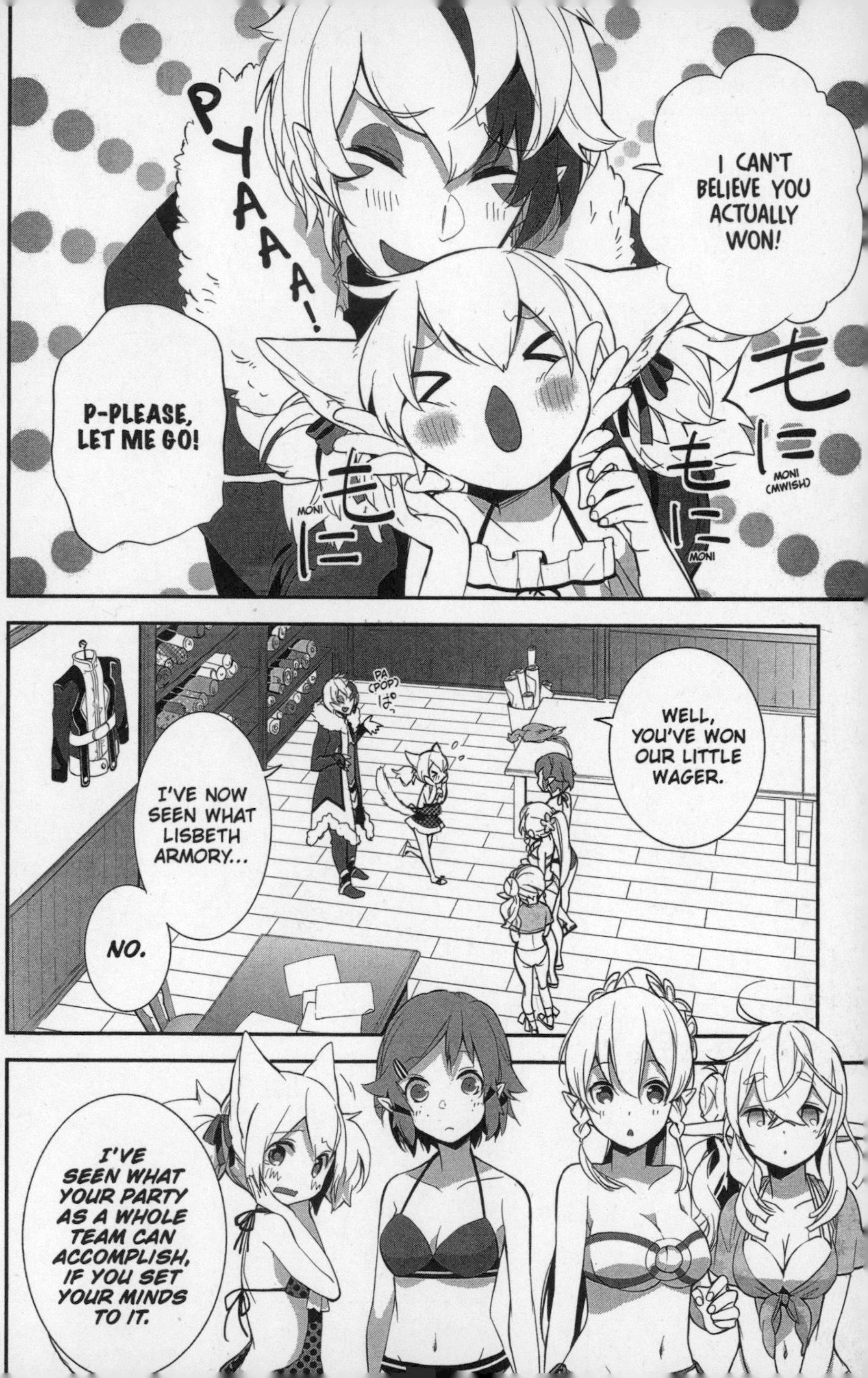
I CAN'T BELIEVE YOU ACTUALLY WON!
PYAAA!
もに
MONI (MWISH)
もに
MONI
もに
MONI
P-PLEASE, LET ME GO!
WELL, YOU'VE WON OUR LITTLE WAGER.
PA (POP)
ぱっ
I'VE NOW SEEN WHAT LISBETH ARMORY...
NO.
I'VE SEEN WHAT YOUR PARTY AS A WHOLE TEAM CAN ACCOMPLISH, IF YOU SET YOUR MINDS TO IT.

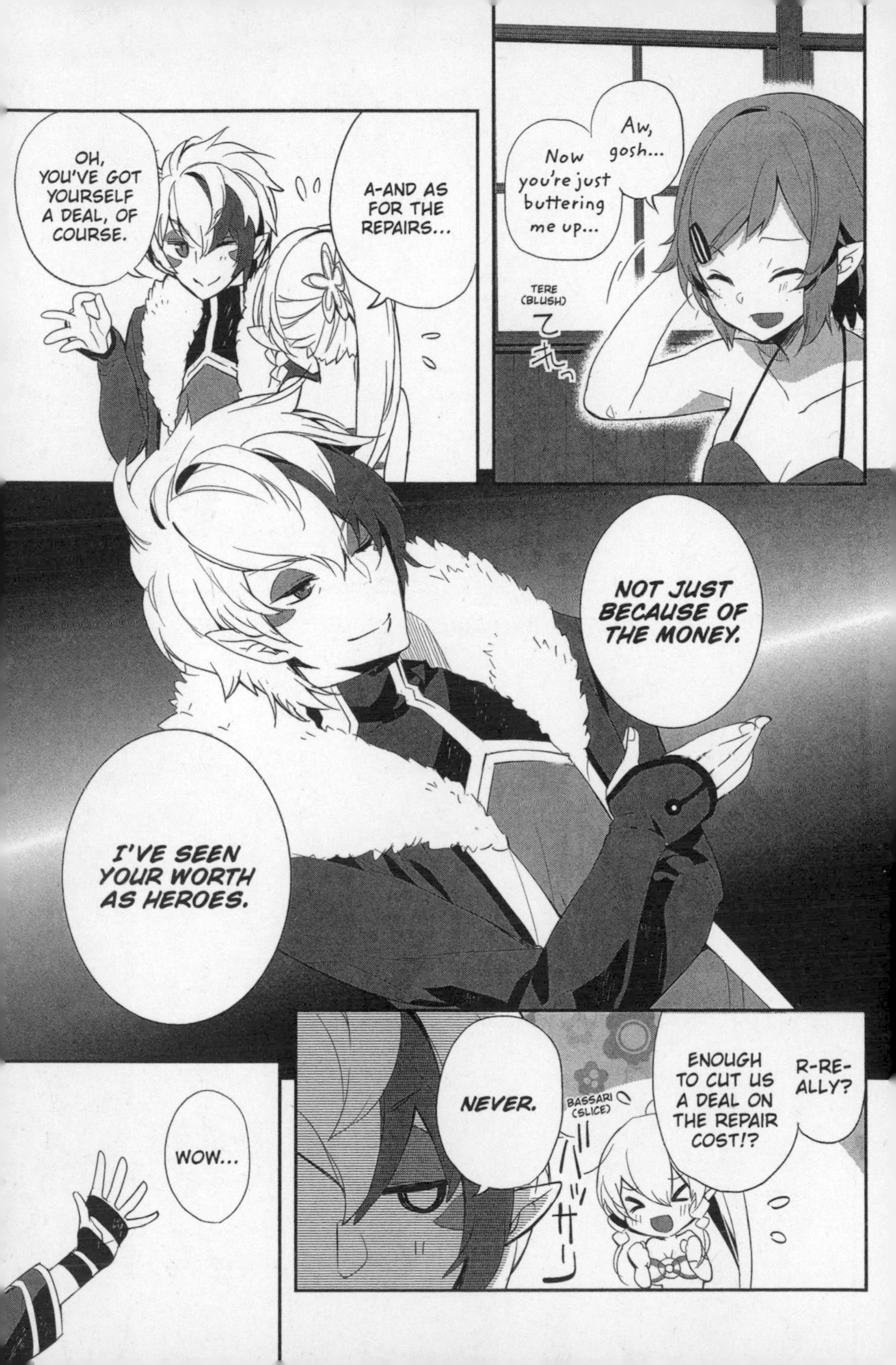
Aw, gosh... Now you're just buttering me up...
TERE (BLUSH)
A-AND AS FOR THE REPAIRS...
OH, YOU'VE GOT YOURSELF A DEAL, OF COURSE.
NOT JUST BECAUSE OF THE MONEY.
I'VE SEEN YOUR WORTH AS HEROES.
R-REALLY?
ENOUGH TO CUT US A DEAL ON THE REPAIR COST!?
NEVER.
BASSARI (SLICE)
WOW...

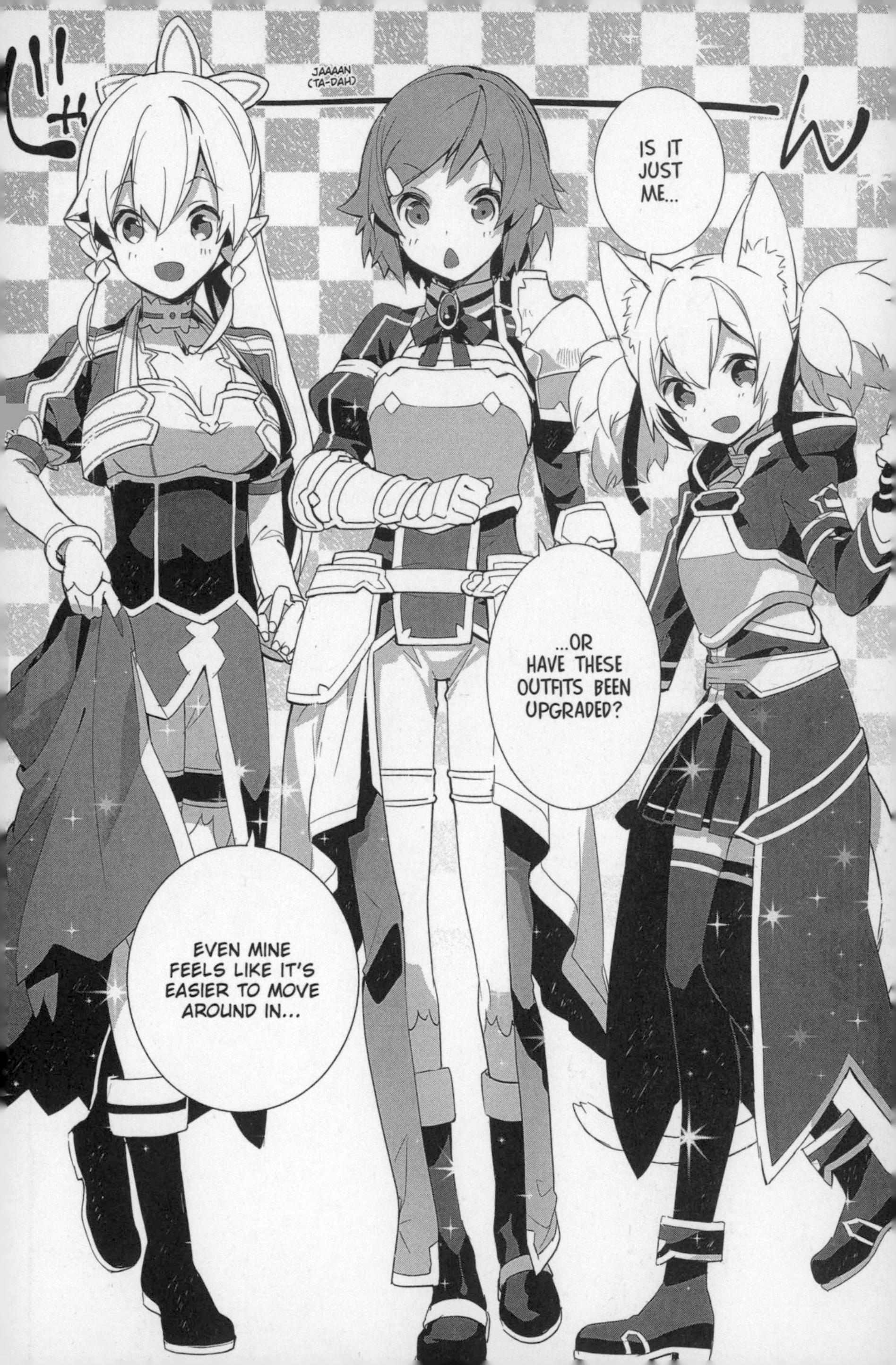
JAAAAN (TA-DAH)
IS IT JUST ME...
...OR HAVE THESE OUTFITS BEEN UPGRADED?
EVEN MINE FEELS LIKE IT'S EASIER TO MOVE AROUND IN...

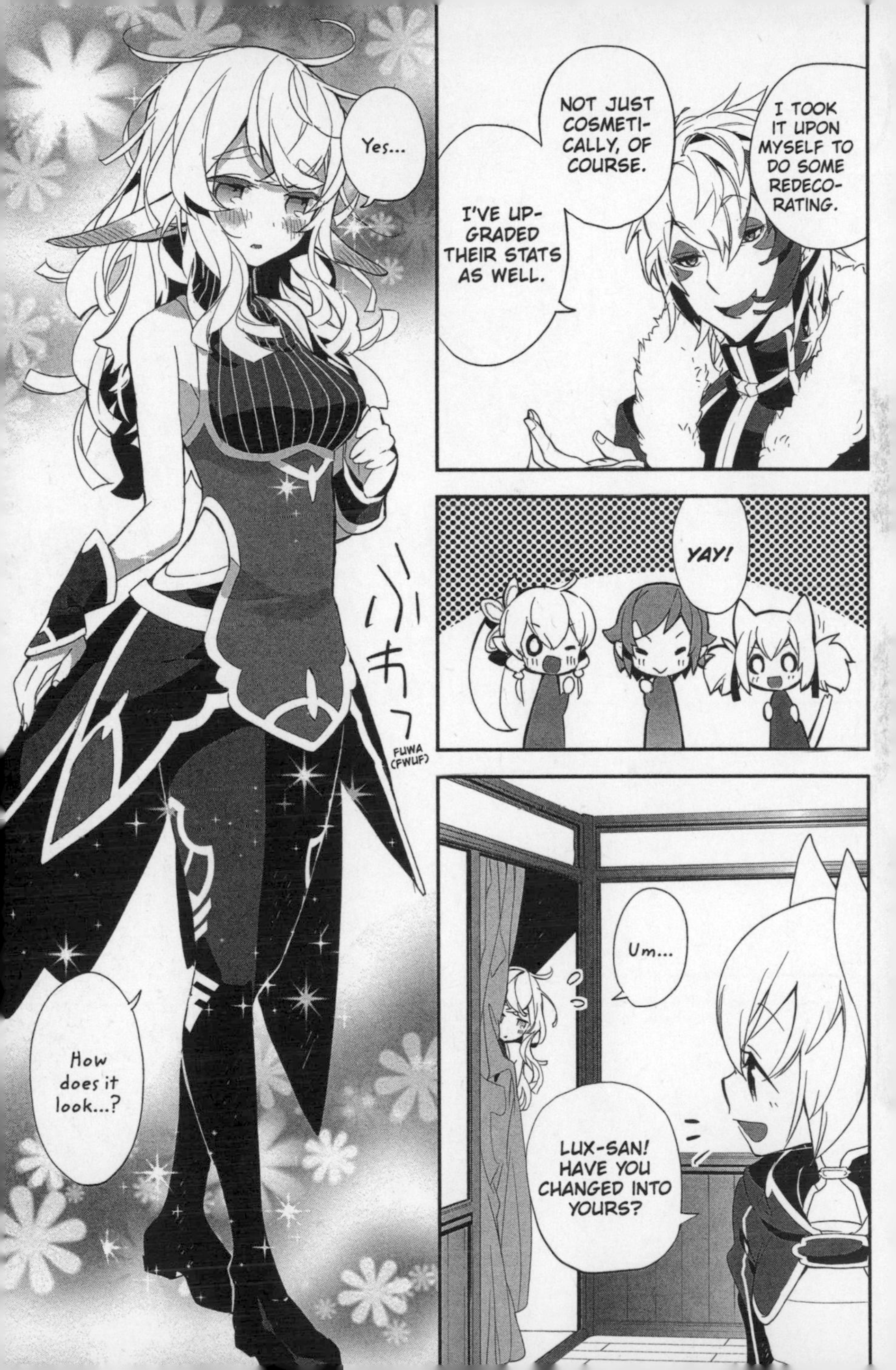

I TOOK IT UPON MYSELF TO DO SOME REDECO-RATING.
NOT JUST COSMETI-CALLY, OF COURSE.
I'VE UP-GRADED THEIR STATS AS WELL.
YAY!
LUX-SAN! HAVE YOU CHANGED INTO YOURS?
Um...
Yes...
How does it look...?
FUWA (FWUF)

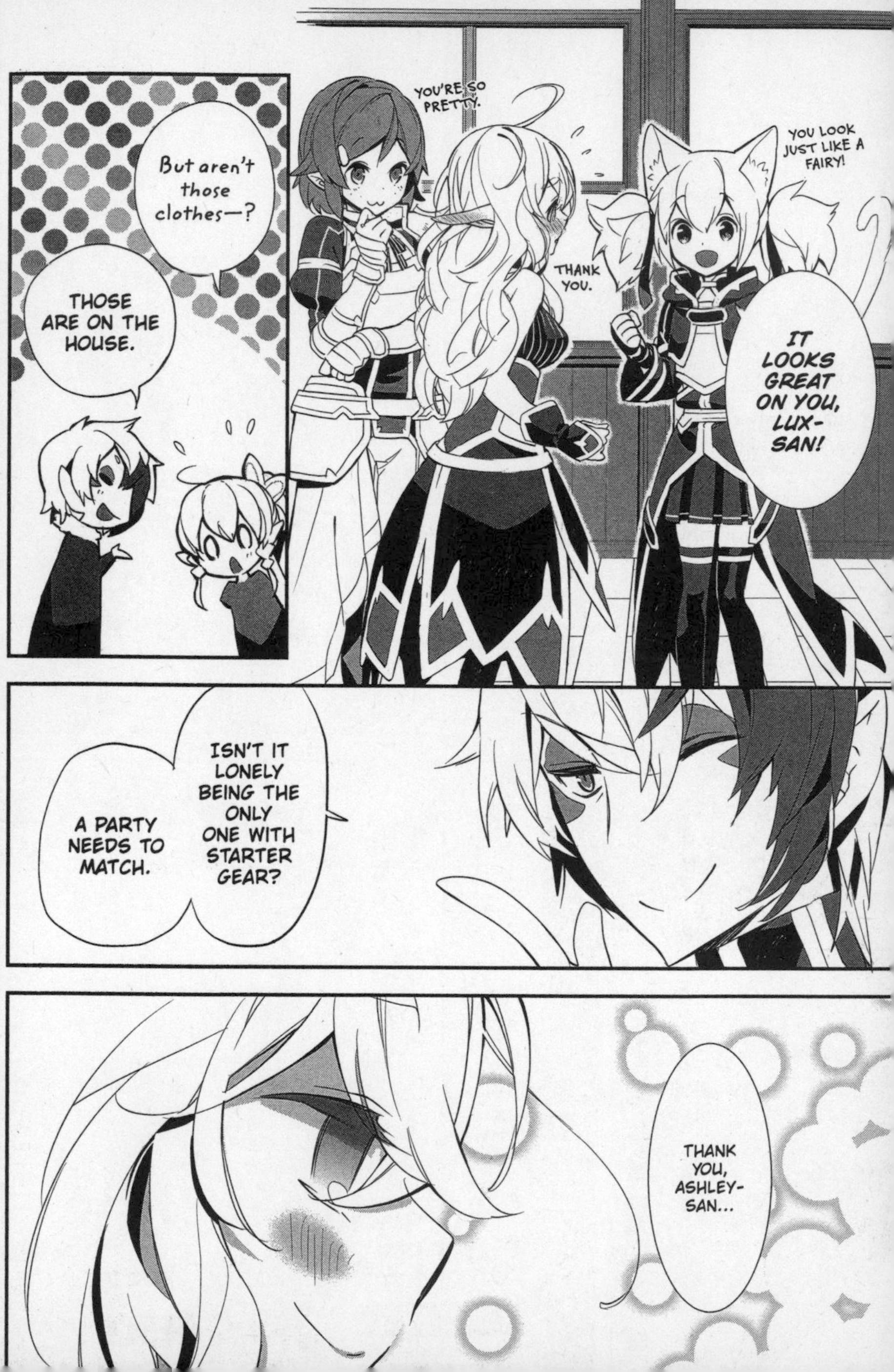
YOU LOOK JUST LIKE A FAIRY!
IT LOOKS GREAT ON YOU, LUX-SAN!
YOU'RE SO PRETTY.
THANK YOU.
But aren't those clothes—?
THOSE ARE ON THE HOUSE.
ISN'T IT LONELY BEING THE ONLY ONE WITH STARTER GEAR?
A PARTY NEEDS TO MATCH.
THANK YOU, ASHLEY-SAN...

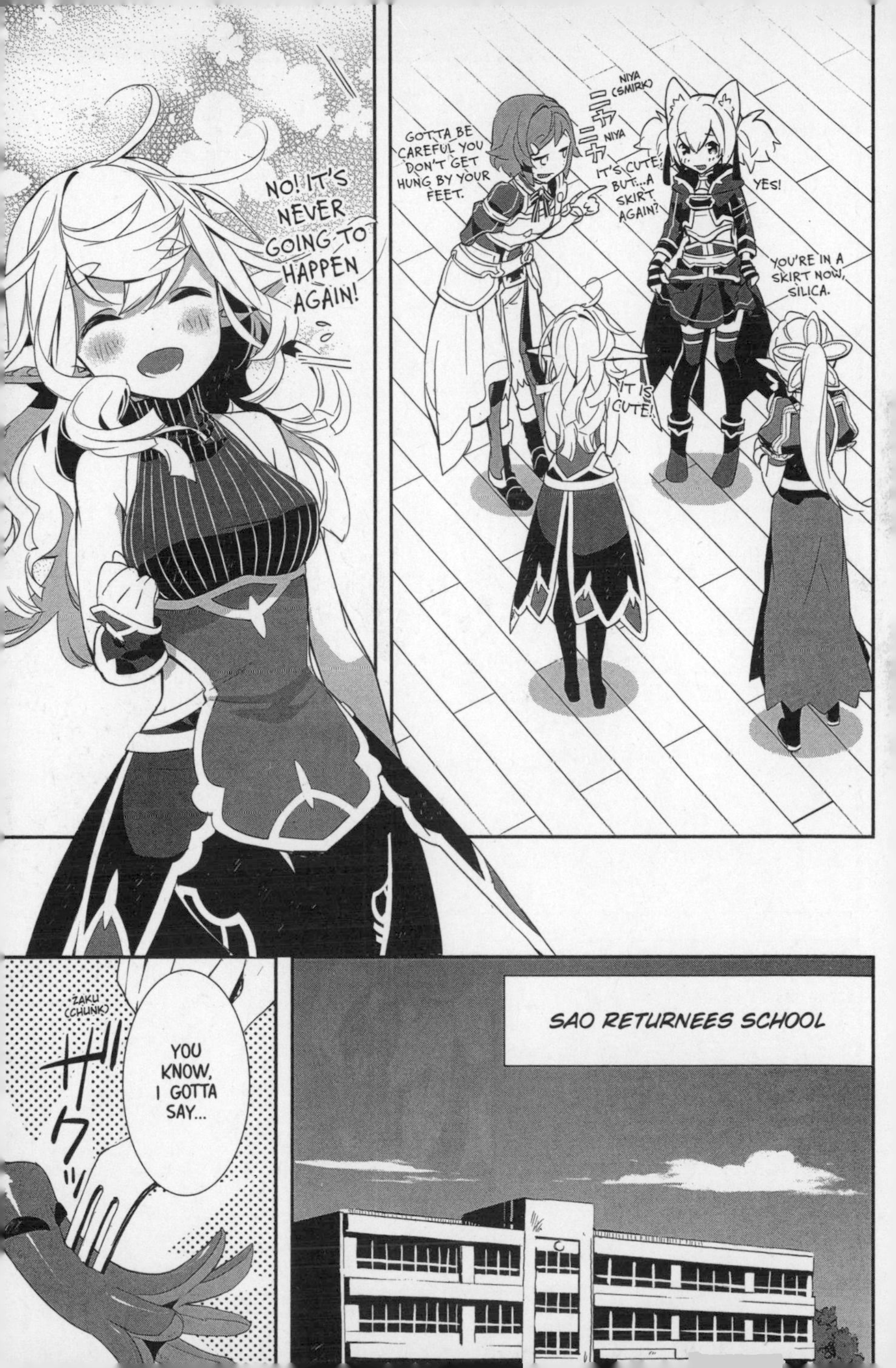

YOU'RE IN A SKIRT NOW, SILICA.
YES!
IT'S CUTE! BUT...A SKIRT AGAIN?
NIYA (SMIRK)
NIYA
GOTTA BE CAREFUL YOU DON'T GET HUNG BY YOUR FEET.
IT IS CUTE!
NO! IT'S NEVER GOING TO HAPPEN AGAIN!
SAO RETURNEES SCHOOL
ZAKU (CHUNK)
YOU KNOW, I GOTTA SAY...

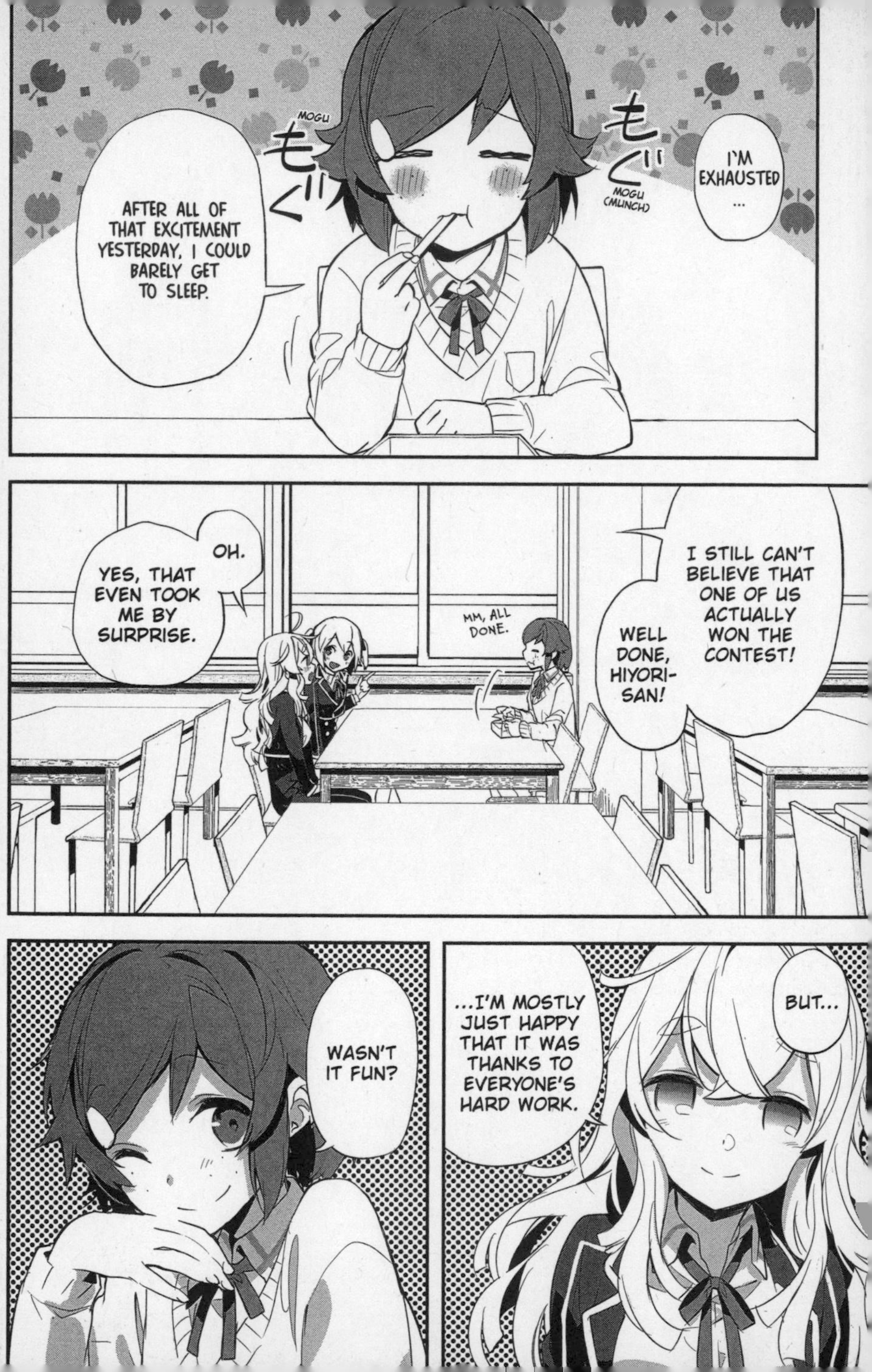
I'M EXHAUSTED ...
もぐ MOGU (MUNCH)
もぐ MOGU
AFTER ALL OF THAT EXCITEMENT YESTERDAY, I COULD BARELY GET TO SLEEP.
I STILL CAN'T BELIEVE THAT ONE OF US ACTUALLY WON THE CONTEST!
WELL DONE, HIYORI-SAN!
MM, ALL DONE.
OH.
YES, THAT EVEN TOOK ME BY SURPRISE.
BUT...
...I'M MOSTLY JUST HAPPY THAT IT WAS THANKS TO EVERYONE'S HARD WORK.
WASN'T IT FUN?

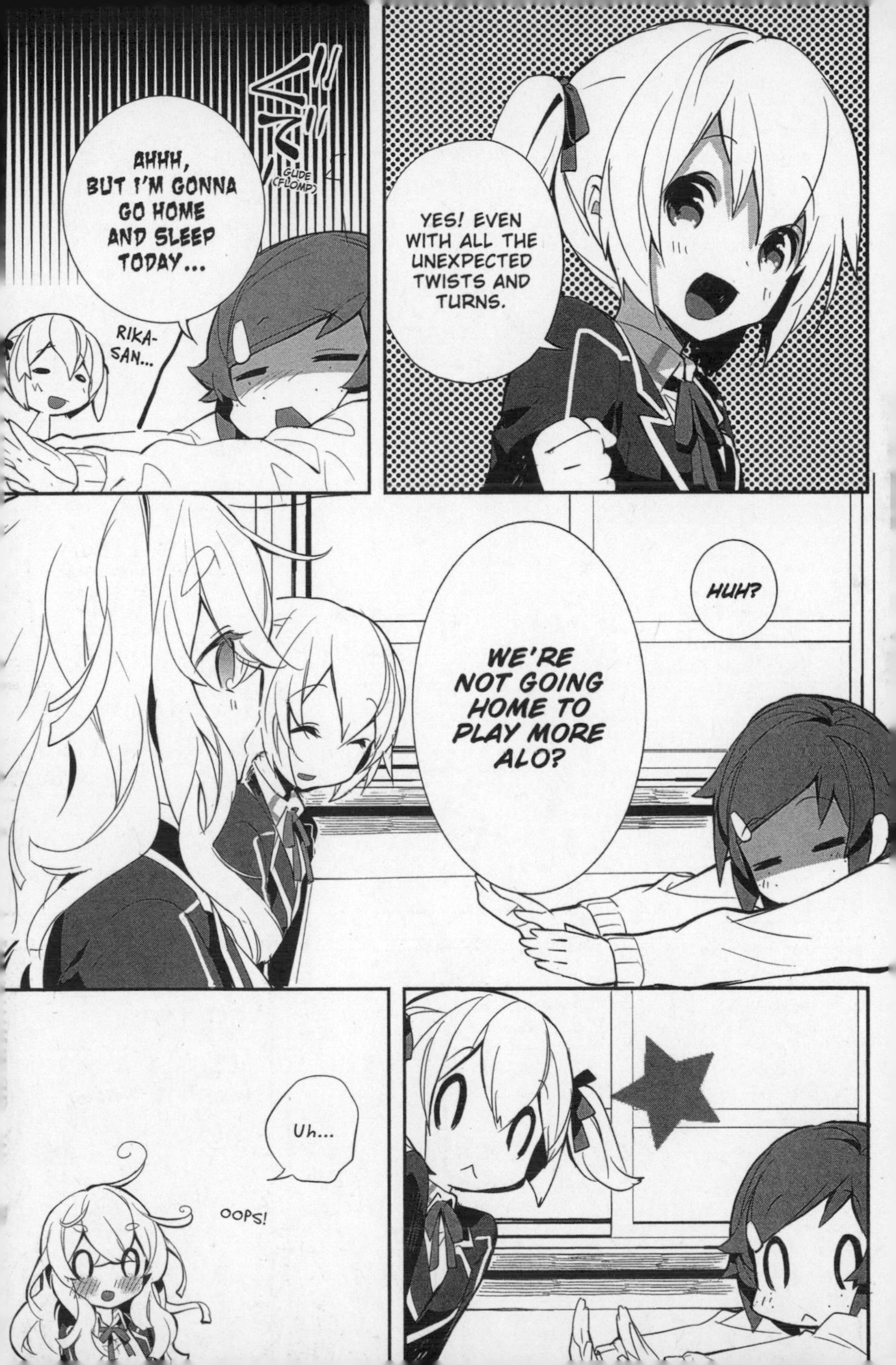
YES! EVEN WITH ALL THE UNEXPECTED TWISTS AND TURNS.
AHHH, BUT I'M GONNA GO HOME AND SLEEP TODAY...
GLIDE (FLOMP)
RIKA-SAN...
HUH?
WE'RE NOT GOING HOME TO PLAY MORE ALO?
Uh...
OOPS!

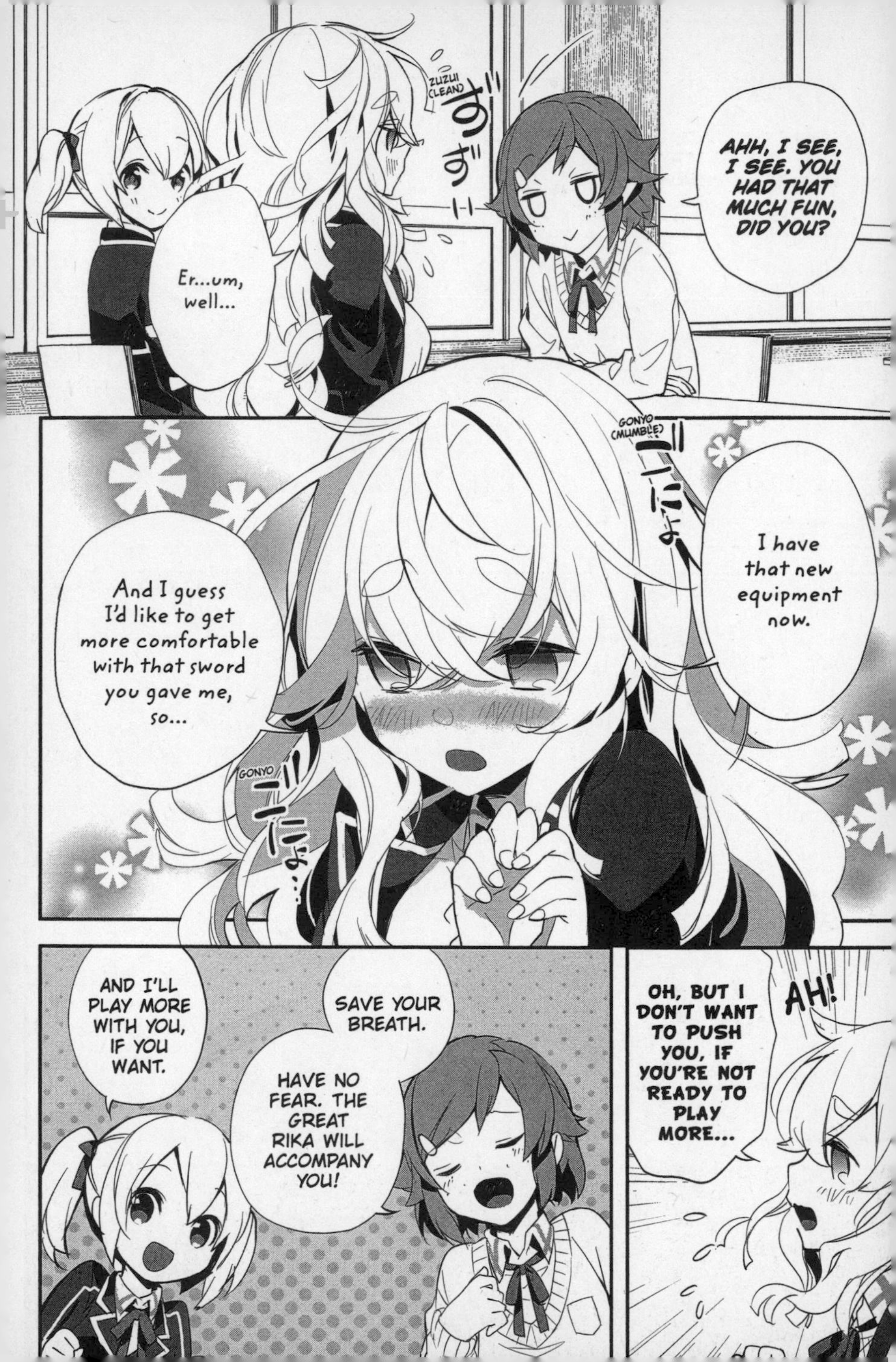
AHH, I SEE, I SEE. YOU HAD THAT MUCH FUN, DID YOU?
ZUZUI (CLEAN)
ずずい
Er...um, well...
GONYO (MUMBLE)
ごにょ
I have that new equipment now.
And I guess I'd like to get more comfortable with that sword you gave me, so...
GONYO
ごにょ...
AH!
OH, BUT I DON'T WANT TO PUSH YOU, IF YOU'RE NOT READY TO PLAY MORE...
SAVE YOUR BREATH.
HAVE NO FEAR. THE GREAT RIKA WILL ACCOMPANY YOU!
AND I'LL PLAY MORE WITH YOU, IF YOU WANT.

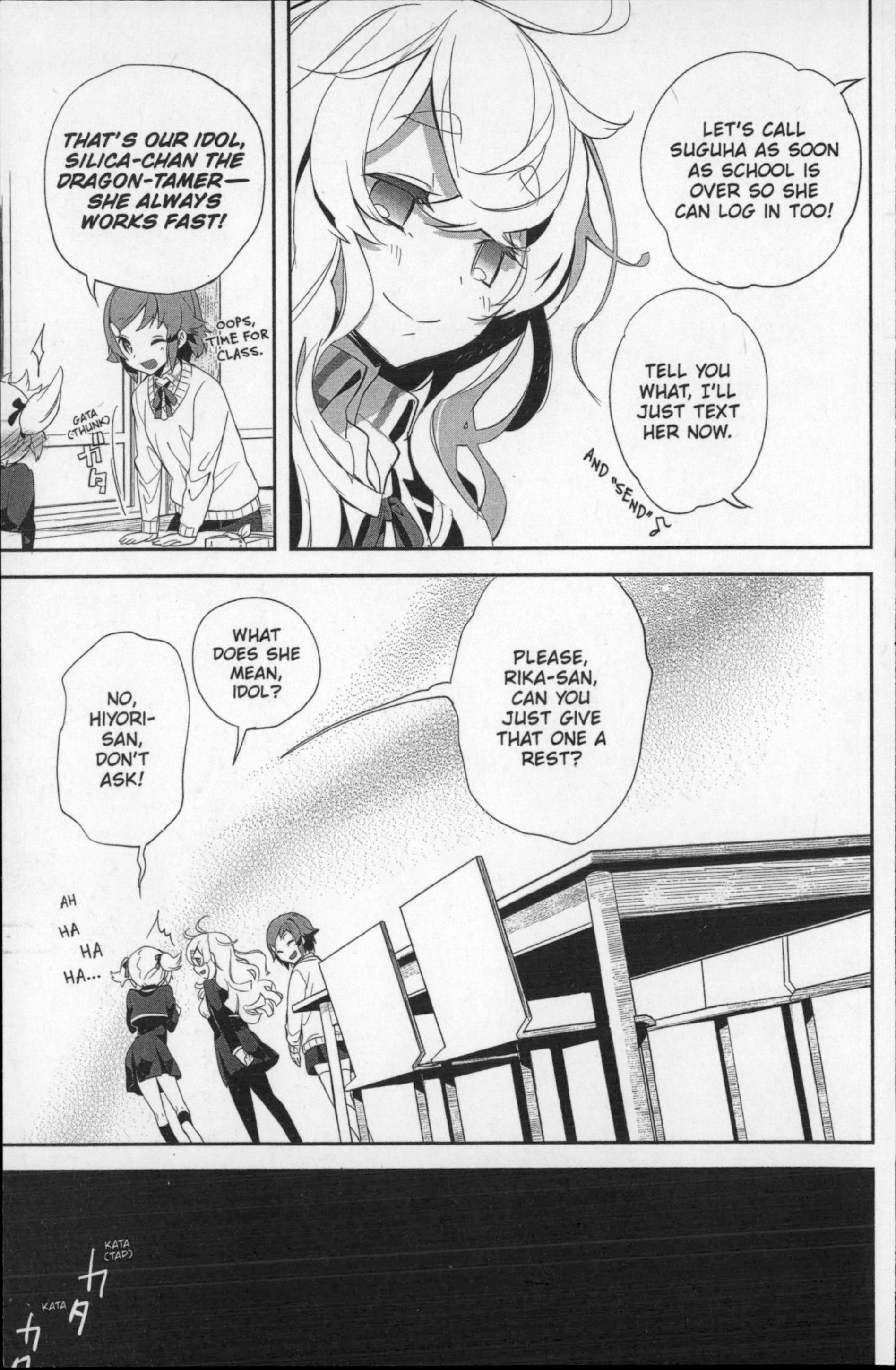
LET'S CALL SUGUHA AS SOON AS SCHOOL IS OVER SO SHE CAN LOG IN TOO!
TELL YOU WHAT, I'LL JUST TEXT HER NOW.
AND "SEND"♪
THAT'S OUR IDOL, SILICA-CHAN THE DRAGON-TAMER—SHE ALWAYS WORKS FAST!
OOPS, TIME FOR CLASS.
GATA (THUNK)
ガタ
PLEASE, RIKA-SAN, CAN YOU JUST GIVE THAT ONE A REST?
WHAT DOES SHE MEAN, IDOL?
NO, HIYORI-SAN, DON'T ASK!
AH HA HA HA...
KATA (TAP)
カタ
KATA
カタ

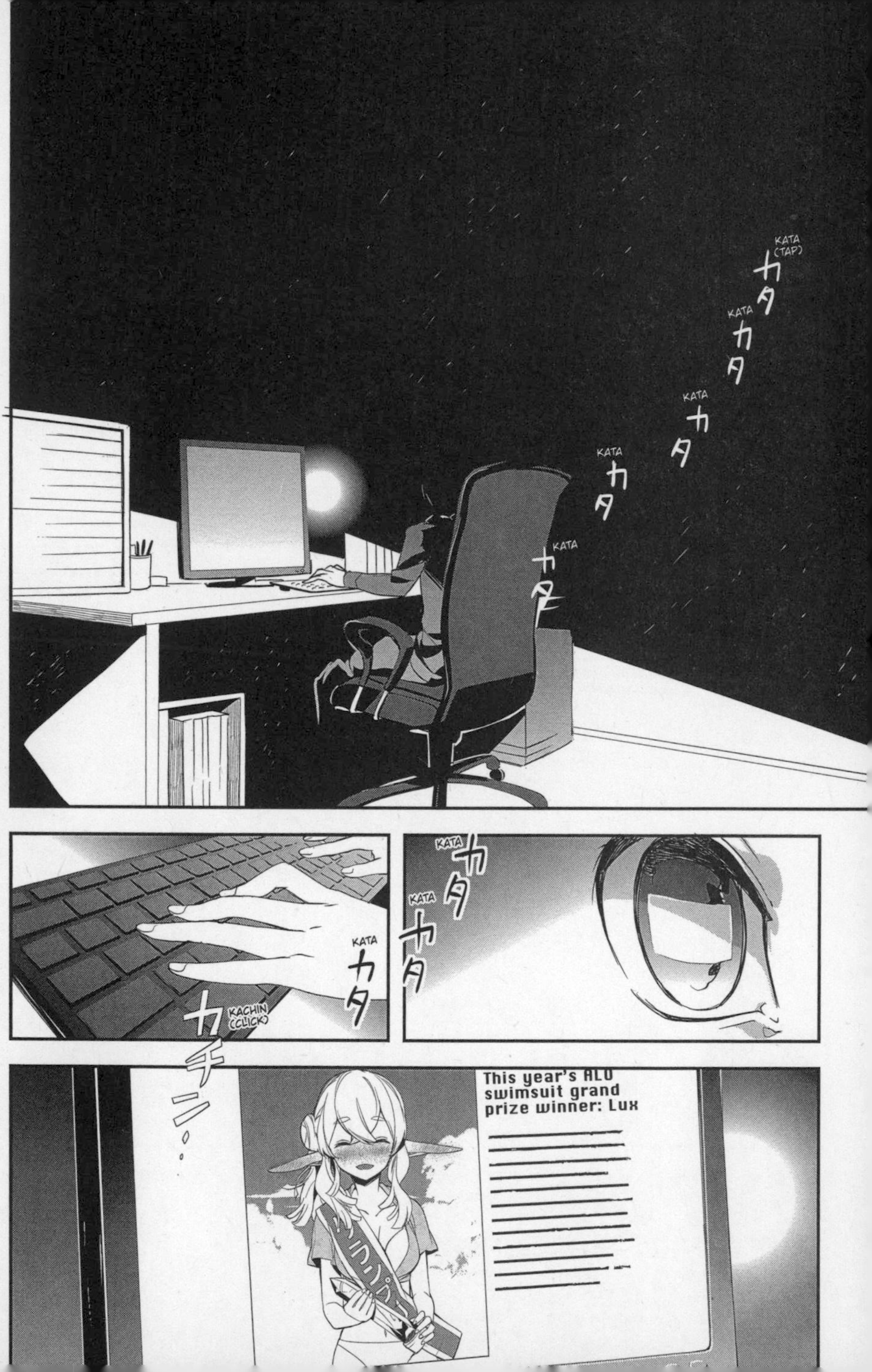

KATA (TAP)
カタ
KATA
カタ
KATA
カタ
KATA
カタ
KATA
カタ
KATA
カタ
KATA
カタ
KATA
カタ
KACHIN (CLICK)
カチン。
This year's ALO swimsuit grand prize winner: Lux

SWORD ART ONLINE
GIRLS' OPS

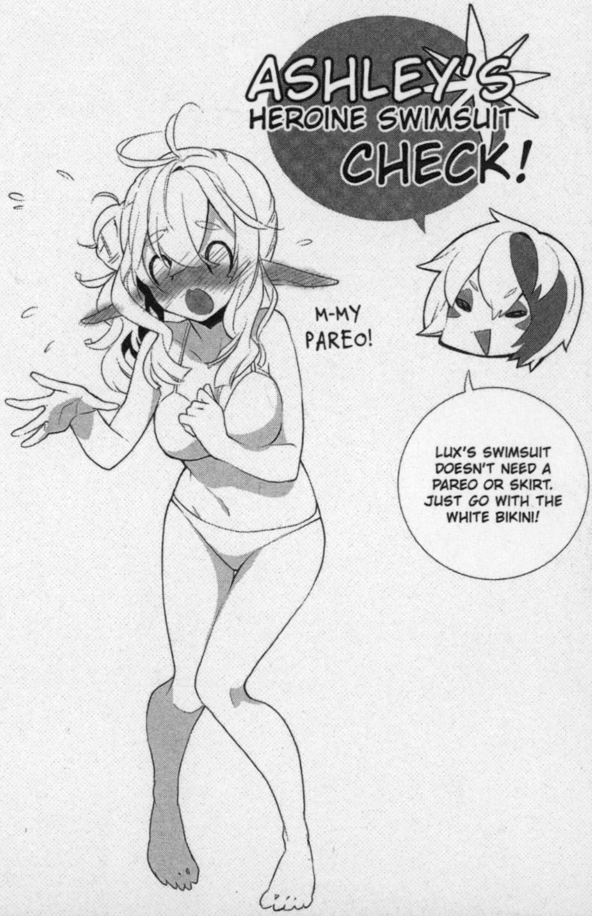
ASHLEY'S HEROINE SWIMSUIT CHECK!
M-MY PAREO!
LUX'S SWIMSUIT DOESN'T NEED A PAREO OR SKIRT. JUST GO WITH THE WHITE BIKINI!

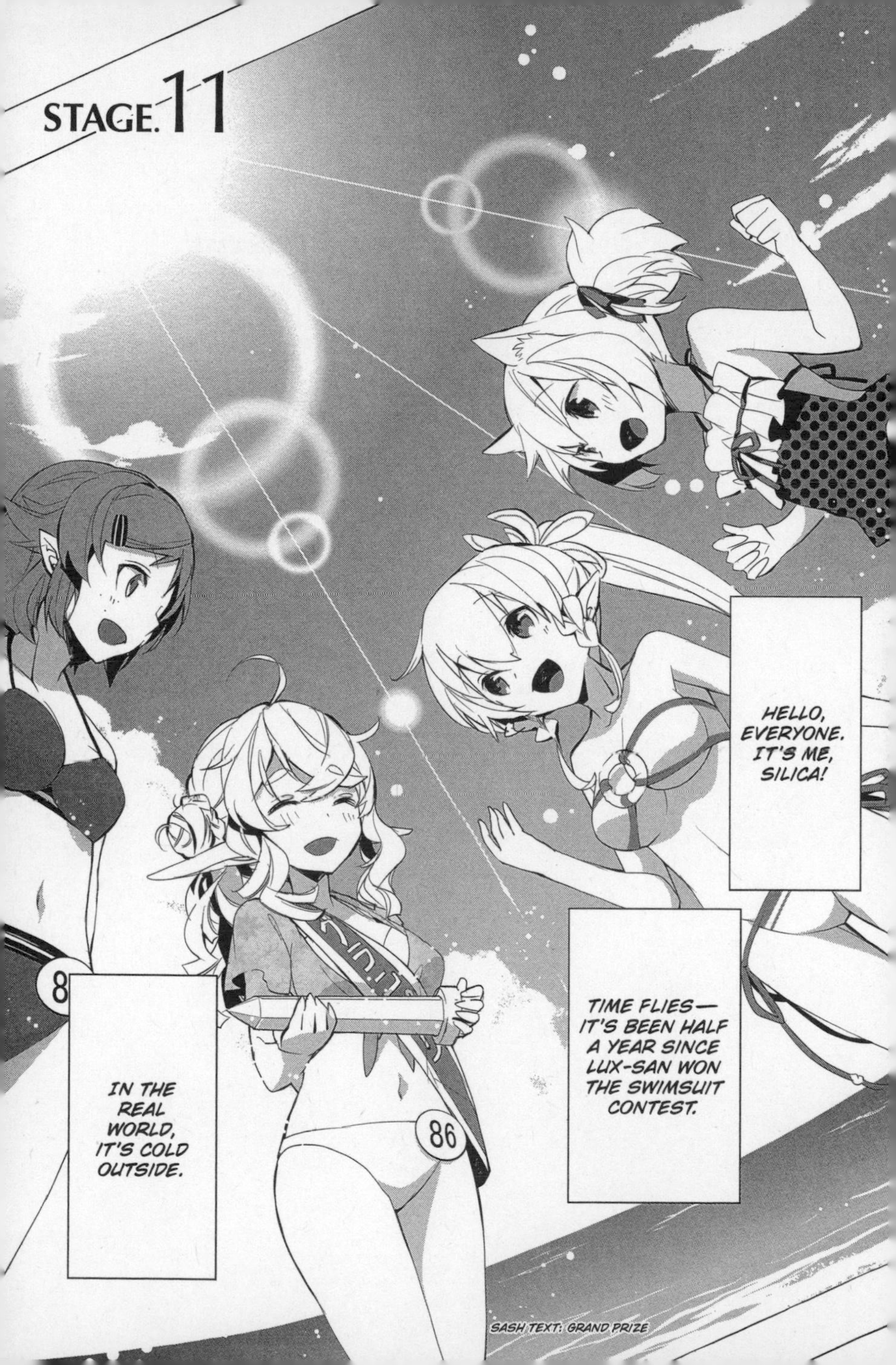
STAGE. 11
HELLO, EVERYONE. IT'S ME, SILICA!
TIME FLIES—IT'S BEEN HALF A YEAR SINCE LUX-SAN WON THE SWIMSUIT CONTEST.
IN THE REAL WORLD, IT'S COLD OUTSIDE.
86
SASH TEXT: GRAND PRIZE

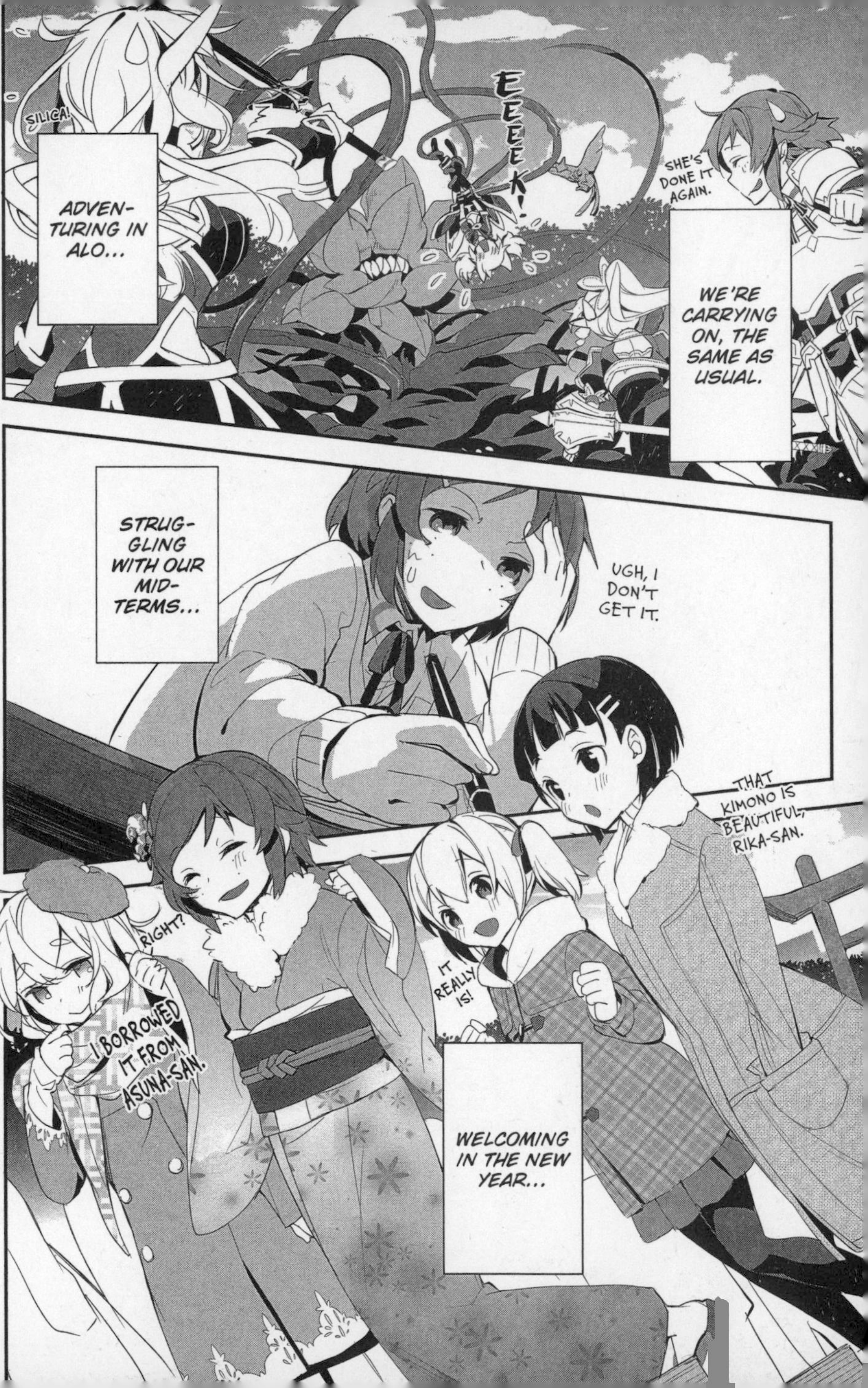
SILICA!
ADVENTURING IN ALO...
EEEEEK!
SHE'S DONE IT AGAIN.
WE'RE CARRYING ON, THE SAME AS USUAL.
STRUGGLING WITH OUR MIDTERMS...
UGH, I DON'T GET IT.
THAT KIMONO IS BEAUTIFUL, RIKA-SAN.
IT REALLY IS!
RIGHT?
I BORROWED IT FROM ASUNA-SAN.
WELCOMING IN THE NEW YEAR...

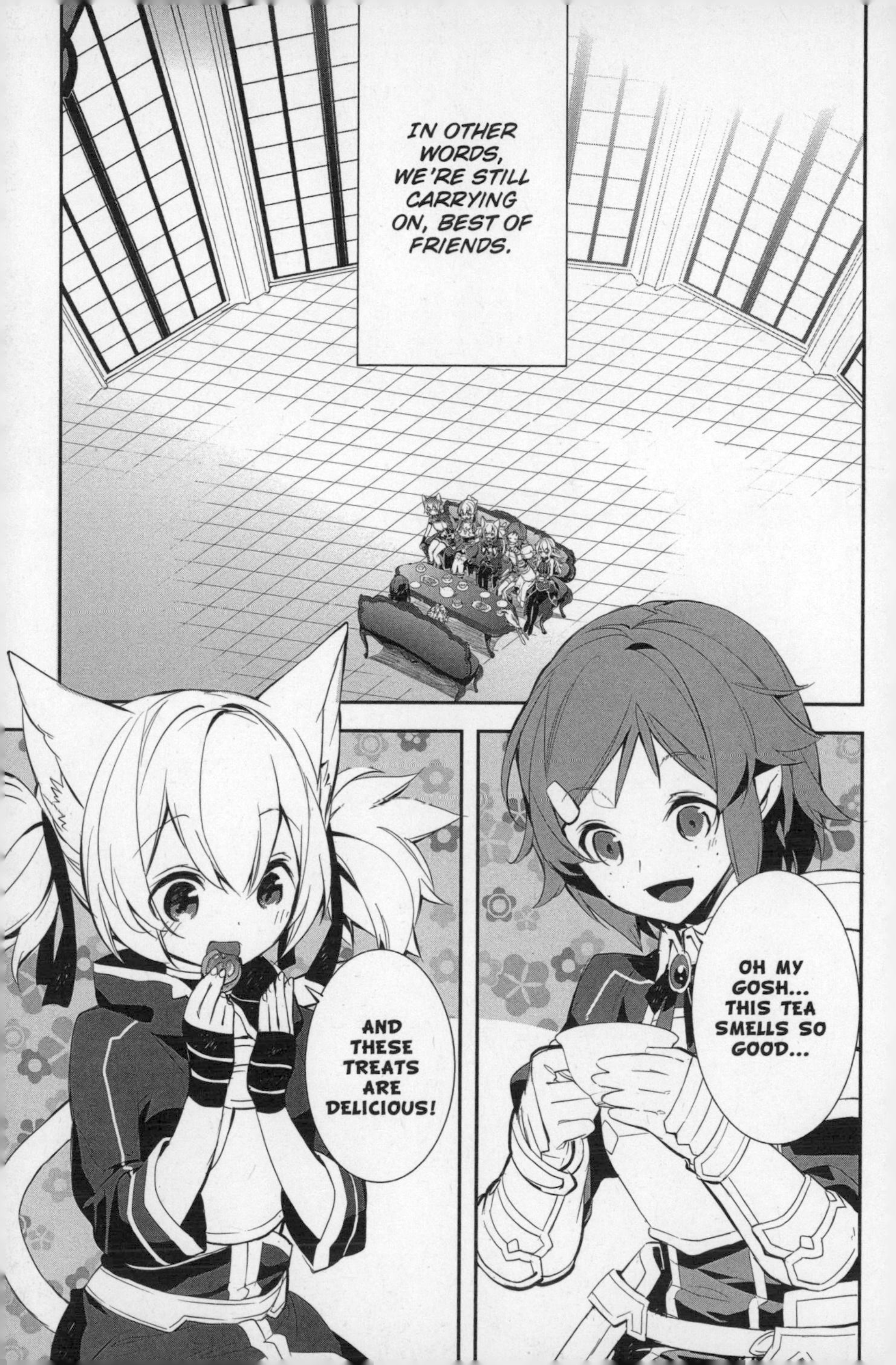
IN OTHER WORDS, WE'RE STILL CARRYING ON, BEST OF FRIENDS.
OH MY GOSH... THIS TEA SMELLS SO GOOD...
AND THESE TREATS ARE DELICIOUS!

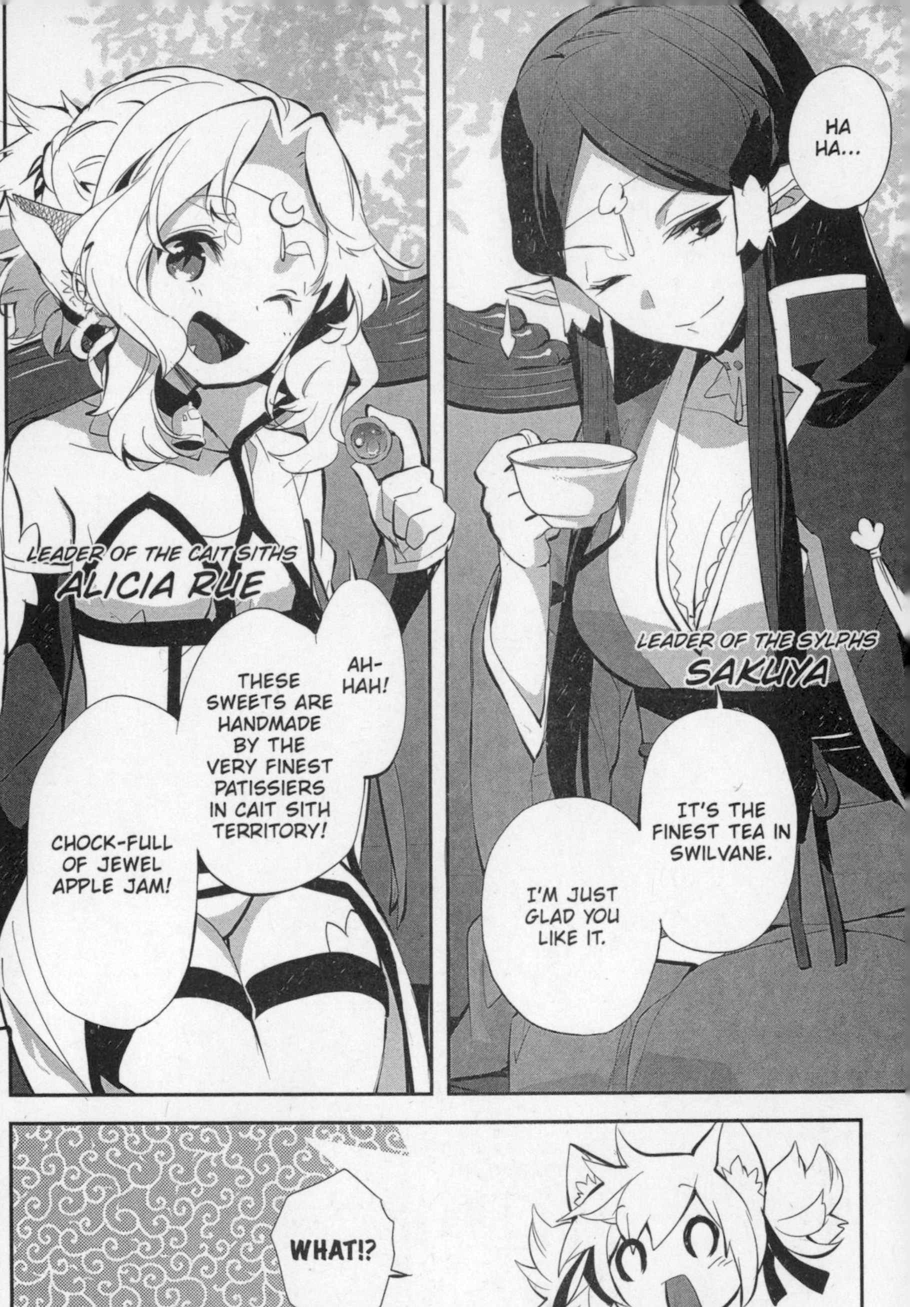
HA HA...
LEADER OF THE SYLPHS
SAKUYA
IT'S THE FINEST TEA IN SWILVANE.
I'M JUST GLAD YOU LIKE IT.
LEADER OF THE CAIT SITHS
ALICIA RUE
AH-HAH!
THESE SWEETS ARE HANDMADE BY THE VERY FINEST PATISSIERS IN CAIT SITH TERRITORY!
CHOCK-FULL OF JEWEL APPLE JAM!
WHAT!?

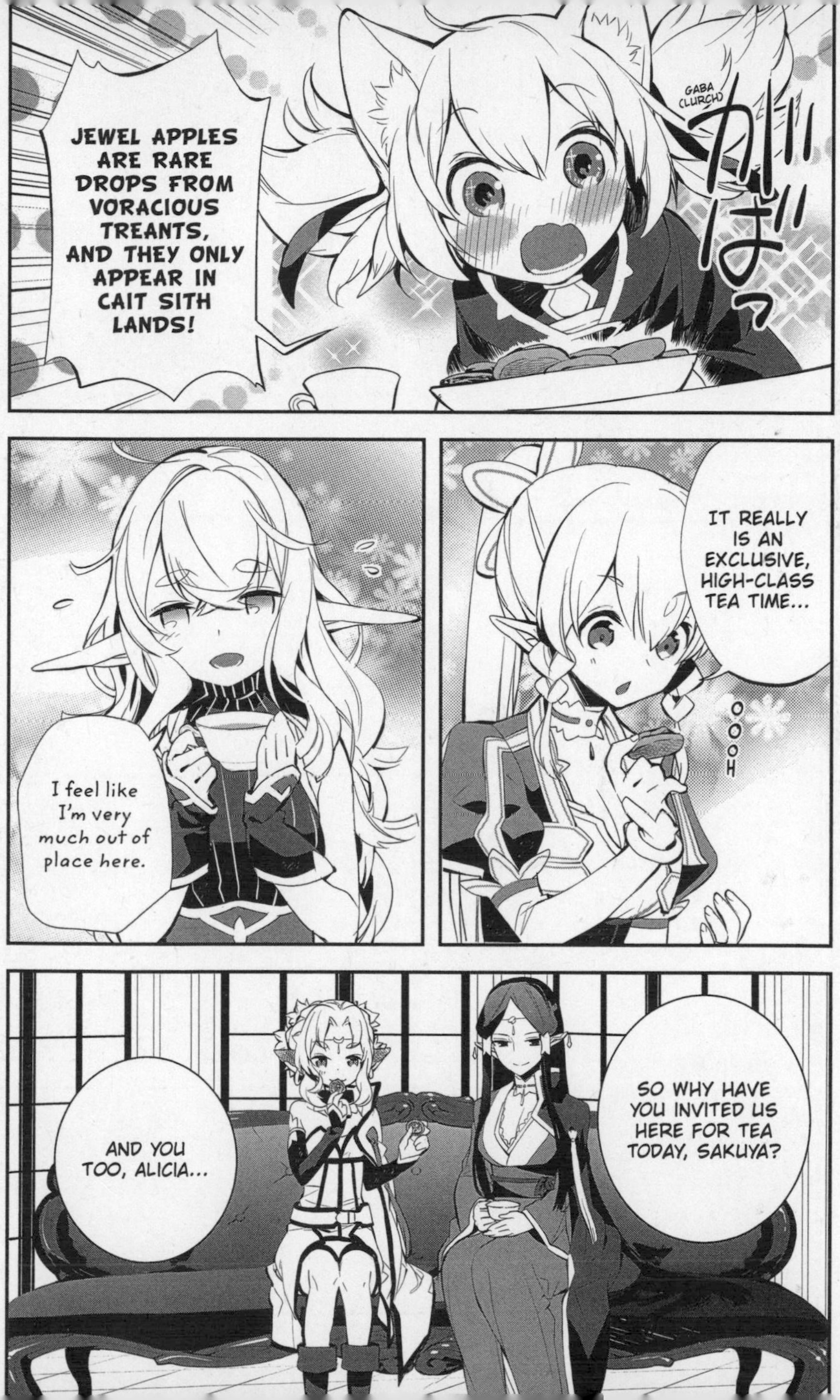
JEWEL APPLES ARE RARE DROPS FROM VORACIOUS TREANTS, AND THEY ONLY APPEAR IN CAIT SITH LANDS!
GABA (LURCH)
がばっ
I feel like I'm very much out of place here.
IT REALLY IS AN EXCLUSIVE, HIGH-CLASS TEA TIME...
OOOOH
AND YOU TOO, ALICIA...
SO WHY HAVE YOU INVITED US HERE FOR TEA TODAY, SAKUYA?

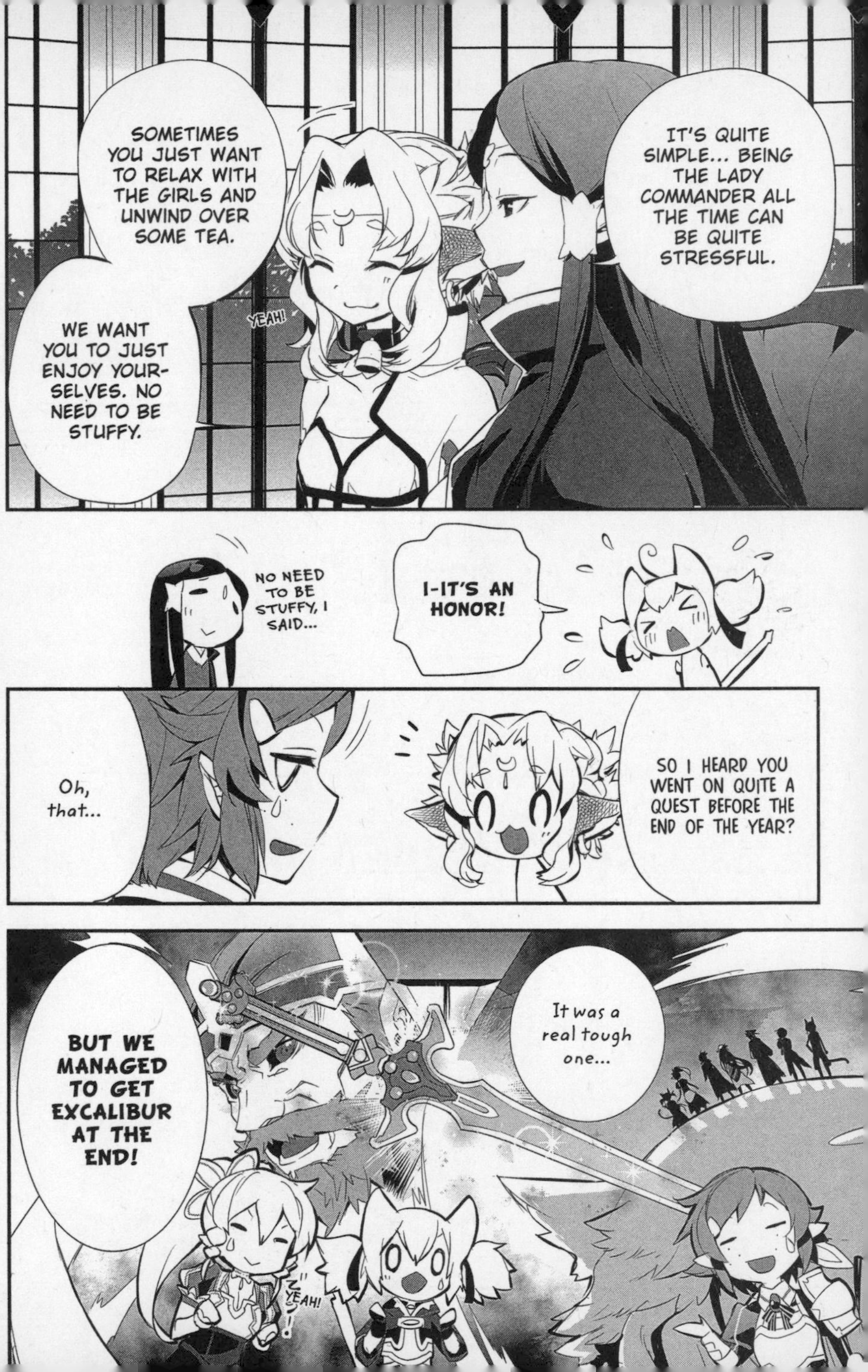
IT'S QUITE SIMPLE... BEING THE LADY COMMANDER ALL THE TIME CAN BE QUITE STRESSFUL.
SOMETIMES YOU JUST WANT TO RELAX WITH THE GIRLS AND UNWIND OVER SOME TEA.
YEAH!
WE WANT YOU TO JUST ENJOY YOUR-SELVES. NO NEED TO BE STUFFY.
I-IT'S AN HONOR!
NO NEED TO BE STUFFY, I SAID...
SO I HEARD YOU WENT ON QUITE A QUEST BEFORE THE END OF THE YEAR?
Oh, that...
It was a real tough one...
BUT WE MANAGED TO GET EXCALIBUR AT THE END!
YEAH!

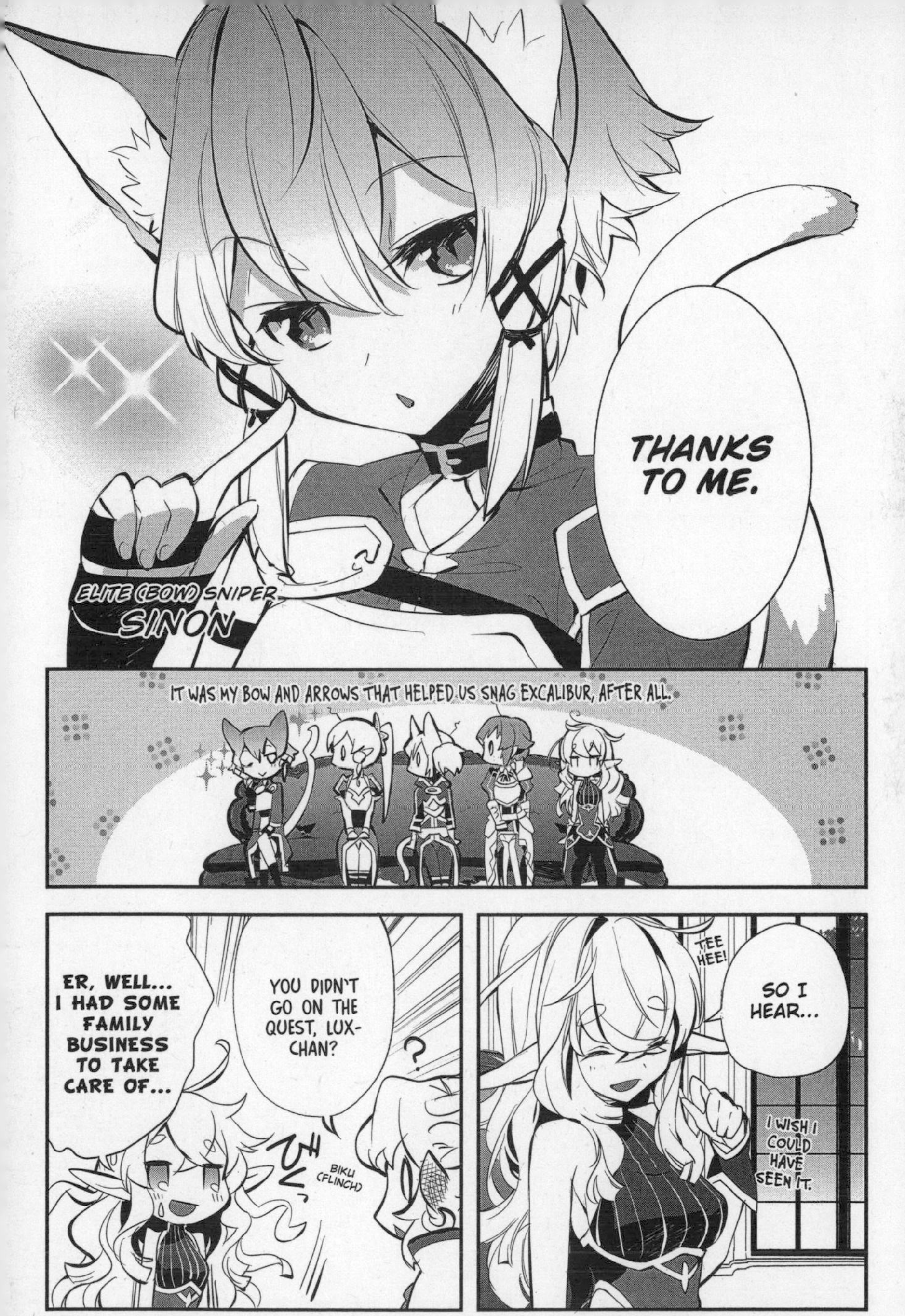
THANKS TO ME.
ELITE (BOW) SNIPER
SINON
IT WAS MY BOW AND ARROWS THAT HELPED US SNAG EXCALIBUR, AFTER ALL.
SO I HEAR...
TEE HEE!
I WISH I COULD HAVE SEEN IT.
YOU DIDN'T GO ON THE QUEST, LUX-CHAN?
?
BIKU (FLINCH)
ER, WELL... I HAD SOME FAMILY BUSINESS TO TAKE CARE OF...

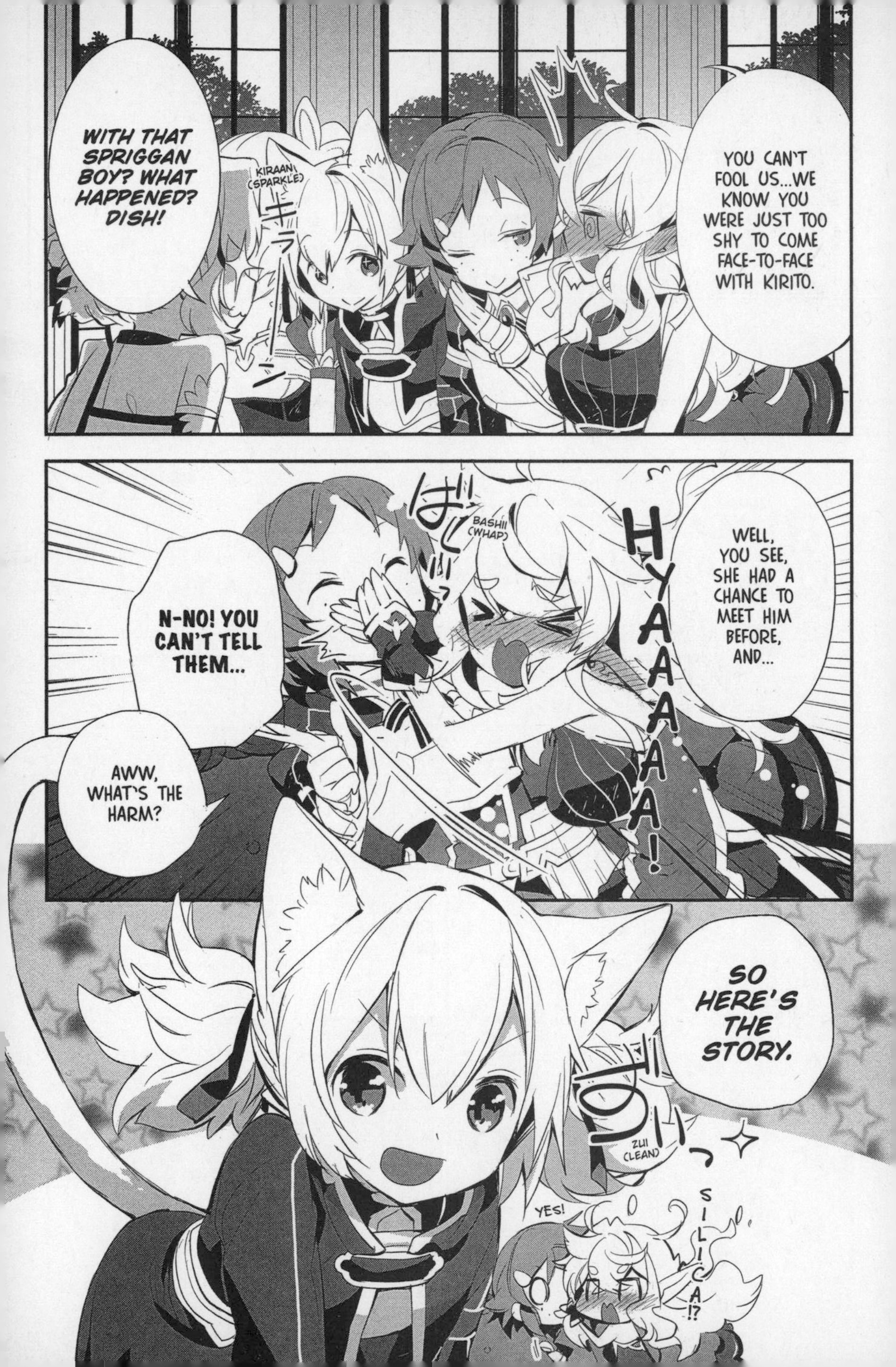
YOU CAN'T FOOL US...WE KNOW YOU WERE JUST TOO SHY TO COME FACE-TO-FACE WITH KIRITO.
KIRAAN (SPARKLE)
WITH THAT SPRIGGAN BOY? WHAT HAPPENED? DISH!
WELL, YOU SEE, SHE HAD A CHANCE TO MEET HIM BEFORE, AND...
HYAAAAAAAA!
BASHI! (WHAP)
N-NO! YOU CAN'T TELL THEM...
AWW, WHAT'S THE HARM?
SO HERE'S THE STORY.
ZUI CLEAN)
SILICA!?
YES!

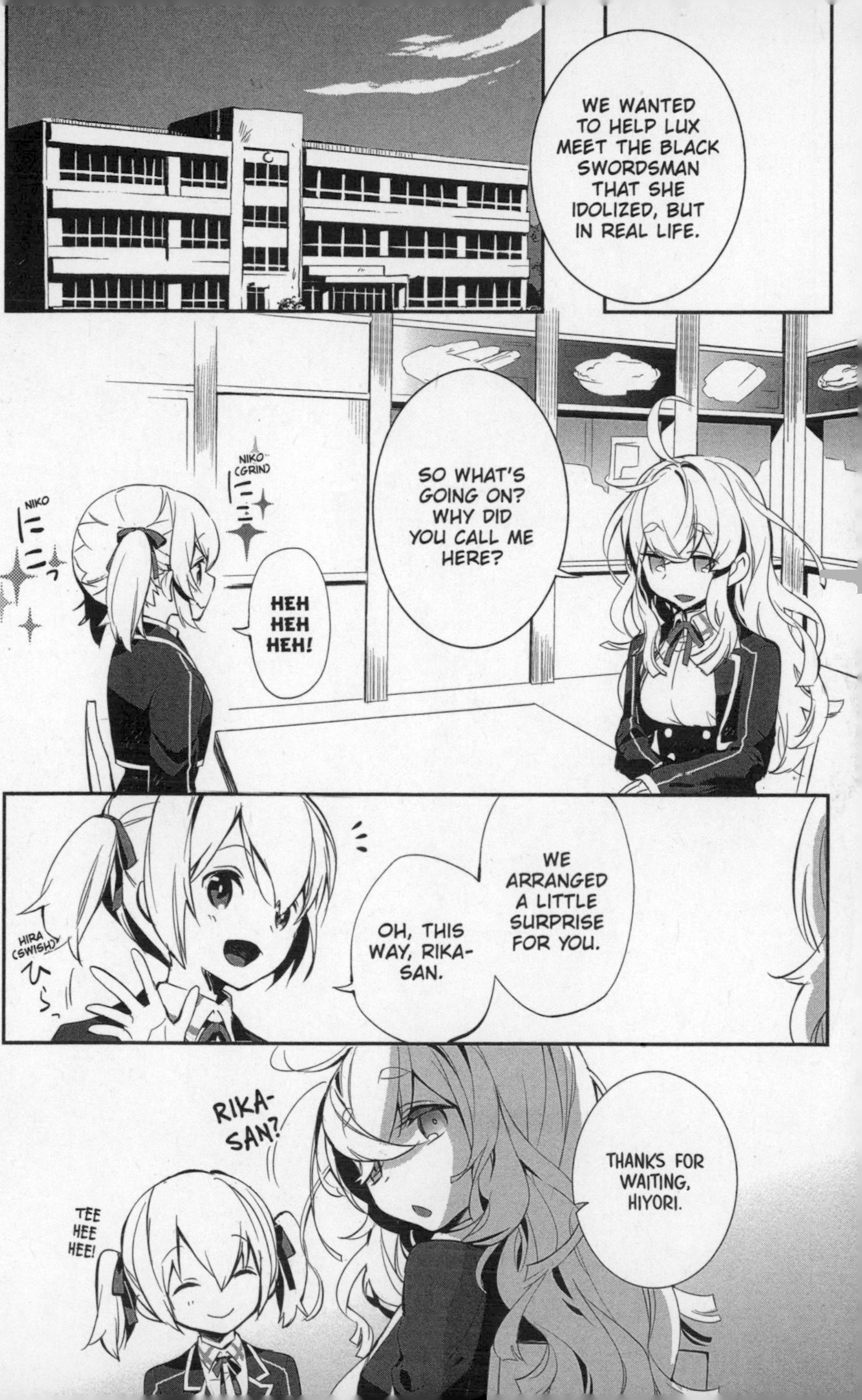
WE WANTED TO HELP LUX MEET THE BLACK SWORDSMAN THAT SHE IDOLIZED, BUT IN REAL LIFE.
SO WHAT'S GOING ON? WHY DID YOU CALL ME HERE?
NIKO... (GRIN)
NIKO
HEH HEH HEH!
WE ARRANGED A LITTLE SURPRISE FOR YOU.
OH, THIS WAY, RIKA-SAN.
HIRA (SWISH)
THANKS FOR WAITING, HIYORI.
RIKA-SAN?
TEE HEE HEE!

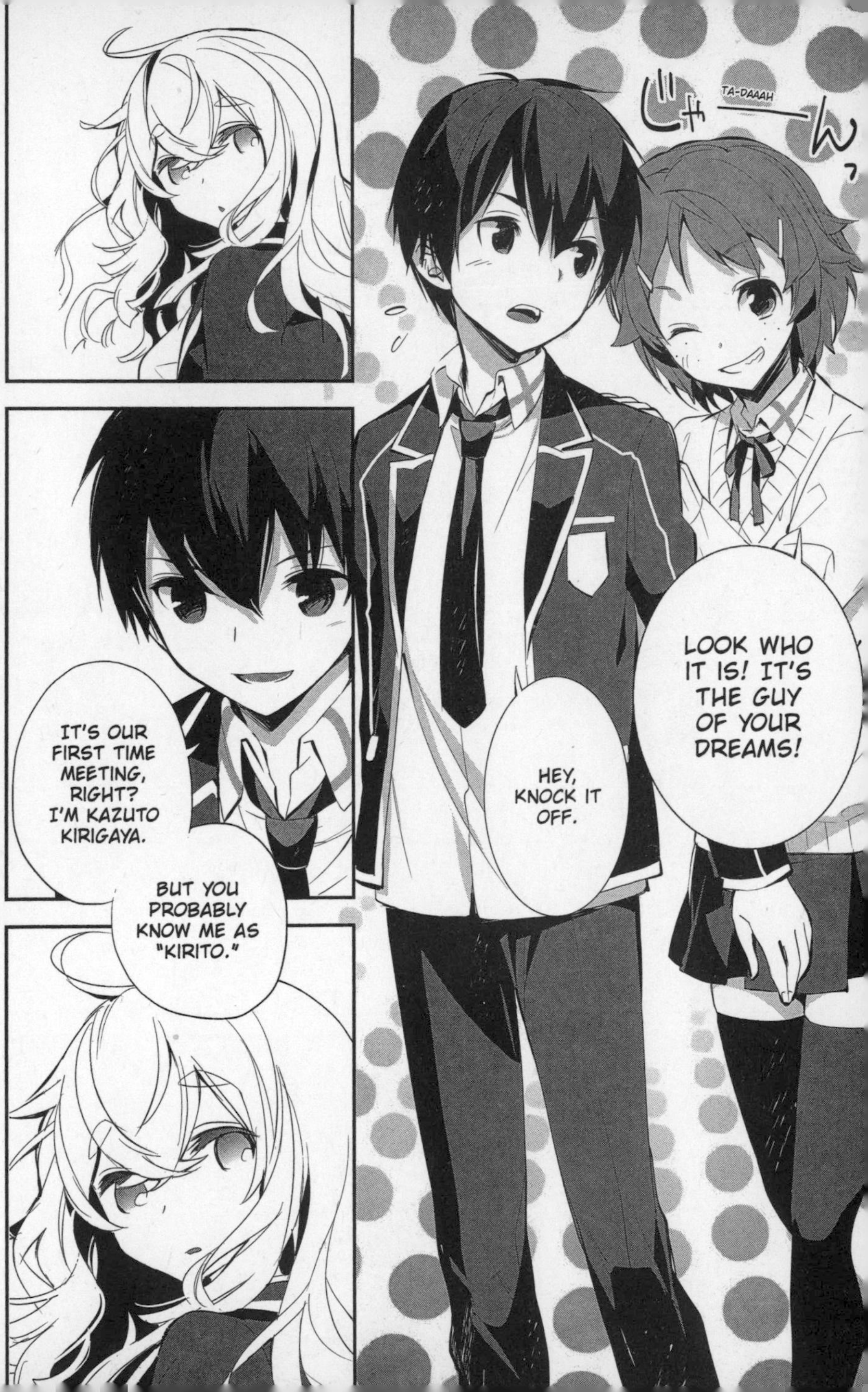
TA-DAAAH
LOOK WHO IT IS! IT'S THE GUY OF YOUR DREAMS!
HEY, KNOCK IT OFF.
IT'S OUR FIRST TIME MEETING, RIGHT? I'M KAZUTO KIRIGAYA.
BUT YOU PROBABLY KNOW ME AS "KIRITO."

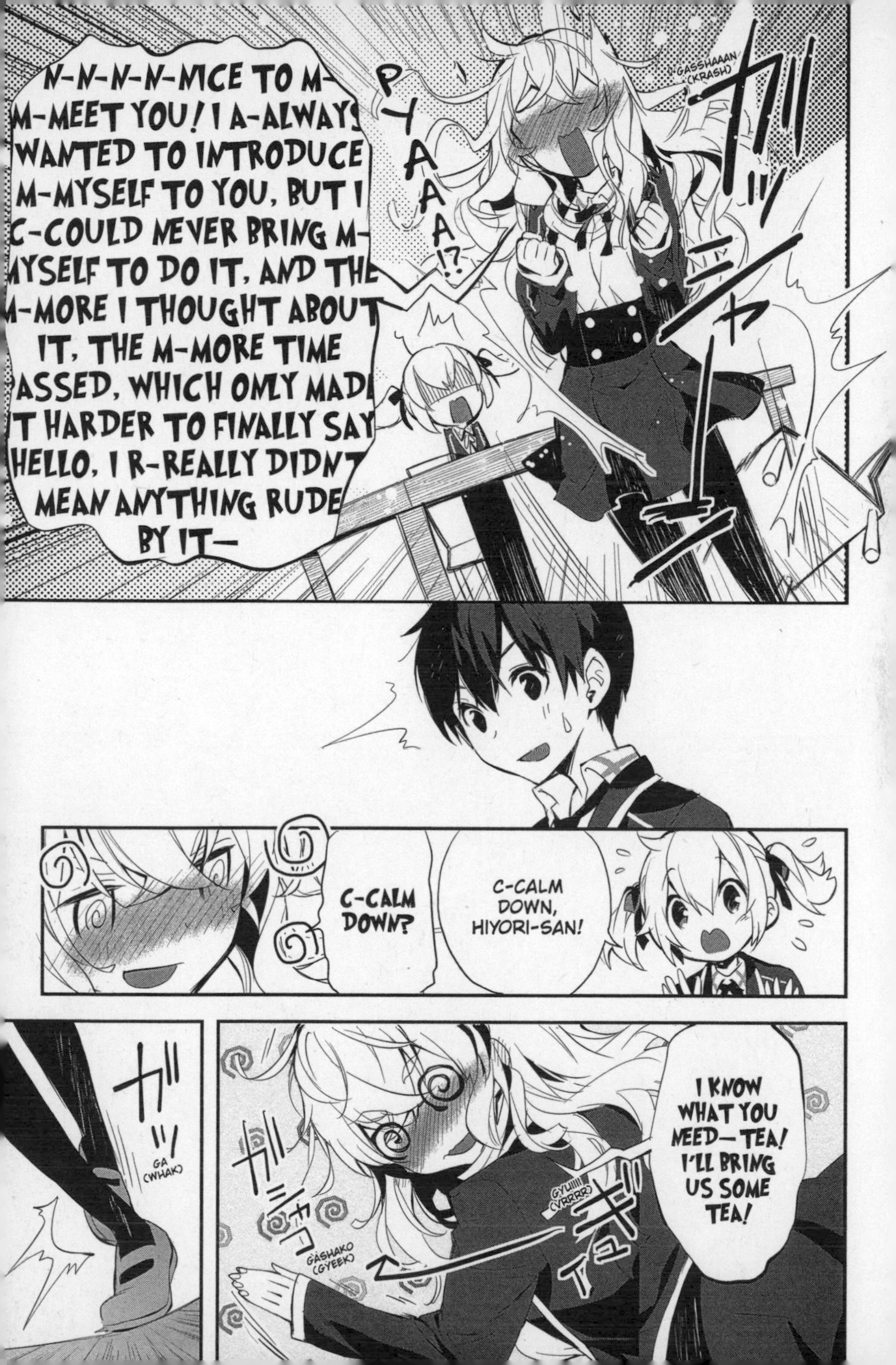
GASSHAAAN (KRASH)
PYAAA!?
N-N-N-N-NICE TO M-M-MEET YOU! I A-ALWAYS WANTED TO INTRODUCE M-MYSELF TO YOU, BUT I C-COULD NEVER BRING M-MYSELF TO DO IT, AND THE M-MORE I THOUGHT ABOUT IT, THE M-MORE TIME PASSED, WHICH ONLY MADE IT HARDER TO FINALLY SAY HELLO. I R-REALLY DIDN'T MEAN ANYTHING RUDE BY IT—
C-CALM DOWN, HIYORI-SAN!
C-CALM DOWN?
I KNOW WHAT YOU NEED— TEA! I'LL BRING US SOME TEA!
GYUIIII (VRRRR)
GASHAKO (GYEEK)
GA (WHAK)

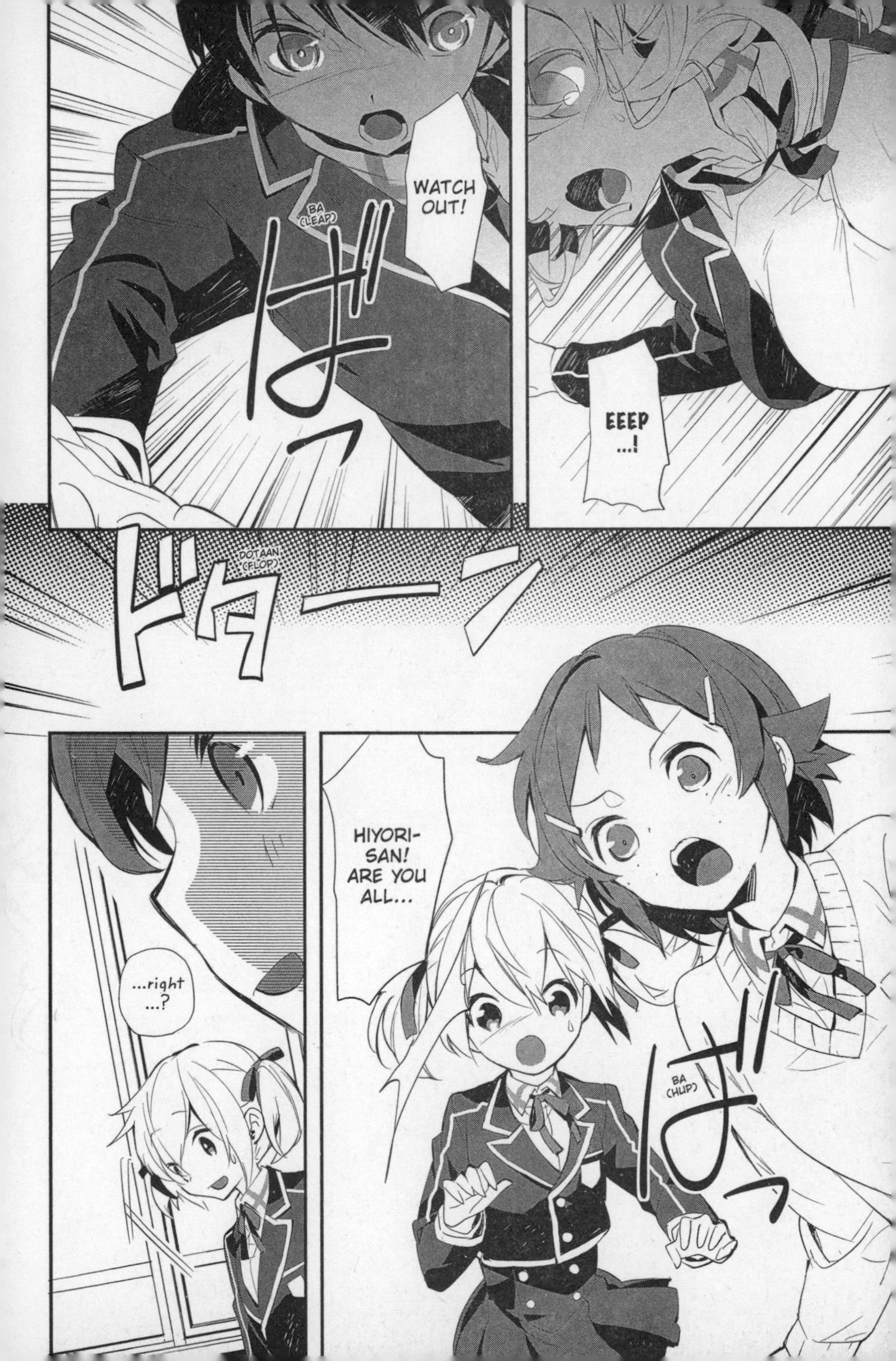
EEEP
...!
WATCH OUT!
BA (LEAP)
DOTAAN (FLOP)
HIYORI-SAN! ARE YOU ALL...
BA (HUP)
...right ...?

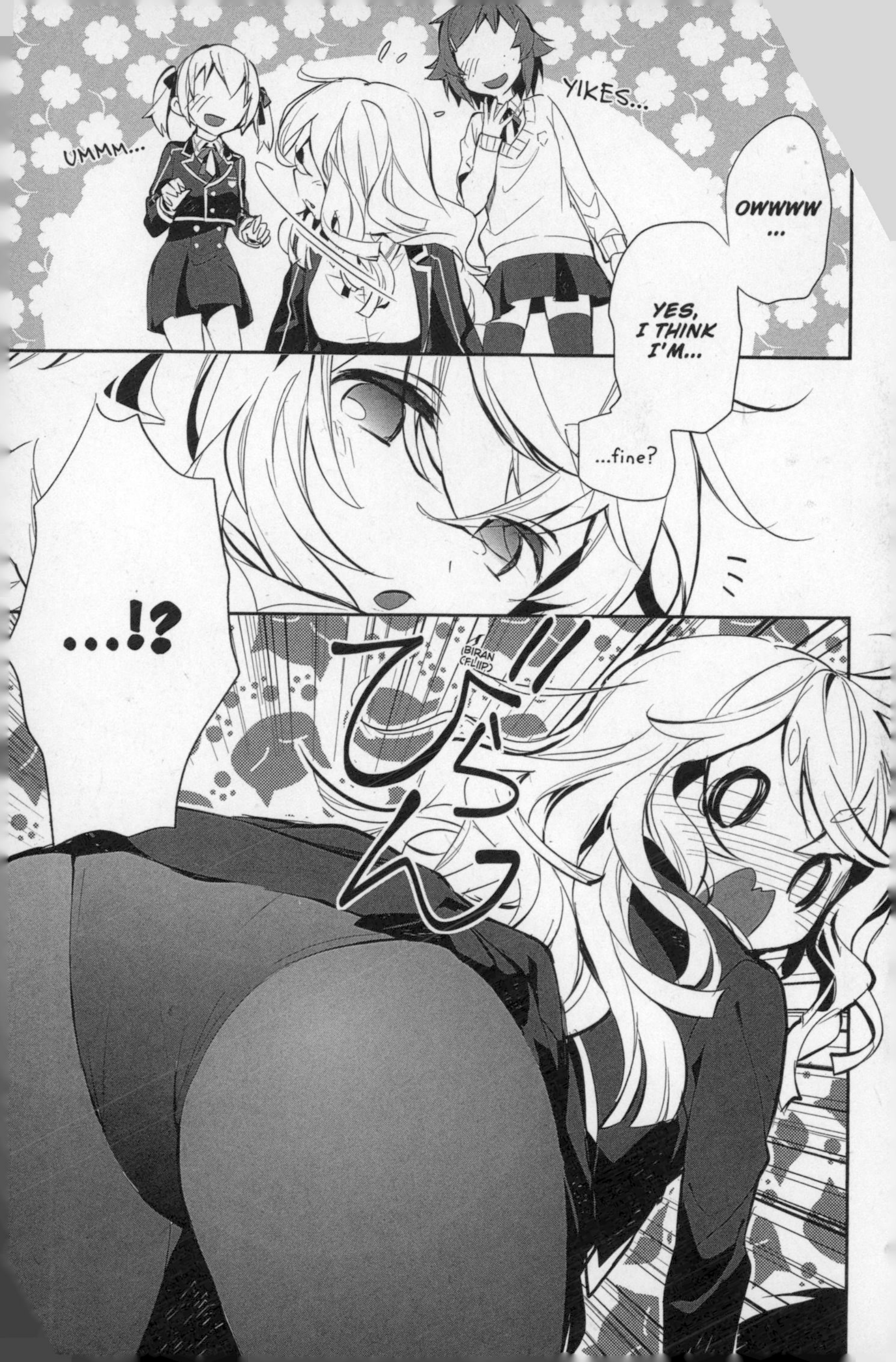
YIKES...
UMMM...
OWWWW...
YES, I THINK I'M...
...fine?
...!?
(BIRAN (FLIIP)
びらん

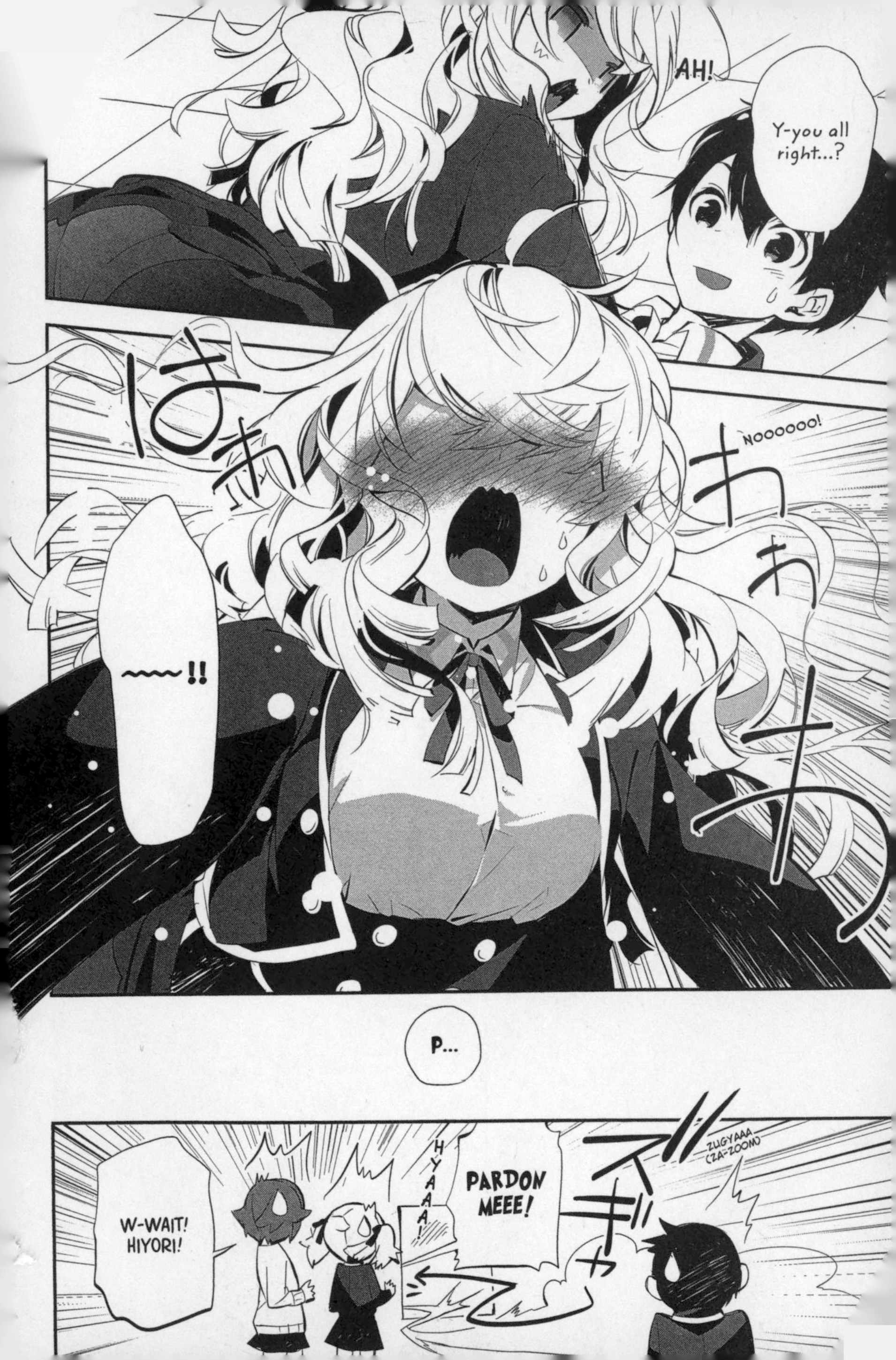
AH!
Y-you all right...?
NOOOOOO!
~~~!!
P...
PARDON MEEE!
HYAAA!
ZUGYAAA (ZA-ZOOM)
W-WAIT! HIYORI!
~~~

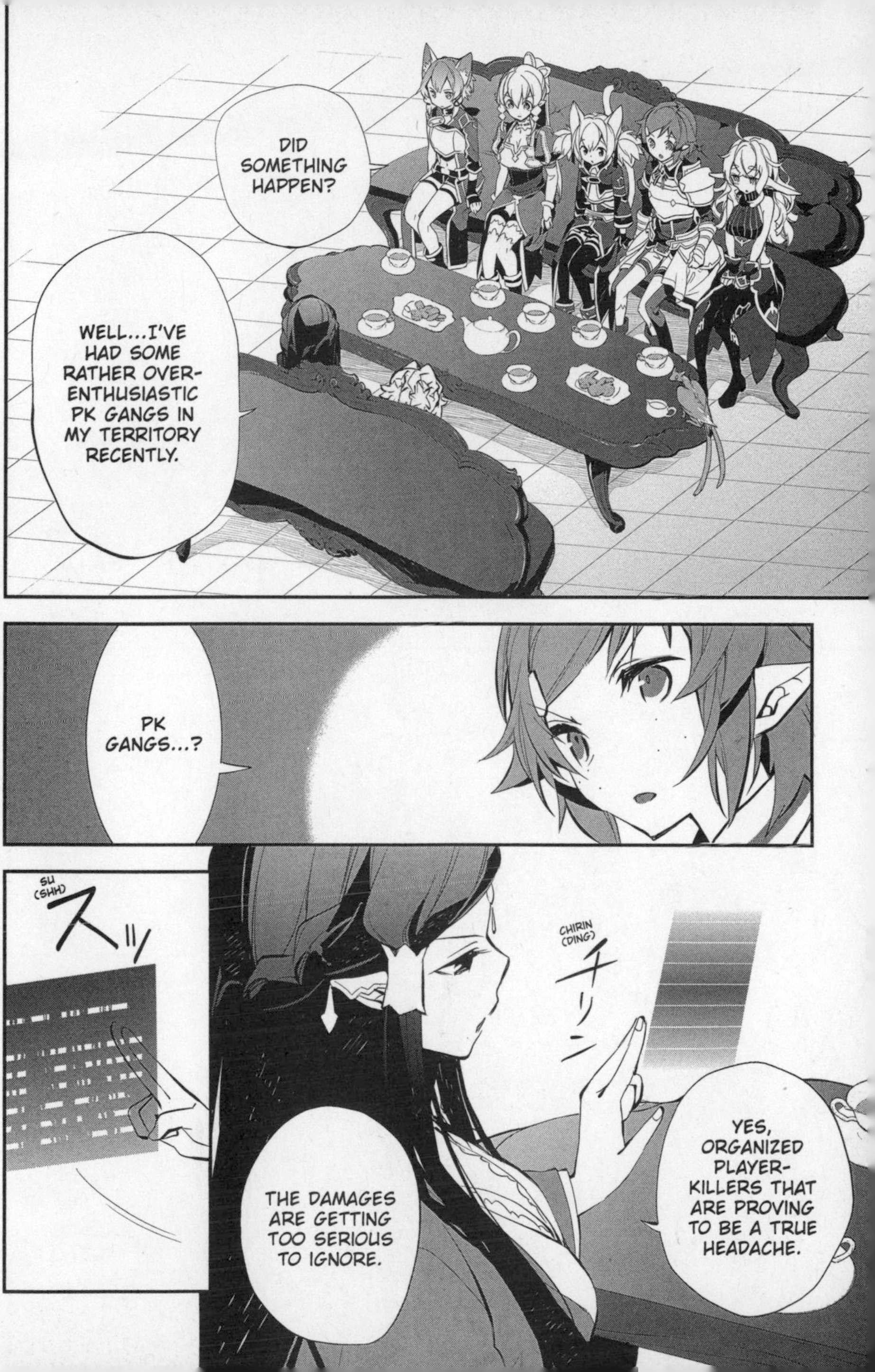
DID SOMETHING HAPPEN?
WELL...I'VE HAD SOME RATHER OVER-ENTHUSIASTIC PK GANGS IN MY TERRITORY RECENTLY.
PK GANGS...?
SU (SHH)
CHIRIN (DING)
YES, ORGANIZED PLAYER-KILLERS THAT ARE PROVING TO BE A TRUE HEADACHE.
THE DAMAGES ARE GETTING TOO SERIOUS TO IGNORE.

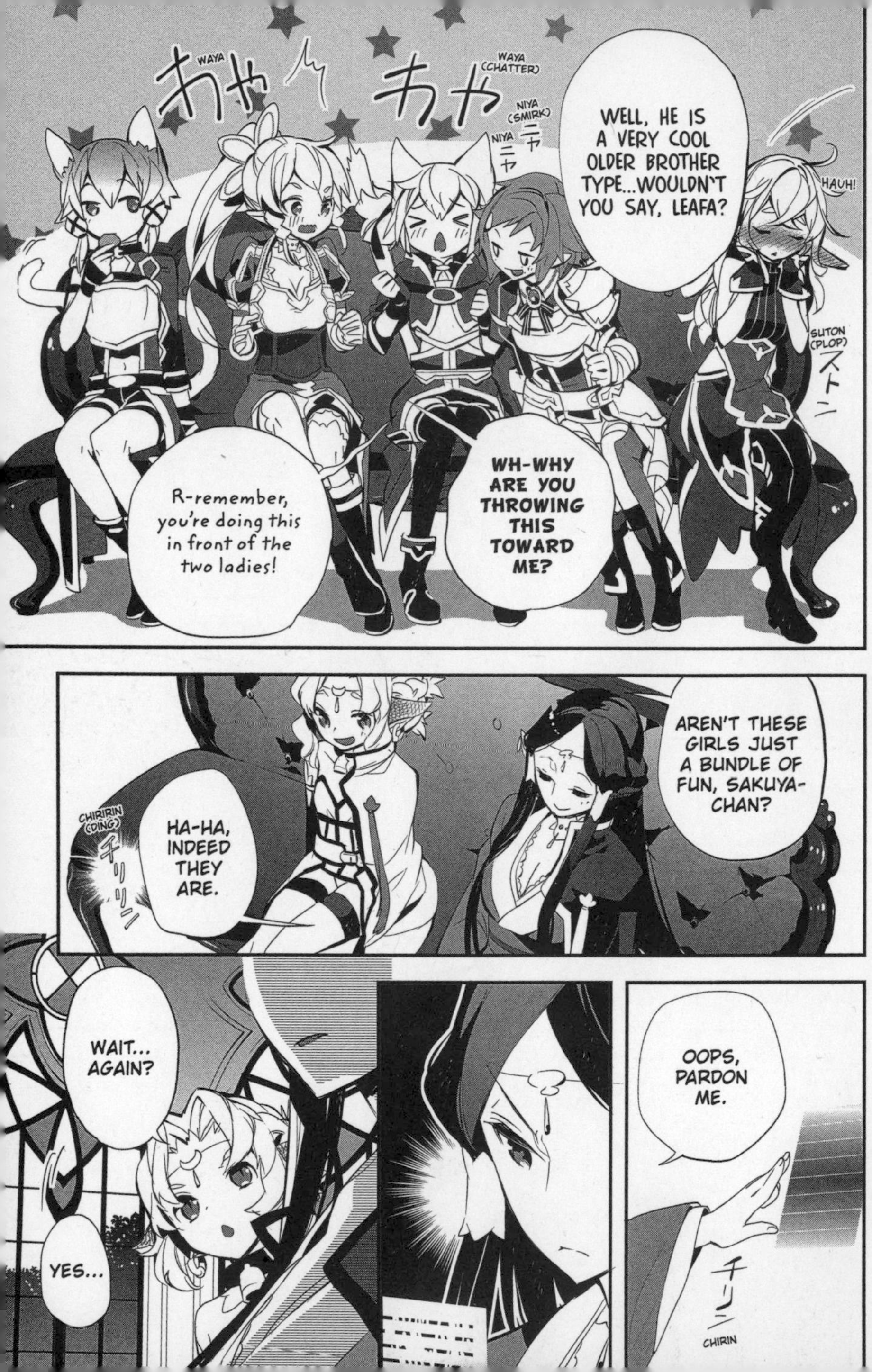
WELL, HE IS A VERY COOL OLDER BROTHER TYPE...WOULDN'T YOU SAY, LEAFA?
HAUH!
NIYA NIYA (SMIRK)
WAYA WAYA (CHATTER)
SUTON (PLOP)
WH-WHY ARE YOU THROWING THIS TOWARD ME?
R-remember, you're doing this in front of the two ladies!
AREN'T THESE GIRLS JUST A BUNDLE OF FUN, SAKUYA-CHAN?
HA-HA, INDEED THEY ARE.
CHIRIRIN (DING)
OOPS, PARDON ME.
CHIRIN
WAIT... AGAIN?
YES...

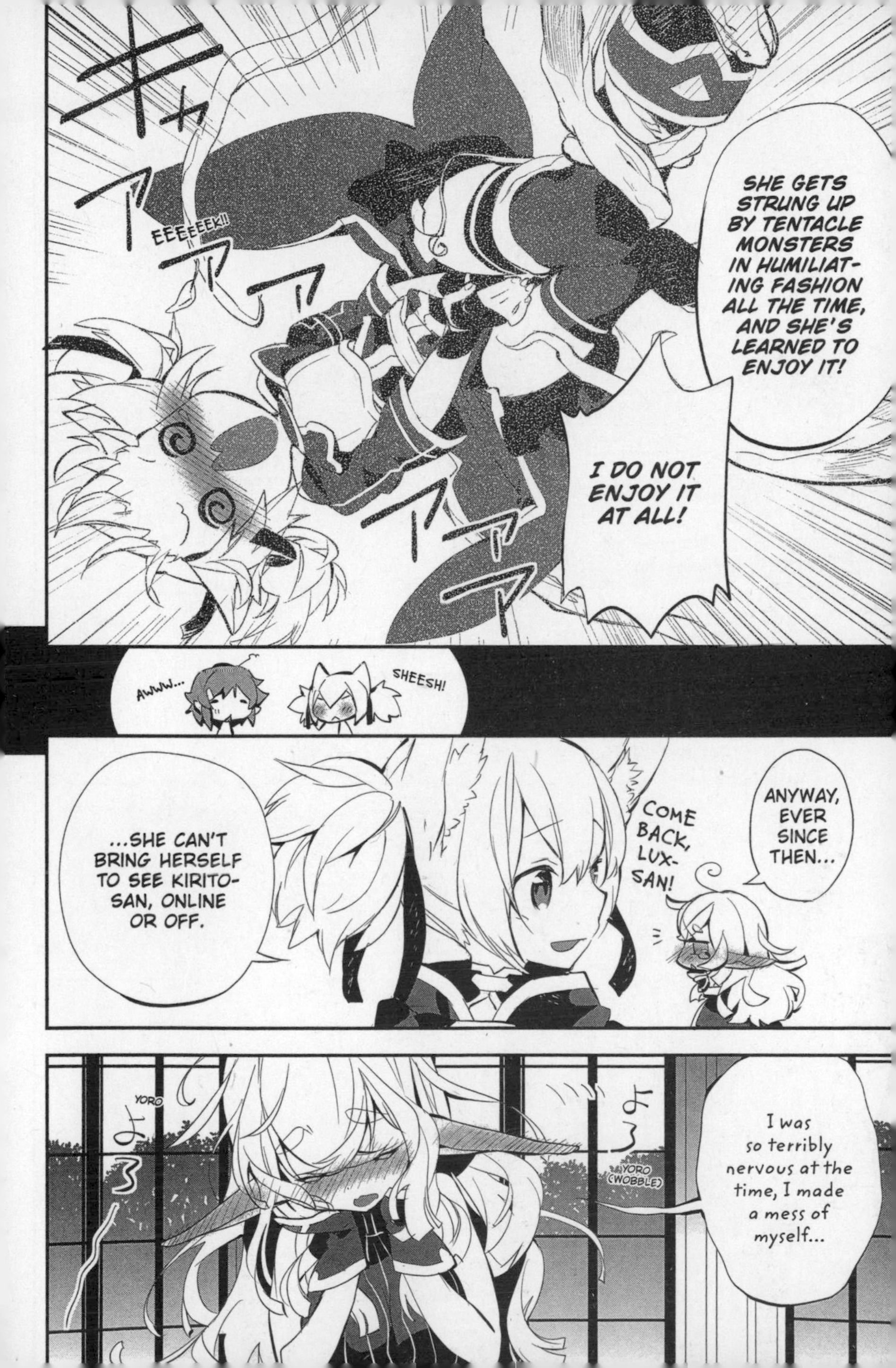
SHE GETS STRUNG UP BY TENTACLE MONSTERS IN HUMILIATING FASHION ALL THE TIME, AND SHE'S LEARNED TO ENJOY IT!
I DO NOT ENJOY IT AT ALL!
EEEEEEEK!!
SHEESH!
AWWW...
ANYWAY, EVER SINCE THEN...
COME BACK, LUX-SAN!
...SHE CAN'T BRING HERSELF TO SEE KIRITO-SAN, ONLINE OR OFF.
I was so terribly nervous at the time, I made a mess of myself...
YORO (WOBBLE)
YORO

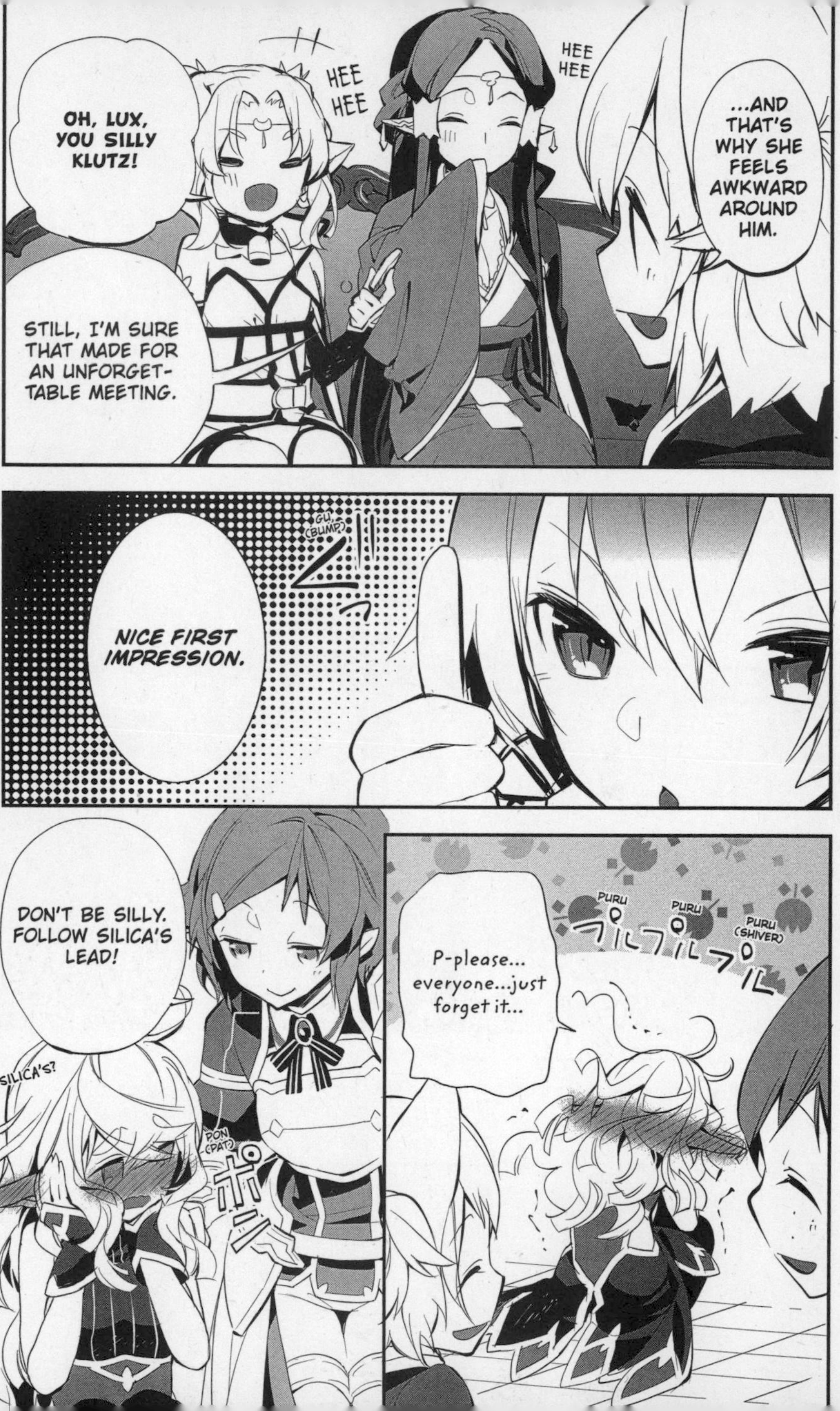
...AND THAT'S WHY SHE FEELS AWKWARD AROUND HIM.
HEE HEE
HEE HEE
OH, LUX, YOU SILLY KLUTZ!
STILL, I'M SURE THAT MADE FOR AN UNFORGET-TABLE MEETING.
GU (BUMP)
NICE FIRST IMPRESSION.
PURU PURU PURU (SHIVER)
P-please... everyone...just forget it...
DON'T BE SILLY. FOLLOW SILICA'S LEAD!
SILICA'S?
PON (PAT)

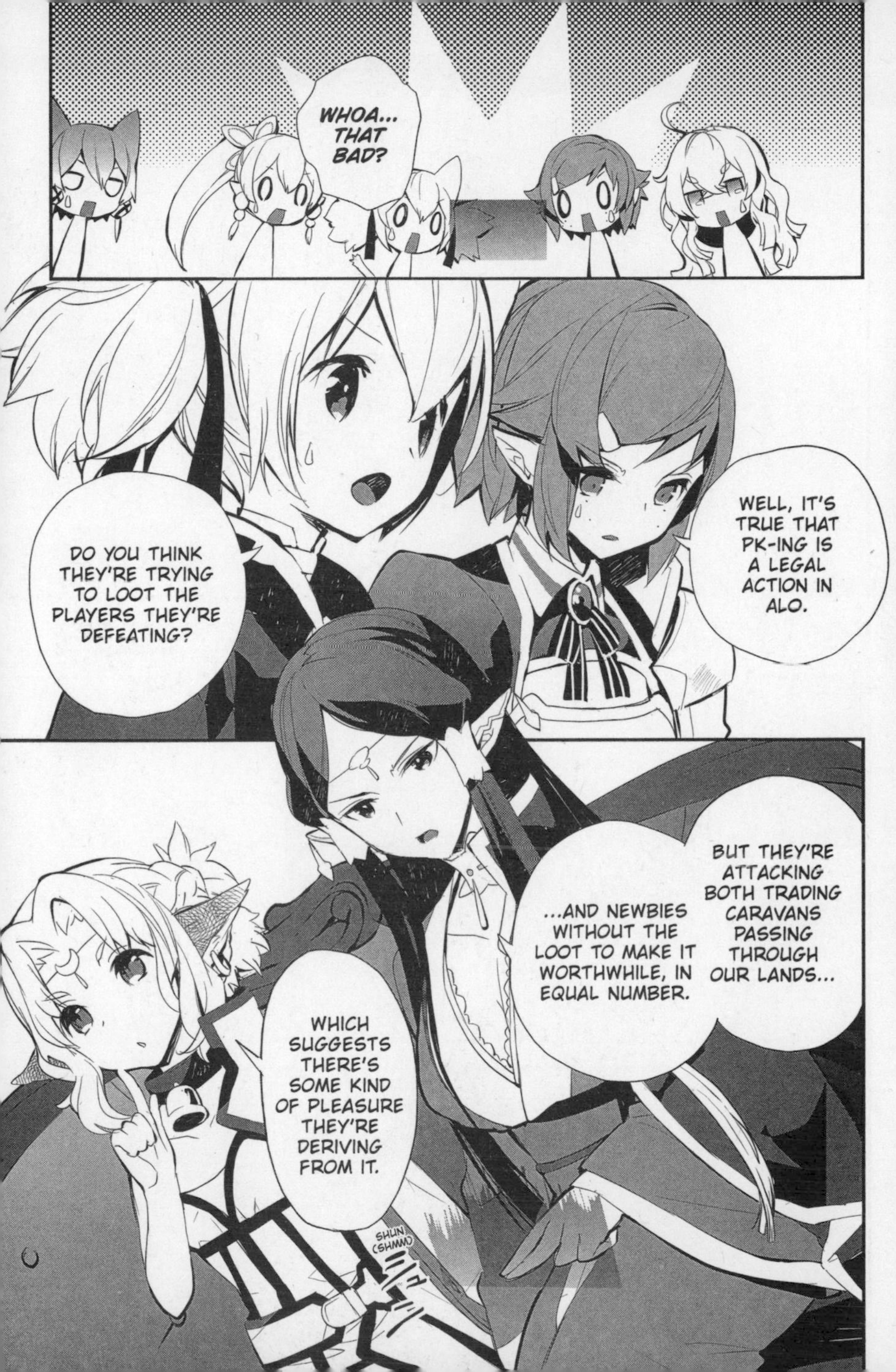

WHOA... THAT BAD?
WELL, IT'S TRUE THAT PK-ING IS A LEGAL ACTION IN ALO.
DO YOU THINK THEY'RE TRYING TO LOOT THE PLAYERS THEY'RE DEFEATING?
BUT THEY'RE ATTACKING BOTH TRADING CARAVANS PASSING THROUGH OUR LANDS...
...AND NEWBIES WITHOUT THE LOOT TO MAKE IT WORTHWHILE, IN EQUAL NUMBER.
WHICH SUGGESTS THERE'S SOME KIND OF PLEASURE THEY'RE DERIVING FROM IT.
SHUN (SHMM)

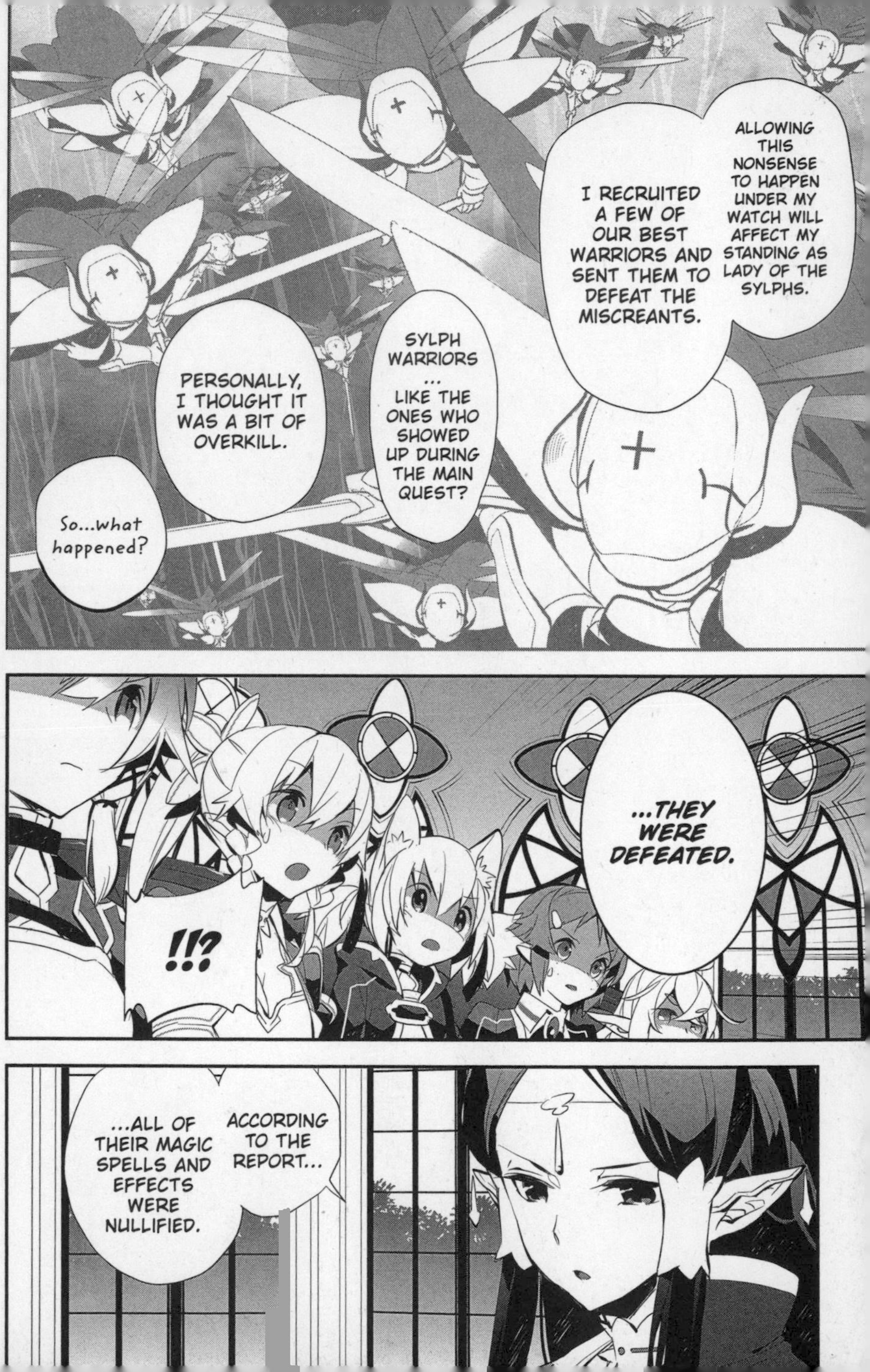
ALLOWING THIS NONSENSE TO HAPPEN UNDER MY WATCH WILL AFFECT MY STANDING AS LADY OF THE SYLPHS.
I RECRUITED A FEW OF OUR BEST WARRIORS AND SENT THEM TO DEFEAT THE MISCREANTS.
SYLPH WARRIORS ... LIKE THE ONES WHO SHOWED UP DURING THE MAIN QUEST?
PERSONALLY, I THOUGHT IT WAS A BIT OF OVERKILL.
So...what happened?
...THEY WERE DEFEATED.
!!?
ACCORDING TO THE REPORT...
...ALL OF THEIR MAGIC SPELLS AND EFFECTS WERE NULLIFIED.

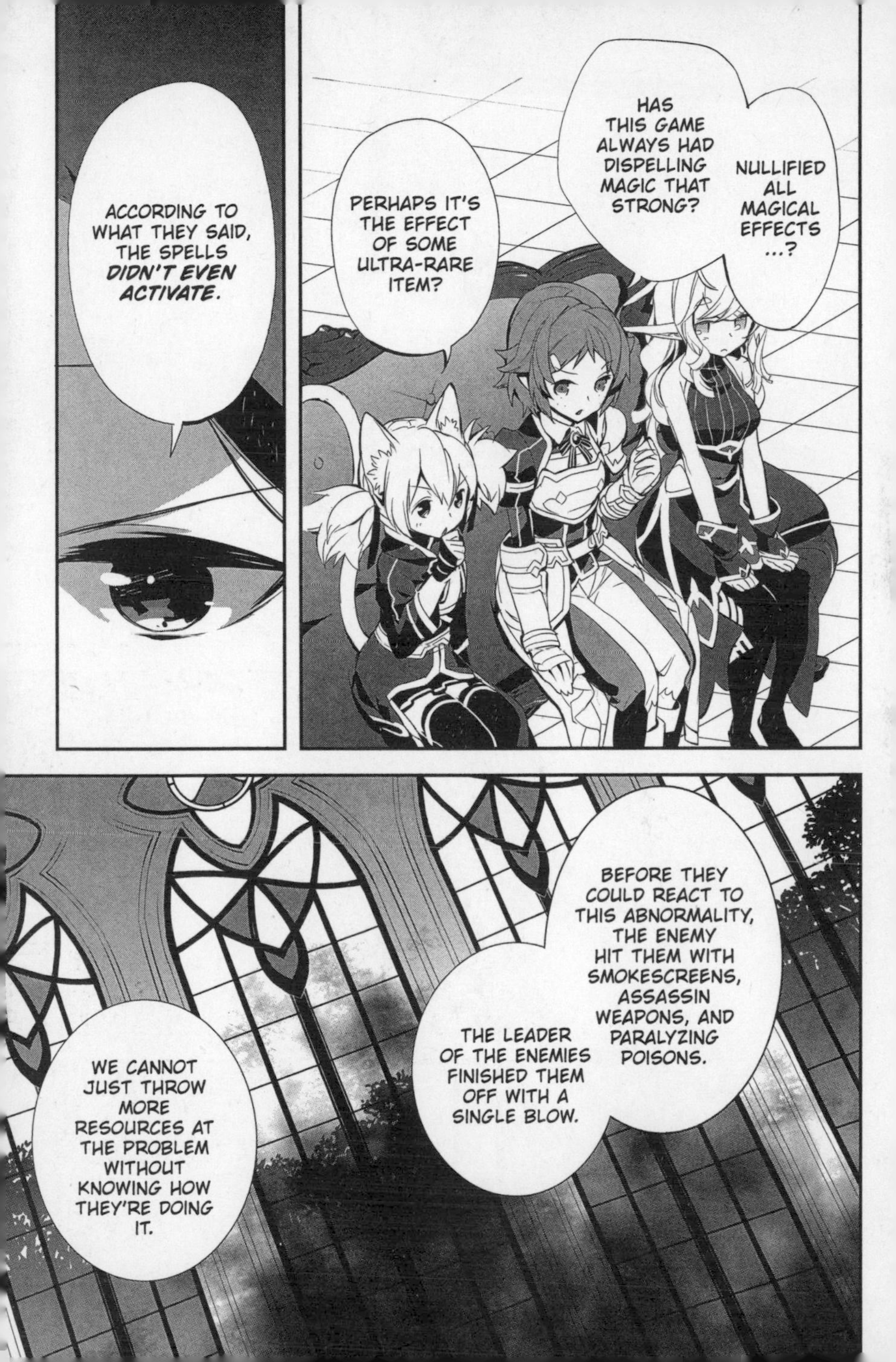
NULLIFIED ALL MAGICAL EFFECTS ...?
HAS THIS GAME ALWAYS HAD DISPELLING MAGIC THAT STRONG?
PERHAPS IT'S THE EFFECT OF SOME ULTRA-RARE ITEM?
ACCORDING TO WHAT THEY SAID, THE SPELLS *DIDN'T EVEN ACTIVATE*.
BEFORE THEY COULD REACT TO THIS ABNORMALITY, THE ENEMY HIT THEM WITH SMOKESCREENS, ASSASSIN WEAPONS, AND PARALYZING POISONS.
THE LEADER OF THE ENEMIES FINISHED THEM OFF WITH A SINGLE BLOW.
WE CANNOT JUST THROW MORE RESOURCES AT THE PROBLEM WITHOUT KNOWING HOW THEY'RE DOING IT.

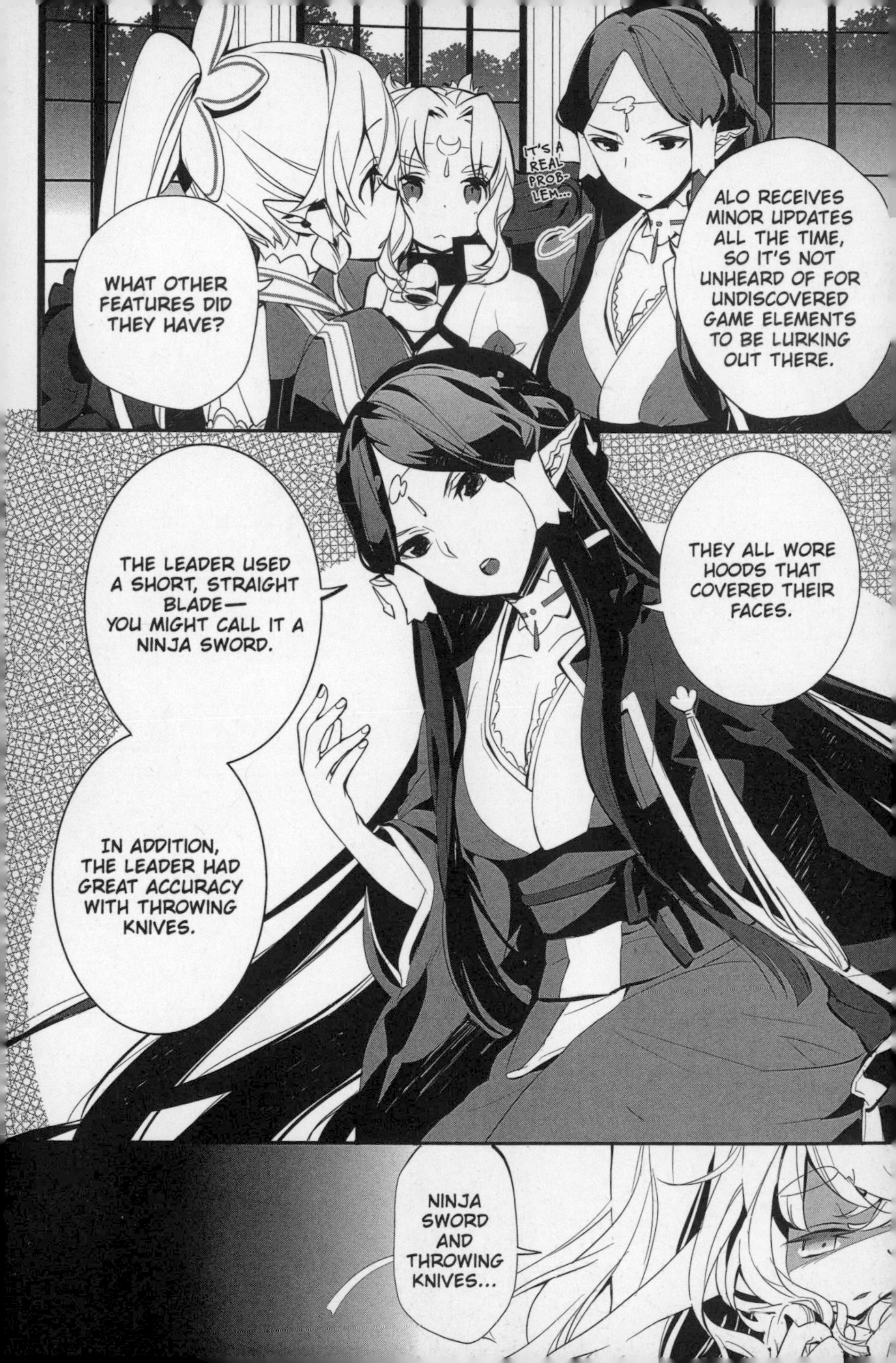
ALO RECEIVES MINOR UPDATES ALL THE TIME, SO IT'S NOT UNHEARD OF FOR UNDISCOVERED GAME ELEMENTS TO BE LURKING OUT THERE.
IT'S A REAL PROB-LEM...
WHAT OTHER FEATURES DID THEY HAVE?
THEY ALL WORE HOODS THAT COVERED THEIR FACES.
THE LEADER USED A SHORT, STRAIGHT BLADE— YOU MIGHT CALL IT A NINJA SWORD.
IN ADDITION, THE LEADER HAD GREAT ACCURACY WITH THROWING KNIVES.
NINJA SWORD AND THROWING KNIVES...

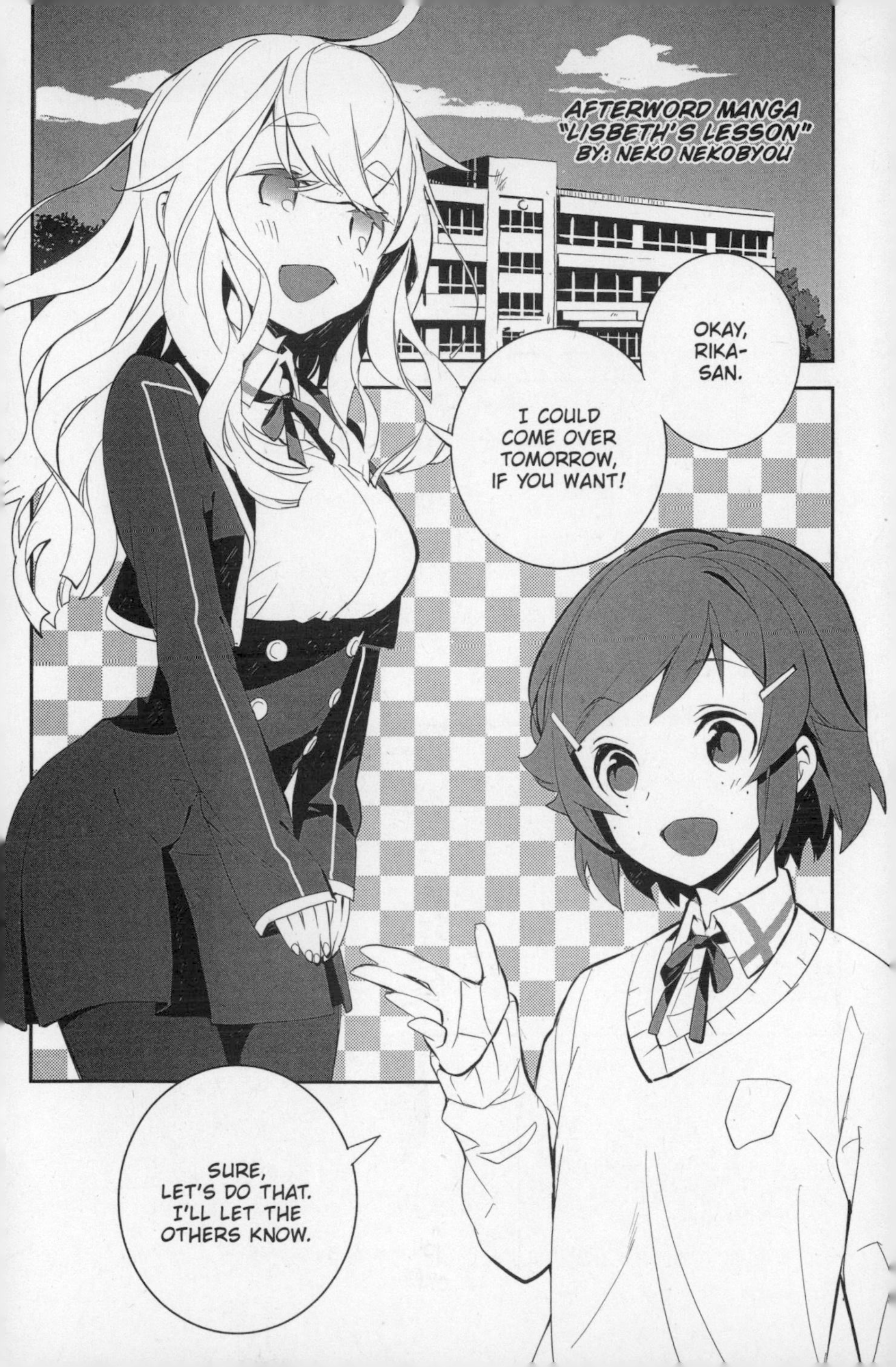
AFTERWORD MANGA
"LISBETH'S LESSON"
BY: NEKO NEKOBYOU
OKAY, RIKA-SAN.
I COULD COME OVER TOMORROW, IF YOU WANT!
SURE, LET'S DO THAT. I'LL LET THE OTHERS KNOW.

SWORD ART ONLINE

GIRLS'OPS

SWORD ART ONLINE
GIRLS' OPERATIONS

To be continued in the next volume!

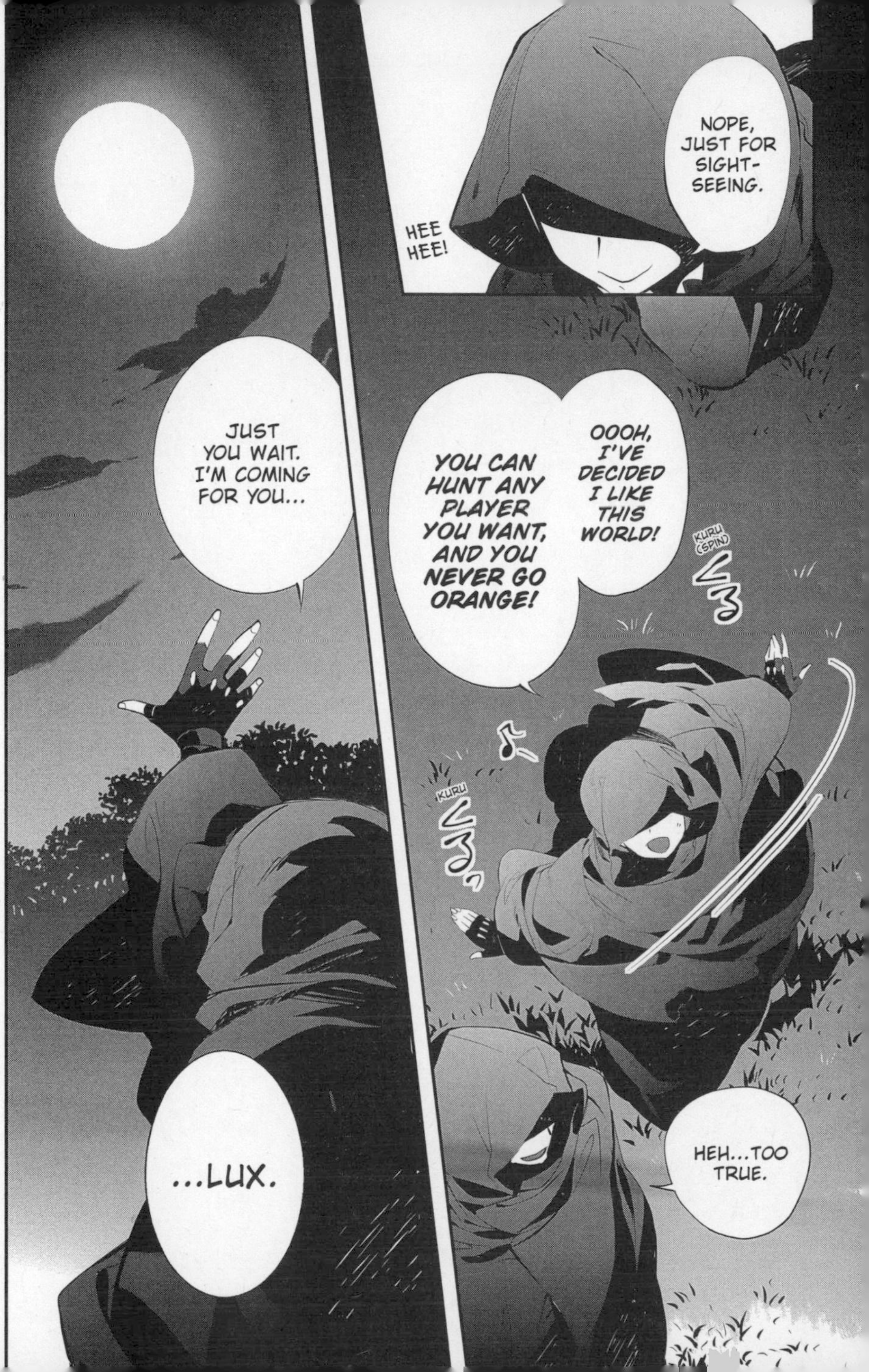
NOPE, JUST FOR SIGHT-SEEING.
HEE HEE!
OOOH, I'VE DECIDED I LIKE THIS WORLD!
YOU CAN HUNT ANY PLAYER YOU WANT, AND YOU NEVER GO ORANGE!
KURU (SPIN)
くる
KURU
くるっ
HEH...TOO TRUE.
JUST YOU WAIT. I'M COMING FOR YOU...
...LUX.

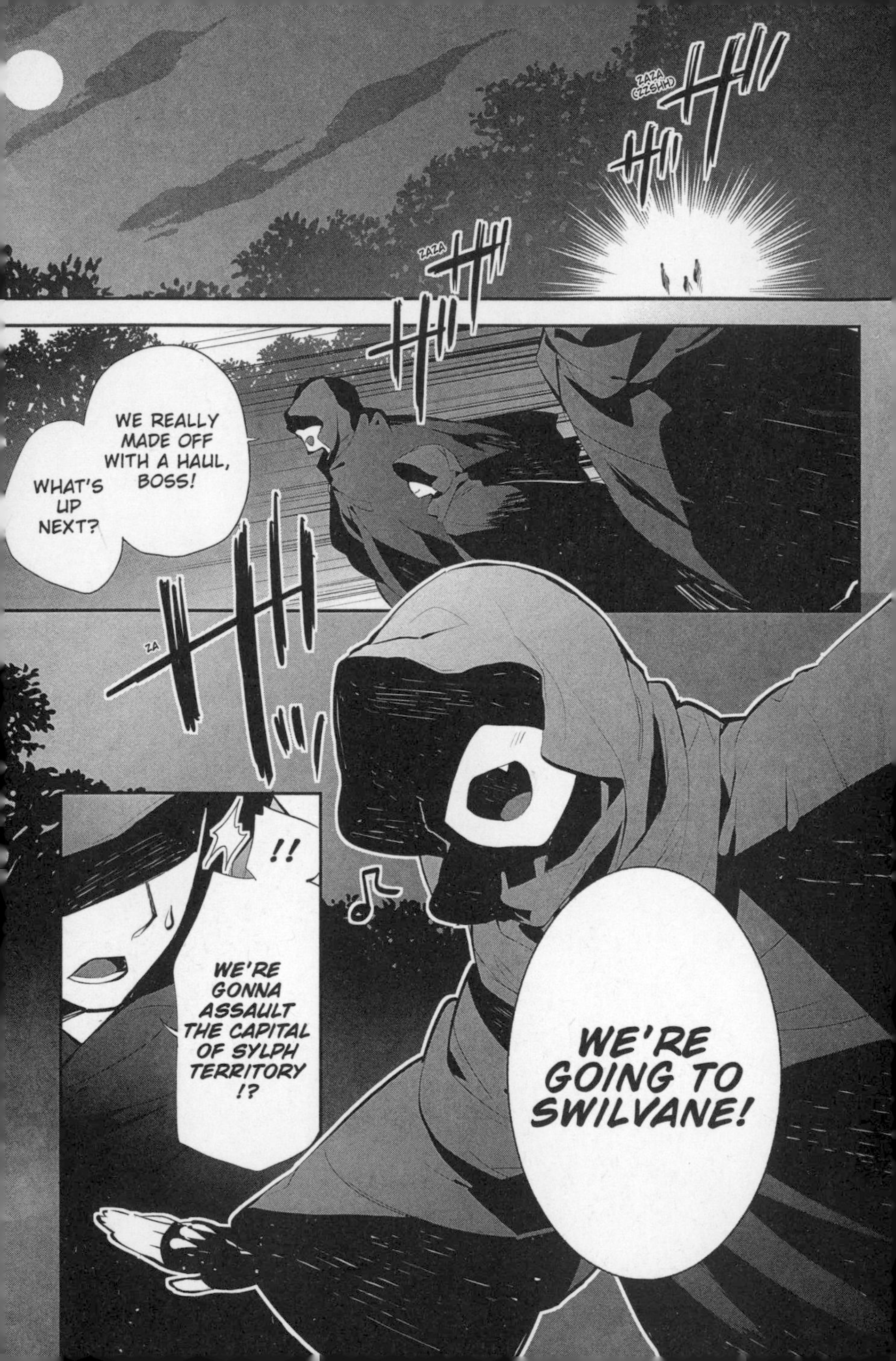
ZAZA (ZZZSHHD)
ZAZA
WE REALLY MADE OFF WITH A HAUL, BOSS!
WHAT'S UP NEXT?
ZA
WE'RE GOING TO SWILVANE!
!!
WE'RE GONNA ASSAULT THE CAPITAL OF SYLPH TERRITORY!?

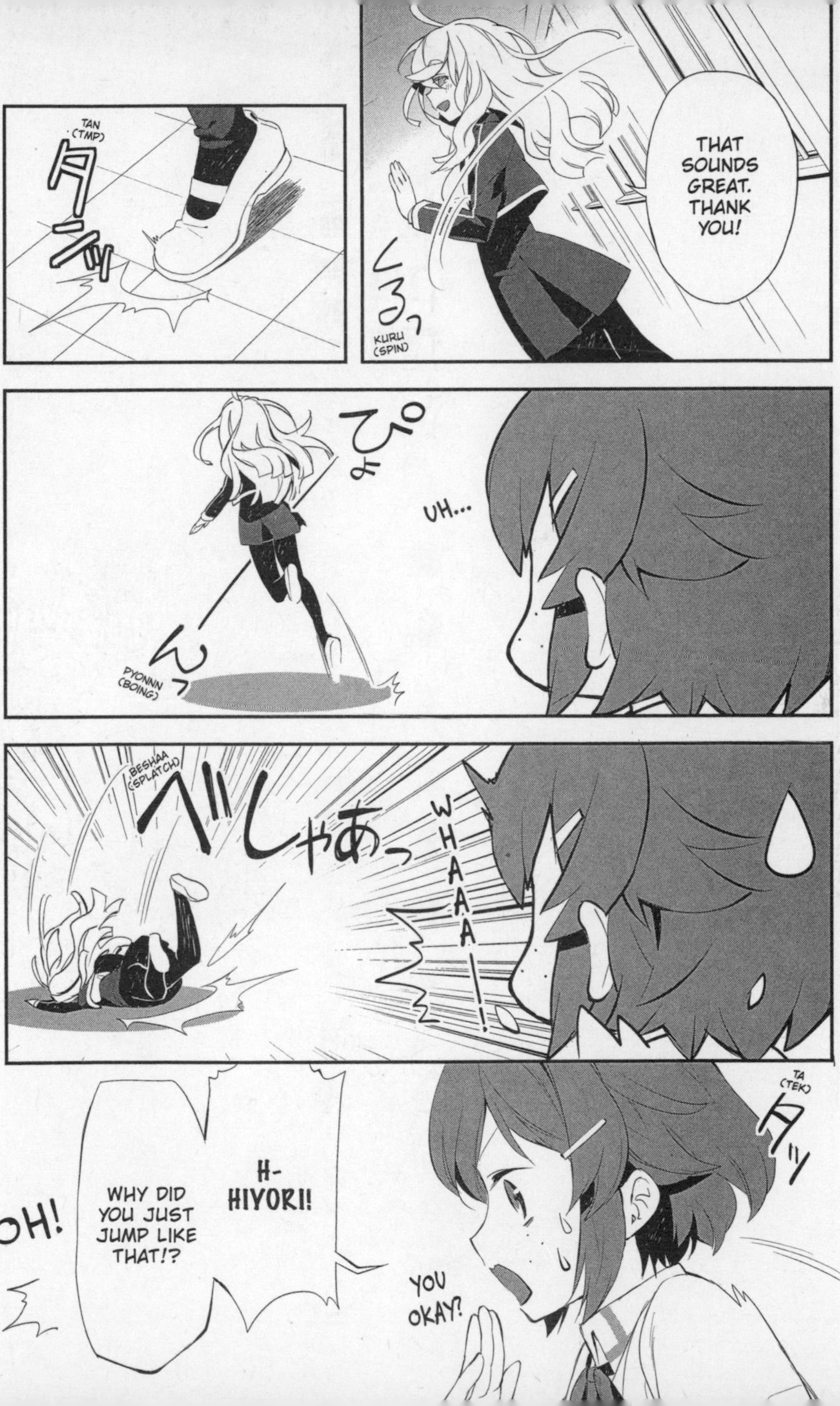
THAT SOUNDS GREAT. THANK YOU!
KURU (SPIN)
TAN (TMP)
UH...
PYONNN (BOING)
WHAAAA!!
BESHAA (SPLATCH)
TA (TEK)
YOU OKAY?
H-HIYORI!
WHY DID YOU JUST JUMP LIKE THAT!?
OH!

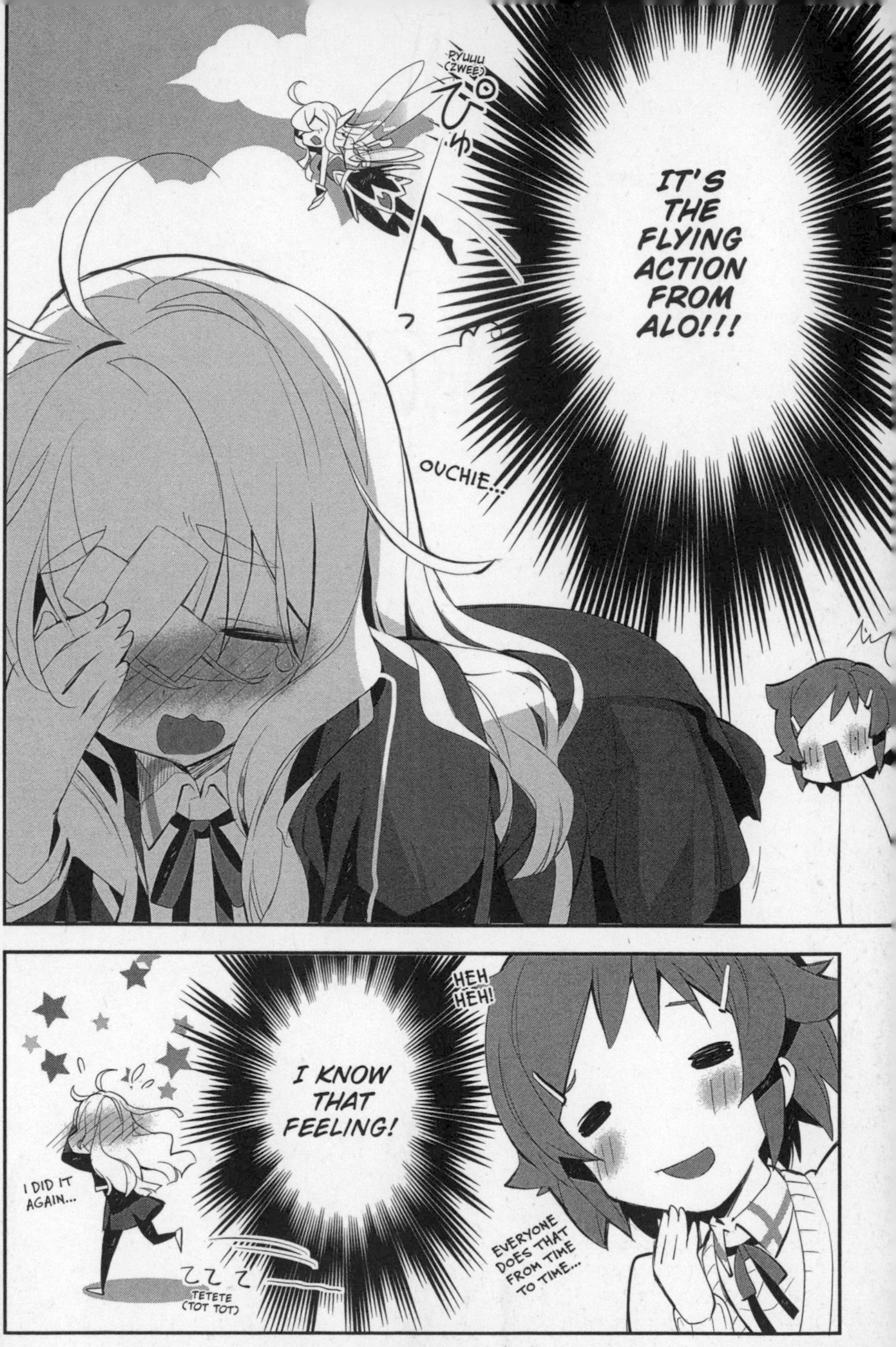

IT'S THE FLYING ACTION FROM ALO!!!
PYUUU (ZWEE)
OUCHIE...
HEH HEH!
I KNOW THAT FEELING!
EVERYONE DOES THAT FROM TIME TO TIME...
I DID IT AGAIN...
TETETE (TOT TOT)

Special Thanks!

YAJI

REKI KAWAHARA-SENSEI

ABEC-SENSEI

SHINGO NAGAI-SENSEI
(I DIDN'T HAVE ENOUGH TIME, SO I ASKED HIM TO WRITE
FOR ME, STARTING WITH THE SWIMSUIT CONTEST ARC.
THANK YOU FOR THE WONDERFUL SCENARIO!!)

KAZUMA MIKI-SAMA

TOMOYUKI TSUCHIYA-SAMA

EVERYONE WHO READ THIS BOOK!

TRANSLATION NOTES

PAGES 6-7
Yakisoba: A dish of soba (buckwheat) noodles that are cooked with a savory sauce and typically served with pork, cabbage, and ginger. Yakisoba is considered a quintessential summer food and is often found and consumed at summer festivals.

PAGE 112
Pareo: A kind of long skirt worn traditionally in Tahiti. The pareo has become a common accessory to a variety of ladies' swimwear.

SWORD ART ONLINE: GIRLS' OPS 2

ART: Neko Nekobyou
Original Story: Reki Kawahara
Character Design: abec

Translation: Stephen Paul
Lettering: Brndn Blakeslee & Lys Blakeslee

SWORD ART ONLINE: GIRLS' OPS
© REKI KAWAHARA/NEKO NEKOBYOU 2015
All rights reserved.
Edited by ASCII MEDIA WORKS
First published in Japan in 2015 by KADOKAWA CORPORATION, Tokyo.
English translation rights arranged with KADOKAWA CORPORATION, Tokyo, through Tuttle-Mori Agency, Inc., Tokyo.

English translation © 2016 by Yen Press, LLC

Yen Press
1290 Avenue of the Americas
New York, NY 10104

Visit us at yenpress.com
facebook.com/yenpress
twitter.com/yenpress
yenpress.tumblr.com
instagram.com/yenpress

First Yen Press Edition: January 2016

Yen Press is an imprint of Yen Press, LLC.
The Yen Press name and logo are trademarks of Yen Press, LLC.

The publisher is not responsible for websites (or their content) that are not owned by the publisher.

Library of Congress Control Number: 2015952589

ISBN: 978-0-316-26899-8

10 9 8 7 6 5 4 3 2

BVG

Printed in the United States of America

Comments in support of

SWORD ART ONLINE GIRLS' OPERATIONS

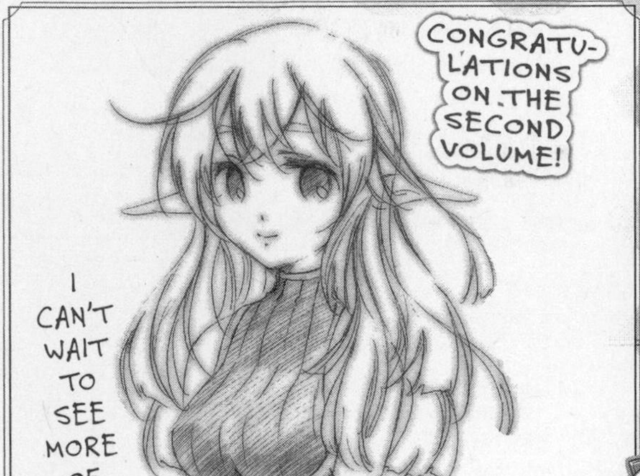

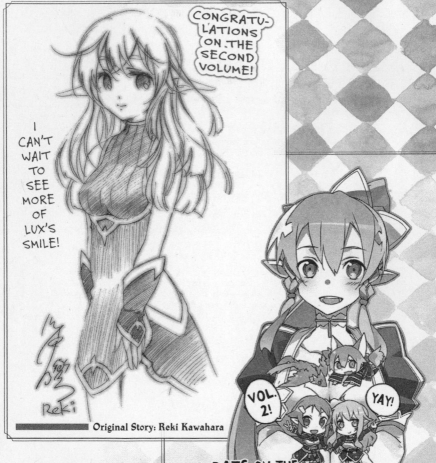

CONGRATU-LATIONS ON THE SECOND VOLUME!
I CAN'T WAIT TO SEE MORE OF LUX'S SMILE!
Reki

Original Story: Reki Kawahara

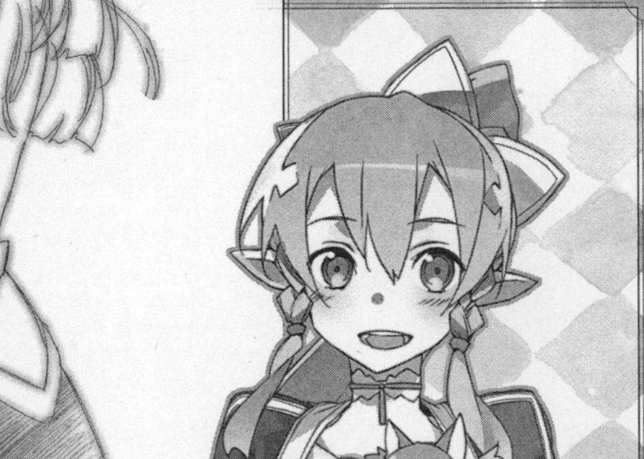

VOL. 2!
YAY!
CONGRATS ON THE RELEASE OF VOLUME 2 OF *GIRLS' OPS!*
abec

Character Design: abec

002

SWORD ART ONLINE
GIRLS' OPERATIONS

ART: NEKO NEKOBYOU
ORIGINAL STORY: REKI KAWAHARA
CHARACTER DESIGN: abec